The Attentive Listener

Three Centuries of Music Criticism

Edited by
HARRY HASKELL

PRINCETON UNIVERSITY PRESS
PRINCETON, NEW JERSEY

© Harry Haskell, 1996

First published in the United States of America
by Princeton University Press, 41 William Street
Princeton, New Jersey 08540

Published in Great Britain by Faber and Faber Limited,
3 Queen Square, London WC1N 3AU

All Rights Reserved

Library of Congress Cataloging-in-Publication Data

The attentive listener: three centuries of music criticism /
edited by Harry Haskell.
p.   cm.
Includes index.
ISBN 0-691-02641-6 (cl: alk. paper)
1. Music — History and criticism.   I. Haskell, Harry.
ML55.A88   1996
780'.9–dc20   95-46364

Princeton University Press books are printed on acid-free paper
and meet the guidelines for permanence and durability of the
Committee on Production Guidelines for Book Longevity
of the Council on Library Resources

Printed in England by Clays Ltd, St Ives plc

1 3 5 7 9 10 8 6 4 2

For Ellen

It's not just spending part of the night going over and over the various incidents of the opera, the form of the musical numbers, the names of the characters, dreaming about it if one falls asleep and still thinking about it when one awakes. Alas, no, this is not all. We critics must also give a more or less intelligible account of something that we have often not understood; turn something that has bored us into an amusing story; explain the why and wherefore, the excesses and shortcomings, the strong and weak points, the soft and hard, of a work sketched in flight, one that did not sit still for its portrait-painter for as long as it takes to make a clear photograph.

Hector Berlioz, *Evenings in the Orchestra* (1853)

Writing about music is about as easy as sculpting with fog.

From an unsigned review in the *Manchester Guardian Weekly*, 9 January 1994

Contents

Acknowledgements

(The numbers refer to articles in this anthology.)

19 From *E .T. A. Hoffmann's Musical Writings*, ed. David
   Charlton, trans. Martyn Clarke. Reprinted with the permission of Cambridge University Press.

25 Reprinted in part from Leon Plantinga, *Schumann as Critic*
   (Yale University Press). Copyright © 1967 Yale University.

29 By permission of Oxford University Press.

44 Courtesy of Florence Jonas.

46 By permission of Marion Boyars Publishers Ltd.

63 © Paul Zsolnay Verlag Gesellschaft m. b. H., Wien/Hamburg,
   1966.

68 © R. Piper & Co. Verlag, München, 1976.

69 © 1982 Giulio Einaudi Editore S. p. A.

72 © Times Newspapers Ltd., 1928.

76 From Theodor W. Adorno, *Gesammelte Schriften in 20
   Bänden*, vol. 18. © Suhrkamp Verlag, Frankfurt am Main, 1984.

79 Copyright © 1937 New York Times Company. Reprinted by
   permission.

82 By permission of G. Ricordi & Co.

86 By permission of the publishers B. Schott's Söhne, Mainz.

91 Originally published in the February 1959 issue of *The
   Atlantic Monthly*.

94 © The Telegraph plc, London, 1969.

95 Courtesy of Joachim Kaiser.

96 © Editrice La Stampa S. p. A., Turin, Italy.

97 Courtesy of the Universidad Nacional Autónoma de México.

98 © 1986 *Le Monde*.

99 By permission of Oxford University Press.

100 © The *Observer*.

Preface

The art of criticizing music is as old as music itself. One need look no further than Plato or St Augustine for evidence that musicians in antiquity found critics close at hand, ready as ever to dispense censure or praise. The popular image of the critic as a professional fault finder is comparatively modern. The Greeks, who gave us the word *criticism*, construed it more liberally as the act of deciding or judging for oneself. In that light, critics are simply ordinary people who happen to possess extraordinary powers of discrimination. In judging for themselves, critics implicitly challenge the rest of us to formulate our own standards of judgment.

Today's harried newspaper critic, pressured by deadlines and sub-editors clamouring for newsworthy copy, seems only distantly related to the arbiters of taste who once handed down judgments with Olympian authority. Yet in the age of mass culture, when music is everywhere and opinions are cheap, the musical journalist has a vital role to play in prodding us to stop, listen, and reflect upon the sounds that we too often take for granted. If critics can no longer claim to be the anointed guardians of artistic truth, they have assumed a function which is at once more mundane and more essential to the well-being of contemporary musical culture: that of catalysts, *provocateurs*, teachers, and even sometimes advocates. They are, or should be, our most attentive listeners.

Once when I was a newspaper critic, someone asked me at a concert if I had come to enjoy the performance or to review it – the assumption clearly being that one couldn't do both. There are indeed critics who seem to have forgotten how to enjoy listening to music, but you won't find them in this book. Nor will you find critics whose conception of their niche in the musical ecosystem is limited to toppling cultural monuments from their pedestals or railing against declining tastes and standards; such critical debunkery has already been comprehensively anthologized in Nicolas Slonimsky's classic *Lexicon of Musical Invective*. What this book offers instead is a highly personal selection of writings by critics of disparate cultures and points of view who share a deep engagement with music and a strong urge to articulate their responses to it in words.

Music and words: what the Germans call the 'Ton-Wort' problem bedevils music critics as persistently as it does composers and librettists. Words and music are in some respects natural enemies, or at best unnatural allies. Music, it is said, subverts literal meaning; it transcends prosaic thought and resists rational explication. Words clip music's wings; they pull it down to earth and tether it to the unyielding logic of verbal semantics. Music, Mendelssohn suggested, is not too vague for words but too precise. It was this realization that prompted the musicologist-critic Hans Keller to devise a method of partially nonverbal music criticism which he labelled 'functional analysis'.

Many a musical journalist, struggling to write precisely and meaningfully about the art, would gladly trade a thousand words for a single example in musical notation. Yet even if most readers of criticism were musically literate, which is far from true today, quoting a passage from a score to illustrate a point would not solve the music–word problem. For music does not reside alone in notes on a page, or even in the sounds performers produce. Music is also, crucially, what goes on inside each listener's head. All critics can do is to try to connect, to find metaphors in their own experience which resonate with other listeners. Good criticism acts like a sounding board: in receiving, amplifying, and transmitting vibrations, it prolongs and deepens the experience of music. It is successful if it strikes a sympathetic chord, jiggles the imagination, brings the reader nearer to the ineffable essence of music, whether on an intuitive or an intellectual level.

Early musical journalists were well aware that writing about music is always in some sense an exercise in futility. Yet it hardly ever occurred to them to question the *possibility* of meaningful criticism. Their mission – for to them criticism was a calling, not a mere profession – was to 'instruct the public taste' and to promote enlightened discussion. William Ayrton, who edited one of England's first musical magazines, prefaced the *Harmonicon* in

1823 with a desideratum that still rings true today:

> If the Public once turn their thoughts to the art, and consider it a little abstractedly, they will not only heighten the pleasure which they derive from its production, but become qualified to exercise a direct and beneficial influence over all that it shall in future produce. To afford some materials for thinking, is one of the objects of those pages in the HARMONICON that are dedicated to the Review of Music.

This anthology, too, is meant to afford some materials for thinking. I have cast my net wide with an eye to taking in as many individual voices as space permitted. And, because comparatively little music criticism in other languages is available to English-speaking readers, I have made a special point of exemplifying regional traditions of critical writing throughout the Western world. There are articles not only from England, Western Europe and the United States, but from Russia, Eastern Europe, Scandinavia, Latin America and Canada as well. My aim has been twofold: to give general readers and students a clearer picture of the evolution of music criticism and its place in Western culture over the past three centuries; and to illustrate the richness, variety and vitality of music criticism as both an intellectual enterprise and a literary genre.

The secondary literature on music criticism is vast and burgeoning, yet we still lack a comprehensive, up-to-date history of the subject. The best general treatment in English, Max Graf's *Composer and Critic*, is nearly fifty years old and reflects the perspective of a critic whose career began before the turn of the century. Readers seeking a more concise overview may turn to the classic article on criticism in *The New Grove Dictionary of Music and Musicians* by the senior British musicologist Winton Dean. In preparing this anthology I have kept both accounts in mind, guided by Dean's definition of criticism as 'current discussion, in the daily and periodical press, of contemporary musical trends'. The implication is not that writing about aesthetics, musical form and analysis, and similar topics does not qualify as criticism in a broader sense; merely that it operates on different assumptions and therefore falls outside the parameters of the present volume.

Journalistic criticism was largely the creation of the eighteenth century, and so I have chosen *circa* 1700 as my point of departure.

The rationalistic world view of the European Enlightenment, coupled with a new-found emphasis on the works of man rather than those of God, fostered the growth of a genuinely critical spirit that transformed writing about music from a narrowly scholastic discipline into a broadly humanistic one. At the same time the proliferation of musical magazines, most notably in Germany and France, afforded critics regular access to the steadily expanding musical public. From Joseph Addison's brilliantly satirical attacks on Italian opera in the *Spectator* to Baron Grimm's pungent criticisms in the *Correspondance littéraire* and Friedrich Rochlitz's magisterial essays in the Leipzig *Allgemeine musikalische Zeitung*, it was a century of lively debate centring on profound philosophical questions of taste and style.

The nineteenth century added a host of new issues to the critical agenda, while fostering a more democratic tone that suited the tastes and interests of the increasingly prominent middle-class audience. No longer confined to specialist journals, music criticism won a place in the columns of daily newspapers and other general-interest periodicals. The personalized, romantic note sounded by E. T. A. Hoffmann's celebrated essay on Beethoven's Fifth Symphony echoed down the decades in the criticisms of such masterful stylists as Heinrich Heine, Vladimir Odoyevsky, Arrigo Boito, Willy (Henry Gauthier-Villars) and George Bernard Shaw. Henceforth, for better and for worse, critics (like composers and performers) would be personalities in their own rights, read and renowned for their literary flair as well as their musical insights. It was a rare composer in the nineteenth century who did not turn his hand to journalism from time to time, and the best of these composer-critics – Hector Berlioz in Paris, Robert Schumann in Leipzig, William Henry Fry in New York, Hugo Wolf in Vienna, Bedřich Smetana in Prague, César Cui in St Petersburg – served with distinction both music and letters.

As the forces of nationalism gathered momentum in the late 1800s, increasingly pluralistic and self-conscious musical cultures began to emerge in Eastern Europe and elsewhere. Critics like Josef Foerster in Slovenia, Mihaly Mosonyi in Hungary, Józef Sikorski in Poland, Halfdan Kjerulf in Norway, and Vladimir Stasov in Russia championed the work of native composers and the cultivation of distinctive national styles based largely on indigenous folk traditions. Yet the influence of Germanic composers remained paramount and perennially controversial. The close of the century was dominated by the great Wagner–Brahms debate, which found lasting expression in Shaw's exuberantly polemical prose and in the erudite writings of his redoubtable antagonist, Eduard Hanslick, conservative Vienna's arbiter of musical taste for five decades.

The convergence of strong, vivid personalities, momentous issues, a thriving and relatively untrammelled press, and a bourgeois public hungry for musical culture made the nineteenth century a golden age of music criticism. Never again would critics – or composers, for that matter – enjoy such ready access to the ear of the musical layman. Never again would music occupy such a central position in Western culture. As the twentieth century progressed, the disintegration of traditional tonality and the widening rift between 'serious' composers and the public thrust some critics into an unfamiliar and problematic role: that of advocate and even apologist for contemporary music. Writers like Claude Debussy in France, Hans Heinz Stuckenschmidt in Germany, Ivan Sollertinsky in the Soviet Union, Paul Rosenfeld in the United States, and Willi Schuh in Switzerland felt called upon to plead the case for living composers, unlike most of their predecessors, whose readers by and large took contemporary music in stride.

Recent years have seen a growing interest in music criticism on the part of scholars. Musicologists, reacting against the 'positivistic' emphasis on quantifiable data, are urging a return to a more critical, less value-free approach to musical scholarship. Cultural and intellectual historians have discovered that critics can be valuable barometers of popular taste and fashion. Courses in critical writing and the history of criticism are now offered at many music schools. An international team of scholars is industriously indexing nineteenth-century music periodicals. All in all, it seems an opportune time to take stock and celebrate the achievements of three eventful centuries of music criticism.

Compiling an anthology is a voyage of discovery. The material eligible for inclusion in this one was practically boundless. Some critics, clearly, were too famous or too important to leave out. Others I wanted to include because they were personal favourites or because they represented a significant tradition or point of view. From the outset I intended the anthology to be cosmopolitan in scope and, as far as possible, to focus on critics who not only had something meaningful to say about music but said it well. I wanted it to be an anthology that invited browsing and reflection, as well as providing primary source material for students of music, social and intellectual history, literature, aesthetics and criticism, and Western culture in general.

Reluctant to impose an arbitrary thematic framework on an already subjective selection of critics and articles, I opted for a straightforward chronological organization, while attempting to give form and coherence to the anthology by focusing on a few issues of central importance in music history. These themes were not preselected but emerged from a more or less systematic survey of critical writing in hundreds of books, journals and newspapers. Thus, each article in Part I relates to one of three broad topics that preoccupied critics and musicians throughout the eighteenth century: operatic reform, national styles and the nature of musical taste and criticism. The nineteenth century was captivated by the cult of personality that surrounded the romantic composer and the charismatic virtuoso. Programme music, cultural nationalism and the breakdown of the monolithic concept of taste are other recurring themes of Part II. As the Balkanization of musical culture continued in the twentieth century, the critics in Part III increasingly turned their attention to the value of tradition, the changing relationship between music, musicians and society, and the impact of modern technologies on composers, performers and audiences.

These, then, are the leitmotivs of *The Attentive Listener*. Like the selection of articles, they are meant to be suggestive rather than comprehensive. Although space restrictions dictated that many articles be abridged, I have tried to do so without distorting either the substance or the style of the critic's argument. Textual notes and the paragraphs introducing each article often refer readers to discussions of related topics elsewhere in the book. On the whole, however, I have kept annotations to a minimum. Here and there I have been unable to locate the source of a quote or elucidate a topical allusion, and I would welcome comments and corrections from better-informed readers. Most of the translations are my own. Several of those credited to others are taken from previous publications; the rest were prepared especially for this anthology by Mirka

Zemanová, George Schoolfield, Jaap Schröder, John Gingerich, Richard Miller and Anthony Phillips. I have also profited from the good counsel of Lili Tunks, Marica Tacconi, Larry Kenney, Stephen Hinton, James Deaville, Joseph Horowitz, Scott Burnham, Robert Jackson, Allen Forte, Richard Warren, Michael Tenzer, Helen Sprott, Andrew Clements and Michael Durnin. To each of them I am most grateful. I am also happy to acknowledge the generous financial support of the Hinrichsen Foundation.

PART I

The Eighteenth Century

1

Joseph Addison, [On Italian Opera]

Spectator, no. 18 (21 March 1711)

Addison (1672–1719) was England's first great music journalist, though few reputations rest upon a slenderer foundation: the bulk of his music criticism appeared in the *Spectator* in 1711 and 1712. Addison satirized the weaknesses and absurdities of contemporary operas and stagecraft, reserving his sharpest barbs for the Italian operas that had lately taken England by storm. He exerted a strong influence on Continental critics such as Scheibe and Mattheson (who translated many of Addison's essays in his magazine *Die Vernünftler* in 1713), and his call for the creation of national schools of opera was echoed by critics down the ages.

... Equitis quoque jam migravit ab aure voluptas
Omnis ad incertos oculos & gaudia vana.

Hor.[1]

It is my Design in this Paper to deliver down to Posterity a faithful Account of the *Italian* Opera, and of the gradual Progress which it has made upon the *English* Stage: For there is no Question but our great Grand-children will be very curious to know the Reason why their Forefathers used to sit together like an Audience of Foreigners in their own Country, and to hear whole Plays acted before them in a Tongue which they did not understand.

   Arsinoe was the first Opera that gave us a Taste of *Italian* Musick.[2] The great Success this Opera met with, produced some Attempts of forming Pieces upon *Italian* Plans, which should give a more natural and reasonable Entertainment than what can be met with in the elaborate Trifles of that Nation. This alarm'd the Poetasters and Fidlers of the Town, who were used to deal in a more ordinary Kind of Ware; and therefore laid down an establish'd Rule, which is receiv'd as such to this Day, *That nothing is capable of being well set to Musick, that is not Nonsense.*

   This Maxim was no sooner receiv'd, but we immediately fell to translating the *Italian* Operas; and as there was no great Danger of hurting the Sense of those extraordinary Pieces, our Authors would often make Words of their own which were entirely foreign to the Meaning of the Passages they pretended to translate; their chief Care being to make the Numbers of the *English* Verse answer to those of the *Italian*, that both of them might go to the same Tune. Thus the famous Song in *Camilla*,[3]

Barbara si t'intendo, &c.

Barbarous Woman, yes, I know your Meaning,

which expresses the Resentments of an angry Lover, was translated into that *English* Lamentation

Frail are a Lover's Hopes, &c.

And it was pleasant enough to see the most refined Persons of the *British* Nation dying away and languishing to Notes that were filled with a Spirit of Rage and Indignation. It happen'd also very frequently, where the Sense was rightly translated, the necessary Transposition of Words which were drawn out of the Phrase of one tongue into that of another, made the Musick appear very absurd in one tongue that was very natural in the other. I remember an *Italian* Verse that ran thus Word for Word,

And turn'd my Rage into Pity;

which the *English* for Rhime sake translated,

And into Pity turn'd my rage.

By this Means the soft Notes that were adapted to *Pity* in the *Italian*, fell upon the Word *Rage* in the *English*; and the angry Sounds that were tuned to *Rage* in the Original, were made to express *Pity* in the Translation. It oftentimes happen'd likewise, that the finest Notes in the Air fell upon the most insignificant Words in the Sentence. I have known the Word *And* pursu'd through the whole Gamut, have been entertain'd with many a melodious *The*, and have heard the most beautiful Graces, Quavers and Divisions bestow'd upon *Then*, *For*, and *From*; to the eternal Honour of our *English* Particles.

4

The next Step to our Refinement, was the introducing of *Italian* Actors into our Opera; who sung their Parts in their own Language, at the same Time that our Countrymen perform'd theirs in our native tongue. The King or Hero of the Play generally spoke in *Italian*, and his Slaves answer'd him in *English*: The Lover frequently made his Court, and gained the Heart of his Princess in a Language which she did not understand. One would have thought it very difficult to have carry'd on Dialogues after this Manner, without an Interpreter between the Persons that convers'd together; but this was the State of the *English* Stage for about three Years.

At length the Audience grew tir'd of understanding Half the Opera, and therefore to ease themselves intirely of the Fatigue of Thinking, have so order'd it at Present that the whole Opera is perform'd in an unknown Tongue.[4] We no longer understand the Language of our own Stage; insomuch that I have often been afraid, when I have seen our *Italian* Performers chattering in the Vehemence of Action, that they have been calling us Names, and abusing us among themselves; but I hope, since we do put such an entire Confidence in them, they will not talk against us before our Faces, though they may do it with the same Safety as if it were behind our Backs. In the mean Time I cannot forbear thinking how naturally an Historian, who writes Two or Three hundred Years hence, and does not know the Taste of his wise Fore-fathers, will make the following Reflection, *In the Beginning of the Eighteenth Century the* Italian *Tongue was so well understood in* England, *that Opera's were acted on the publick Stage in that Language.*

One scarce knows how to be serious in the Confutation of an Absurdity that shews itself at the first Sight. It does not want any great Measure of Sense to see the Ridicule of this monstrous Practice; but what makes it the more astonishing, it is not the Taste of the Rabble, but of Persons of the greatest Politeness, which has establish'd it.

If the *Italians* have a Genius for Musick above the *English*, the *English* have a Genius for other Performances of a much higher Nature, and capable of giving the Mind a much nobler Entertainment. Would one think it was possible (at a Time when an Author lived that was able to write the *Phaedra* and *Hippolitus*)[5] for a People to be so stupidly fond of the *Italian* Opera, as scarce to give a Third Days Hearing to that admirable Tragedy? Musick is certainly a very agreeable Entertainment, but if it would take the entire Possession of our Ears, if it would make us incapable of hearing Sense, if it would exclude Arts that have a much greater Tendency to the Refinement of humane Nature: I must confess I would allow it no better Quarter than *Plato* has done, who banishes it out of his Commonwealth.

At present, our Notions of Musick are so very uncertain, that we do not know what it is we like; only, in general, we are transported with any thing that is not *English*: So it be of a foreign Growth, let it be *Italian*, *French* or *High-Dutch*, it is the same thing. In short, our *English* Musick is quite rooted out, and nothing yet planted in its stead.

When a Royal Palace is burnt to the Ground, every Man is at Liberty to present his Plan for a new one; and tho' it be but indifferently put together, it may furnish several Hints that may be of Use to a good Architect. I shall take the same Liberty in a following Paper, of giving my Opinion upon the Subject of Musick, which I shall lay down only in a problematical Manner to be considered by those who are Masters in the Art.

1 'Now even the knights have ceased to take their pleasure through the ears, but have switched their whole allegiance to the unsure eyes and empty joys.' Horace, *Epistles*, 2, 1, 187–8.
2 Thomas Clayton's *Arsinoe, Queen of Cyprus* (1705) was the first all-sung opera in the Italian manner staged in England.
3 Bononcini's opera, first produced in Naples in 1696, enjoyed a run of sixty-three performances in London between 1706 and 1709. The libretto was translated and adapted by Owen Swiney.
4 According to Burney, *Almahide* (1710) was the first opera performed in England wholly in Italian and by Italian singers. Italian and English texts were printed side by side in the libretto books.
5 *Phaedra and Hippolytus* by Edmund Smith (1707).

2

Johann Mattheson, Preface to *Critica musica*

Critica musica, vol. 1 (1722)

Published in Hamburg between 1722 and 1725, *Critica musica* was the first periodical devoted exclusively to music. Mattheson (1681–1764) was distinguished not only as a writer and composer, but also as a theorist, singer, lexicographer and translator. The Hamburg of his day was a thriving commercial and cultural centre; Mattheson himself served as private secretary to the British ambassador. The preface to the first volume of the magazine reveals, in characteristically vigorous and rough-hewn language, his stern devotion to the Enlightenment ideal of rationalistic criticism.

A critique, critique et demi.[1]

The beauty of a garden cannot prevent weeds from sprouting. The richer the soil, the more the bad burgeons forth among the good. As soon as one thinks he has diligently eradicated the weed, it creeps back into the light the next morning. Hitherto I have taken some pains in the wondrously beautiful garden of music, leaving no stone unturned in my efforts to yank out, with all my strength, the old, deep-rooted, rigid, thorny, stiff, unruly, wild, barbaric shrubbery and chuck it out of the way. Sometimes I thought it would not come back again so easily, having been burnt to ashes, root and branch, as it were, in the fire of reason. But see! I cannot yet take proper pleasure in my work, for hardly is the garden clear in one spot when the nuisance bursts forth afresh in another, and (so it please the gods) causes the old pest to come back with new vigour, in changed appearance – here in philosophical guise, there in the shape of modern ignorance.

I see now that this goal cannot be achieved all at once or with a single work. Accordingly, I have decided to undertake it in stages so that something better may perhaps be accomplished. I have fewer doubts about this course of action because, as things stand today, people seldom read an entire book, whereas a couple of monthly magazines can easily be read right through to the end. In this way, too, the attack is always new and may by repetition, almost like a constant drop of water, finally wear many holes in the rock. Moreover, honest reports of many events and such matters will be met with in this criticism, which will not only disabuse many budding musicians of their false principles and inculcate better ones in their stead; it also will place clearly before their eyes the weaknesses of many an Old Master. Now and then there might also be occasion to report some musical news, unusual occurrences, notices, anecdotes and observations about opera, concerts, special topics, etc., and in passing to offer recommendations and surveys for the benefit of all: hitherto this has been lacking, and much good is to be hoped from it.

Anyone who has a contribution to make shall do so: for the works of other virtuoso critics shall gladly be inserted when it is appropriate. But my chief aim will always remain this: to examine all kinds of musical writings and issues – new and old, published and unpublished, domestic and foreign, German, French, Italian, Latin, English, etc. – in the manner of the *Acta eruditorum*,[2] but in even somewhat greater detail. I will aim not only to give a report and summary of each piece of writing (even the occasional rare one), so that everyone may know what the gist of the book is without buying it;[3] but also to praise its good points, reject the pernicious errors, and convey the more beneficial precepts instead. Likewise, if the reader follows our work from the beginning, in time some generally edifying lessons and ideas about composition will no doubt be added, in an unexceptionably critical manner. In the meantime, we shall not commit ourselves to present the foregoing material in any particular order but shall introduce topics as they arise, whether the authors are old or new. Each author, however, shall be treated separately, without interruption, in a special issue of the magazine; hence each issue must bear a special title and deal coherently with the same material to the very end. Now that everyone hopefully has enough information about our plan, we will get on with our work without further preamble.

1 'To criticism, and then some' – a nod, perhaps, to the French critics whom Mattheson admired.
2 A German periodical founded in 1682 and published in Leipzig.
3 Even if some of them can be had for nothing, the truth of the classical proverb has struck home: as a rule, not much that is rare is to be found in rare books (author's note).

3

Anonymous, 'Defence of Operas'

Gentleman's Magazine (July 1735), reprinted from
Universal Spectator (5 July 1735)

Eighteenth-century music criticism was not confined to specialist journals; general-interest publications such as the *Mercure galant* in France, the *Gentleman's Magazine* in England, and the *Journal des Luxus und den Moden* in Germany (see no. 16) increasingly found room for it as well. The music historian John Hawkins became a regular contributor to the *Universal Spectator* some time after the magazine published this garbled but pointedly moralistic account of Handel's *Alcina*

The first Design of the Stage was to discountenance Vice and encourage Virtue, by shewing both in their true Light; and so far Theatrical Entertainments deserve Encouragement, whether the Moral be given in plain Sense, a sublime Stile, or join'd to Musick; which last, indeed, has often been ridiculed for its Absurdity in making Heroes sing their Anger and Resentment as well as their Love; but it is equally unnatural for Men to talk in Rhime or Blank-Verse, to govern Kingdoms, &c. in measured Periods, as to sing their Orders, or defy their Enemies in Musick. These are Cavils of low Wits, who mistake the Design of the Stage, which is to convey a Moral in the most agreeable Manner, and to allure us to Virtue by flattering our Senses, while it improves our Minds; for this Reason the Theatre is allowed to call upon the Sister Arts, Poetry, Painting and Musick. If then an Opera, or a Poem set to Musick, gives us, in some pleasing Allegory, a Lesson of Morality, it must be preferable to the comick Vein or the tragick Stile; the first sets us too much upon the merry Vein to consider the Moral; the Incidents of the latter too much affect us to let us consider the Design of the Poet; or, in attempting the Sublime, he often becomes unintelligible: Neither of these Inconveniencies can be objected to the Pieces set to Musick, the Harmony of which keeps us attentive at the same Time, that more than one Sense is entertained; the Language intelligible, and in a just Mean between the Rant of Tragedy, and the low Wit of

Comedy; besides the Operas of the *Italian* Poets, from whom our Operas are taken, have more delightful Allegories, and more excellent Morals than our modern Writers.

What put me on these Reflections was, a young Gentleman's being very severe on Operas in general, and that of *Alcina* in particular;[1] he could find no Allegory in the whole Piece, and nothing of a Moral. I differed from his Opinion for the following Reasons. The Poem of *Alcina* is finely set to Musick by the inimitable Mr *Handel*, and is taken from *Orlando Furioso*, Book 6, 7. The several Characters in the Fable convey most useful Lessons; it figures to us the Violence of youthful Passions, which hurries us beyond the Bounds of Reason; and makes good the old Proverb, *Repentance treads on the Heels of Sin*; it proves that neither the Counsel of Friends, nor the example of others, can stop the giddy head-strong Youth from the Chase of imaginary or fleeting Pleasures, which infallibly lead them to cruel Reflections, and too late Repentance. The Character of *Alcina*'s Beauty and Inconstancy, proves the short Duration of all sublunary Enjoyments. *Rogero*, the Hero of the Opera, being attack'd by monstrous Forms, figures the Vices which continually war upon us, and his resisting them for some Time, shews the first struggling of a virtuous Mind; for *Nemo repente nequissimus*.[2] *Alcina*'s Change into Deformity by Virtue of an enchanted Ring, which *Melissa*, a Sorceress had given *Rogero*, figures to us Remorse of Conscience awakening Reason, which strips vicious Pleasures of their Paint and gaudy Trappings, shews them in their innate Deformity, and causes our Abhorrence.

---

1 Handel's opera was performed eighteen times at Covent Garden between 16 April and 2 July 1735. The characters to which the writer refers are the sorceress Alcina; Ruggiero, a knight whom she has bewitched; and Melisso, the governor of Ruggiero's betrothed.
2 No one turns bad suddenly.

4

Johann Adolph Scheibe, [A Plea for German Opera]
Critischer Musikus, no. 16 (1 October 1737)

One of the most influential music theorists and writers of his time, Scheibe (1708–76) is remembered today for his rejection of J. S. Bach's music as 'bombastic' and 'confused'. That criticism appeared in Scheibe's journal, *Critischer Musikus*, a few months before this rousing plea to German musicians to cast out the Italians and assert their true musical identity. In his faith in good taste and the imitation of nature, Scheibe was both a child of the Enlightenment and a harbinger of Gluck's operatic reforms.

> *He is all too blind*
> *Who has all the knowledge in the world but understands not*
> *himself.*
>
> Opitz[1]

Is it to be credited that we Germans have so little understanding of the powers bestowed on us by nature? That we are guilty of negligently squandering our treasures, only to reward the fripperies of foreign ingrates? And that countless, increasingly ludicrous prejudices have brought us to the point where we do not esteem our virtues and inborn capacities but almost totally reject them, while marvelling at – and even preferring – the depravities and unnatural practices of other nations?

To be sure, our fatherland has none the less produced the kind of men who, if they have not surpassed foreigners in the arts and sciences, have at least been esteemed their peers. And in our day especially we can boast of men in philosophy, rhetoric, poetry, and at last in criticism as well who can hold their own with the sharpest minds in France and England. Indeed, we can go so far as to flatter ourselves that we possess within our own borders the greatest philosophers ever seen.

Having come so far in these arts and sciences, it is surprising that alongside such virtues we deem two others – namely, music and theatre – worthy of no better examination and respect, although reason and nature have commended them to us for praiseworthy delight and edification. In most people's eyes, theatre remains an object of utter contempt.

In music we have reached the point where we no longer have need of foreigners to produce our pieces, and where we see the beauties of Italian and French music being practised by our own people with greater understanding, diligence and experience. Yet still we detect a certain lack in performances of our pieces, a lack which at present we take not the slightest trouble to correct nor ever dream that we would remedy it if only we were willing to take a closer look at ourselves.

Nature and reason demand that for music to be complete, the vocal parts must consist of soprano, alto, tenor and bass; for not only is the harmony thereby fuller but also the contrast arising therefrom is one of the most notable amenities. Furthermore, we can express all the singers' characters without offending against verisimilitude – something which is impossible with unison or similar voices. So universal is this principle that unless it is taken into account in the truest sense, no complete piece of church music, no opera, no oratorio, no other vocal piece, pastorale or serenade can be written and performed without being deprived of one of the greatest beauties that flows irrevocably from reason and nature.

Most of my readers will no doubt wonder that I am expounding to them a truth so old and universal; but their surprise will soon end if they will permit me to take them into most of our musical theatres.

We await the first character to appear on stage. The symphony comes to an end, the curtain is raised. A voice is heard, womanish but powerful, emanating from a body whose costume presents to us the portrait of a hero. Let us first check in the libretto to see whether this character is made up as a female, an Amazon, or someone from Topsy-turvy Land. No, nothing of the sort: it is Alexander the Great. What? Alexander the Great? Since when has this mighty world-conqueror changed into a weakling, or perchance a woman?[2]

Who then is this man on his knees who sighs so movingly, so womanishly, and so cravenly in a weak alto voice for the favour of his lovely goddess? Is it not one of Alexander the Great's pages? Absolutely not. It is haughty Hephästion, one of the celebrated king's most distinguished generals – Hephästion who, in his wisdom and valour, smites down all that stands in his path.

But here comes another character. Let us see who this is, lamenting in a screeching soprano the cruelty of fortune and the pitilessness of a married lady. Surely he must be a libertine sponger? Far from it. He is virtuous Lisimachus, who subdued a lion with no weapon but his bare hands; who, by dint of virtue and patience, most gloriously reclaimed the royal favour which the envy of his enemy had denied him.

At last we are going to hear a chorus of heroes. What? Nothing but sopranos and altos? Has Alexander then conquered the world with an army of women?

Such are the virtues of Italian opera, which we have imported and adopted in Germany and for which we go to great expense to order women singers and castrati all the way from Italy. What would it avail the poet to produce a better dramatization and characters? For inasmuch as all are sung by womanly – or womanish – voices, they would lose their very natures. This lunacy is already so widespread that practically everywhere in Germany one hears nothing but sopranos and altos in serenades and songs, and even in religious oratorios, though one seldom hears decent basses and tenors. Italian opera and music have nothing else to offer; for since the Italians themselves have no basses and tenors, we want (out of a peculiar conceit) to make our imitation of them complete and even to match their shortcomings, without considering that we are rendering ourselves unnatural in the process.

German men are more partial to the tenor and bass voices than are men of other nations. Our strongest singers are in these categories, making us the envy even of Italy. But we are far too careless, and far too prejudiced against 'foreigners', to heed these advantages. Instead, we demand a steady supply of Italian sopranos and altos, straying further and further from the laws of nature and reason. Consequently, the nearer our greatest masters of music come to good taste, the further we put it behind us ...

I do not on that account reject all Italian singers, male and female. The glory that several of them have earned is far too great, and the great skill that they have continually proved in various noteworthy demonstrations deserves the just admiration of every rational person.

But the overriding question remains: Would we in Germany not also have female singers – singers who would do just as much hon-our to theatre, palace, and church as foreigners – if we sought them out and supported them with a modicum of training and the requi-site funds? Surely experience shows that we would indeed find women of that sort, if only we were willing to provide for them. The main thing is that we should value ourselves more highly and do more to encourage our compatriots. Would we not thereby do ourselves credit? Would we not rightly conserve many treasures which we have needlessly squandered, as well as furnishing a noble art with all manner of skilled souls who lack training and support?

In Germany we find not only palaces but also imposing cities which spend large sums on music every year and maintain huge bands of singers and instrumentalists. Hence it is clear that a very great number of male and female singers may be found in Germany … I shall offer a proposal for musical training designed to test the possibility of bringing up young people of both sexes so as to ensure the advancement of vocal music and the banishment of haughty Italians from our borders.

A complete choir, for use in the theatre as well as in church and chamber music, can consist of no fewer than eight persons. I break it down as follows: a pair of sopranos, a pair of altos, a pair of tenors, a higher bass, or so-called baritone, and finally a lower bass. These eight persons must all be skilled. But since the choirs would still need to be filled out, chapel boys could easily be recruited in the palaces, or schoolboys in the cities. Among the eight lead singers, women must be engaged for the soprano and alto parts, as their voices will be more natural and have greater stamina and puri-ty. For the tenors and basses, one must select men who have voices which are sturdy, natural, and clear.

One way of establishing a choir of this sort on a continuing basis and at the same time of creating a beneficial surplus of skilled men and women singers – which would make our neighbours pay as much attention to us as hitherto we have paid to the Italians – would be as follows:

One chooses several young girls whose poverty already com-mands our compassion and whose upbringing is a Christian duty of the authorities. One does the same with several poor boys. Those who show a special talent for music will soon distinguish them-selves from the rest. Assuming that their musical proclivity is accompanied by clear, strong, natural voices, they are placed under the supervision of a pair of skilled singers who, in addition to having good taste, are competent in the rudiments of music. These teachers must instruct the students with great care not only in singing but also in the essential and practical rudiments of music, so that they learn not only how to sing but also to judge how they ought to sing. At the same time they must be introduced to pure, clear diction and fitting gestures. Finally, they must also be trained in the most essential languages, namely, German, Italian and French. Knowledge of these languages can often be very useful; moreover, it is in very poor taste for a singer to sing in a language of which he knows nothing ...

The Italians have learned very well from long experience how useful it is to take precautions of this sort. They derive such a marked profit from their musical nurseries that they are more and more motivated to support their foundations and established customs.[3] And in sending their boys and girls abroad, they not only gain great renown but make themselves virtually indispensable. If their constitutions and temperaments – and perhaps their customs as well – permitted, they would certainly be just as careful and diligent with the lower voices.[4]

And so it is right, is it not, that we use the powers bestowed on us by nature, that we proffer our gifts, that in our church music we praise and extol the highest being in a multitude of voices and in perfect harmony, that in our songs we express the laws and qualities of character ordained by nature, and finally that we let our own people recover their rights, provide for them rationally, and confer upon them, to our own glory and profit, the same rewards that we grant to other peoples out of sheer negligence.

1 Martin Opitz, the poet, critic and metrical reformer.
2 Alexander the Great was a popular operatic subject for Baroque composers. Handel's *Alessandro*, for instance, had been produced in Hamburg in 1726.
3 Many Italian *ospedali*, charitable institutions which served as orphanages and hospitals, offered musical tuition for children. Systematic musical education along the lines Scheibe proposes was, however, a long way in the future.
4 According to the latest reports out of Italy, good singers, male and female, are also quite rare. Those who have good voices learn a few arias by heart and are proficient in them, but they understand virtually nothing about music. The castrati are exceedingly haughty and scarcely know how unruly their behaviour is (author's note).

5

Friedrich Wilhelm Marpurg, [The Attentive Listener]
Critische Musicus an der Spree (27 May 1749)

Fashionable eighteenth-century audiences were accustomed to being told what to think about music; Marpurg urged them to open their ears and judge for themselves. A prolific, learned, and often lively author, Marpurg (1718–95) produced a large body of books and periodicals, starting with *Der critische Musicus an der Spree* (The Critical Musician on the River Spree), paying titular homage to Scheibe's *Critischer Musikus* (see no. 4). Burney rated Marpurg's writing highly; this article illustrates his entertaining, unpretentious style.

Attentiveness on the part of listeners is unquestionably one of the best means of stimulating the lofty ambition of skilled virtuosos, or of other well-bred persons devoted to music, and thereby of raising the level of good taste. But attentiveness is not simply a matter of keeping quiet during a concert, of not playing cards and appearing to listen without distraction. Nor is it enough to refrain from disrupting the Muses' agreeable strains with trampling feet or disorderly chatter. We owe the performer's skill a clearer sign of our approval. The enticing tones with which he delights us deserve the honour of a compliment. To prick the concert artist's zeal and encourage music lovers in this way does not yet seem to be altogether fashionable. Here and there people are still accustomed to listening to everything with frigid and phlegmatic indifference.

After demurring briefly, charming young Phyllis allows herself to be prevailed upon to play. At once people gather around the piano, grouping themselves according to their social class. Her dexterity is wonderful; she does credit to her teacher. But in her stolid listeners she elicits no response. One after another they retire to their seats in respectful silence. Doris sings incomparably. The range of her voice, the delicacy of her trills, the purity of her diction – everything about her is extraordinary. Yet her lifeless listener does not realize it, or is not cultured enough to let it be seen. Not until he is shown a roll of tobacco does he open his mouth: its taste is more familiar to him than musical taste. All at once he shakes off his stoical slumber. Then the others wake up, each one putting in a word as his nose catches a whiff of this celebrated plant. Hitherto they have sat stiff and motionless, like Christmas dolls wrapped up on their chairs – except, perhaps, for an idler who, not yet knowing the ways of the dandy, began to tell sparkling-eyed Lisette about the locusts in Hungary as soon as the piece was over; or another fellow who played with his pocket watch (which he had just redeemed for the third time from a squalid usurer), giving all and sundry an excuse to ask the time. This insensitivity, this failure to listen to tonal refinement with a serious and somewhat dignified demeanour, is becoming the rule; and if someone is moved and wishes to show his approval to several performers – or, to avoid arousing jealousy, to the whole lot of concert artists – by complimenting them publicly, he must keep it to himself, unless he wants to pass for a buffoon from France in the eyes of the simpleton.

In the end it is no wonder some listeners are tongue-tied and insensitive. Their conception of what is good and bad in music is so uncertain that they cannot decide whether they should praise or find fault. Under the circumstances they play it safe and hold their tongues. We tend to ascribe great intelligence to people who say little or nothing; they are invariably mistaken for the most thoughtful connoisseurs of music. If they opened their mouths, however, they would let their secret out at once. Everyone would see that they are not what we took them to be, and their weakness would lie exposed to the eyes of the world. But why do these people not endeavour to acquire some knowledge of musical taste? Then they would have the pleasure of being able to use their own judgment in giving the good or the bad its due. If someone in their group brought up a musical topic, they could take part in the discussion. They would know why one aria is better than another and how this player differs from that one, even though both may deserve applause and one player's merit does not detract from the other's.

It would not be enough for them that some distinguished man considered a certain piece pretty and clever. They would speak out of their own convictions and would not feel obliged to stop admiring the piece as soon as the distinguished man pronounced it ugly because it had aged a bit. We all know that even distinguished people can be wrong. Many a man, when his shares have risen and he is in a good mood, pleased with himself and his ducats, tends to consider anything he hears, even the most simple-minded street song, to be a most wonderful work that Apollo himself could not have composed more elegantly. But catch this man, whose mood changes with the weather, on his Sabbath, on that gloomy day when he is feeling down on himself, and in that melancholy moment place before him the most finely crafted masterpiece: he will condemn it, and all the numskulls will go along – not because they are truly convinced that he is right, but because they are incapable of judging for themselves. So-and-so has said it, and that is enough for them.

Furthermore, how many such seducers of the hoi polloi are not guided more often by other motives – favouritism, prejudice, yes, even ignorance? Titius of E. likes nothing but what Lucil does. Lucil is his hero. So blinded is he by prejudice that Lucil seems scarcely mortal. Everything Lucil writes is unbeatable; everyone else's music revolts him. If you want Titius to despise Lucil's piece, tell him Barus wrote it. But if you want him to praise Barus unwittingly and unwillingly, scratch Barus's name off the title page and put Lucil's in its place: satisfaction guaranteed. Sempronia will not admit that any music is beautiful unless it resembles the songs, minuets and peasant dances she already knows. If someone sings her an ode in which the composer has been carried away and mixed serious expression with a touch of vaudeville, she will smile behind her fan and let her friends know that she would not remain aloof if some man were to serenade her beneath her window. At once these good friends learn this pastiche by heart. It wins approval – and too often the greatest connoisseurs will betray their taste to please Sempronia. No wonder people who as yet have no taste, who do not know how to distinguish ugliness from beauty, acquire misconceptions. No wonder good taste is not yet so widespread as not to require some instruction from time to time.

For the benefit of those who still have not taken in the concept of beauty in music, on behalf of these budding connoisseurs, I propose to translate into our language a little foreign tract, which apparently has not yet been widely circulated in our country, and to bring it out in these pages in instalments. This matter of good taste in music is so essential, and to my knowledge so little has been written about it (apart from the superb treatise of the renowned

Herr Scheibe),[1] that it would be irresponsible not to make such a document thoroughly familiar to our worthy music lovers. Herr Grandvall,[2] the author of this tract, had, when he prepared it, been appearing on the lyric stage in Paris to great acclaim for nearly twenty years. During that time he took part in performances of a fair number of operas, both good and bad. His longstanding involvement with music and with the best intellects in the field, the mature insight he has acquired over many years, and diligent reflection put him in a position to venture an experiment concerning good taste in music, and the encouragement of a noblewoman at court induced him to publish it. Many people, to whom the French theatre is not yet well known, will gain sufficient knowledge of it from this document. I shall begin to serialize it in the fifth number. Should annotations be needed here and there, I will supply them. I desire nothing more than that everyone may acquire sound ideas about the true beauty of music, and that nothing be approved or rejected without good reason. For this, rational judgment is required, nothing more.

1 Scheibe's *Critischer Musikus* had been republished in one volume in 1745.
2 Nicolas Racot de Grandval, French composer and writer. His *Essay sur le bon goust en musique* (Essay on Good Taste in Music) appeared in 1732.

6

Marc-Antoine Laugier (?), 'Zoroastre'
Sentiment d'un harmoniphile, part 2 (1756)

By the mid-1700s France had a long tradition of music criticism, but *Sentiment d'un harmoniphile sur différents ouvrages de musique* (A Music-Lover's View of Various Musical Works) was the first French magazine devoted to the subject. Like its German models, it aspired to be both topical and philosophical. Its authorship has been attributed to Marc-Antoine Laugier (1713–69), a stalwart defender of French music against the criticism of Rousseau and others (see nos. 9 and 12). This essay testifies to France's musical awakening and accurately describes the innovative part Rameau played in it.

Mediocre talents, always satisfied with themselves, regard their creations as masterpieces. Everything of theirs seems to bear the stamp of immortality. Fondness blinds them to the imperfections in their works, like fathers who dote upon their children, showering praise even on their faults and letting their budding defects grow until it is too late to root them out. Great geniuses, on the other hand, are like strict fathers who let nothing slip by them. Dissatisfied with their work, they are always searching for ways to do better. However sublime a piece may be, if it does not live up to their expectations, they put it back on the anvil to beat it into a new shape.

Several examples spring to mind. Despite the success that *Castor et Pollux* scored when it was new, M. Bernard, the author of the words of this tragedy, recast his work to give it greater interest.[1] M. Rameau in turn made the necessary corrections in the music, and their opera became a masterpiece.[2] *Zoroastre*, tragedy by messieurs de Cahuzac[3] and Rameau, needed considerable reworking and the authors set to it with pleasure. What immense richness there is in the harmony of this opera! Admirable symphonies, sublime choruses, striking arias! Everything in it is worthy of the celebrated musician who composed it.

The overture to an opera may be considered either as a symphony, bearing no relation to the drama; or as a depiction of one part of the piece; or as a characteristic tableau of the entire drama. In the first case, it serves simply as a frontispiece to the work; in the second, it introduces the main themes and sets the stage for the opening scenes; and in the third case, it is a résumé of the whole plot. M. Rameau is the first musician to conceive overtures of the last type. Before him, these sorts of symphonies were always based on the same model; so great was the force of precedent that no one dared to stray from the beaten path. Now that the yoke has been shaken off, great care is taken to give the overture some connection with the drama, and works demanding no scene-painting start with a brilliant concerto: ballets, for example, in which each act is a self-contained drama.

In *Zoroastre*, the overture is a superb tableau which sets forth the principal elements of the plot. An awesome symphony announces, in its harshness, the oppression of the peoples and their laments under the tyrannical power of the barbarous Abramane. The benevolent character of Zoroastre, who comes to break their chains, is expressed in the second part of the overture. Sorrow gives way to hope, soon to be followed by a lively joy that marks the gratitude of the oppressed toward their liberator ...

The music of *Zoroastre*[4] makes an incontestable case for French music against the claims of its enemies.[5] To appreciate it fully, one must be perfectly conversant with the language the music expresses, assuming the performance to be perfect (as it seldom is in France today) with respect both to the voices and to a taste and spirit in keeping with the expressions. There is no proportion among the voices in the choruses. Some shout; others sing out of tune; others, like the basses, can be heard too little or not at all. There is no proportion in the orchestra either. The first violins play louder than the seconds; some sections of the orchestra are too weak, their numbers being too small to realize the contrasts between soft and loud; or else they have poor instruments with strings that are too thin. Some of the young musicians are not very attentive, slurring notes on a single bow when they should be bowed separately. The same is true of the wind instruments: when they should dominate or be equal to the voice, the accompaniment comes out; then, when it really needs to come out, the effect is spoiled.

This is what we have come to. Now, how can we expect our music to give as much pleasure as might if it were executed perfectly? In spite of that, ask the good Italian musicians in Paris what they think of our music on the basis of *Zoroastre* alone. First of all, concerning the only two ariettes – or, more correctly, the only two airs – in it, they will agree that we are their peers in this genre, especially when the lively tempo permits us to make use of simple unisons. The flavour of these ariettes depends solely on our poets: they will be animated, playful and comic when the poets want them to be. Our recitative is lyrical and expressive, and if it is poorly done, the fault lies with the singers. Some of them would rather be known for their voices than for their spirit and feeling, while others sacrifice everything to feeling, using song and speech, notes and noise, indiscriminately. Italian recitative, by contrast, is neither lyrical nor expressive, and if some people claim that it is notated declamation, it's because they cannot excuse it otherwise; after all, even the Italians merely listen to it in order to follow the plot, and stop listening once they know the words. The symphonies of our operas are worthier and more distinguished than those of the Italians. We can cite, for instance, the symphonies of M. Rameau, which are presently making the rounds of theatres all over Europe, and throughout the world as well. As for the choruses, those in *Zoroastre*, like those in all the author's other operas, are universally admired, as much as some which redound to the glory of other French musicians.

1 In fact, *Castor et Pollux* had a lukewarm reception at the Paris Opéra in 1737. After extensive revisions by Rameau and the librettist, Pierre-Joseph Bernard, it was a notable success in 1754.

2 Misfortune seems to have dogged all of M. Rameau's tragedies. Apart from *Hippolyte et Aricie*, for which the abbé [Simon-Joseph] Pellegrin wrote the poem, all the rest have been reworked by the authors (author's note). [*Hippolyte et Aricie* too was revised during its initial run – Ed.]

3 Louis de Cahusac. *Zoroastre* was staged at the Opéra in 1749 and again in 1756.

4 This opera, by virtue of the great number of varied sets and machines it requires, could have presented a most magnificent and truly grand spectacle. A few of the sets were tolerably well executed, but the rest were mediocre, and the way they were deployed – by means of ropes crossing the theatre from side to side – was often extremely awkward. The stagehands could be heard shouting, 'Push, pull!' to one another during an interesting scene, in plain view of the audience. It's high time we paid attention to remedying such blemishes, which disrupt the show and expose it to ridicule (author's note).

5 Let us always be given music like that of the fourth act of *Zoroastre* and it will not be 'so much the worse for us' that we have a national music, as M. Rousseau said at the end of his *Lettre sur la musique française* (author's note). [Rousseau's 'letter' of 1753, a key document in the Querelle des Bouffons (see nos. 7 and 9), is translated in Strunk, *Source Readings*. – Ed.]

7

Friedrich Melchior Grimm, [Obituary of Jean-Philippe Rameau]

Correspondence littéraire (1764; repr. Paris, 1877)

Among the most celebrated of the Encyclopedists, Grimm (1723–1807) wrote about music with passion, penetration and wit. Born in Regensburg, he moved to Paris in 1749 and embroiled himself in the Querelle des Bouffons (see no. 9) on the side of the Italians. *Le petit Prophète de Boehmischbroda* (1753), a satirical putdown of French opera, made his name a byword in musical circles. That same year he joined Diderot and several others in founding the *Correspondence littéraire*, a lively chronicle of opinion and events, where this deliciously double-edged appreciation appeared shortly after Rameau's death on 12 September 1764.

Jean-Philippe Rameau, storied in the annals of French music, has just died at the age of eighty-two.[1] He leaves us several theoretical works on music, a large number of operas, a collection of harpsichord pieces, and other musical creations. In France Rameau suffered the fate of all great men: he was persecuted long and mercilessly. Because someone named Lully had made plain, pious settings of Quinault's lyric poems during the reign of Louis XIV, Rameau was accused of destroying good taste in singing, and of dealing a mortal blow to French opera. His works all fell flat at first, and although they subsequently recovered, his champions were none the less regarded as heretics and almost as bad citizens. Later, when Italian music made inroads in France, Rameau's bitterest enemies traded their rancour for the blindest admiration and, unable to abide Lully, set Rameau's name and fame in opposition to the champions of Italian music. This too was treated as a patriotic affair: it was an insult to the nation to prefer a music from beyond the Alps to that of a Frenchman – and an old man at that. From that time on, every journalist, especially those who had written most slanderously about poor Rameau, hailed him as Europe's foremost musician once a month in print.

Europe, however, scarcely knew the name of her foremost musician; she knew none of his operas, nor could she ever have tolerated a production in her theatres: in the end all she knew of her foremost musician boiled down to a few dance tunes, which French dancers from time to time carried to foreign countries, where more often than not some orchestra leader went to the trouble of correcting them in order to give them a bit of style, taste and grace. It must be admitted that our press causes as much mischief with its praise as with its insults; our most mediocre characters are promoted and extolled more in three months than other countries' greatest men are in their entire lives; and since this foolish admiration is compounded with ignorance, we persuade ourselves that neither genius nor talent exists elsewhere, because the *Mercure de France* and the *Avant-Coureur* don't mention them. The *Gazette de France*, in announcing Rameau's death, says that his name and works will constitute an epoch in music – in French music, the paper should have said, for I'll be hanged if Rameau and all his notes have ever counted for anything elsewhere in Europe. If Europe has lost her foremost musician, she is in precisely the same position as the Jews are *vis-à-vis* their Messiah, whom they have never been able to acknowledge in the eighteen hundred years since they put him to death, no matter how tortuously they try to apply to him the meaning of their prophecies.

Rameau left several theoretical and highly obscure works on the principle of harmony. The journalists say he made discoveries of the greatest importance on this subject – one more service he performed for the art of music, unbeknown to all the conservatories of Italy and all the schools of Germany. I realize that the inventor of counterpoint was as great a genius as Pythagoras; but I fail to see what purpose M. Rameau's alleged discoveries will ever serve. In his operas this famous man crushed all of his predecessors by dint of harmony and notes. Some of his choruses are very beautiful. Lully only knew how to sustain a vocal line with a continuo; Rameau added orchestral accompaniments to his recitatives practically everywhere. It is true that they are in rather poor taste, that they almost always serve to smother the voice instead of supporting it, and that it is this which has forced the actors of the Opéra to emit those shouts and shrieks that are so excruciating to delicate ears. One emerges from a Rameau opera drunk with harmony, and stunned by the noise of the voices and instruments: his taste is always Gothic, his style always heavy-handed in both its grace and its forcefulness. He was never at a loss for ideas, but he didn't know what to do with them; his recitative, like Lully's, is a *mélange* of nonstop absurdities and a few felicitous declamations. As for his airs, since the poet demanded no more of him than that he play around with words like 'lance', 'vole', 'triomphe', 'enchaîne', etc., or that he imitate the nightingale's song with flageolets and other childishness of that sort, there is nothing to say. If he had been able to finish his training in some school in Italy, and to learn what style and thought in music are, what composing is all about, he never would have said that all poems were the same to him, and that he would set the *Gazette de France* to music. He could have created music in his country, but he succeeded only in imitating – and crushing – Lully.

Rameau was by nature hard-hearted and unsociable, a stranger to all human feelings. I was present one day when he said he could never comprehend why people wished that the duke of Burgundy[2] would demonstrate kingly qualities. 'What difference does that make to me?' he said naively. 'I won't be around any more when he's on the throne.' 'But your children ... ?' He simply did not understand that one could be interested in one's children beyond one's own lifespan. His guiding passion was avarice. He cared nothing for reputation, awards, glory; he wanted money and he died a rich man. He was as remarkable in his appearance as he was famous for his works. Much taller than M. de Voltaire, he was equally pale and gaunt. Some years ago M. de Carmontelle[3] sketched him from memory the way people used to see him on his endless public walks; that little engraving is cleverly done and very true to life.

1 In fact, Rameau died just shy of his eighty-first birthday.
2 The dauphin Louis, grandson of Louis XIV and father of Louis XV.
3 Louis Carmontelle, the painter and engraver.

8

Johann Adam Hiller, 'Report on the Comic Opera *Lisuart und Dariolette*'

Wöchentliche Nachrichten und Anmerkungen die Musik betreffend, no. 33 (10 February 1767)

The *Wöchentliche Nachrichten und Anmerkungen die Musik betreffend* (Weekly Reports and Remarks Concerning Music) has been called the first modern music magazine. Published in Leipzig from 1766 to 1770, it was the brainchild of Hiller (1728–1804), a prolific writer, concert promoter, and composer who virtually created the German Singspiel. This tongue-in-cheek 'review' of his own opera, first performed at the Rannstädter Thor on 25 November 1766, reflects Hiller's cosmopolitan sympathies and a sensibility which today might be termed 'middle-brow'.

We promised our readers a more detailed description of this piece, and it is right that we keep our word. Neither poet nor composer shall be showered with praises by us: both are too close to us to shield our effusions from charges of bias. Nevertheless, we can give the reader an idea of both the poet's and the composer's work without offending the modesty of either man. We shall start with a few brief observations.

We Germans are still unfortunate enough to have no Singspiels or operas in our mother tongue. Where does the blame for this lie? Surely one need look no further than the fact that the Germans' genius is not sufficiently respected, drawn out and encouraged. The Italians and their language have taken over the greatest courts in Germany and their musical stages, and even if in some courts a German genius has had the good fortune to invest the post of kapellmeister with glory, the German language always seems to be the least of his worries. 'Of course,' they say, 'the German language isn't fit for music.' This complaint rests on a very flimsy foundation. The most that can be said with confidence is that German does not sit quite as comfortably with music as Italian does, and that therefore we still do not have many good librettos in German. Both statements are true; but the first problem can be overcome in part and the second *in toto*. The infelicities of the language will pretty much disappear if the poet is attentive and takes care not to consider everything that can be twisted into verse equally suitable for setting to music. All languages have poets to thank for their improvement, and so too it is up to ours to acquit our language of a charge which, were it founded, would bring discredit on all of their poetry. It would be still more conducive to correcting the defects of the language if Germans cultivated good singing more assiduously – if we trained singers ourselves and inured them over time to the good diction which is beneficial to singing.

Here we have just one comment to make: one of the major infelicities of our language is that so many syllables end not with vowels but with consonants. But cannot a skilful singer, equipped with a nimble tongue and light diction, do much to correct these defects by always enunciating the vowel very clearly and slowly, and so uttering the clustered consonants all the more quickly – in short, by imagining that all syllables ended with vowels and that all the following consonants belonged to the following syllable? Likewise listeners, whose ears are pampered and seduced by *bravura* and glitter, could contribute to this improvement of the language if they were more enamoured of emotion and expression. These are qualities to which our musical language is perfectly adapted, whereas Italian has the advantage in the *bravura* department. And while it is true that we sometimes sacrifice beauty on this account, we may also have less musical claptrap to listen to.

A few words more about the dearth of German librettos. A good libretto must use the language of feeling and have a suitable prosodic structure. Our old poets were especially careful in respect of the latter, but too often they neglected the former. Today the opposite is true: the language of feeling appears to have become the poet's native tongue, but the mechanism of their verses is often all the more unmusical. It is true that in order to produce a good libretto, a poet must also be to some degree both a musician and a composer. Since this combination is undoubtedly to be found only in the rarest cases, one would wish that the outstanding treatise by the lawyer Krause, *On Musical Poetry*,[1] were read more widely and diligently. No treatment of this subject could be more thorough, comprehensive and beautifully written. Even Metastasio could use it as a model, the more so since his metres readily lend themselves to imitation in German. The French poets are much poorer models for the librettist. Even when they don't lack feeling, there is always too much scene-painting and epigrammatic wit in their poetry. Moreover, they are a long way from understanding the musical period the way Metastasio does, as the editor of the *Essay on the Union of Poetry and Music*[2] showed them not long ago. As a result, good German singers, skilful and attentive poets, successful and tasteful composers – who, as even foreigners admit, are now more plentiful here than ever – in the end could well supply us with good German Singspiels, if the German fatherland would cast its eyes more on its children. Since this may still be hoped for at present, perhaps efforts which we have deemed minor are in fact worthy of note.

Let us now consider the piece that has been performed here on Herr Koch's stage,[3] *Lisuart und Dariolette*, or *The Question and the Answer*, in somewhat greater detail. Its poetic structure is modelled on the so-called comic operas or comedies with interpolated songs that have recently become fashionable in France. From time to time people still object to singing in the theatre on the grounds that it is unnatural. This is not the place to rebut this objection, and perhaps after all it is not even necessary. But let French poets judge whether it is any more more natural to hear a piece half-sung and half-spoken (as they would have us believe) than to see a knight running beside his horse with one leg in the stirrup and the other on the ground. It is fashionable enough in France, and we follow suit. The author of *Lisuart* at first composed his piece merely as a postlude, without songs, but at length the style now coming into vogue moved him to try on this French coat, though in the event he gave it more of an Italian than a French cut. In many of his arias, especially those sung by the knight Lisuart and the princess Dariolette, a noble and highly musical feeling prevails. The duet sung by this same pair toward the end of the third act, 'So should I call you mine', would hold its own in the greatest Italian opera. The other roles, such as those of the equerry Derwin and the ladies-in-waiting, are comic roles, though not grotesquely so. The arias, or rather ariettas, of these characters are not quite in the mould of the knight's and princess's serious arias, but this is not so essential here, since the composer can help himself by varying the pace and, in general, the style of performance.

In this piece, too, the composer has been meticulously true to the poet. He has sought to present all of Lisuart's arias, as well as several of Dariolette's, in a style commensurate with the serious taste and customary character of a well-crafted aria ...

If only Germans took more account of their own genius, their own taste, and did not cling so hard to imitation! If foreigners must indeed be held up as models, we should not be turned into either French or Italians; rather, French and Italians should be turned into Germans. Perhaps from time to time the French produce a piece whose design is good and workable for us. One accepts it, but one does not believe that all songs which sound beautiful to French ears, and their endless little airs, must also sound beautiful to ours. The French audience is always vocal, but ours is not so presumptuous. It wants to be moved and delighted by music; admittedly, an air delights it too now and then. Therefore, a French design cast in an Italian mould would be more entertaining and pleasing to our taste every time, even if one were forced to keep up the fashion to half-speak and half-sing a piece. For no long-winded proof is needed that our taste in music is more in accord with the Italian than with the French ...

1 *Von der musikalischen Poesie* (1752), by Christian Gottfried Krause, dealt with setting words to music.

2 *Essai sur l'union de la poésie et de la musique* (1765), by François-Jean, marquis de Chastellux.

3 The impresario H. G. Koch, for whom Hiller wrote most of his Singspiels.

9

Michel-Paul-Guy de Chabanon, 'Letter on the Musical Properties of the French Language'

Mercure de France (January 1773)

Opera was a central and contentious issue in the tangled artistic politics of the late eighteenth century. In the 1750s the Querelle des Bouffons pitted partisans of French and Italian opera against each other in a war waged largely through pamphlets and journalistic jeremiads. Among the leaders of the pro-Italian forces were Grimm (see no. 7) and Rousseau; the latter's *Lettre sur la musique française* (1753) elicited many rejoinders, including this belated one by the theorist, composer and violinist Chabanon (1729/30–92), a close friend of Rameau.

Sir: I read in the second *Mercure* of October that M. Gluck, renowned for the Italian operas he has set to music, has just cast an acquisitive eye on our language and applied his talent to a French libretto.[1]

M. Gluck's enterprise is remarkable in that it contradicts the forceful assertion of M. Rousseau.[2] The foreign artist, following the author of *Ernelinde*,[3] has lifted the embargo on our language. But not merely does he deem it worthy of assisting his art: he prefers it to all other languages. This startling conclusion, especially coming from a foreigner who is not blinkered by chauvinism, has put me in mind of discussing the possible justifications for it, as well as the arguments which have been advanced against it. Before beginning this discussion, allow me to make some general observations.

It has been said that all men are discontented with their lot. All peoples are so with their language: we moderns envy the language of the Romans, the Romans envied the language of the Greeks. Everyone complains about his share.

I have often heard it asserted that one language is pre-eminent over another; but at heart such claims are merely the judgments of society, and they have all of society's fickleness. As a rule they are based on *aperçus* rather than profound examination, on appearances rather than reasoned proofs. I would have languages be judged as men are, by their works ...

I would like those who judge a language by its physical properties to determine its essential character according to their observations. After all, if this character exists, conferred by the inherent structure of the language, it is obvious that every writer must adapt to it and follow it. One would, I think, criticize a writer who strove to be effusive in a language made for concision. His writing would be bloated, like a frog in a skin which is too tight and refuses to stretch.

But what language is there whose character and properties have been determined, such that one cannot find in it quite the opposite properties and an altogether different character? Cicero is effusive, Tacitus concise. Which of the two better understood the character of his language? Both, with equal success, lent it the character of their genius.

What can one say about our French language? Naturally obscure on account of the difficulty and ambiguity of its relative pronouns, it has won praise for its extreme clarity. No one questions this advantage; it is the language of the *philosophes* and consequently of reason. How can one explain the contradiction between the language's inherent flaw and the major virtue it has acquired? It is because writers have concentrated their efforts on the language's weakness; from its inherent flaw they have derived one of its means of perfection. The language is what writers make of it ...

Concerning the musical properties of the French language, the public is of three minds:

1 Our language is musical, but Lully created the only music of which it is capable.

2 The language lends itself to the forms of modern song, but these forms are unworthy of the dignity of opera.

3 We are unsuited to good music of any kind and are condemned never to sing.

When we have dealt with these three views, it will only remain for us to set forth our own in response to M. Gluck's.

I fear I must point out, sir, that Lully did not create the musical genre which he is alleged to have invented: he merely imported it from Italy, where it was well established. Anyone who is taken aback by this proposition need only recall Corelli's music: his French style teaches us what Italian music used to be. In order to become French, it merely had to become old-fashioned, since the Italians had changed their musical language while we hung on to ours.

After all, what difference does it make whether this music was adopted or created in our midst? Is it the only music that suits us? That is the question.

The public itself provides the answer. Lully's music must indeed have lost its appeal, since so little of it has been allowed to survive when Quinault's works are revived in the theatre. What a strange twist of fate for the two authors! It used to be that people supported Quinault for Lully's sake, or so it was believed. Today it is Quinault's works which, escaping from obscurity, bring back fragments of the old music which otherwise were destined to perish[4] ...

Let us move on to the second view, according to which we should not applaud at an opera that which we applaud at an Italian comedy.

It may seem startling, sir, that in music we draw a distinction between two districts of Paris which we would hardly draw between two disparate climates ... But I was forgetting that different forms of entertainment are in question, and the dignity of opera is involved ...

It remains for us to discuss a third view. This one is the most formidable; not that I believe it to be the truest, but the merit and fame of its author[5] lend it a force almost equal to that of truth ...

'Our language,' says M. Rousseau, 'composed of mixed sounds and sounds which are mute, unvoiced, or nasal, having few open vowels and many consonants and articulations, is completely contrary to music.'

I would like to talk with M. Rousseau to find out exactly what he means by 'mixed sounds'; I do not have a sufficiently clear idea of what these words mean to respond to them. Our language undoubtedly does have many mute sounds. They help make our speech more graceful and varied; I believe they even correlate exactly to certain parts of song, as I shall endeavour to prove a little later on. Here I am content to point out that M. Rousseau, who finds the

Italian language so sweet *because it is always eliding one vowel against another*, should find ours even sweeter, because a pleasanter and more natural sort of elision is continually being made between a mute syllable and an open vowel. Let us condense this to an example, citing the one M. Rousseau supplies:

Teneri sdegni, è placide è tranquille

Repulse, è cari vezzi, è liete paci.

If you pronounce all the vowels without elisions, you proceed from hiatus to hiatus and render the pronunciation jerky. Elide them, and you truncate – disfigure – the words by taking away one of their essential syllables; besides, you tire the ear with the constant iteration of endings in *e*.

Let us compare this with an elision of a mute syllable:

Oui, je viens dans son temple adorer l'Eternel.

The words *temple* and *adorer* preserve their full and correct pronunciation; and the mute, by a smooth elision, disappears softly and melts into the following vowel.

Next M. Rousseau claims that 'the lack of brightness in vowels makes it necessary to compensate in the notes, and that unvoiced language makes for noisy music.'

It seems to me that this should have quite the opposite result.

The lack of brightness in vowels cautions against putting any in the sounds of the music. M. Rousseau himself, elsewhere in his letter, in this way deduces the character of the appropriate music from the character of the language.

'The pace of our music must be slow and tedious. If one tried to make it move even a little faster, it would scurry along like a stiff, bony corpse rolling on the pavement.'

I search our language for reasons that would force our music to be slow. I find that the language has a surfeit of short syllables. How does speech which is light and swift necessarily produce song which is sluggish and lazy? Must one always deduce backwards from language to music? But why is this reverse reasoning reserved for us alone?

'I suppose', M. Rousseau continues, 'that the same language would have bad prosody, weakly marked, and lacking in precision; that the longs and shorts would not relate simply to each other in duration and number in such a way as to make the rhythm pleasing, exact and regular; that some longs are more or less long, some shorts are more or less short, some syllables are neither short nor long, etc.'

Here M. Rousseau is merely assuming to be true all the reproaches he has made against the French language. You may be startled to find that his accusatory tactics can be turned to its defence. If it were necessary to attribute to our language pre-eminence over all others in music, perhaps one would merely need to repeat to its advantage what its adversary has said against it. But we are not there yet; let us not anticipate our line of reasoning.

'Our prosody,' it is said, 'is not marked at all' – and yet it is impossible to alter the value of a syllable without offending the ear.

'Our prosody,' it is said again, 'is bad' – and yet when the verses of Racine, M. de Voltaire or Quinault are well declaimed, the result is a pleasure for the ear which M. Rousseau has surely felt as keenly as anyone.

But, it is added, *we have longs which are more or less long, shorts which are more or less short, syllables which are neither short nor long*. Dionysius of Halicarnassus[6] says the same of Greek, sir. If these words indicate an inherent flaw, an anti-lyrical flaw, in the language, what becomes of M. Rousseau's extravagant eulogies of Greek, which he finds so musical and harmonious? Besides, music itself has longs which are more or less long, shorts which are more or less short, semibreves, minims, crotchets, quavers, etc. How would such a marked correlation between language and music make them incompatible? ...

Does it not seem to you, sir, that the faults found in music are too often attributed to language? M. Gluck himself commits this injustice: he attributes the frequency of *roulades* which he censures in Italian song to the frequency of vowels in the Italian language. But there is no need whatsoever to make *roulades* on vowels and the language is innocent of this charge. If Italian song degenerates into *roulades*, it is because composers defer to performers who are anxious to show off their *bravura*, and because audiences in Italy have become accustomed to look upon opera as a kind of concert to which they listen only sporadically. Hence the composers are less aware of how out of place *roulades* are in a tragic air. Hence they have an actor sing for a long time without giving a thought to his interlocutor, who, while the air is going on, is merely another spectator in the theatre. Hence they prolong the *ritornellos* and multiply the *da capos* with no regard for the plot, the actor's performance, or his appearance. None of these defects of Italian opera would be tolerated in France. Our refined and exacting taste weighs the parts as a whole and subordinates the music to the theatrical plot. This is what makes me think that we are bound to take opera further than foreigners have done; maybe it is also what has given M. Gluck the desire to dedicate his talents to us.

But does our language lend itself to a genre of music which can please both foreigners and ourselves? This question brings me back to my theme and leads me to set forth my view.

I believe, sir, that music is more independent of languages than we imagine. I consider it a language itself, distinct from every other; a universal language, essentially unchanging, to which dialects bring only negligible differences, if any at all ...

If the music of every people is a natural dependency, a necessary consequence of the language it speaks, why does music change while language remains the same? The Italians have sung in a French style; and we, who speak the language of Quinault, are a world apart from that of Lully ...

I have collected several songs of the savages of Canada. Their melody is the same as ours: will it be said that their language is the same as well?

Ah! Who, sir, does not see that music, as I have said, is a language distinct from every other? Each people has created for itself a conventional language in order to be understood, a language whose formation is the result of chance: for there is no logical reason why we should call bread *pain* instead of *artos*, as the Greeks do. The chief forms of music, on the contrary, arise neither by chance nor by convention; they derive from the laws of nature – that is, from our constitution – which make them necessary, unchanging, universal. The relationship between musically combined sounds and our senses is a mystery impenetrable to reason. No one can explain why such and such a sequence of sounds produces a melodious song; why from the rhythm expressed by this song there results a movement that makes it necessary for our bodies to follow. There is no logic to these effects; but in every country, in every climate, every well-constituted man feels them. The coarsest and most uncouth peasant has a sense of song and rhythm: children acquire it at birth ...

The proof that song does not derive its appeal and power from its relationship with language is that one can be ignorant of the language of a country and still love its music. The Armenian whom M. Rousseau mentions in his letter does not understand a word of Italian, but he does understand and appreciate the Italian airs that were sung to him ...

But, someone will say, how can we explain the difference between Italian song and French song, even modern French song, if it does not result from the character of the two languages? But how can we explain the difference between modern and ancient Italian song, if the character of the music is determined by that of the language? ...

Take the truly lovely airs from our comic operas and join them skilfully to Italian words, or translate some beautiful Italian airs into fluent French. If the performances are faithful to the music, I wager that both translations will be successful. A beautiful song is a marketable commodity all over the world; it is a diamond which holds its value and is suitable for anyone's jewel box.

In the alliance of music and words, sir, music plays the role of those favourites whom everyone treats as subjects, but who secretly govern their masters. It is as a consequence of this servitude of language that the same words are repeated so often in an air. I know that reason protests this custom, which it labels abuse, but music justifies it. Because it is essential to the workings of music to retrace the same phrases, to let them be heard several times in the same and different keys, the same words naturally recur throughout the same song; and the ear, once seduced by the charm of the sounds, becomes less scrupulous as to the privileges of language and reason ...

Must I give examples of good music which is unfaithful to prosody? I can find them in every language ...

Le Devin du village[7] is full of faults of prosody. I choose this work by preference, because no one can suspect its author of transgressing through ignorance. It must be that M. Rousseau, ardent zealot of the privilege of languages, felt that music too has privileges which can sometimes be given preference, since he is unfaithful to the quantity of a language which he speaks and writes so well.

What can one deduce from all this? That the observation of quantity is, for music, a fetter from which we try as hard as we can to free ourselves. But this fetter would be nothing if there existed a language whose vague, indeterminate, flexible and changing prosody lent itself to the needs of the composer. The words of this language would have no fixed and real value. Its longs would be more or less long, its shorts more or less short, many of its syllables would be neither short nor long; they would resemble the syllables *do, re, mi, fa, so, la, ti, do*, which Italian, French, and German musicians pronounce long or short, according to the demands of the melody.

Have you noticed, sir, that in tracing the characters of a prosody truly desirable for music, I have merely repeated word for word what M. Rousseau said of our prosody? But I fear that M. Rousseau (who, in speaking this way, thought he was denying our advantages) supposed us to have advantages which we do not have. I have already said that I cannot admit that our prosody is indeterminate, since it is true that it is impossible to alter the value of our syllables without offending the ear. Moreover, I do not agree with M. Gluck that our language is more musical than any other, but merely that it can adapt itself to good music as well as the next.

If I had to assign to it some special properties suitable to the art of song, I could find them in the very qualities which have been criticized as contrary to music. Its mute endings, for example, are directly related to *sons perdus* in music, on which the voice fades away and finally expires like a mist.

The grammatical order of our constructions also favours music in that it favours clarity of discourse. The more readily the meaning of the phrase is explained, the more easily the mind grasps the song's relationship to the words.

Such, sir, are the observations I wished to convey to you. May this article, if it must be contradicted, at least draw on its author only critiques which enlighten but do not afflict him! It would be unfortunate if, on matters of the least importance, one could not venture an opinion without losing a night's sleep ...

1 Gluck's *Iphigénie en Aulide*, to a libretto by Marie Françoise Roullet, was produced at the Paris Opéra in 1774. Gluck had already written several French *opéras comiques* for Vienna.

2 'I predict that the tragic genre will not even be attempted.' *Lettre sur la musique* (author's note). [A translation of Rousseau's letter is in Strunk, *Source Readings*. Chabanon's quotations are substantially, though not literally, accurate. – Ed.]

3 François-André Philidor. *Ernelinde*, produced at the Opéra in 1760, wedded French forms to Italianate music.

4 What has been preserved of Lully's works are mainly recitatives; but, strictly speaking, recitatives are not music. For the rest, we readily agree that Lully wrote some pieces of an interesting simplicity, such as the beginning of the prologue of *Amadis*. We do not believe that we are wronging this artist by comparing him to Corelli (author's note).

5 M. Rousseau (author's note).

6 'On Literary Composition' (author's note). [See Dionysius of Halicarnassus, *The Critical Essays*, Loeb Classical Library, 2:105–9 – Ed.]

7 Rousseau wrote both words and music for the popular *Devin du village* (1752).

10

François Arnaud (?), 'The Evening Wasted at the Opera'

(1776); from Arnaud, *Oeuvres complètes* (Paris, 1808)

Arnaud (1721–84), one of the most gifted writers of his generation, devoted his considerable talents to the cause of operatic reform. In Gluck's works he saw an ideal marriage of the French and Italian styles, though he was anything but an uncritical admirer of either country's operatic traditions. This essay – usually said to be by Arnaud but sometimes attributed to the writer and composer Pascal Boyer – was published as a pamphlet in 1776. I have omitted or summarized the lengthy footnotes in the original.

Alceste was being given for the fifth time, and I was seeing *Alceste* for the fifth time.[1] The opera was just beginning when one of my neighbours turned to me and said, 'That's a sad sort of music.'

'You mean the music is sad?'

'Right.'

'But do the words really seem cheerful to you?'

'What's the difference? That's just one more strike against it.'

'No doubt monsieur does not like tragedy?'

'Good thinking! Since when has tragedy been sung?'

'It was with the Greeks.'

'Bah! The Greeks were Greeks.'

'Yes, monsieur, and everything else was barbarian ...'

'Oh!' said another man, 'this is a rum sort of opera. They told me it had no dances.'

'What? Here's one, my friend, and to such a noble, touching, religious air – an air which should transport you to the midst of temples, place you at the foot of altars, and inspire the most profound contemplation.'

'You call that a dance?'

'What? Surely you wouldn't want priests and priestesses to worship and pray while executing *entrechats*? Don't all these movements, perfectly in harmony with the orchestra's, depict what they ought to depict, express what they ought to express? Come, monsieur, have the goodness to tell me what feelings or ideas are aroused in you by *cabrioles, entrechats, gargouillades*, and *moulinets*. Believe me, the sort of thing you have in mind should only be found at the fair: read your *Noverre*[2] ...'

'But, monsieur, not a single cadenza! Where does the chevalier Gluck get his aversion to cadenzas?'

'But, monsieur, how is it that cadenzas have moved you to such tender concern? What great pleasure can shakings of the voice, convulsions of the throat, quick and long vibrations from one note to another give you? Even if this alleged *agrément*[3] were fitting to represent either the warbling of birds or the shuddering of leaves gently shaken by a light wind, would that be any reason to require that it constantly be tacked on to all phrase endings? Tell me, is that not the oddest abuse, and of all musical pedantries the most impertinent and ludicrous?'

'Here's a nice chorus,' said a fourth man, 'but it's pilfered from *Golconde.*'

'Wait a minute, monsieur. At the end of the second act there's one of the loveliest airs ever heard on any lyric stage, an air which contains the most moving and joyful modulation that art has yet borrowed from nature. Well, this same inflexion, this same turn of phrase, is found in an air from M. Sacchini's *Olimpiade*. But you must know that *Alceste* saw the light of day long before the creation of both M. Sacchini's *Olimpiade* and of *Golconde* – the day, that is, when it was performed, engraved and published.[4] Oh, if you only knew how much has been stolen from the poor chevalier Gluck! Naturally, people found it easier to pilfer from him than to imitate him ...'

'I believe, monsieur, that this is the air you were just telling us about. One must admit that the accompaniment is charming. Oh, yes, it's a charming thing, this accompaniment!'

'What are you saying, monsieur? What! This orchestra, full at first of groans, sobs and tears, and then of movement, action and life; this orchestra, which should represent all of nature, sharing in the actress's predicament and all of her emotions – this you call a charming thing! Ah, monsieur, you have neglected the education of your ears with a vengeance. Come here often; and if this music doesn't educate them, don't bother to come back unless Lully's innocuous sing-songs are on the stage, or Rameau's learned *melogryphes*,[5] or Philidor's noisy pastiches.'

'Would to God,' exclaimed an old officer, 'would to God we *could* have those sing-songs of M. Lully! But that would take actors, and unfortunately we no longer have any.'

'There is some truth in what monsieur has just said. Since Lully's music, like that of almost the entire French school, did nothing for the actors, the actors had to do everything for the music. Hence those gestures of the head, arms and eyebrows, those languorous *ports de voix*, those weak cadenzas, those *inhuman* cries, those sounds ripped from the bowels and accompanied by deathly rattles, and that whole heap of affectations and simperings that we indulgently took for *expression* ...'

'I must admit', said a young man, 'that in thinking about what the music of *Orphée* did for M. Legros, and what that of *Alceste* is doing for Mlle Levasseur today,[6] I'd be tempted to believe that the chevalier Gluck's manner is indeed more animated and theatrical than other composers'. But what's an opera without song?'

'Ah, what a barbarian! ... A thousand pardons, monsieur, for my hot temper. I wanted to let off steam, not to offend you. So you believe there is no song in this opera? Could it be because there are neither ditties, nor carols, nor romances, nor vaudevilles, nor hymns, nor drinking songs?'

'Hah! I couldn't care less about such trifles. I'll have you know, monsieur, that my ears were opened long ago.'

'Monsieur, monsieur, let's not turn up our noses. All these little things have their value and price in their place; but here ... !'

'Here I want something other than what I hear. And to be perfectly frank, it was hardly worthwhile for M. the chevalier Gluck, who was quite aware of the strides music has taken in France, to make two trips from Vienna to Paris just to bring us operas without ariettes.'

'Ah, monsieur, in the name of Apollo and all the Muses, leave the pretentious ornaments, tinsel and extravagances to Italian music, which has long been dishonoured by them. Take care not to covet false and worthless riches, and do not invoke a manner which is forsworn by whatever *philosophes*, people of spirit, and enlightened amateurs there are in Italy. What! Will you approve if, just when the emotions for which your soul has been prepared should be brought to a climax, the actor amuses himself in embellishing vowels and stands with his mouth open in the middle of a word, as if under a spell, spewing forth a flood of inarticulate sounds? Of all the absurdities you can swallow, is this not the greatest and most offensive? What would you say of an actor who clowned around while he was declaiming a tragic scene? Or of an orator who, instead of thundering, fulminating and overwhelming his listeners, stitched all the waggish rhetorical figures he knew together end to end? When it's just a question of amusing my ear to while away my spare time, then by all means warble away prettily with the canaries and nightingales as long as you please. But to reduce music to cheap tricks, when my soul demands emotions, is a blatant mockery of good sense and propriety. It's an insult to both art and nature.'

'I grant you your ariettes,' said another young man who was listening to me attentively and with interest. 'But can an opera do without *cantabiles*?'[7]

'Have you already seen this opera?'

'No, but I've seen connoisseurs ...'

'Ah, monsieur, why don't you make up your own mind? Why defer to a few people who quite often have neither knowledge of nor feeling for the true beauties of the arts, but who manage to intimidate you by randomly dropping certain technical terms to which they have never attached any distinct and precise meaning? Trust your own impressions, not second-hand opinions. Judge this music the way we judge smells and colours, without listening to pedants, cold-hearted people, and all the assassins of the arts who would mark the artisan's path off-limits to the artist and substitute method for freedom, the goddess of genius. Investigation, discussion and analysis are doubtless necessary whenever one has to deliver an opinion on works of rational argument. But where the fine arts are concerned, if you think or reason before applauding and shouting out, something is wrong either with the artist or with your organs. See how quickly the applause breaks out all over the hall. Look around, raise your eyes to the loges: they were yawning before, today they are crying.'

'Just a moment, just a moment, monsieur the eternal admirer,' burst out a man who was weeping with anger when all the sensitive persons were weeping with compassion. 'You are going to hear a piece whose praise I invite you to undertake ... Here it is. Well, what do you have to say about it, messieurs? Four whole verses on the same pitch, on the same note![8] Could anything be more worthless? Is this not the antithesis of music?'

'It's true that the nature of music, especially theatrical music, is to capture the expression of the passions, to embellish it, reinforce it and make it more perceptible. But the figures on stage are *ghosts*, and there are no passions after death. These verses do not lend themselves to a different declamation, and in stripping them even of their natural and ordinary expression, the chevalier Gluck shows us how much feeling and respect he has for propriety. However, since it is not merely a question of imitating, and since the imitation must be done in music, keep one ear on the orchestra and you will see that the composer attaches to this monotonous declamation a harmony which is highly varied, expressive and picturesque, a harmony which is bound to move any sensitive person and to instil terror and wonder in those who combine sensitivity and artistic knowledge.

'How can it be that *Iphigénie* and *Orphée* have not accustomed you to listening to the orchestra more attentively? This indifference is only excusable in the rest of your operas where, except in a handful of pieces, the instruments accompany the voice the way a valet accompanies his master, not the way the arms, hands, eyes, the gestures of the face and the whole body, accompany the language of feeling and passion.'

'It's no use admiring, praising, and making speeches. We know that your chevalier Gluck is considered merely a composer of the second rank.'

'By whom, monsieur, if you please?'

'By everyone in Italy and the rest of Europe.'

'That's news to me. But one thing I do know is that the author of the best treatise ever written on dramatic music – an Italian author, Neapolitan no less[9] – compares the chevalier Gluck's operas to

Raphael's masterpieces; that the same author, having urged the Jomellis, Piccinnis, Traettas and Sacchinis at last to bring real music back to the stage – music which paints the passions and speaks to the heart – holds the chevalier Gluck up to them as a model; and that it is on the *Alceste* of the same chevalier Gluck that this writer-*philosophe* bases his entire theory. I also know that the Englishman who is the most profoundly versed in the history and science of music, Dr Burney, calls the chevalier Gluck the Michelangelo of music. Nor has the illustrious citizen of Geneva[10] concealed his admiration for the talent and works of this great artist. Here is how M. Wieland,[11] one of the most celebrated writers of Germany, expresses it ...

'But I see you blush and blanch by turns. I shan't go on, monsieur. It was not my intention to annoy you; I merely wished to undeceive you. So I will content myself with telling you that M. the chevalier Gluck is in neither the first nor the second rank of composers. He is in a class by himself, and it's not likely that many musicians will join him there. Farewell, messieurs. You have deprived me of a great pleasure. If thirty performances of this opera are given, I shall really have seen it only twenty-nine times. *You have made me waste an evening.* But if I have destroyed your prejudices, I console myself and pardon you.'

---

1 Gluck's opera was originally presented in Italian in Vienna in 1767. A French version, largely rewritten, opened at the Paris Opéra on 23 April 1776.
2 Jean-George Noverre, the reform-minded choreographer who devised the dances for the Vienna *Alceste*.
3 Ornament.
4 Sacchini's *Olimpiade* was first staged in Padua in 1763, Monsigny's *Aline, reine de Golconde* in Paris in 1766. Hence the speaker's claim for the priority of *Alceste* would seem to be ill-founded.
5 An apparent neologism, from the Greek for song-writing.
6 Joseph Legros sang Admetus and Rosalie Levasseur the title role in *Alceste*. Arnaud, in a note, says that previously she had portrayed only light-hearted characters.
7 In a note, Arnaud explains that he has in mind a special kind of measured musical verse exemplified by Gluck's *tragédies*.
8 In the famous Underworld Scene (Act 3 of the French version), the infernal gods address Alcestis in monotone phrases of 'Malheureuse, où vas-tu?'
9 Antonio Planelli cited *Alceste* as the ideal tragic opera in *Dell'opera in musica* (1772).
10 Rousseau.
11 Christoph Martin Wieland, the poet and dramatist.

11

Nicolas Etienne Framery (?), 'On the Best Means of Naturalizing a Taste for Good Music in France'

Journal de musique, no. 5 (1777)

In the 1770s tension between francophiles and italophiles in France centred on Gluck and Piccinni, whose operas were perennially popular in Paris. Framery (1745–1810), a prominent critic and librettist, waved the banner of Italian music in the *Journal de musique* and *Mercure de France*. Although the following article is unsigned, Framery's hand is suggested by the mention of the Paris Conservatoire, an institution for which he lobbied strenuously and which he helped to found in 1795.

I do not propose to discuss which music is the best. My taste agrees with the sentiments of everyone in Europe in preferring Italian music. Since M. Gluck's masterpieces have brought M. Rousseau himself to recognize that our language was capable of all the musical beauties,[1] it seems to me that it is only a matter of determining the best means of importing the true taste of Italy to France and, if possible, of bringing it to perfection.

In the famous war that the *bouffons*[2] incited in 1753 and 1754, everyone naturally held fast to his own opinion. But since that era of ferment and strife, the party of the old music has seen more than three-quarters of its defenders die without being replaced; whereas a new generation, so to speak, of young amateurs has arisen, all of whom have embraced the party of Italy. Some have made up their minds intelligently; most have done so out of a desire to be fashionable and to follow the crowd. Needless to say, it is the latter who have the loudest voices. Others applaud only when they are moved, but these people are always ready to clap and shout 'bravo' at the top of their lungs, whether or not the singing is in tune, and whether the music is well or badly written ...

Music, painting, all the arts which depend on taste are everywhere subject to the errors of ignorance, to the blind whims of the masses, and, what is worse, to the false judgments of those would-be amateurs who, without truly liking the arts or having ever cultivated them, join a party, pass judgment without knowledge, speak without understanding, applaud with a yawn, and thrive on destroying performers' reputations.

What is even more astonishing is that today, when public opinion in France seems to be unanimously in favour of Italian music, no one is trying to gain more than an imperfect understanding of it. The English have long had a bona fide Italian opera, both comic and serious, performed in Italian, for which they import composers and actors from Italy at great expense. The Italian colony of a sort, which always exists in the centre of London, guards and perpetuates Italian taste in all its purity. M. Burney[3] judiciously observes that this is why even English composers who have never gone to Italy imitate the Italian style better than our musicians who have spent long periods there.

It is the same with the sensitivity of the ear and delicacy of taste in music as it is with accent in language. We pick them up by habit, without noticing it, from the people we live with. A boy transported to Paris little by little loses his native accent, but picks it up again when he goes home. So it is that Italians who move to France, and who often find themselves called upon to make music with Frenchmen, in the end pick up their taste. French composers who have gone to study in Italy bring back an Italian style, but often manage to lose it after living in France for a few years.

In Italy renowned male singers and celebrated divas scrupulously avoid giving lessons for fear that the vocal defects of their students will lead their imagination astray and pollute their brains. Lovers of classical Latinity, eager to preserve its taste in all its refinement, take care to read only the Augustan authors. What a frightful hodge-podge of styles and genres must be produced in our heads by the habit of listening now to music in the Italian taste by French composers, now to music from Italy performed by French singers, now to a few Italian ariettes executed for better or worse, and now to operas whose motley mode of performance puts one in mind of seaports, or those big fairs where foreigners from every land assemble and everyone speaks his own language, some replying in Greek to proposals made in English, others in Arabic to offers made in Spanish.

We have reason to hope that a new troupe of Italian *bouffons* will soon be seen at the big opera house. This will be one more step toward the understanding we need; but why can't we hear serious operas? They have their flaws and we may be unjustly biased against them, but one cannot judge them without knowing them. It is unthinkable that Metastasio's masterpieces, adorned by the music of Sacchini, Piccinni, Anfessi, Paisiello and the rest, would not yield new pleasures for true amateurs and valuable instruction for our librettists, composers and the whole nation.

To ensure the progress of the art, it seems to me that our next desiderata should be a conservatory, a general music library open to the public at all times, and a genuine academy of music in Paris, with branches in Naples, Rome, Bologna and Venice ...

If the ideas I have just outlined hastily can ever be realized, perhaps then we will see borne out the comment of one of our musicians who was trained in Rome: 'Go to Italy,' he was wont to say, 'it is the font of truth. I have not given up hope that the Italians will one day come here to learn, but I shall not live to see it.'

1 Rousseau's conversion is reflected in his later essays on Gluck's *Alceste* and *Orphée*.
2 The Italian company whose presence in Paris fomented the Querelle des Bouffons.
3 Charles Burney, the English music historian (see no. 15).

12

Georg Joseph Vogler, 'On the State of Music in France'

Betrachtungen der Mannheimer Tonschule, vol. 3
(March–May 1781)

Vogler (1749–1814) served as court chaplain and assistant kapellmeister in Mannheim, a city known for its musical establishment, particularly its famously disciplined orchestra. Vogler founded his Tonschule, or conservatory, in the early 1770s and went on to teach Weber, Meyerbeer and others. Although most of his writing was of a theoretical nature, the *Betrachtungen der Mannheimer Tonschule* (Observations of the Mannheim Conservatory) had the very practical goal of giving amateurs the skills they needed to form musical judgments.

One can but marvel that the French nation, whose sharpness of mind, sensitivity, and strength of imagination, at least in affairs of the heart, are not to be gainsaid, still lags behind all other nations when it comes to music.

Music came from the Greeks to the Romans, and in Italy it always held the upper hand – its true place. But lately – within the past fifty years, no more – the Germans have begun to master that great, sublime, complicated thing called harmony. Moreover, they have finally begun to restrain their impetuosity, to dampen the fire which threatened to break out in Gothic wildness, to sweeten their strong spice. And I speak not as a German but as a connoisseur when I maintain that they are capable of accomplishing everything – *everything* – in any kind of performance, be it playing an instrument, demonstrating their vocal skill, or composing a great masterpiece.

If we look into the past in search of the French nation's musical capability, we shall soon lose our way.

It is as true as it is remarkable that at the time the Corelli sonatas were published, there was no virtuoso in the great city of Paris, or in all of France, capable of playing them.[1]

It is equally true that three talented musicians were selected to be sent to Rome and kept there on salary for a whole year, merely to acquaint themselves with these new harmonic developments. For a full year after they returned to Paris, these initiates were the only ones who could play this music.

Lully, an Italian by birth, who in his day was as great a violinist as a composer, lit the lamp for the French and opened the first chapter in their musical history.

Rameau wrote the second chapter. He, however, applied his mathematical acumen to write a method, and he could win over the inquisitive mind with truths just as convincing as the happy deceptions he practised on the pleasure-loving ear with his limpid song.

To be sure, his method was not yet complete; all possible materials for his harmonic school had not yet been assembled and put on display. And to be sure, his song was nothing like the graceful songs of his Italian contemporaries, or even the pure songs of the Germans. An old stiffness, a predilection for chorale-like minor keys, still lingered behind the prettily and precisely delivered words. Only his choruses, which have survived to this day, had substantial beauty.

Rameau, however, is always a rarity. He puts to shame all dull practitioners who sing without ideas – that is, compose without principles – as well as the high-flying theorists, those mute organ pipes who are useful to the architect for their symmetrical beauty but can never produce a pleasing sound with all their columns of figures.

France's opera, supported by an important royal foundation, its day-to-day existence guaranteed for more than 120 years,[2] adorned with dances, sets, costumes (advantages of which no other lyrical theatre in Europe can boast) – France's opera lay in a deep slumber. Every old man learned to hum Lully's and Rameau's songs one by one and every child tried to babble along, producing almost the same effect as the unison violins and the bass, moving along so softly with the violas, in the opera.

Now French ears had to be awakened, shaken up, and made aware.

This was Gluck's destiny. He came to Paris and launched an ardent attack, bringing his *Iphigénie en Aulide*, a lyrical drama based on Racine's tragedy.[3] Now it was time to herald a new era – an era, inevitably, of opposition. All scholars, aestheticians, connoisseurs of the first rank, and – let us not forget – that generous patron of the fine arts, worthy daughter of the immortal Theresa,[4] appreciated the German composer's beautiful creations. Having raised recitative from the depths of flabbiness, Gluck rejected the venal modern *ritornello*; employed all the instruments (especially the winds); made portraits and musical paintings (only plausible ones); let the torrent of passion rage for three hours, instead of frosty, commonplace intermezzos; and showed what music is capable of when it is turned into drama. His subsequent operas, *Iphigénie en Tauride* and *Armide*, made a similar impact, as did his Italian operas *Alceste* and *Orphée*, which were translated from the Italian and adapted for the French stage, where they have always been repeated to acclaim.

From this time on, all old operas were banished from the theatre. No one will abide the old, dried-out, stiff French music any longer.

The Parisian public, which comprises the keenest artistic judges of dramaturgy, cannot abide a mediocre libretto, and the most beautiful music does not please them if it clothes dull words, insipid bilge, or particularly tedious plots. Pastoral or tragic opera must always be a drama corresponding to the characters.

After this great era and the violent displacement of old music, the celebrated Piccinni from Naples was written up here; his *Roland* was performed seventy-five times to universal acclaim.[5] The works of this good-natured, melodious composer, and various compositions of Philidor and Grétry, now alternated with Gluck's.

At present, Gluck is still occupied with the *Danaide*, to a libretto by Baron von Tschudi, which is awaited here with cheerful impatience.[6]

All ballets are woven into the drama and the ludicrous sight of a conjuror dawdling around on stage, having nothing to do with the heroic characters of the preceding act, is disappearing in Paris.

Now, how different the French are from the Italians with respect to taste can be judged from this: picture a stage without sets on which a pair of women and a pair of castrati are standing woodenly. Their costumes are all wrong, there is no scenery, no sensible and fitting dances, and their recitatives are poor, lacking in declamation and metre. After the orchestral introduction, they take turns singing their *passaggi* and showing off their vocal agility. The public doesn't take the slightest interest in what they may have wanted to say. People yawn during the recitatives and chat during the vulgar arias. Nobody listens; they play games in the loges, drink coffee, eat supper. Sometimes, out of sheer disgust, they even close the window to the theatre, until the highlight of the concert moves them to silence for perhaps five minutes, eliciting scattered applause for the rondo which the castrato trots out every day, like a hobbyhorse. (Every other season the castrato, like a doll, has a different spangly gown cut to order by many kapellmeisters in various places.)

After such recitatives, scratchily accompanied by a solo cello, and a thousand similar absurdities, who can abide anything more? Aren't librettos of a fashionable (and for the most part repulsive) cut just so much offensive nonsense?

If one were to examine the impression the play makes on the undeceived nature – heedless of habit, oblivious to fashion, free of prejudice – then beauties would be revealed more decisively and flaws would be more thoughtfully avoided.

Each and every poet and harmonist must approach his work as if it were incumbent upon him to invent an entirely new drama and not, as unfortunately happens every day, to dash off an insipid copy of the every-day fare we're used to.

When I think over the impression my first opera made on me (a pet idea which I always entertain), I discover the language of feeling, which has a quite different rationale than that suggested by the obfuscating costume.

I had always heard people speak about opera – about the excellent singing, splendid music, etc. I was so eager and yet so taken in by the enthusiastic reports that I could form no conception of it – and so formed a conception which exceeded anything imaginable.

It was one of the most splendid Italian operas. With matchless eagerness, I lay in wait for the beginning, and I heard a symphony which was quite lovely – but a symphony of a kind that I had heard many times before, and which was so little distinguished from the ordinary that it seemed to me unconnected to what followed.

How few overtures there are which have their own character and, with this authentic local beauty, put the listener in the position of feeling, of being full of, the expression which is the theme of the play.

When the curtain went up, I heard a recitative, an aria, then another recitative, and another aria, until finally another set appeared and people – who bore no relation to the previous ones who had sung the arias – began to jump around: this was called the first ballet. After this oracular leaping, which couldn't mean anything since it related to nothing, came another concerto, as it seemed to me, then another dance, and finally more song.

The wretched recitative that left everyone yawning, the arias just so many bars long, measured off with pedantic yardsticks, and the speechless, meaningless intermezzos still couldn't persuade me that I was at the opera, or even (who could imagine it?) at a play. Without giving another thought to either one, home I went from the theatre-concert, my ears full of melodies, my heart cold, my head empty, and I marvelled that I should now have seen an opera.

Just hear even one opera in Paris; hear those performers who don't forget the drama for a second. Oh, what a difference there is between singers who are supposed to act and true actors who sing!

One aspect of the old style has stuck with French opera composers: sometimes they get carried away by the object of their expression and lay too heavy a hand on the voices, reminding us of the old days with certain trills – a minor fault of which they will be cured in time and which, for the price of a thousand other dramatic benefits, can and should be forgiven.

The Parisians' enthusiasm for opera is unparalleled. Performances are given three times a week, winter and summer, without interruption and are well attended for the most part, depending on the popularity of the piece.

The French enthusiasm for musical drama – and everyone strives to be receptive to its beauty – spoils nearly all concerts for that nation, accustomed to expression, striking harmony and meaningful song, and full of knowledge of the theatre. Everybody wants to feel, no longer to marvel. And if something else does please them, it is anything but weighty fare. Put off by the size of the musical dramas, the women (whose verdict is worth more here than anywhere) now pay the homage of warm acclaim to a quite small, insignificant rondo – the more artless, gallant, insipid and trifling it is, the surer they are to like it. Their spirit is preoccupied with the opera's captivating effect; they leave their soul in the theatre and bring only their ears to the concert.

Of course, this particular brand of amateurishness, taken to extremes, cannot be reconciled with highly refined concert music, which, though it has neither words nor a definite object of expression or portrayal, is equally deserving of our attention by virtue of a well-made harmony, a tenderly executed adagio, or an instrumentalist's dazzling dexterity. And at present this music is misunderstood in Paris.

The famous Concert des Amateurs, which had no peer in Europe, is defunct, perhaps because so many amateurs of harmony were called to sea by the war, that gloomy age full of unresolved dissonances. In these concerts the clever symphonies of the celebrated Herr Gossec were performed to universal acclaim. The Concert Spirituel was only held on high feast days, when the theatres stayed closed[7] ...

To hear beautiful singing, one must travel to Italy; musical drama can be seen only in Paris; and only Germans are capable of painting with tones, penetrating all the passions on the stage, but always sounding from the lips of the Graces.

1 Arcangelo Corelli's first collections of violin sonatas were published in the 1680s.
2 Louis XIV founded the Académie Royale de Musique, known as the Opéra, in 1669.

3 First produced at the Opéra on 19 April 1774.
4 Marie Antoinette, Gluck's patron in France.
5 Niccolò Piccinni's *Roland* was first given at the Opéra on 27 January 1778.
6 Gluck's *Echo et Narcisse*, to a libretto by Ludwig von Tschudi, had in fact been staged at the Opéra on 24 September 1779.
7 The Concert Spirituel was founded in 1725, the Concert des Amateurs in 1769; both concert series buttressed Paris's reputation as the musical capital of Europe. Vogler is referring to Louis XIV's war with Holland and Spain, which ended with the Treaties of Nijmegen in 1678–9.

13

Johann Friedrich Reichardt, 'On Musical Performance'

Musikalisches Kunstmagazin, no. 3 (1782)

Reichardt (1752–1842), a founder of modern musical journalism, was an outstanding figure of the German romantic movement and a friend of such luminaries as Goethe, Tieck, the brothers Grimm and Hoffmann (see no. 19). From 1782 to 1791 he edited the *Musikalisches Kunstmagazin* (Musical Art Magazine), a lively blend of criticism, history and aesthetics, and new compositions. Reichardt's early renown as a violinist and lutenist no doubt sensitized him to the demands of performance; the Toscanini-like standards of orchestral playing that he advocates here far exceeded the abilities of most contemporary ensembles.

The flood of composition textbooks is endless, and yet a true composer has never been produced and trained by them. By contrast, people are utterly unconcerned with performance, which really can be taught and learned. Yet if performances were perfect, or at least better, if one could hear the works of the great masters performed in their own spirit, there would be no need for all the composition textbooks, which merely (and often wrongly) gloss the existing masterworks. True performances of these works would make a far more telling and fruitful impression on the ear and heart than all the rules which the intellect prescribes and which guide – or misguide – our view of the scores. Performance today is for the most part so wrongheaded that score-reading remains almost the only recourse for training young composers. But unless this is supervised by a competent, insightful and broadminded composer, it can point young composers in altogether the wrong direction. Often the eye can take great satisfaction in the painstaking artistic composition of a piece, enjoying the manifold transpositions, imitations, inversions, etc. in its development, the concision of each individual voice, and so expect the piece to produce a wonderful effect; and yet the effect, if not positively bad, can be utterly different. Conversely, a score can seem empty and contemptible to the eye and yet make a great and potent effect.

All such misunderstandings would be avoided if people became acquainted with musical works through accurate and true performances. Only to the most insightful, multi-faceted and prescient artistic spirit is a score more than the description of a picture is to a friend of the painter. The most accurate description of the most genuinely noble painting always evokes quite a different picture in the mind's eye and (curiosity aside) arouses emotions that are but weak; but place the viewer in front of the painting and at first glance he has gained infinitely more than in all the foregoing description and all the subsequent analysis and dissection of the work. Likewise, rules are wholly intelligible – as well as useful – only for someone who has already had several encounters with the work from which they were derived. But this cannot happen without the truest performance. Therefore, composers who are not lucky enough to have an orchestra to hand with which they can work directly, with their whole beings, should make it their most urgent business to consider how to bring about better performances of their works. This may be more easily said than done. In order to perform a noble piece entirely in the spirit of the composer, the performing musician must possess almost all of the composer's abilities and knowledge, save creativity. He must understand the piece, have an appreciation and feeling for its purpose, and know what means to use to make its performance more intelligible and to achieve its purpose. In addition, he must possess the skill to apply and exercise all those means easily and surely.

If the performing musician is to achieve all this straight away, then from the cradle on he must be treated differently than he has been up to now and every last player[1] in an orchestra of a hundred must be a true artist.

I lack heart and faith to propose ways and means to this end, and to reflect with hope on their application and exercise. Instead, I will try another course with my proposals: I will address the architects of musical buildings, the instrument makers and composers.

1 These rankings in our orchestras already demonstrate the shortcomings of our practice. Apart from the leader, all the players are of the same rank and each must contribute equally for the work to be presented powerfully and truly. By the same token, each player can – and does – spoil the work. A note which the composer places at the right time in an otherwise insignificant voice for a special effect, if performed with the most perfect purity and clarity, with exactly the right strength or weakness, length or shortness – often this alone makes the whole piece what it should be. If this one note is wrong, the piece comes to nothing, or to something quite different (author's note).

14

Anonymous, 'From a Letter from Hamburg'

Carl Friedrich Cramer, ed., *Magazin der Musik*, vol. 2 (1784)

As the eighteenth century drew to a close, musical magazines shed some of their weighty philosophical baggage to make room for articles of a more popular and topical nature. Reports of musical events throughout Europe, and from as far afield as Philadelphia, were an important feature of Cramer's *Magazin der Musik*, published in Hamburg from 1783 to 1786. The unflattering picture of Hamburg's musical life painted by this anonymous correspondent casts an interesting sidelight on the observations of Mattheson and Scheibe (see nos. 2 and 4).

Sir: May I request that you insert the following in your popular magazine? It is, I trust, very useful to everyone and it especially concerns musicians, if not music. For several years there has been such a torrent of virtuosos visiting Hamburg, so much ballyhoo in the local papers, so many concerts advertised, so much to read about music-loving in this town, that it would be no wonder if whole orchestras and opera companies picked themselves up and moved here in order to entertain such a musically inclined public, at once so wealthy and so enamoured of luxury. All virtuosos who come here think that they will be received with open arms, that concerts and – better yet – money and gifts will immediately be in store for them, and that they will be sent on their way showered with plaudits and praise. This is what the puff pieces in the newspapers would lead one to expect – yet the truth is quite the opposite! There is not a single musical patron here, not a single champion of the fine arts. We have music lovers aplenty, but not just now among our wealthy citizenry. Merchants have better things to do than to take an interest in arts that don't turn a profit. Scholars, for the most part, live on the glory of their art. Women sing and play, sometimes quite nicely (and a few very well), but none rises to the level of patron, and few could if they wanted to. There are a few concerts here, but they aren't public ones, nor are they as important as concerts in Berlin, Leipzig or Vienna.[1] Moreover, they are hard pressed to survive on a subscription, which never amounts to enough even to hire mediocre singers.

Once the elder Bach had the best and most frequent concerts, and after him Herr Ebeling in the Handlungsakademie,[2] but the latter have been discontinued on the grounds that it was detrimental to the academy to entertain its students with good music for a couple of hours every week in polite society. Bach retired and hasn't been presenting any more music in the concert hall for a long time. Furthermore, in the summer all the so-called *beau monde* lives in the gardens, but in the winter the *clubs, assemblées, lotteries, piqueniques,* balls and banquets are so many and so well established that finding a few free hours to sneak in a concert is an unspeakable bother. No concerts can be held during the day on Sundays: orthodoxy forbids it. Three or four days a week are mail days, when no businessman, bookkeeper or shop clerk ever has time to think about concerts. The rest of the week is taken up with comedies. So that leaves only Sunday evening, when everyone is recovering from the wining and dining, gambling losses and business deals – and gearing up for another round.

What hope is there for poor music? As a rule, either the comedy house, which is freezing cold, or the concert hall, where admission is dear, is chosen for a virtuoso's concerts. The good virtuoso suffers greatly from both. The costs of everything from the permit to the lighting are exorbitant. So many advertisements, posters, hired hands, and then the comedy house or the hall, lighting and finally – the music! Then the municipal musicians have to be paid. If they wish, however, they can send substitutes, who often play wretchedly and make the virtuoso's life miserable, if he has any pride at all and is accustomed to good music. Nine times out of ten the concerts are failures and the artist, who thought he was putting bread on the table, has in fact laid out a considerable sum for the day and takes home nothing but an empty purse.

'But the puff pieces in the newspapers!' O my good virtuoso, don't you see that the purpose of all this frantic hullabaloo is to attract amateurs? Just ask all those fine people who could hardly tear themselves away from the rich part of town, where there were plenty of amateurs but all too few rewards. The virtuosos come, armed with introductions to a few well-known connoisseurs and dilettanti, and often without introductions. Now Bach or the concert promoters are standing at the abyss. They bring in artists to play in their concerts (for people want to know who the miracle-worker is) to cries of 'Bravo! Bravo!' Playbills are passed around and advertising is arranged. Then the cry is 'Hired! Hired!' The virtuoso makes a rough estimate: 100,000 residents, rich, well-to-do, accustomed to amusements and luxury – therefore the house is sure to be sold out! He takes the plunge and plays – most of the time to empty seats. Buying a ticket is seen as an act of charity; there's talk of begging, pestering, etc., and the man upon whom such a virtuoso thrusts himself is hard put to commend, praise and help him. I've heard many people complain about this, and even louder are the complaints of the poor, swindled virtuosos, half a dozen or more of whom (often of the same instrument) are often colliding with each other here and taking hard knocks. Nevertheless, I must say in defence of the Hamburger that he has been deceived by many an incompetent, many an ingrate, and, yes, many a fraud, as the affair of the bogus Vanhall shows.[3] This makes people cautious; and if a Lolli, Schick or Mara comes,[4] the whole city doesn't race to their concerts. First people want to hear what the upshot is. 'They will give more concerts.' And therefore the virtuoso must stay here four, six or eight weeks, paying out of his own pocket, for a net profit of some fifty to a hundred marks. He's come all this way just to see Hamburg!

I call upon those who have been coming here for eight years and more to vouch for the truth of every word I've written. Please, sir, out of love for many fine, good-natured musicians who are not wealthy, publish this in your journal as a warning. I'm not afraid of being contradicted, or at least no one will dare sign his name to a rebuttal. For who can dispute an established fact? I consider it my duty as a good Hamburger to make this known, having enjoyed many happy hours here every year when business brings me to town. For many a musician has fallen into great difficulty, indeed distress, because he imagines that this paradise for merchants is also a paradise for virtuosos. In fact, even great virtuosos of the first rank have never left Hamburg enriched unless they were already rich when they came here.[5]

I have the honour to be, etc.,

J. G. V. from H.

1 Actually, public concerts had been offered in Hamburg since at least the mid-1600s. The short-lived series organized by C. P. E. Bach, to which the writer alludes below, began in 1768.
2 Christoph Daniel Ebeling, a teacher of history and Greek at the Handlungs-akademie, translated Burney's *Present State of Music in Germany* into German.
3 The Bohemian composer Johann Baptist Vanhall. I have been unable to trace this incident of false impersonation.
4 The sopranos Gertrud Mara and Margarete Schick, and the violinist Antonio Lolli.
5 In a lengthy footnote, Cramer somewhat apologetically confirms that the situation in Hamburg is every bit as bad as the correspondent contends.

15

Charles Burney, Review of *Observations on the Present State of Music, in London*, by William Jackson of Exeter

Monthly Review, series 2, no. 6 (October 1791)

Historian, critic and chronicler, Burney (1726–1814) was the most cele-brated English writer on music of his time. The accounts of his musical tours on the Continent and his *General History of Music* are remarkable both for their literary quality and for their erudition. Burney's views on criticism can be gleaned from his comment in the latter work that 'when every phrase or passage in a musical composition is to be analised and dis-sected during performance, all pleasure and enthusiasm vanish'. This book review – one of many he wrote for the *Monthly Review* on a wide range of subjects – attests to the brilliance of his pen and mind.

As critical reflections on the fine arts seldom come under our notice, they are a relief to us after the more dry and uninteresting labours of investigation. The remarks of able professors of any art or science come with weight; and from the reputation and productions of the author of this pamphlet,[1] we expected information and ingenuity. Many of his sentiments, however, militate so violently against the general opinion of the lovers and judges of music throughout Europe, and are so decisively delivered, that it seems incumbent on us to examine the principles on which they are founded.

Mr. Jackson boasts a claim to *candour*, for 'not mentioning the name of any living professor'; which will hardly be granted by intelligent musical readers, who can no more help thinking of HAYDN, when *symphonies* are mentioned, than of HANDEL, when *oratorio choruses* are in question. He says, 'if he may judge of the sensations of others by his own,' the public is *not* pleased with what it applauds with rapture. Why does it then applaud? What artist can bribe the whole public? Our House of Lords, which is the highest court of judicature in Great Britain, and from which there is no appeal, is supposed to be out of the reach of individual influence; and the enlightened public, in every kingdom, is the supreme judge of such productions of art as are exhibited for its amusement. Cabal and party, in a small circle, may triumph over judgment and good taste: but what, excepting sterling merit, can bias the public at large, for any considerable time?

According to Mr. J. our present musical pleasure is, 'by some awkward and unfortunate circumstances, derived from *polluted sources*'; and, as a wonderful discovery, he tells us, 'that PERFECT MUSIC is the uniting *Melody to Harmony.*' Now this is a *truism* so incontrovertible, that we believe it has never been disputed since the present rules of composition have been invented.

The invariable language of the enthusiastic admirers of Handel, and of every thing ancient in music, has long been, that the moderns *neglect harmony* for air: – but the whole tenor of Mr. Jackson's pamphlet is to prove, that 'melody is best qualified to exist alone, and that modern music has *no air*.' Mercy on us! have we then neither soul nor body? – and have we been so mistaken, as to fancy we have received delight from music, which has neither melody nor harmony to support it? Unluckily for our author, that music which he condemns in so summary a manner, and which, in this country at least, he says, 'is in a fair way of shortly being totally without melody,' is the favourite music of all the most cultivated and polished nations of Europe.

This severe censure is repeated in the next page. 'VOCAL MUSIC had once nothing but harmony to subsist on: by degrees, melody was added; but now it is very near being lost.'

'In the grand opera, *songs* may be considered as *pathetic*, *bravura*, something *between the two*, which has *no name*,² and airs called *cavatina*. Generally the last have most melody, and the first sort have least: but it is scarce worth while to ascertain which has most, where all are defective.'³ This is a brave assertion! – and are all the composer, performers, and hearers, of taste and judgment, to go to Exeter to ask Mr. J. how to please and be pleased? Is there no air, no elegance, no melody, in the productions of a Sarti, a Cimarosa, or a Paesiello? Very few opera airs are now printed, nor indeed were there many performed, in the last year: but that was more owing to particular circumstances, than to the barrenness of the times. Mr. J. perhaps condescends, though, it may be, not with much disposition to be pleased, to go to an opera once in two or three years; and calculates the whole progress of the art by what he happens to hear, or not to hear, during that one night's performance. Surely, prejudice, envy, a provincial taste, or perhaps all together, prevent candid attention; otherwise, some ingenuity, spirit, grace, and elegance, might have been discovered even in the worst operas, serious or comic, that have been brought on our stage: – but the writer seems wholly to confine his idea of melody to the symmetric measure and monotonous repetition of passages in a Vauxhall ballad,⁴ a dancing minuet, or a gavot. A TUNE that can be carried home, and interwoven in an English song, seems the grand *desideratum*.

Now the *tunes* in the English operas of highest favour, which were composed 'when melody still existed,' have been furnished by the Italian opera; and that still continues, as much as ever, to supply our national theatres with melodies which delight both *gods* and men.

Mr. Jackson is equally dissatisfied with the pertinacious adherence to Handel, and with the enthusiasm with which the flights of Haydn into new regions of melody and harmony, are admired. What are we to do? Are we to hear no music in our concerts but elegies, and ballads which the clown 'can whistle o'er the furrow'd land,' as well as they can be executed by the greatest professor? A liberal and enlightened musician, and bearer of music, receives pleasure from various styles and effects, even when melody is not so vulgarly familiar as to be carried home from once hearing; or even when there is no predominant melody, if a compensation be made by harmony, contrivance, and the interesting combination of the whole ...

Mr. Jackson's whole artillery is now pointed against the present *instrumental music.*

'The old CONCERTO (says he) is now lost, and modern full-pieces are either in the form of OVERTURES or SYMPHONIES. The overture of the Italian opera never pretends to much; that of the English opera always endeavours to have an air somewhere, and the endeavour *alone* makes it acceptable.' – Civil again! Richter's eternal repetitions, and Abel's timidity, are praised,⁵ for they are no more: – 'but later composers, to be grand and original, have poured in such floods of nonsense, under the sublime idea of *being inspired*, that the present SYMPHONY bears the same relation to good music, as the ravings of a bedlamite do to sober sense.'

Now, might not the ingenious writer as well have said, at once, that the authors of these *floods of nonsense* are HAYDN, VANHALL, PLEYEL, and MOZART, and the admirers of them tasteless idiots, as leave us to guess who he means? If he had gone a little farther, and had assumed the *title*, as well as the style, of SUPREME DICTATOR in the republic of music, what would he have told us that we do not already know? This was one of the times, we suppose, when he '*shrunk from the matter.*'

Modulation, measure, discord, and all such *paltry shifts*, are condemned in the lump; and even poor *Pianissimo*, which, though it moves on tiptoe, and with its finger on its lips, and is 'so delicate as almost to escape the ear,' does not escape the lash. Soft and loud, quick and slow, concord and discord, are *all in the wrong*, whenever applied to any thing but ballads and elegies: all other musical productions are *untuneable*.

This complaint of want of *tune* is more usually the croak of ignorance than the voice of knowledge. In the concertos of old masters, of which Mr. J. laments the loss, are there not fugues, and other entire movements, without a single phrase of melody? Yet these had their place, for the sake of variety, and were heard with pleasure. It is the perpetual want of variety which stimulates the composers to try every thing. Old masters did the same, as far as they dared: but so much has been tried, that little now of what is called natural, is left; and art, and sometimes caprice, and whim, are forced to supply the rest. To tread in the steps of our predecessors, in music, would be justly called plagiarism. The public accommodates itself to the music of the times, which chiefly offends those who are old enough to remember that of the last age; which was likewise censured by those of a former period.

We have heard or read somewhere, that Dr. Pepusch, Dr. Greene, and other learned musicians, established the *Academy of Ancient Music* soon after Handel's arrival in England, to check that composer's torrent of innovation, which began to overflow the country.[6] The public, however, for the honour of the nation, not seconding their endeavours, he was suffered to deluge the land; nor have either *drains* or *dams* been since able to diminish, nor to keep in bounds, the streams that flowed from his fountain of invention.

Handel was, at this time, a young man, and little known in any other part of Europe; so that we had the courage and merit of feeling his worth, without adopting it as a foreign fashion: but not to approve and admire Haydn, whose works have been in as great favour at Vienna, Madrid, Lisbon, Paris, and in the several capitals of Italy, as at the court of his patron, Prince Esterhazy, in whose service he had been engaged, as we have been told, for 25 years before he came hither, would have disgraced our musical taste. Indeed, it seems likely that the productions of Haydn will be admired and imitated *all over Europe*, as long as those of Handel have been in England only.

We are not certain that our present musical doctors and graduates are *quite up* to Haydn yet: but the public are so unanimous in applauding, that they cannot help giving at least a silent vote of assent to the justice of the praises so enthusiastically bestowed on him ...

1 William Jackson, composer, writer and organist of Exeter Cathedral.
2 The author surely forgets that there is such a thing frequently in an Italian opera as an *aria graziosa* (author's note).
3 Why a *cavatina*, which means nothing more than an air without a second part, should have more melody than a pathetic, rapid, or graceful air, we know not. In

times when Mr. J. allows melody to have been in its most flourishing state, in *da capo* days, there were no *cavatinas* (author's note).
4 The popular strophic ballads performed at Vauxhall and other pleasure gardens.
5 The composers Franz Xaver Richter and Carl Friedrich Abel.
6 The Academy of Ancient Music was founded in 1726 to promote the revival of 'ancient church music'.

16

Anonymous, 'On Fashion in Music: Second Letter'

Journal des Luxus und den Moden (July 1793)

From 1786 to 1827, Germany's rising bourgeois class turned to the *Journal des Luxus und den Moden* (Journal of Luxury and Fashions) for information and guidance. Everything 'fashionable' fell within its purview, and although music featured less prominently in its pages than literature, theatre and art, coverage of the subject was by no means nugatory or uninformed. This article shows how Mozart was seen by some fashion-conscious music-lovers in the 1790s.

Fashionable composers of our day can rightly be divided into two classes, namely, instrumental and vocal. In song, only Herren v. Dittersdorf, Mozart and Martini can lay claim to this epithet.

I venture to offer a brief description of these three composers.

Among them, Herr v. Dittersdorf[1] unquestionably has the greatest claim on the ear of the people, including polite society and connoisseurs – as soon as he renounces strict rules and declamation and sets store only by comedy, good theatrical effect, songs that are easy to understand and memorize (so that the performer isn't always forced to follow the conductor anxiously and listen to the orchestra), and the other hallmarks of his style. Take, for example, the arias from *Doktor und Apotheker*, 'Wine is a Specificum – Lovers need no witnesses' and 'If you want to catch a girl,' and the like from this composer's other operas. Yet Herr v. Dittersdorf knows how to give a good twist to the most commonplace theme, the most notorious of which, 'If it helps not, at least it harms not' (otherwise known as 'Blotting paper and carbon paper'),[2] from *Das rote Käppchen*, with the obbligato violin solo, furnishes a good example. However, in every respect the most superior opera by this composer appears to me to be *Die Liebe im Narrenhause*.

Mozart appears to be enjoying much more prestige and approval among the public since his death than was allotted him during his lifetime. Now he is called incomparably great. The vast majority of those who can't understand him at all Frenchify his name and exclaim in ecstasy, 'Ach, by Mausard – how heavenly!' But this approval isn't pure; it doesn't come as genuinely from the heart as the approval bestowed on Dittersdorf. It springs from the shouts of half-baked experts, parroted by their pupils and followers, and from these 'experts' spring up factions which side with Dittersdorf or Mozart wherever the two composers' operas are given. Mozart's talent appears to me to be an original spirit, one which in any case is still searching for compositions which are bizarre, striking and paradoxical, melodically as well as harmonically, and avoids natural flow so as not to become common.[3] Now, if such a talent is sufficiently skilled in everything that harmony puts into the composer's hands, and if the fire of youth has burned out and been replaced by a man's modest reflection and healthy self-abnegation, so that beauty is often sacrificed lest there be too much spice and one effect harm the other: such a man is surely a great man for his own time and for posterity. But what true connoisseur will assert that this description fits Mozart? His song is overladen with a surfeit of harmonies, accompaniments and tricky intervals which are often very hard for the singer to remember and intone. His instrumental accompaniments demand a meticulous and precise orchestra, and they make their effect only after frequent rehearsals; only then can one follow and find pleasure in the composer's ideas; only then can one see that he was no run-of-the-mill talent but a genius who worked according to a plan which has no place for harsh modulations, incorrect imitations and convoluted accompaniments.[4] His gift for characterization cannot be denied – witness *Don Giovanni* and *Figaro*.

Now I come to Martini.[5] It is not easy to imagine a composer having greater success than this Italian has had with Singspiels like *Una Cosa rara* and *L'Arbore di Diana*, which have been given on all the German and Italian opera stages. And he has earned his success justly, in view of the high esteem in which he is held by both public and connoisseurs. His song is agile and flowing without being commonplace or watery; simple mood and elegant turns of phrase make it new, and all this causes one to listen to the songs from both operas with consistent pleasure. But when this composer tries to write in grand-opera style, he is weak and insipid, like most Italians. Witness the grand arias in the two operas and his cantata *Il Sogno*, which has become well known. Here I must return again to Mozart's lovely opera *Die Zauberflöte*. In this one finds in all the little arias and duets, in addition to Martini-esque charm, a higher and nobler song; in the grander arias, finales and the like, Mozart's original talent is compounded of so many new turns of phrase, of so much fire and power of imagination, that this opera can, so to speak, count in all respects as the most perfect that the three afore-mentioned composers have bestowed on us.

What is all a jumble in all of these composers, and in all new the-atre works (with the sole exception of Schulz's theatre songs, which are unfortunately distorted by Cramer's miserable settings),[6] is cor-rect declamation. So it appears that declaiming badly is a second characteristic of fashionable taste in music. But what does not mere-ly appear to be fashionable taste but really is so, is this: English dance and waltz movements.[7] As a result one hears people shouting at the top of their lungs in the parterre, boxes and concert hall: 'That's pretty, that's delightful!'

Why Salieri, who is so beloved on account of his operas, is not found here here shall be told in the following letter, which is also devoted to fashionable instrumental composers.

1 Carl Ditters von Dittersdorf was renowned for his Singspiels, the first of which, *Doktor und Apotheker* (Doctor and Apothecary), was premièred in Vienna in 1786. *Die Liebe im Narrenhause* (Love in the Madhouse) and *Das rote Käppchen* (The Red Cap) followed in 1787 and 1788.

2 'Löschpappier und Blaupappier'. I have been unable to discover the source of this alternative title.

3 All the same, I must say that his last work, *Die Zauberflöte*, is altogether different and presents a great model of lovely, noble and simple song (author's note). [*The Magic Flute* was produced in Vienna in 1791, the year of Mozart's death – Ed.]

4 I believe that Mozart would have discarded this, too, had he lived longer. The over-ture to *Die Zauberflöte* and his last three quartets attest to this; in time, moreover, he would no doubt have acquired all the aforesaid attributes of greatness. Unfortunately, however, he died too soon (author's note).

5 Vicente Martín y Soler (1754–1806) was born in Spain but spent most of his life in Italy, hence the writer's erroneous assumption that he was Italian.

6 J. A. P. Schulz, prolific composer of songs and operas. Carl Friedrich Cramer (see no. 14) edited the vocal score of Schulz's *Aline, reine de Golconde* (1790).

7 The craze for the waltz and other triple-metre dances had spread to England by the late 1700s.

17

Friedrich Rochlitz, 'Difference of Opinion about Works of Music'

Allgemeine musikalische Zeitung, no. 32 (8 May 1799)

For half a century, from 1798 to 1848, the Leipzig-based *Allgemeine musikalische Zeitung* was Europe's most authoritative journal of musical news and commentary. Its influence was due in large part to the stature of Rochlitz (1769–1842), who edited the magazine for its first two decades. Although the *AMZ* had a far-flung network of correspondents and contributors, it was Rochlitz who gave the journal the intellectual depth and the breadth of coverage for which it was known. In this article he turns away from the monolithic concept of 'good taste' and recognizes a plurality of opinions – though some, in his view, remained more valid than others.

About the products of no art are so many opinions offered as about works of music. This is natural. The great variety of its products, the common and often public use of music, the universal yet varying effect it has on men, etc., explain this phenomenon.

About the products of no art are such different opinions offered as about works of music. This too is natural. Differences of opinion increase with the number of opinions and of judges on any subject, for in spiritual, as in material, creation, total uniformity is an impossibility. This explains the large number of differences of opinion. There is nothing visible about music which would allow its works to be juxtaposed and compared and from which some agreement would necessarily arise. This explains the extent of the differences of opinion about works of music. As different as may be the opinions as to the worth of, say, a painted rose, they are nevertheless all in complete agreement on one point: for everybody has seen roses in nature, compared the painted with the natural, and expresses his opinion, which may be very unartistic but is never altogether wrong. A sublime piece of music is heard; it makes an impression – according to the listener's subjective sensitivity, to be sure, but still essentially the impression it should make, and none other – on all who hear it. But we must already know our own feelings, must already be capable of bringing the changes in our frame of mind to consciousness and articulating them, in order to be able to judge them and what provokes them. He who cannot do this should surely refrain from all judging. But it is human nature to pass judgment on everything – and human weakness to like nothing better than to pass judgment on that which we do not understand. And so we judge nevertheless, and from this a great difference of opinions must certainly arise.

As a rule, these popular opinions are utterly despised; but we may at least deduce from them that a musical product which makes no impression upon the mass of people who are merely capable of feeling, even if they are not educated in art, is certainly not good – although it is not for that reason bad; and that one which does make an impression upon them is certainly not bad – although it is not for that reason good.

So much may be deduced from them, but no more. On the contrary, the desire to be all things to all people has often begotten musical monstrosities, of which I shall mention only today's not infrequently theatrical church pieces and the fad for heroic-burlesque operas.

Since the differences of this very popular opinion are so easily explained, so natural and necessary, and since nothing more appears to result from this than what has already been mentioned, we therefore come to differences of opinion among those who are comprised under the names of connoisseurs, artists and amateurs, and whom we wish to include in the category of men who are not only capable of feeling and sensitivity but are also more or less acquainted with the means by which music arouses feelings – with notes and their relationships.

From these people, at least, some harmony of opinion about works of music, at least in the essentials, is to be expected. But here too experience teaches the contrary. In Paris Gluck's most perfect conceptions are wholeheartedly booed by one party, while another is sent into raptures by them and adores the composer. In the same city Rameau was ridiculed by one party while another praised him to the skies. And it cannot be denied that both parties belong in our category. In Vienna heroic opera, in which the masterpieces of a

Hassler, a Salieri and others were given, is falling to rack and ruin because the biggest party won't listen to it, taking its chief delight instead in the dance-songs of a Wenzel Müller.[1] Here too private interests can play so great a part that it would be unkind to cite them as the sole cause of the whole phenomenon, and unjust not to grant this party its place in that category. Whence, then, this difference?

Some clever English writer (Sterne, if memory does not deceive me)[2] divides travellers into four classes. (Jean Paul,[3] following his lead, does the same for walkers.) The first class contains the most pitiful travellers, those who are motivated by vanity and a desire to be fashionable. The second class contains the learned, who travel for the exercise and not so much to enjoy as to digest what they have already enjoyed. The third class comprises those who see the world through the eyes of landscape painters; the fourth, those who cast not just an artistic but a holy eye upon creation, who transplant the other world on to this world of blooming things and set the Creator among his creatures. In somewhat similar fashion, one could also toss listeners and judges of music into four classes. Of course, many of these statements about them can also be applied to people of any sort who contemplate works of art.

In the first class, as I said, sit the pitiful souls who listen to – or rather, are present at – music only out of vanity and a desire to be fashionable. They have a seat and a voice at the opera and concert – a seat, so that they may display themselves and their elegant attire; a voice, so that they may chat. During an enchanting solo performed by Viotti which they don't hear, they extol one by Kreutzer which they haven't heard.[4] To them the opera house and concert hall are nothing but a spacious place where the smart set turns up dressed as splendidly as possible. The performer's most stirring passage merely moves them to whisper more furtively, the most powerful chorus merely to widen their circle of conversation and raise their voices a little louder. They pay no more attention to a Mara[5] than to their fancy hats, and they find nothing more remarkable and 'special' about Joseph Haydn than that he is a skinny little man, etc. But to them, all right and wrong in music are governed by the opinions of others and by today's conversation. With them this is not narrow-mindedness but voluntary confinement: they neither want to be nor to have anything more, even if they could; and so

66

they too belong in that category. By the way, people of this sort are most commonly found among the great and distinguished of the two sexes.

In the second class belong those who listen attentively but merely with the intellect, so to speak, and who go by the name of connoisseurs (whether through usurpation or possession I do not know) and prefer having it to themselves. Many of them shrink from virtually all music that is being written today. It displeases them without exception – why? Because it is not the way it used to be, at least in the first half of the century. Like certain scholars who have passed their examination, they have completed their course for their whole lifetime with their early schooling. What then delighted them – with good reason, perhaps – is now not merely good but uniquely good. As a result of this prejudice, contemporary music moves them but little – so little that they can easily get along without it. The more candid among them compare the effect of contemporary music with that of the older music. The latter, they find, never bears comparison with the former; but they do not reflect that the cause lies inside themselves and that their opinion is derived merely from the music's effect on them. Their excitability has cooled down, and they think that contemporary music has no excitement. They protest that the music of their youth still delights them when it is revived; but they do not reflect that this pleasure is rooted in the association of their ideas – that it is not the music alone which sweeps them along but the awakening (even if ever so secret), the effect (even if unconscious) of thousands of sweet memories of happier years, happier loves, etc.

Many others in this class do not willingly miss the performance of a new piece of music; they read diligently and extensively; but they go out for one reason alone: for the occasional pleasure of spotting a false fifth, a forbidden octave, or the like in the work of one or another of our accepted masters ... By the way, men of this ilk (for indeed there are no women of this ilk), in the nature of things, are to be found almost only among superannuated artists and musical scholars.

Here too belong the virtuosos who are nothing more than virtuosos. For they are interested only in the good or bad execution of difficulties and so-called magic tricks, just as tightrope walkers are interested only in keeping their balance on the high wire ...

The third class comprises those listeners and judges of music who hear merely with their ears – good, harmless little people of both sexes. They love music because it makes their blood run faster and sets their feet to dancing, as it were; they love music which makes this happen. They value compositions because they can provide an almost sure-fire antidote to boredom, whether in company or in solitude; they value compositions which provide this. A suite of charming dances, a merry sonata, humorous variations on a favourite air, military music, and especially pretty, charming, cheerful songs, and opera arias and duets in that style – this is chiefly what holds their love and interest. Music that lasts longer and makes demands, that is more deeply engaging, that cannot be sung so easily on the way home – this is not for them, is nothing to them. They have not enjoyed listening to Mozart's *Zauberflöte* without Papageno's songs, to Salieri's *Axur* without the intermezzo, to Joseph Haydn's symphonies without the so-called minuets. Paisiello they approve of, Martini[6] more, bits and pieces of Dittersdorf most of all. They are honest enough to understand that the rest is not for them, but many are also egotistical enough to dismiss it contemptuously and censure it.

Incidentally, as a rule these listeners and judges are not to be despised or laughed at, as earnest scholars and amateurs are wont to do: for they really are devoted to something belonging to the essential nature of music and they generally regard that which lies in their ken from a far more correct angle, judge it far more correctly, than, for example, the virtuoso in the second class. Young, vivacious, cultivated women are the principal members of this class; and since young, vivacious, cultivated women have a strong influence on young, vivacious, cultivated (or uncultivated) men, as well as manipulating the susurrations of the *vox populi*, they are beginning to play a very important part in deciding the fate of the work of art, and hence the fate of the artist, and hence too the fate and the course of artistic culture itself ...

In the fourth class, oft overlooked, almost always unconsulted, stand those who listen with their whole soul. They proceed from the correct foundations about art in general. To them art is one of the means to perfection and refinement of taste. What science is supposed to achieve by directing learning toward reason, this, they believe, art is supposed to achieve by mirroring feeling in its depictions. The former points man toward his highest aspiration; the latter makes him more inclined to reach out to it. The former can make him freely decide to approach the aspiration; the latter makes the decision easier to carry out. The former sharpens his sense of purpose and shows the way; the latter makes the purpose glorious and praiseworthy and smooths the way. In the opinion of these people, art is not the teacher and educator, or even the servant, of human sensuality; nor is it the bridge over which man is to cross from sensuality to freedom. But if science demonstrates what pure nature (abstracted from the empirical, free of what Lessing called 'resistant matter') is supposed to be, art shows what it is. Both guides, science and art, thus take man between them, so to speak, and lead him to the temple of perfection and freedom. As these people conceive of art in general, so also do they conceive of music: music too should be as they wish it to be, and so it is, if it is true music. Such judges do not despise that which lies outside the essence of music, but they view it with indifference unless it is used and applied as a means to the end of all art. That is why to them the humblest folk song, innocent and merry, which makes men merry is worth more than the concert which is nothing but a convoluted display of difficulties, devoid of feeling. Merry men usually are or are becoming better: but those who are blinded by amazement are and remain naught but ciphers. The most learned fugue which is merely a well-calculated textbook contrapuntal treatment of a trite theme is not an object of contempt to them, but neither is it any different from the *variorum* anthologies of classical authors which are nothing but *variorum* anthologies – the foundation of a good mind. They cling neither to the new nor to the old but to the good, that is, to that which aims at and approaches the highest purpose of art. They always distinguish this from that which is merely correct, and when something is good they are ready to excuse minor breaches of correctness as human weakness, without a lot of fuss. The opinions of the third class do not rouse their indignation, and they use the critics of the second class to enrich their knowledge and amend their experiences. Their opinions about works of music not infrequently agree with the opinions of the second and third classes; the viewpoint from which they consider these works, never. They understand the opinions of the two classes very well, but usually theirs are not understood in return. They are tolerant toward the others and for the most part are treated with intolerance. Freely and decisively, they judge a piece of music to be absolutely contemptible or absolutely praiseworthy, out of feeling for the dignity of an art which is reviled on the one hand and glorified on the other. As for a piece which belongs to neither category, they prefer to withhold their opinion, since they wish no spark of native genius to be snuffed out, since they cannot explain their opinion in a few words, and since they know that not everyone has the inclination – or time – to listen to their explanations. But they hold the maxim 'De gustibus non est disputandum'[7] to be a lie.

1 A composer of popular Singspiels and solo songs.
2 In 'Preface – in the Disobligeant' to *A Sentimental Journey*, Sterne divides travellers into classes, though not precisely the ones Rochlitz describes here.
3 In the second part of *Die unsichtbare Loge* (author's note).
4 The violin virtuosos Giovanni Battista Viotti and Rodolphe Kreutzer.
5 Gertrud Mara, the German soprano.
6 Vicente Martín y Soler (see no. 16).
7 'There is no arguing with taste.'

PART II
The Nineteenth Century

18

Leigh Hunt, ['Pantomime with Its Tongue Cut']

Examiner (30 July 1809)

Essayist, critic, and poet, Hunt (1784–1859) earned a place in music history with his penetrating and vivacious reviews of opera performances in London. Most appeared in the *Examiner*, the weekly newspaper that Hunt and his brother founded in 1808 as an outlet for their liberal views on politics and art. William Hazlitt and Charles Lamb were among the other regular contributors. Like Addison (see no. 1), Hunt deplored contemporary opera librettos, but he had a higher opinion of Italian opera *qua* music.

Lyceum

A new opera, attributed to Mr. Siddons, called the *Russian Impostor*, or *Siege of Smolensko*,[1] has been produced at this Theatre. It is founded on the story of an adventurer named Pugatscheff, who personates the wretched Alexis, son of Peter the First, and aims at the Russian crown. The music, by Mr. Addison, is in a style of pleasing common-place, and of course little calculated to advance the reputation of the English opera: however Mrs. Mountain used it so as to recall her best powers, and to eclipse her formidable rival Mrs. Bishop; and Mr. Phillips gave an additional specimen of his taste and feeling in the ballad department.[2] I was going to say, that it is a pity Mr. Bishop[3] was not requested to compose for the *piece*; but the *poetry* comes across my mind, and I congratulate him. However calculated his talents are to do honour to his country, I would rather see him writing for dances, than for dramas like these – rather see him giving grace to bodily elegance, than to mental deformity. The opera itself is indeed below criticism. Fancy a common spectacle at the Circus, a tyrant, an escape, and a battle, with words and songs added by one of the Circus poets, and you have a complete idea of the production. It is a pantomime with its tongue cut. One circumstance struck me very forcibly in the midst of the speeches and sentiments, and this is, that in knowing one half of any sentiment in such dramas, you infallibly know the remainder; and I am confident, that the manager would save a great deal of time, and the audience be quite as well informed, if one of the candlesnuffers were employed to stand, like the ancient Greek chorus, by the side of the actors, and cut short the speeches, particularly the sentimental ones, by one half; as thus – when an army, that is to say, a dozen of men, lift up their swords and cry, We swear to –, the chorus or candlesnuffer will say, as pithily as possible, *et cetera*, and thus the author will at once gain in conciseness, and the audience comprehend all that might have followed respecting freedom and one's country, sentiments that require the merest hint in a mind of the least generosity. A musical instrument might be employed with equally explanatory powers, in a song; as for instance, a flute might play tweedle-dee after every two lines in which the words [sic] *heart* or *woman* is used; a bassoon follow up a tyrant's resolutions by a groan; and a trumpet burst forth at the end of every line concluding with *charms*, as the audience are then fully prepared for *alarms*. Thus, one of the songs in the present piece relates the story of a lover, whose corpse is thrown up on shore at the feet of his mistress, who – etcetera; – and another says, that the heroine's bosom is as pure as ice, but alas, it is also – etcetera. In one or two instances, however, it may be dangerous to interfere, where, for example, instead of having the whole meaning in half a sentence, there is no meaning at all, as in the case of one of the Russian lovers before us, who talks of snow being *enrolled* on a temple, a word of which it is impossible to discover the significancy till you come to the rhyme *cold*, when you find it perfectly 'convenient, 'greable, and aproposs,' as Foote[4] says. – All this is highly entertaining; but then it is truly lamentable to reflect, what an absolute dearth of *sound study* and *sound ambition* there is, even amongst the best educated dramatists of the present day.

1 By John Addison and H. Siddons, produced at the Lyceum, 22 July 1809.
2 Rosoman Mountain, Elizabeth Sarah Lyon Bishop and Thomas Phillips.
3 Henry Bishop, the most successful English stage composer of his day.
4 Samuel Foote, the eighteenth-century comic actor and dramatist.

19

E. T. A. Hoffmann, 'Casual Reflections on the Appearance of This Journal'

Allgemeine Zeitung für Musik und Musikliteratur (9 and 16 October 1820), from David Charlton, ed., *E.T.A. Hoffmann's Musical Writings* (Cambridge, 1989), trans. Martyn Clarke

One of the giants of German literary romanticism, Hoffmann (1776–1822) composed a good deal of music which is all but forgotten. His writings about music, however, have stood the test of time, notably his imaginative reviews of Beethoven's works in the *Allgemeine musikalische Zeitung*. In this piece, published in a short-lived Berlin periodical, Hoffmann offers his credo as critic, whom he sees as mediating between artist and public. It makes an interesting contrast to the views of Johann Mattheson (no. 2) and W. J. Henderson (no. 59).

What is that incantatory formula with which authors customarily conclude their prefaces? 'And now go forth, my dear child, which I have cherished and protected with such care,' etc. And since nothing is more natural, it has become the convention to compare the intellectual with the physical act of giving birth.

Upon both lies the curse of original sin, that is to say the pain and torment of labour, counterbalanced by paternal pride and an abundance of blind love for the new-born creature. In truth, however, it is not a child which the author of a finished book sends out into the world, but a fully grown man whose whole physique lies open to view, within and without. With a work such as that just making its first appearance here, the situation is different again, totally different. The publisher builds as pretty a cradle as he can, the editor places the embryo in it, and as soon as the tiny creature begins to stir he asks suitable godparents, just like real godparents, to provide the infant with the necessities of life, care and upbringing. The thing may now develop and thrive according to its nature right under the eyes of the invited guests. There is an extended christening feast, and it is the responsibility of the hosting godparents to ensure that the food remains elegant and tasty, and that the drink never lacks fire and spirit; then the guests will not stay away, and the little one sitting at the front also eating and drinking will enjoy nourishing and palatable food and will continue to grow into a healthy adult.

But why this sour expression, my dear composer?

'Yet another new anatomical slab on which our works will be clamped down with their limbs forcibly stretched out and dissected with ruthless cruelty. Ha! I can already see false relations and hidden consecutive fifths severed from the flesh of their harmonic context and quivering under the glinting knife of the anatomist!'

So what is the source of your displeasure? Oh my dear old composer! I am convinced that you will write, or must already have written, a work which proceeded directly from your innermost heart. If it was perhaps an opera that you wrote, then first you absorbed the poetic idea underlying the whole with all its deepest implications; then the genius of music stirred its powerful wings; and even the fetters now and then imposed upon it by inferior passages of the libretto were unable to curb its bold flight, as it carried upward into higher regions every radiance of that poetic idea. All love, all yearning, all desire, ecstasy, hate, delight, despair seemed transfigured in the splendour of music's higher realm, and the human heart, stirred in a curious way, perceived the divine even amid the worldly. I believe that in the sacred hours of inspiration it was given to you to conceive the music in such a way as your controlling, ordering intellect deemed most truthful. Yes, intellect! I am afraid that this sometimes rather grumpy taskmaster cannot be ignored. He examines the supports of our building with a sharp eye; if he finds them too thin or weak he kicks them down, and if the entire edifice collapses he says that it was of no value anyway! It is better for it to be done by our grumpy friend within us than by others from outside! Enough, my dear composer. You have done a thorough job, I am sure, and it goes without saying that you are perfectly aware of having composed your music in accordance with its underlying idea, in that way and no other. So here you find your work not lying on an anatomical slab under the murderous hands of a barbaric anatomist, but standing before an allied spirit who casts a sharp eye over it and, instead of ruthlessly cutting it to pieces, puts into words all that he discovers in it, the entire edifice with all its wonderful intricacies. Do not say, dear composer, that it is hardly a pleasure to have everything one has thought and felt analysed like a mathematical problem. It is the pleasure of being fully understood by a kindred spirit which prevents any concern about such pedantic analysis from arising. Think of your work, my dear composer, as a beautiful and imposing tree which has sprung from a tiny seed and now extends its blossom-laden branches high into the blue sky. Curious people stand and stare and cannot understand the miracle by which the tree came to grow in such a way. But then this kindred spirit comes along who is able, by means of a mysterious magic, to let the people see into the depths of the earth, as through crystal, so that they discover the seed, and realize that from this very seed the entire tree sprang. Indeed they will see that tree, leaf, blossom and fruit could take only that form and colour and no other.

You will appreciate, my dear composer, that I was just reflecting on the form which criticisms of musical works should take, and that I prefer to consider as such only those essays which really penetrate to the heart of the work and reveal its deepest impulses; they not only cheer the composer, should the trumpet of his praise not always sound, as well as his fellow artists, but they also acquaint others with much that they would otherwise miss. What is certain is that criticisms of this sort can lead people to *listen* well. Listening well is a skill which may be acquired, if one is so disposed, but composing well oneself is certainly not. The latter activity presupposes a small matter which one shrewd old composer candidly referred to in a polite letter to a young gentleman of quality, who had asked in great desperation how in the name of heaven he could set about delighting the world with a musical masterpiece. The musician replied: 'If only Your Lordship would be so good as to possess genius, then everything would etc. etc.'

Finally I must confess to you, my dear composer, that it strikes me as very curious how often a few songs or an album of polonaises or, had they not gone out of fashion, minuets, can bear criticism very well, far better than many works lasting three hours, by which time one has heard enough and more than enough. Even a whole bush of rootless sprigs stuck into the loose soil can never become a vigorous, living tree.

There is nothing more gratifying than to give voice to one's feelings about an art which is so dear to one's heart; but how is this to be achieved? Talking is far better than writing, but it seems that one must write, since it is nowadays well-nigh easier to find people who read than people who listen; and musicians will always much prefer to listen to notes than to words, and suffer as unwillingly in speech as in music those excessively audacious modulations which the winged word all too lightly permits itself. One must ensure, however, that the dead letter carries within it the power of coming to life in the reader's mind, and making his heart respond to it! So does this also mean articles on musical subjects not based on any particular work? Nothing is more boring than articles of that sort, you say? Quite right! Especially in the style in which they are couched in *Hildegard von Hohenthal*[1] by the hero of the novel; he lectures his aristocratic pupil, for whom incidentally he bears a not entirely respectable affection, on the mathematical aspects of musical science in such a way that one cannot understand how she could bear such a pedant! Everything has its proper time and place. When a house is built, scaffolding is necessary; it would indeed be strange, however, to seek and find the architect's merit not in the building but in the scaffolding! There is a way of discussing musical matters, whether in speech or in writing, which satisfies the initiated without being incomprehensible to the people in the temple forecourt. The latter in fact may well derive considerable pleasure and unwittingly receive a measure of enlightenment without putting on priestly vestments at all ...

1 By Wilhelm Heinse, published in 1795–6.

20

Anonymous, 'To the Editor [of the *Quarterly Musical Magazine and Review*]'

Quarterly Musical Magazine and Review, vol. 6 (1824)

Modelled on the great literary magazines of the period, the *Quarterly Musical Magazine and Review* (1818–28) set the stage for a rapid expansion of England's musical press. Its editor, Richard Mackenzie Bacon (1776–1844), aspired to raise the level of musical taste and education in Great Britain. He addressed his magazine to the lay reader, taking a dim view of critics who were 'too often weak in judgment though fluent in objection'. The author of this letter seeks his advice about making judgments in an era of shifting aesthetic standards.

Perditur haec inter misero lux.
Hor.[1]

Sir: Some how or other I have wrought myself into a belief that I derive considerable enjoyment from listening to good music, well performed. Perhaps you will say there is nothing extraordinary in this: no more there is with respect to the belief; but with respect to the fact I really begin to suspect there is something more extraordinary in it than you may at first imagine: and it is upon this subject that I want to consult a public censor like yourself, in the hopes of being relieved from the doubts which at present beset me. As the matter now stands, if I were not pretty obstinately bent on maintaining my belief, I should soon become exceedingly sceptical, so many occasions arise to make me question whether all excellence be not imaginary. In order to bring the subject for your counsel into a more tangible shape, I must have recourse to examples of such circumstances as cause these musical misdoubtings in my mind, and from which I hope to be relieved by your magisterial judgment.

Let me, therefore, suppose myself at one of the most celebrated concerts in the metropolis, for in such a place are congregated all the most able professors, as well as the principal professing amateurs. Here I listen with great delight to the performance of a concerto by a gentleman who appears to me to possess all the requisites of a great artist – power, delicacy, energy, incomparable facility, and that which marks a man of true talent, a distinguishing style of his own. In the midst of my admiration of what appears to me so excellent, my attention is attracted to the observations of a person near me, who, with eyes twinkling with the exultation of self-approving judgment, with busy gesticulation, and great volubility of tongue, determines there is nothing in all this but what any body may do who will sit down and practise; and laments that such worthless pretensions should be tolerated. I look around to examine the persons whom he addresses, and find amongst them men whose judgments should direct them to a wiser and more just conclusion; but I perceive great gravity in their countenances, whilst their silence and gently indicated smile seem to confirm the opinion of the critic, and consequently to increase the animation of his oratory. In a few days afterwards I attend another concert, where another person takes his station at the instrument, and to my poor notion performs a piece without displaying one single quality which announces distinguished talent – no power of contrast – no passion – no sentiment – none of the stronger impulses which mark elevation of conception – but a mere monotonous dexterity, wholly void of character. I look around me, and I perceive my amateur critic in high exultation, pointing out the excellences of the performance to men, to whom I am bound to concede the right of passing judgment. I observe them to give smiles and nods of approbation, and the face of the critic assumes the settled dignity of authority.

Here, Mr. Editor, you will perceive my poor judgment quite adrift, without rudder or compass, and left in an open sea, buffeted by the winds of conflicting opinion. I had thought, in the simplicity of my heart, that I had formed my taste upon the best models, after mature consideration, and under the guide of men of the first eminence; but I find there is nothing certain in this mortal life. Being, however, desirous of improving my judgment, I make inquiries about this critic, in the hopes of finding my way to his acquaintance, and obtaining a few aids from the abundance of his information; and to my surprise I find he is a lawyer. Here I am doubly confounded; for what chance is there that my judgment should have any approximation to correctness, when I discover that this gentleman's taste and knowledge in the fine arts are built on the solid basis of the common law of the land? I know the wise modesty of the Chancellor would disclaim the fame of such unusual combination, and at least doubt his fitness for this double seat of judgment; but as I discern no vacillation in the mind of this arbiter elegantiarum, and see that he is abetted by men who should value their reputation in the art, my ideas are fallen into very lamentable confusion, from which I beseech you to relieve me ...

Further, Mr. Editor, being a harmless sort of man, I have occasionally the advantage of being at quartet parties, which generally consist of a mixture of amateurs and professors. Here again I am puzzled; for having been accustomed to hear with delight the compositions of Haydn and Mozart, I observe with great regret that these works are not unfrequently [sic] treated with a disregard somewhat bordering on contempt, and particularly by the amateurs. The reason of this, no doubt, is, that those gentlemen have more leisure for philosophical reflection and for diving into the hidden mysteries of the art, than the rest of the world. I had foolish-ly conceived that a noble consistency in the whole, with a nice adaptation of the parts to the main intention, was a great beauty in this species of composition – that bold thoughts should be artfully connected by the polished links of fine taste – and that when the imagination has wantoned in the luxuries of beautiful melody and rich harmonies, the judgment should have ample matter for delight-ful occupation at every repetition of the performance, in tracing the ingenious modes by which genius effects its well-arranged designs. But I find I am altogether mistaken. If in more recent compositions I fancy I perceive extravagance and want of consistency, 'Delphines inter sylvas'[2] – that I am not naturally, or by concealed art, led into the thought that is forced upon my attention; I am given to under-stand by modest imitation, that these are bold strokes of genius, which none but the initiated are capable of appreciating; and that it will be a long time before the greatness of eccentric genius becomes intelligible to the mass of mankind. If in the limitation of my facul-ties, I fancy myself to perceive indigestible crudities, which true judgment would never have introduced at all, but if introduced should at least have the excuse of being a foil to subsequent beau-ties, I am again informed there are mysteries of profound genius even in this, which the improvement of the human faculties is here-after destined to develop. If baldness stares upon me, I am saga-ciously informed that this is true simplicity: so that you see, Mr. Editor, I am really in a state which threatens a total dissolution to my taste, unless you furnish me with some efficacious remedy ...

I happened to be seated a short time ago in the midst of a body of critics, when a production of the unintelligible species, although by a great man, was, after numerous rehearsals, performed. I paid great attention to it, and kept my eyes pretty constantly upon the faces of these cognoscenti, in order, if possible, to provide myself with a clue to the many mysteries which were presented to my ears. But I could find none; nor could I discover any specific intention which the author had proposed to himself in the heterogeneous sounds which assailed my ears, except it were a witty essay upon the judg-ment of critics. However, at the conclusion of the piece, the whole body put themselves into an agitation of applause, although they had been unable to fix on one single rallying point during its perfor-mance. I humbly proposed some questions suitable to my unassuming capacity, in order to come in for some small portion of the delight which these gentlemen so unequivocally displayed. My answers were according to the pattern of the quartet party; and I was given to understand that such music could only be appreciated by the limited elect, and that it would be years before the public could be made partakers of these exalted pleasures ...

A short time afterwards, I was present in the same circle, when a new work was produced by a man of unquestionable genius, and which appeared to me to possess in an eminent degree that 'lucidus ordo'[3] which characterizes the works of truly great men. There was grandeur of conception, masterly art, a perfect knowledge of all the instruments, refined taste, bold and free imagination, wrought with profound judgment into the noblest effects – at least so it appeared to me; for during the performance I felt that kind of internal exultation by which the mind is elevated at the acting or recital of heroic deeds; but I saw nothing of this in the countenances of the critics who surrounded me ...

The first of these gentlemen I afterwards found was a clergyman, who thrums a little upon the piano forte, and who having mingled with certain learned Thebans, has taken the persuasion into his head that he is not less appointed to direct poor souls in the way to heaven, than to direct poor musicians in the way to compose.

The second was a philosopher of the pointed toe, vulgariter, a dancing master, who from the employment of his kit had risen to a part in a quartet; and from thence to the office of critic, par eminence, in all matters of composition. Nor is there any thing unreasonable in this, since it is the philosophy of the Verulam[4] school to build up its noble fabric from the most simple foundations, and gentlemen of this calling begin and prosecute their operations below all others.

The third was a merchant, who by taking a part now and then in an inexplicable quartet, without any knowledge of music but from intuition, had warmed himself into a belief that he had reached the highest point of Parnassus, and was a thoroughly inaugurated priest of Apollo.

The fourth was a man who had made many efforts in the way of composition, which had so completely shewn an utter destitution of imagination, originality, and science, that it would be cruelty not to let him amuse himself with the shadow, where the substance was so entirely beyond his grasp. The fifth was an amateur flute-player; but I rather think he must have been an amateur flageolet-player, since he must have reached the very extremity of music to have made himself so high a judge; and as height and depth in the learned languages are synonymous, it could not be doubted but his profundity must be amazing. Besides as expiration is absolutely necessary for a performance on his instrument, and as expiration cannot take place without inspiration, he must be considered as one of the inspired, for the depth of his knowledge in music could be accounted for on no other principles. The sixth was my already described causidico-musico-critico-amateur; at least this was the information communicated to me by a friend; but I have some doubts that he must have been mistaken; for the confidence with which these gentlemen spoke and acted makes me fully persuaded they must be the truly great and learned critics of the age, by whose verdict all musical merit must be decided. With this conviction, you will easily imagine, Mr. Editor, how much my poor judgment must be perplexed, and how much I stand in need of your magisterial counsel to direct it into its proper course.

With the most profound respect,
I remain, Sir, your servant and admirer,
ADELOS[5]
London, May 11, 1824.

1 'Amidst these things the light of day wanes before my wretched eyes' (*Satires*, 2, 6, 59). Horace, anxious to return to his country estate, is importuned by advice-seekers.
2 Dolphins in the woods.
3 Ordered clarity.
4 The school of Francis Bacon, Baron Verulam, a champion of inductive reasoning.
5 Greek: secret.

21

William Ayrton, [Beethoven's Ninth Symphony]
Harmonicon (March and April 1825)

Ayrton (1777–1858) was one of London's most prominent musical citizens in the early 1800s. Composer, opera impresario and writer, he began his career as a critic for the *Morning Chronicle* in 1813 and a decade later launched the monthly *Harmonicon* as a forum for what he called 'fair, manly and open Criticism'. His reservations about Beethoven's last symphony were echoed by other writers of the period; Adolf Marx (see no. 22) was virtually alone in approving of the unorthodox choral finale.

Previously to the re-commencement of these concerts, the Phiharmonic Society[1] had three private meetings in the months of January and February, for the purpose of trying, with the full orchestra, new compositions, and deciding on their fitness for public performance. Amongst these were, a symphony by Mr. Cipriani Potter, an overture by Mr. [John] Gross, Weber's overtures to *Preciosa* and *Euryanthe*, and a Grand Symphony recently composed for the society, by Beethoven.[2] All of these we shall have to notice when they are regularly before the public. But much curiosity having been excited by the latter composition, from the pen of so great a master, we shall anticipate in part our regular criticism on it, by observing, that it manifests many brilliant traits of Beethoven's vast genius; that it embodies enough of original matter, of beautiful effects and skilful contrivances, to form an admirable symphony of ordinary duration: but that unfortunately, the author has spun it out to so unusual a length, that he has 'drawn out the thread of his verbosity finer than the staple of his argument,' and what would have been delightful had it been contained within moderate limits, he has rendered wearying by expansion, and diluted his subjects till they became weak and vapid. When we add that the time which it is calculated this composition will take in performing, cannot be much less than an hour and twenty minutes, our readers, though they have not heard it, may almost judge for themselves of its inadequacy to fix the attention of any audience, or to produce such an effect as the admirers of Beethoven must earnestly wish ...

The new symphony of Beethoven, composed for, and purchased at a liberal price by, this society, was now first publicly produced. In our last number we mentioned it, and we see no reason for altering the opinion we there offered. We must, however, correct our statement as to its duration. At a rehearsal, where so many interruptions occur, it is next to impossible to ascertain exactly the length of a piece: we now find this to be precisely one hour and five minutes; a fearful period indeed, which puts the muscles and lungs of the band, and the patience of the audience, to a severe trial. In the present symphony we discover no diminution of Beethoven's creative talent; it exhibits many perfectly new traits, and in its technical formation shews amazing ingenuity and unabated vigour of mind. But with all the merits that it unquestionably possesses, it is at least twice as long as it should be; it repeats itself, and the subjects in consequence become weak by reiteration. The last movement, a chorus, is heterogeneous, and though there is much vocal beauty in parts of it, yet it does not, and no habit will ever make it, mix up with the first three movements. This chorus is a hymn to joy, commencing with a recitative, and relieved by many *soli* passages. What relation it bears to the symphony we could not make out; and here, as well as in other parts, the want of intelligible design is too apparent. In our next we shall give the words of the chorus, with a translation; in the present number our printer has not been able to find room for them. The most original feature in this symphony is the minuet, and the most singular part, the succeeding trio, – striking, because in duple time, for which we are not acquainted with anything in the shape of a precedent. We were also much pleased by a very noble march, which is introduced. In quitting the present subject, we must express our hope that this new work of the great Beethoven may be put into a produceable form; that the repetitions may be omitted, and the chorus removed altogether; the symphony will then be heard with unmixed pleasure, and the reputation of its author will, if possible, be further augmented ...

1 Founded in 1813 to present regular concerts of orchestral music.
2 In 1817 Beethoven accepted the Society's invitation to write two 'grand symphonies', but in the end he delivered only the Ninth. It was first heard in London on 21 March 1825, the première having taken place in Vienna on 7 May 1824.

22

Adolf Bernhard Marx, 'Lost Loves, or German Composers in Paris'

Berliner allgemeine musikalische Zeitung, vol. 4 (1827)

Editor of the influential *Berliner allgemeine musikalische Zeitung* from 1824 to 1830, Marx (1795?–1866) was widely respected as a critic and teacher, less so as a composer. He played a key role in the nineteenth-century Bach revival and was a perceptive champion of Gluck and Beethoven. In this fanciful dialogue (see no. 10 for another example of this fictionalized form), he imagines himself backstage at a performance of Gluck's *Iphigénie en Aulide* at the Paris Opéra in 1774.

Berlin, 9 November 1827

The Königstadt Theatre today having performed an opera recently arrived from Paris, Hérold's *Marie, or Secret Loves*,[1] I dutifully went in and fell asleep.

But I must have missed the right entrance, for unexpectedly I found myself between the wings and witnessed a spirited conversation that two people, unaware of me, were having in French one wing over, in a strangely refined yet exotic dialect that sounded archaic: 'Monseigneur,' a young, spirited voice asserted, 'Monseigneur could not imagine the *succès* this German has had with it. Grétry[2] himself, who took ill at the dress rehearsal, hasn't experienced anything like it.'

'Was he cheered with *éclat*?' the other man asked in a brusque, disapproving tone.

The younger man: 'What do you mean, cheered? Was it an opera, then, a high-society entertainment? The whole parterre was in ecstasy; people forgot the opera, forgot themselves. Oh, you should have seen them, those French of ours, who alone know what *noblesse* of feeling is. The whole house joined in, on my honour! Well now, Achilles has an aria[3] in which he draws his sword for his princess like a real French chevalier:

Calchas, pierced by a mortal blow –

'All of a sudden a noise, a flash of lightning – all our gendarme officers involuntarily ripped out their swords, like so many of the Myrmidon prince's[4] soldiers. Oh, those French of ours! There's only one nation for *noblesse* and art!'

The elder man: 'Bah, what an exaggeration! He didn't have a single motif that was *touchant*. The king[5] prefers the Italians.'

Y.: 'I have the honour to tell you that the queen has awarded him an honour; just yesterday –'

E.: 'Ah, the Austrian woman! Her countryman – she'll never become French – everywhere favouring foreigners who crowd around her, everywhere – '

Y.: 'Monseigneur will forgive me if I have the honour to assure him that Monsieur Gluck is far from being a valet. He consorts with the most distinguished persons, as if he knew better and they had nothing to say. He doesn't worry about anything. Even at the rehearsal the day before yesterday, Vestris[6] comes with the order that at Iphigenia's triumphal procession the king wishes to see a *divertissement* arranged by Vestris. And Gluck refuses!'

E.: 'But would he be so rash as to forget the public's preference, the *succès* of his own opera?'

Y.: 'That's what all the directors tell him, even the chamberlain himself (I saw it with my own eyes). "The public? The king?" Gluck cries excitedly. "Do they know what an opera calls for? Should the plot be interrupted with these childish games? They should be swept away!"'

E.: 'What arrogance!'

Y.: '"*Mais moi, le dieu de la danse!*" Vestris breaks in, in a passion. "They may dance that way in heaven," Gluck retorts, "but not in my opera, not if I don't want them to!"'

E.: 'And he gets his way?'

Y.: 'He gets his way.'

E.: 'Ah, the clever rascal! He counts on the queen's pardon, he implores her – '

Y.: 'Oh, not a bit. Doesn't he speak to her as well the way nobody speaks even to a princess? That's what makes him irresistible: he forgets her and himself for the sake of his opera. Even the actresses hate him sometimes and yet listen to him submissively. Do you hear?'

In the dimly lit theatre I now saw Gluck with a female singer, gesturing vehemently. They too were talking about the first performance of *Iphigénie en Aulide* the day before.[7]

'Away with these outbursts of emotion, Madonna! They have nothing to do with this. What, by all the gods – is Clytemnestra a love-sick Italian girl? Don't speak to me of applause! Does the crowd know what it wants? You are worthy of rising above this. Now, do you know what the scene is about? You are suffering the fate of the Atrides and the ancient hatred of the gods! Jesu Maria, what are you after, then, with your tenderness and sweetness? Come here and I'll tell you. You have – *Clytemnestra* has arrived with her daughter. Her husband, venerated like a god as Zeus is beloved of Juno, has deceived and betrayed her; he threatens his own flesh and blood. His beloved daughter, born to might and sovereignty, is to be sacrificed to ambition, to Calchas's greedy knife. And all of this unexpectedly comes crashing down on her queenly mother's heady triumph. Do you feel that, Madonna? Seize on it. Now Iphigenia departs, fearing for her mother's life, threatened by grief and suicide. Grief? Suicide? She gives no thought to them! What is Calchas to her, or the king or the gods? She rebels against them and the world with her "Mighty Gods, I call you to witness! No, I will not endure it." No wild passion, I say! I beg you, no hand-wringing! Just feel the queen inside yourself. And now she rushes after her daughter. The women hold her back as she runs – not a glance, not a word in their direction, Signora! What are they to the queen, who ignores the resistance of the Greeks, of the king, of God? By all that's holy, not a glance! The women are nothing but undergrowth snaring the pursuing conqueror's foot. Thither Iphigenia hastens after her soul,[8] consumed with the "No, I will not endure it." All those words – "You dare to stop my steps, perfidious ones" – thrown away! Only with the "Ah, I succumb" does she come to herself, succumbing to this consciousness and "to my mortal grief". Now I beg you, my dear, understand the crashes and groans in my orchestra. It penetrates your impotence; the impulse urges you on. Don't get up yet. In the women's arms, on the ground, with misty eyes, speak like this: "Ah, my daughter – ." What are you looking for? You can barely lift your arms – it's a vision, your glance strays. Away with this resolution! Can you not forget yourself, seeing that Clytemnestra has vanished? Not a word? *I* say to you: Everything will hang on your trembling lips, your silent word will strike like thunder, all the Hesperian sweetnesses are nothing there! And now get up. Now comes the moment that begets Clytemnestra's capitulation to the avenger Aegisthus, Agamemnon's murder, Orestes' cruel fate.[9] Now – '

Here fate interrupted the desiccated yet strangely courteous Monseigneur with a message from the queen. Gluck was distracted, clearly perturbed, and had to suppress his impatience. At length he seemed to understand that the queen was sending for him and wished to hear one of his scenes, which had greatly moved her the day before and still wasn't quite clear to her.

'You see, Signora – yes, the queen understands me. She is worthy of hearing my opera! I hasten to her. Oh, this true sovereign, this Armida, who with her noble charm could conjure love even out of the long-dead French heart! Truly, if her whole people were to rebel against her in a fit of rage, she would only rule more nobly and gently! She awaits me and from her I obtain satisfaction!'

He hastened away and so spared himself witnessing a conversation between the two theatre impresarios, who were having a spirited discussion about a coup to fill their cashboxes.

'He hasn't been crowing any longer since the *Siege of Corinth*. His *Guillaume Tell* isn't ready, though arrangements are being made for him to take up Meyerbeer's *Ranz des vaches*.[10] It's not pulling them in any more and the singers are making a killing. The little German wants to roll in gold too – here comes the young composer! Now, Monsieur, is the third act not ready yet? You've been promised the honour of a performance for four weeks now. Mademoiselle Cuiccidora doesn't disdain to undertake a role of yours – indeed, she wants to insert her favourite concert aria with a Turkish chorus. And you keep her waiting?'

Only now could the other impresario get himself introduced to the young, blond, pale-blue-eyed composer, who muttered something about patronage and excused himself. He had not been able to write for two evenings, as there had been a soirée musicale at the home of Duchesse Tronc and he had been obliged to arrange variations on the giraffe piano for Vicomte Bleumourant (which, by the way, he promised to use as an overture for the opera, so that the time hadn't been wasted).

'But,' said the other impresario (who seemed to me, on the whole, the more perceptive of the two), 'will it go with the opera's Swiss costume?'

'Oh,' the young man apologized, 'I've already found a way to bring in the cow dance – it occurs later on anyhow at the consecration and peasants' dance.'

'Not a peasants' dance,' barked the first impresario, breaking in. 'That's old hat, like a rose-festival dance! Something new – you must be original! Couldn't it be a dance for Mamelukes or Osages? Maybe you could get the king of the savages himself!'

'Splendid, unique,' stammered the young man, 'only on account of the costume one would have to consider – '

'Ah, well,' the first impresario interrupted, 'from time to time one still hears that your previous experience was behind the shop-counter.[11] I tell you, I understand this better than you; also Mr. Salto wants to have a *pas de trois* with the sisters inserted. Congratulate yourself – that will bring people in and win them over. You must make it gay, with Turkish music and trumpets – Her Highness doesn't like the harp to be left out. What could you represent? Let's see, er – yes, *le génie de la gloire*, the one *Volupté*, the other *Religion*. *Bon, bon*, that's the ticket! So: where he kneels and the women hop over him, bring on the Rossinian stretta, like this: La la la, tindarada, schneterdeng deng, bum.'

At this point the poor composer was handed a note with which Cuiccidora returned his two arias. In the touching second-act aria she must have a chromatic run of two octaves, like the one Mademoiselle Tut recently sang. The other aria in B-flat was passable, but it must have a better theme and it must definitely begin on B, since that was her best note and in the future she wouldn't appear in any opera unless all of her pieces began on B.

'What a request!'

'Oho, young man,' the impresario interrupted again, 'you must never hesitate to comply with a singer's request.'

'But a new theme! What's wrong with the old one?'

'Yes, as your German poet, the Faust from Weimar, says: "As your poets will it to be, so poetry commands."'[12]

'My head! One came to me yesterday. How does it go now? Oh, my head!'

'That comes from going into raptures.'

'But one can't shut oneself off from that – you wouldn't consider me an artist. I hasten to her, to convince her, to move her!'

(The awakening follows.)

Marie, or Hidden Loves, opera in three acts by Hérold

The Parisian composer's cold, spirit- and art-forsaken music is at all events sufficient as incidental decoration of incidental inspiration, in just such cold and elegant conversation pieces as we receive from Boieldieu and Auber. In the above-mentioned Singspiel,[13] this music is nevertheless supposed to serve for the language of the heart, is supposed to resound like the Swiss mountains, and thereby of course reveals its shallowness and emptiness all the more conspicuously. No wonder that even the public, however much it may have forgotten the true vocation of art, takes a less lively interest in this novelty than in things which are ever so feeble but which move in more auspicious spheres. Does this pronouncement on opera still require formal proof? It has as little right to it as pictures in the fashion journals have to critical elucidation in art pages. To him who expects nothing of opera but an empty diversion for empty hours, one could recommend nothing better; he who seeks something better will readily recall what good operas have yielded for him and dispense with these French operas ...

1 Ferdinand Hérold's *Marie* tallied a hundred performances within a year of its opening at the Opéra Comique in Paris on 12 August 1826. It was first seen in Berlin on 7 November 1829.

2 André Grétry, the popular composer of *opéras comiques*.

3 The third-act aria in Gluck's *Iphigénie en Aulide*, in which Achilles vows to kill the high priest who has decreed the sacrifice of Iphigenia, daughter of Agamemnon and Clytemnestra.

4 i.e., Achilles'.

5 The king and queen were Louis XIV and Marie Antoinette.

6 Gaetano Vestris, the 'god of dance', was ballet master to the French court.

7 At the Opéra, 19 April 1774. Gluck is describing the scene in Act 3 in which Clytemnestra tells her daughter that she is willing to die in her place.

8 i.e., Clytemnestra.

9 These events fall outside the bounds of Gluck's opera.

10 Rossini's *Seige of Corinth* was first performed in 1826, *Guillaume Tell* in 1829. The overture to the latter contains a *ranz des vaches*, or Swiss shepherd's melody; Marx, however, seems to be referring to the 'Ranz des vaches d'Appenzell' which Meyerbeer wrote to a text by Eugène Scribe.

11 An allusion to Meyerbeer's bourgeois Jewish background.

12 A misquotation of the famous lines from Goethe's *Faust*, part 1: 'Gebt ihr euch einmal für Poeten / so kommandiert die Poesie!' which Walter Arndt translates, 'Call yourselves poets by vocation? Then order up your poetry.'

13 Published by Schlesinger in Berlin in a piano arrangement (author's note).

23

Ludwig Rellstab, 'Möser's Symphony Soirée'

(11 February 1828), from Rellstab, *Gesammelte Schriften*,
vol. 20 (Leipzig, 1848)

Berlin's most celebrated journalist in the early 1800s, Rellstab (1799–1860)
was born into a musical family: his father was a music publisher and critic,
his sister an opera singer. As a young man he was imprisoned for lampoon-
ing the popular soprano Henriette Sontag in a novel. A writer of outstanding ability, Rellstab began his newspaper career on the *Vossische Zeitung* in
1826 and four years later founded the weekly journal *Iris im Gebiete der
Tonkunst* (Iris in the Service of Music).

The symphony evenings interspersed with the quartet evenings,
which Music Director Möser[1] has arranged for this winter, are
unquestionably the musical entertainment which has given the cultivated listener the highest pleasure, indeed often genuine edification. The circle of interested friends of music is becoming visibly
more crowded as well, so that the hall, which still had quite a few
seats left at the outset, is already beginning to become more and
more cramped in the standing area.

After a pause began Beethoven's marvellous Symphony in A
major.[2] It appears that this unfathomable master, with his ever-
growing power of creative fantasy, must increasingly have lost his
organizational mastery. Far from wishing to reproach him in the
slightest on that account, we are on the one hand confronted by
this as a proof of his greatness, while on the other hand we of
course recognize the limits which are unalterably set even for the
boldest flight of genius.

In the first Allegro of this symphony there reigns a roaring torrent of joy, which sweeps everything away with it and transports
us on its waves through a romantic wonderland. Every turn
brings new vistas; but just as we do not argue with the Rhine for
being overly long, so here too we ought to forget, in the presence
of so much creative richness, that a smaller treasure of ideas
would have allowed itself to be shaped more easily and more con-

centratedly into a harmonious whole.

The Andante touches with such a deeply melancholy emotion that we can hardly find the peace to form an opinion as to the mood it arouses in us – peace which one needs in order to become aware of the wonderful inventions in instrumentation and of the deeper but still light-handed working out of the theme.

After the bold rhythms and harmonies of the Scherzo, we come to the Finale. Here reigns a colossal energy of the inventing spirit, which can hardly find satisfaction even in extreme measures. It is a chaos filled with cosmic thoughts in which we view with amazement the genius who created it, while at the same time we confess that the elements still appear too much in conflict for us to see the ordered world, founded on the standard and law of beauty. It does not appear to us that a lack of individual conceptual power is to blame here, although we are well aware that many of Beethoven's admirers consider him greatest at these very moments. It seems to us that this is merely based on a very easy confusion of the creator's energy with the results themselves, like a rider who cavorts in the saddle of a wild, intractable steed without being pitched off and appears to be superior to one who has such control over the beast's strength that it can never cut loose capriciously.

These last words of Beethoven's are surely a presentiment of an even deeper development of men's musical capabilities than now exists. But perhaps only in centuries hence will it become possible for a cultivated artwork to be shaped from such materials – materials with which our master's enormous strength now piles up colossuses that recall the wonderful Egyptian sculptures before which we are more astonished than before those of a Phidias, without underestimating the conscious spirit at work in the latter.

1 Karl Möser, composer and violinist, began giving chamber music evenings with his quartet in 1813. They soon expanded into symphony concerts, at which he conducted local premières of several of Beethoven's works.
2 The Seventh Symphony of 1816.

24

François-Joseph Fétis, 'On the Future of Music'

Revue musicale (2 October 1830)

Fétis (1784–1871) was one of the nineteenth century's towering musical intellects. In an age obsessed with progress, both artistic and technological, he argued that musical history was evolutionary and that every era had to be understood on its own terms. The historical concerts that Fétis organized in Paris and Brussels in the 1830s were landmarks of the early music revival. This article for the *Revue musicale* – a weekly journal which he founded in 1827 – attests to his sense of historical flux.

The inevitable effect of political revolutions, such as the ones that broke out in France in 1789 and 1830, is to let the people's ideas burst forth abruptly and to forge a short cut from the starting point to the finish line, avoiding the intermediate steps. A revolution, then, is merely a way of making one's way quickly toward a goal that one would have reached slowly in the normal course of events.

The results of this quickness are not felt in politics alone; they also manifest themselves in the sciences, arts, industry, and indeed everything that lies within the domain of the intellect. New needs are created which must be satisfied, or society will pay the price. In his famous Reformation, Luther did not restrict himself to inflicting a deep wound on the Catholic religion; having substituted the power of reason for that of faith, he opened new paths for men of state, philosophers, scholars and artists. The dawn of the first French Revolution saw the birth of a new, rational chemistry, of a new system of painting and of instrumental power in music.

The most distinguished men are seldom prepared for these sudden changes of ideas. Ahead of their time until the revolution starts, they find themselves lagging behind once it is over. Superior beings, capable of moving with the times and holding their own, are always few and far between. Maturity does not understand the needs of youth, and what it sees as folly may only be the consequence of rebellion. So do our politicians, who three months ago were ardent defenders of liberty, recoil before a greater and mightier liberty that is no longer in harmony with the progressive course they had charted.[1] So do artists of genius, who have urged their art forward out of innovative necessity, conceive nothing beyond the boundaries they have set for themselves. But the river carries away everything in its path. Boundaries to improvement exist only in the minds of those who impose them; there is always something beyond our ken. What is it? you ask. Who can say? God only knows.

If we apply these principles to music, we at once understand the cause of this progress, and of the resistance to it. As far back in time as you care to look, music can be seen struggling against the shackles affixed by the very people responsible for its advances, breaking those bonds and casting brilliant reputations into oblivion to make room for others to arise. This instability is the despair of men with established reputations and accounts for the little strategies and tricks by which they seek to preserve their waning supremacy. But their futile efforts merely postpone the victory of new ideas and abilities for a few days. What do we do when victory is achieved? We wax indignant about 'the madness of the age' and 'reckless innovators'. Music, we grumble, is a 'fashionable art, unworthy of the time we devote to it', and so on and so on.

'Music is a fashionable art': let us take a moment to examine this expression, which has so many different connotations.[2] If by *fashion* is meant certain periodic changes the art has undergone since its inception, it is quite evident that music is fashionable; but in this sense the other arts, the sciences, literature, philosophy and even politics are fashionable as well, since fashion is simply society's seal of approval for new ideas or progress. Music is vague in its subject matter, but its means are vast and its variety infinite. In changing form, it moves forward by adding the unknown to the known. The public's taste for a music of new forms is therefore not fashion but progress. It is not a bit like changing tastes in furniture and clothing: whim alone gives rise to them, and yesterday's cast-offs are soon taken up again. If ever we revert to Lully's operas and Stamitz's symphonies, music will be a fashionable art in the narrowest sense. This art, then, does not simply vary when it changes; it enriches itself by adding new combinations of notes to its storehouse.

The different aspects of music which have undergone successive improvements are: harmony, or the art of writing learned forms; melody, in the absolute sense; melodic forms; the expression of words; the expression of feeling, independent of the words; the disposition of phrases; the division of pieces; rhythm; instrumentation – in short, the effects of sonority in voices and instruments. Each of these aspects has had the upper hand in its turn, and every time a step has been taken in one or another, people are convinced that the goal has been reached, for musicians have never gotten out of the habit of planting the pillars of Hercules[3] in their art. Hence their resistance to new things and, on the other hand, the senseless and headstrong vogue for such novelties among those for whom they represent a new source of pleasures. Some drew the boundaries of art in the present, others in the past, but both were equally unfair and prejudiced.

How many things remain to be done in such a multifarious art! After so many changes, so much progress, who could fail to see, upon reflection, that the goal is receding before us and that the boundaries of art are chimeras? Let us have no doubts: in the end we will convince ourselves, despite the excitement of new discoveries, that the state of music, whatever it may be, is not and cannot be anything but transitional. Another order of ideas will soon begin. Instead of passionately espousing one or another system exclusively, we will enlarge the circle of our pleasures by opening ourselves to all. Musicians and public will be imbued with the spirit of eclecticism, and with it will come variety – a variety all the greater in that the art will enrich itself endlessly with new things, while losing none of the old.

Variety! Since the beginning of music, this has been has been the missing ingredient in the genius of artists and in the experiences of us all. Fixated on a single goal and on artistic boundaries, and prey to the deeply felt prejudices that used to govern everyone, we have always done as much as possible to reduce the immense domain of this art; we have been open only to a certain kind of enjoyment, whereas it was possible to multiply our pleasures. Variety, once introduced in music, will do away with the fatigue – even boredom – which seizes us through the uniformity of the best things. With it, the simplicity and majesty of Palestrina's style, the learned and elegant forms of Scarlatti, the moving language of Leo, Pergolesi, Majo and Jomelli,[4] the dramatic force of Gluck, the incisive harmony of Johann Sebastian Bach, Handel's massed power, Haydn's richness, Mozart's impassioned voice, Beethoven's independent spirit, the suavity of Italian melodies, the energy of German songs, the dramatic aptness of French music, all combinations of voices, all systems of instrumentation, all effects of sonority, all rhythms, all forms – in a word, all the resources of music can find a home in the same work, and their effects will be all the more impressive in that they will be appropriately used.

Variety in making and appreciating music, eclecticism in judging it – this, then, is the future of music. Properly speaking, there will no longer be a school or a manner. Each person will understand that he can – must – take charge of his own aesthetic education, instead of trying to mould himself on other people's. No one style will be preferred at the expense of another, for genius is nothing but audacity, and artists will know that they not only can but must take risks.

1 Louis Philippe, the 'citizen king', disappointed the hopes of French liberals.
2 See no. 16 for another view of 'fashionable' music.
3 In ancient times, marking the boundaries of the known world.
4 Giuseppe Majo, Niccolò Jomelli and Leonardo Leo were all known for their operas in the eighteenth century.

25

Robert Schumann, 'To Chiara'

Neue Zeitschrift für Musik (10 November 1835), translated in part by Leon Plantinga

Schumann (1810–56) was perhaps the most remarkable of the nineteenth-century composer-critics. Influenced by the literary romanticism of Hoffmann (see no. 19) and Jean Paul, he invented a league of artists, the Davidsbündler, who gathered to debate artistic issues of the day. The impassioned Florestan, the gentle Eusebius and Master Raro, the chairman of the league, made their debuts in the *Allgemeine musikalische Zeitung* in 1831. Three years later Schumann helped to found a new journal, the *Neue Zeitschrift für Musik*, to 'take action, so that poetic qualities may again be honoured in this art'. Those qualities are evident in the following essay, one of a series entitled 'Enthusiastic Letters'. It is addressed to Schumann's beloved Clara.

The postman burst into bloom for me when I saw the red 'Milano' stamp glittering on your letter. I too recollect with delight the first time I set foot in La Scala, just as Rubini was singing with Méric-Lalande.[1] For Italian music has to be heard in the company of Italians; German music, of course, can be enjoyed under any sky and best of all in Firlenz, which has almost always kept clear of prejudice, shortsightedness, and pernicious patriotism.

Quite rightly I had read no reactionary intention into the programme of the previous concert, for the coming ones brought hesperidean fare – not top-drawer Rossini, unfortunately. On that occasion Florestan entertained me the most. He was genuinely bored by it, and only his obstinate opposition to certain Handelians and other zealots, who talk as if they themselves had composed *Samson* in their nightclothes, kept him from pitching straightway into the hesperidean music. He compares it with 'fruit dessert', 'Titianesque flesh without spirit', and the like, in such comical tones, to be sure, that one could laugh aloud but for the lofty condescension of his eagle eye. 'Truly,' he said on one occasion, 'to be irked by Italian things has long since ceased to be fashionable. Besides, why flail about with clubs at floral perfume that flits about here and there? I don't know which world I'd prefer: one full of nothing but stubborn Beethovens, or one full of dancing swans from Pesaro. But I'm puzzled by two things. First, why don't divas, who after all never know what to sing (except everything or nothing) – why don't they expend their caprices on little things, perhaps a song by Weber, Schubert or Wiedebein? And then, since German song composers are always grumbling that so little of their work turns up on concerts, why don't they think of concert pieces, concert arias, concert *scenas*, and write something like that?'

The singer (not Maria), who sang something from *Torvaldo*,[2] sang her 'Dove son? Chi m'aita?' with such a wide vibrato that my inner voice replied: 'In Firlenz, my dear. *Aide-toi et le ciel t'aidera!*' But then she came to a sweet passage and the public broke out in sincere applause. 'If German divas', Florestan interjected, 'would only stop acting like children who think they become invisible when they shut their eyes. Instead, they usually manage to hide so quietly behind the score that you can't help paying attention to their faces and noticing how different they are from the Italian divas I saw at the Academy in Milan, who rolled their eyes at each other so beautifully while they were singing that I feared artistic passions might erupt. This last I have exaggerated, but I do long to read something of the dramatic situation in the German singers' eyes, something of the joy and sorrow of the music. Beautiful singing from a marble face makes one doubt the best quality deep inside – as a general rule, I mean.'

You should have seen Meritis[3] play Mendelssohn's G minor Concerto. He sat down at the piano as innocent as a child, then proceeded to capture one heart after another and draw them after him in droves. And when he released them, one was conscious only of having flown past Greek islands of the gods and been deposited safe and sound back in the hall in Firlenz. 'You are a right blessed master in your art,' said Florestan to Meritis at the end, and they were both right ...

You recall that we never considered the bare piano part something rare and original, the way your average youngster prefers the subjectively characteristic to the universally ideal. But, having been heard just now from Meritis and a warmly understanding orchestra, the concerto indeed expresses nothing more than a master feels in unalloyed cheerfulness. At the entrance of the trumpets (if it has no aesthetic connection, it certainly has no unaesthetic one either), someone beside me sat up with a start. One thing I know – that I should never take it into my head to write a concerto in three interconnected movements. Yesterday I quite nicely understood my friend Florestan, who hadn't said a word to me about the concert. I saw him paging through a book and making some sort of annotation. When he left, I read what he had written. Beside the passage he had marked – 'Many things in this world defy description: for example, Mozart's C major Symphony (with the fugue), much of Shakespeare, some of Beethoven' – he had written in the margin: 'Meritis, when he plays M.'s concerto.'

We took great delight in an energetic overture by Weber, the mother to so many limply derivative pens, as well as in a violin concerto played by young ***; for it is satisfying to be able to predict with certainty of someone who is striving that his path will lead to mastery. I shall not entertain you with accounts of pieces which are repeated year in and year out, except for symphonies. I share your earlier observation about Onslow's[4] Symphony in A – that having heard it only twice you now know every bar by heart – without quite understanding why it should be so easy to memorize. On the one hand, I see how the instruments still cling to each other too much and how instruments that are too dissimilar are piled up together. On the other hand, the melodic threads, both primary and secondary, are so strongly perceptible that the obtrusiveness of the latter, with their thick combination of instruments, seems very odd to me. There is something going on here that I can't express clearly, for it's a mystery to me. But perhaps it will stimulate some reflection in you. I feel most at home in the refined ballroom jumble of the Minuet, where everything sparkles with diamonds and pearls. In the Trio I picture a scene in an antechamber, and through the frequently opened ballroom doors the sound of violins penetrates, drowning out words of love. How's that?

This brings me very conveniently to Beethoven's A major Symphony, which we heard recently. In modified rapture, we went afterward late that evening to Master Raro. You know how Florestan sits at the piano and, as if in his sleep, talks, laughs, weeps, stands up and starts all over again, etc., as he improvises. Zilia was in the bay window, with other Davidsbündler scattered in groups here and there. There was a lot of discussion going on. 'I had to laugh,' Florestan began, as he launched into the A major Symphony, 'I had to laugh at a dry old actuary who found in it a battle of giants, and in the last movement their final destruction – though he had to pass lightly over the Allegretto because it didn't fit into his plan ... But most of all my fingers itch to get at those who insist that Beethoven always presented in his symphonies the most exalted sentiments: lofty ideas about God, immortality and the courses of the stars. While the floral crown of the genius, to be sure, points to the heavens, his roots are planted in his beloved earth.

'Now about the symphony itself; this idea is not my own, but taken from an old volume of *Cäcilia*⁵ (though there the setting is changed to the parlour of a count, perhaps out of too great a diffidence for Beethoven – which was misguided) ... It is a most merry wedding. The bride is an angelic child with a rose in her hair, but only one. Unless I am greatly mistaken, in the Introduction the guests gather together, greeting each other with inverted commas, and, unless I am wrong, merry flutes recall that in the entire village, full of maypoles with many-coloured ribbons, there reigns joy for the bride Rosa. And unless I am mistaken, the pale mother looks at her with a trembling glance that seems to ask, 'Do you know that now we must part?' And Rosa, overcome, throws herself into her arms, drawing after her, with the other hand, that of the bridegroom ... Now it becomes very still in the village outside.' (Here Florestan came to the Allegretto, taking passages from it here and there.) 'Only a butterfly flits past or a cherry blossom falls ... The organ begins; the sun is high in the sky, and single long, oblique rays play upon the particles of dust throughout the church. The bells ring vigorously – parishioners arrive a few at a time – pews are clapped open and shut – some peasants peer into hymnbooks, others gaze up at the superstructure – the procession draws closer – first choir-boys with lighted candles and censers, then friends who often look back at the couple accompanied by the priest – then the parents, friends of the bride, and finally all the young people of the village. And now all is in order and the priest approaches the altar, and speaks first to the bride, and then to the happiest of men. And he admonishes them about the sacred resonsibilities and purposes of this union, and bids them find their happiness in profound harmony and love; then he asks for the "I do" that is to last for ever; and the bride pronounces it firmly and deliberately ...

'I don't want to continue this picture, and you can do it your own way in the Finale.' Florestan thus broke off abruptly and tore into the close of the Allegretto; the sound was as if the sacristan was slamming the doors so that the noise reverberated through the whole church.

Enough. Florestan's interpretation has suddenly aroused something in me too, and the letters are beginning to jumble. There is still much I would like to say to you, but I am drawn away. And so bide the interval until my next letter with faith in a better beginning!

Eusebius

A word from me as well. Livia asks me to contribute something about concerts to the **sche Zeitung*. You know how I abhor public music scribblings, especially the good-naturedly arcadian ones. This could perhaps be made tolerable by means of a freer form, perhaps that of a letter. But then the letters would have to turn out very different from those to a certain Chiara.

Florestan

1 The tenor Giovanni Battista Rubini and the soprano Henriette Méric-Lalande.

2 Rossini's *Torvaldo e Dorliska*.
3 Meritis was the name given to Mendelssohn among the Davidsbündler.
4 The English composer George Onslow.
5 A music journal published in Mainz.

26

Vladimir Fyodorovich Odoyevsky, 'Letter to a Music Lover about an Opera by Glinka: *Ivan Susanin*' and 'A New Russian Opera: *Ivan Susanin*'

Severnaya Pchela (The Northern Bee) (7 December 1836) and *Literaturnykh Pribavleniyakh k Russkomy Invalidu* (Literary Supplement to the Russian Veteran) (30 January 1837), from G. Bernardt, ed., *V. F. Odoyevsky: Muzykalno-literaturnoye naslediye* (Moscow, 1956), trans. Richard Miller

A soulmate of the German romantics, Odoyevsky (1803/4–69) is best known as a writer of fantasies in the manner of Hoffmann and Poe. He was also Russia's first music critic of distinction, a personal friend of Serov (see no. 38) and other leading composers, and a founder of the Moscow Conservatory. Like most Slavophiles, Odoyevsky was galvanized by the St Petersburg première of Glinka's *A Life for the Czar* (originally called *Ivan Susanin*) on 27 November 1836 – a date that marked the beginning of Russia's emergence from European cultural domination.

You wanted me to give you my first impression of Glinka's new opera, and that's precisely what I'm doing: I'm writing to you immediately after the first performance, so don't look for strict cohesiveness in my words; I know that at the moment fullness of feeling will hinder fullness of expression; the charming, attractive melodies of the opera still sound in my ear, and I'd rather sing them than speak about them ...

How can I express the astonishment of true lovers of music when they discovered from the first act that this opera settled an important question for art in general and for Russian art in particular, namely, the existence of *Russian* opera, *Russian* music – the existence of *national* music generally? For you, the educated amateur, this question had always been close to decided; you believed that just as a painter knows certain features that define the physiognomy of this or that nation and can draw, for instance, a Russian or Italian face without needing a model, so too a musician knows certain melodic and harmonic forms that define the character of the music of this or that nation and by which we distinguish German music from Italian or even Italian from French. Even before Glinka we had a few happy attempts to find these common forms of Russian melody and harmony ... But never before had these forms been used on such a grand scale as in Glinka's opera. Initiated into all the secrets of Italian singing and German harmony, the composer has deeply penetrated the character of Russian melody! Rich in talent, he has proven by this shining example that Russian melody, by nature now plaintive, now merry, now bold, can be elevated to the tragic style. In the whole opera only the first two measures are taken from a well-known folk song, but after that there isn't a single phrase that isn't original to the highest degree and at the same time native to the Russian ear.

Glinka's opera introduces something that has been long sought but not found in Europe – *a new element in art*, and a new period in its history has begun – *the period of Russian music*. Such a feat, we swear solemnly, is an act not only of talent but of genius! ...

There have already been fourteen performances of this opera and each time the theatre has been full, and several journal articles have variously commented upon it. In these lines I do not intend to assume the stern countenance of an implacable judge and pass final sentence, but wish only to share with you the impression the opera has made on me; I saw the effect it had on you, saw your tears, and am certain that these lines will find a warm response in your gentle and educated soul.

For my part it is very difficult, having picked up the pen and being full of sweet recollections of *Ivan Susanin*, to write down a few horrible judgments that, unfortunately, are rather common in Petersburg; but, however reluctantly, it is best to relate them at the beginning: at least it will be over with! So long as there appeared compositions in the Russian spirit, so long as many noble journalists reiterated that now Russia has found its originality, now a Russian grasps what is Russian, his own, etc.; so long as only composers and journalists were saying such things, their optical illusion had a complete success. But when a Russian, noble and educated, with an ardent soul and sublime talent, understood the Russian national spirit; when, having seen the cloudless sky of Italy,[1] he recalled his gloomy native sky, and having heard the works of Bellini, Rossini and Donizetti in their native countries he recalled the plaintive song of a Russian and created the gentle Antonida and the angel Vanya[2] – and finally, saying a sorrowful farewell to his beloved dream, exposed it to universal ridicule – the optical illusion vanished, the curtain that had impenetrably hidden the Petersburg upper crust and their judgments split open, and an era of true over-turning of general opinions arrived.

Until now, the European glory of all operas that appeared on the Petersburg stage secured the judgment of our 'fashionable' people, who would say, 'That is marvellous, *mais c'est délicieux!*' and thus only confirm the general opinion that they were great connoisseurs of music; a few of them were even so fortunate as to manage to learn by heart a few simple motifs of Rossini and Bellini. Of course, these are trifles, but trifles that you meet at every step and do not give you a minute of rest. And these great arbiters have bred like locusts in Petersburg; they even call Petersburg a musical city and drone on that not going to the opera or preferring this or that to the opera is barbarism.

At last there appears *Ivan Susanin* and everybody says, 'This is our composition, we ourselves must render an opinion of it.' But poor music-lovers! They had forgotten that in this instance there is as yet no general opinion, no European praises of the composer, that there are no fine phrases in the French journals to come to their aid, and they would have to figure out what to say by them-selves.

Many said, '*C'est mauvais,*' you can hear that on any street, '*dans tous les cabarets ... *' Others were more generous and announced that 'the opera is rather good, but how can one compare it with our dear Bellini, Rossini!' And then they enthusiastically sing a theme – from Bellini or Rossini, you think; but not at all: our music-lover, in proof of his words, can sing only the triumphal march from *Fenella*![3] And these people bellow their judgments of music at pub-lic meetings! ... And there are still others, the most pitiable remains of the upper crust, who feel the whole charm of Glinka's work but do not dare to speak their opinion aloud, lest they compromise themselves. This smoke of judgments has with nary an exception filled the halls and the stalls, and a Russian man does not know where to turn if, wiping away a sweet tear drawn by the music of Glinka, he wishes to avoid the baneful grin in a frock coat and velvet lapels and a *lorgnette élastique* in his hand ... There has been so much talk, for so long, about Russicism and Russianness and nationality; but it is now clear that the upper crust has remained nothing but a pitiful, characterless and unscrupulous imitator ...

It is indisputable that Italian, French and (later) German music, having reached a full development, have received broad renown, and that from them a general European music has formed. It has so taken root everywhere, it is listened to so intently, that the usual unsophisticated sounds of native music cannot make an impression on the majority of people.

This situation has presented Mr. Glinka with a significant problem. Guided by the general music, he has had to transmit entirely faithfully the native sounds and thereby place Russian music on the same level as the national melodies of Western Europe. This is extraordinarily difficult, as anyone who listens at all to our melody will easily appreciate. Nowhere in the world is there a more individual, incorrect, and at the same time harmonious conjunction of sounds as in Russian melody. In this Mr. Glinka has succeeded; he has understood these melodies and conveyed them in an elegant whole, having appended to them a remarkable orchestration which would do honour to any opera by Auber, Halévy, Bellini, or Donizetti. But he has shown even more with this composition: he has shown that he wields the pen of music with a firm hand, that it never betrays him, regardless of how diverse the circumstances of the acts may be. And, indeed, how many contrasts will you find in *Ivan Susanin*! Lightheartedness, family happiness, *a holiday, a wedding holiday*, the quiet feelings of a happy father, the rollicking merriment of Poles dancing a mazurka ... In the course of a minute, sorrow and despair and loss all change. The greatness of the Russian character is lifted high, love for the czar is sharply drawn; a firm decisiveness, ardent faith, and the sorrowful reflections of the lost all combine in the full beauty of Susanin! ...

1 Glinka spent three years in Italy in the early 1830s.
2 Antonida, daughter of the peasant Susanin, who sacrifices his life to protect the czar from the Poles. Vanya (Vanja) is Susanin's adopted son.

3 Auber's *La Muette de Portici* (1828). The Russian censor, fearing the revolutionary character of the story, demanded that the title be changed to *Fenella*, after the heroine of the opera.

27

Castil-Blaze, 'On Musical Imitation'

France musicale (8 July 1838)

François Henri Joseph Blaze, known as Castil-Blaze (1784–1857), virtually invented the musical *feuilleton* – a leisurely journalistic essay designed to show off the writer's personality, knowledge, and literary flair. In his debut article for the *Journal des débats* in 1820, Castil-Blaze promised that his column would be 'devoted exclusively to music … an art full of charm about which periodicals, up to now, have spoken in too vague and fugitive a fashion'. Berlioz, Castil-Blaze's successor on the *Journal des débats* (see no. 33), had recently written a series of articles on musical imitation; this is Castil-Blaze's rejoinder.

Volumes have been published about musical expression and imitation – not that this should surprise you. Yet very few men are really sensitive to music's beauties (whether they know music or not is another matter). Now, there is no greater pleasure on earth than talking about something one doesn't know, explaining something one doesn't understand, analysing something one doesn't feel. No, I'm wrong. There is one pleasure even more exquisite than talking about something one doesn't know: that is, writing about something of which one is perfectly ignorant. And so our literature has been enriched with a large number of 'essays on music', 'reflections on the musical art', 'theories on the prodigious effects of music, from Amphion to M. Halévy', 'learned and amusing dissertations on consonances, dissonances, resonances, assonances … and cadences'; not counting M. the abbé Dubos's classic work on poetry, painting, and music[1] …

Much has been written about music and more surely will be – to the greater glory of the mechanical presses. But all the theories in the world are not worth one miserable little fact. Would you fully grasp the vanity and emptiness of musical theories and dissertations? Open the *Mercure galant* of 1686.

At the first performance of *Armide* (by M. Lully, if you please),[2] the public was seized with delirious enthusiasm and exclaimed in admiration at the rustic tableaux which the composer had offered to the eyes – I mean ears – of his listeners. Nothing could be more beautiful, more expressive, more evocative of nature than the pastoral scene of the third act of *Armide*.[3] That's a fact. Lully, with the audacity of all inventive geniuses, had made so bold as to use two flutes in the accompaniment of a chorus of Naiads; and these two memorable flutes played no fewer than four notes (apiece) in a slow and solemn tempo. Well, these eight notes – or rather four double-notes – of the flute represented a whole new world to the imagination of the astonished Parisians.

Do, ti, la, so and *la, so, fa, mi*, played by two flutes – that meant: a blue sky sprinkled with little silver clouds (*do, ti, la, so*); green lawns, thick and plump (*la, so, fa, mi*); a stream gliding delicately over white pebbles (*do, ti, la, so*); a flock of sheep (*la, so, fa, mi*); a windmill (*do, ti, la, so*); a donkey going to the mill (*la, so, fa, mi*); mown hay (*do, ti, la, so*); a storm, hail, rain, lightning, thunder (*la, so, fa, mi*)!!! Now, I beseech you, write one volume – or several, as you wish – about musical expression and imitation.

This happy discovery of Lully's sounded the reveille for imitative genius. A quarter century after *Armide* people grew bolder, in keeping with the law of progress. When they wished to paint a pastoral scene, they always used two flutes, but these two flutes played sixteen notes instead of eight; and as soon as the two flutes appeared on the horizon the audience on the orchestra floor cried out in unison: 'It's the plain of Saint-Denis!'

After a half century two oboes were added to the two flutes (where wert thou, O clarinet?) – further progress in musical imitation. The thirty-two notes which took care of rustic nature were transformed from minims to crotchets, then to quavers, then to demiquavers, and finally to a continuous trill. The clarinet took its place in the orchestra; then came the piccolo, the flageolet, the three-holed flageolet, the bagpipe, the hunting horn and the valved trumpet, the nineteenth century's preferred instrument of civilization. And pastoral imitation no longer knew any bounds.

From imitating things, people went on to imitating words. The musical pun was invented. I know a singular example. In a mass performed in 1810, the composer wrote the Agnus Dei in pastorale rhythm. His reasoning went like this: *Agnus* means lamb or little sheep, but sheep aren't accustomed to strolling in the Eglise Saint-Roch; they generally graze in the middle of the fields. To put sheep out to pasture, you must have shepherds. Shepherds carry crooks and sometimes bagpipes. Therefore, for the music of the Agnus Dei to fit the words, it's essential to play a pastorale. On with the flutes!

So well is it understood that the flute and the oboe make the poplars tremble and the daisies bloom that a composer would be mercilessly hissed if he took it into his head to paint a pastoral scene with violins. Oh, what sticklers for rules we are! Suppose an opera aria begins with this verse:

The trumpet has sounded the alarm,

If the public doesn't hear half a dozen trumpets in the accompaniment, it will pelt the performer with baked apples. The public loves music, no doubt, but it loves puns even more.

In line with these classical rules of musical imitation, I have witnessed a profound discussion about the ballad from *La Dame blanche*.[4]

See here that fair realm,

Where battlements touch the sky.

Boieldieu made the voice descend an octave on the words 'touch the sky'. Probably this ending seemed more in keeping with the nature of his melodic phrase, and besides it was a fair translation of the vocal inflections the character should make when he wanted to speak about those high ramparts. Whatever the case, Boieldieu's phrase is excellent from the musical point of view, and it approximates spoken dialogue as closely as necessary. A learned critic, however, declared that this was an atrocious contradiction, that the voice should not fall on the words 'touchent les cieux', but on the contrary climb as high as the Château d'Avenel. To descend an octave! Nay, it should rather rise *two* octaves, to scale the battlements! Whence people concluded that Boieldieu understood nothing about musical imitation. That's how much the French understand about the arts and artistic criticism.

For a long time we have restricted ourselves to pastoral imitations in music. We ventured a few kettledrum taps and tremolandos to imitate a storm, a few trumpet blasts to announce a belligerent character, a few horn fanfares to announce a lover of the hunt. But there was no large-scale, perfect imitation except that of the rustic life. This situation could not go on for ever.

Innovators were encountered who said: 'There are more than sheep and shepherds in nature; there are also brigands. Let's make brigands.' Thereupon the imitation of the brigand was created and put on stage. The most familiar way of using the brigand is in a drunken orgy. Moreover, the musical brigand appeared at the same time as the literary brigand. M. Victor Hugo infested the stage with brigands. He invented beautiful young princesses who said in crude verses: 'O my love, my soul, my brigand, how I love you! Brigand, my love, let me hold you to my heart! No, there is no one in the brigand world more lovable than you!' Et cetera.

Musical genius, jealous of M. Victor Hugo's brigands, decided to play its trump card and invented brigand orgies.[5]

'Why do you make brigand orgies?'

'Because brigands go on orgies.'

'Ah! ... have you seen any brigand orgies?'

'No, but I have seen ophicleides, long trumpets, trombones, cymbals, Chinese bells and tamtams, all instruments of brigandage, out of which I'm going to make you a first-class orgy ... '

'Thanks a lot!'

Tasso climbed a hill one day and said to one of his admirers: 'Do you see that lovely countryside, that admirable sky, those masses of greenery, that majestic river, those shepherds' huts, and the city in the distance with its ramparts, battlements and black smoke? Do you see those weapons glancing and that whole tableau of war unfurling ... ? There is my poem.'

Today the musician can say: 'Do you see that copper mine?' 'Yes.' 'Well, there is my music.'

Lastly, reader, will you ask me for a short declaration of principles about musical imitation? I am ready to oblige – and I am going to give you more than you bargained for. I am going to yield the podium to a great master and cite a sublime passage by the author of *Entile*. This passage of Rousseau's sums up in the finest language all one can say about the aesthetic of imitation:[6]

'Imitation in painting is always lifeless because it is deficient in the sequence of ideas and impression which warms the soul by degrees, and because everything is said at first glance. The imitative power of this art, despite its many apparent subjects, is in fact limited to very weak representations. This is one of the musician's great advantages: to be able to paint things which cannot be heard; whereas it is impossible for the painter to paint things which cannot be seen. And the greatest marvel of an art which creates a plot only through movement is to be able to give movement the image of repose. Sleep, the calm of night, solitude, and silence itself are included in music's tableaux.

'Sometimes noise produces the effect of silence and silence the effect of noise – as when a man falls asleep at a flat, monotonous reading and wakes up instantly when there is silence. The same is true of other effects. But art has more fertile and much finer substitutions than this one. It can excite through one sense emotions similar to those which can be excited through another sense; and since the connection is perceptible only when the impression is strong, painting, deprived of this power, has difficulty reciprocating the imitations that music draws from it. *Though all of nature be asleep, he who contemplates it does not sleep; and the art of the musician consists of substituting for the unconscious image of the subject that of the movements which its presence excites in the spirit of the viewer. Music does not represent the thing directly but awakens in our soul the same sentiment that we experience when we see it.*'

1 Jean-Baptiste Dubos, *Réflexions critiques sur la poésie, la peinture et la musique* (1719).
2 At the Paris Opéra, 15 February 1686.
3 The famous Passacaille in the original Act 5.
4 The Ballad of the White Lady, guardian spirit of the Avenel family, from the opera by Boieldieu and Scribe (1825).
5 The 'Orgie des brigands' in Berlioz's *Harold in Italy* was surely uppermost in Castil-Blaze's mind.
6 This passage is taken, freely, from chapters 13 and 14 of Rousseau's *Essai sur l'origine des langues*.

28

Henry F. Chorley, 'Contemporary Musical Composers: Giuseppe Verdi'

Athenaeum (31 August 1844)

A redoubtable figure of conservative taste and often acerbic candour, Chorley (1808–72) was resistant to the innovations of Verdi, Wagner, Berlioz and others. As critic at the *Atheneum* for more than four decades, he was celebrated for what his American contemporary, J. S. Dwight (see no. 30), called 'the peculiar crotchety humors of Mr. Chorley'. He later revised his opinion of Verdi, whom he came to consider as a worthy successor to his beloved Rossini. See no. 31 for Basevi's very different perspective on Verdi.

Recent occurrences and appearances having called the attention of our English public to the modern style, or rather no-style, of Italian singing, it may be as well for the critic to see what is doing in the world of Italian vocal composition; and, since the name of Giuseppe Verdi has begun to circulate widely as the *maestro* most likely to become popular, we avail ourselves of such opportunities as perusal of his compositions here published affords us, to offer a word or two concerning his operas.

But first, we must remind the reader that the distinctive basis of Italian Opera, from its outset, has been melody – melody in recitative, in air, in concerted piece, and in chorus; the dramatic expression of the moment being largely left to the singer. Even in the German musical drama, though the voice has been often assigned tasks too ungracious to be ever well performed, under the notion of rendering it a mere instrument in the composer's hands, and the adaptation of sound to sense has been more closely studied, still melody has been indispensable to success – in the orchestra if not on the stage. Digressing for a moment, we may add that, at certain points, the fusion of the two schools has taken place, as in Mozart's operas. But whether German or Italian, there is no melodist who has not had a way of his own, in part arising from those mysterious instincts and perceptions which defy analysis, in part referable to the executive power or prevailing fashion of the composer's age, and, beyond these, that *je ne sais quoi* which the ear learns to distinguish as surely as the eye decides on the touch of the painter. Now it appears to be the fancy of the modern European school, to throw overboard what is essential, because of the accidental; and, since invention just now seems to be at the lowest ebb of exhaustion, musicians denounce the old manner of satisfying the ear, as mere excitement *ad captandum*.[1] In France, for instance, M. Berlioz does vigorous battle with rhythm, quoting, with admirable inconsistency, Gluck's colossal style against Auber's[2] piquant metres; forgetting that the structure of all Gluck's great melodic pieces is as referable to the *ciaconna*, *gavotte*, and *minuet* taste of his epoch, as M. Auber's liveliest *finale* is to the *galoppe* or the *valse* which has succeeded those more solemn measures. All this while, M. Berlioz, be it noted, whenever he does employ a form in his own compositions (and without form and number, whatever be the mode of arrangement, there can be no musical composition better than the wanderings of the Eolian harp), adopts one of the most hackneyed common-place and frivolity. Then there is Herr Wagner, the young Dresden composer, whose operas we have heard rapturously bepraised, because they contain no tunes which any one can carry away.[3] Yet we do not hear that in declamatory propriety and dramatic fashion he has improved upon Weber, the deepest of German vocal composers, and still the most sympathetically melodious and fascinating. In Italy, as all the world knows, Bellini, eager to throw off the symmetrical forms of Rossini with small expense of study or labour, established a manner striking in its languid *laisser aller*. But, under pretence of dramatizing the style of Italian opera, Bellini's successors, less vigorous in invention, have outdone him in renouncing all firmness and ordinance of construction, producing, it is true, tunes in the canonical number of bars required by the poetic ear, but without the slightest novelty of combination or phrase. In short, Italian invention seems fast advancing towards a point at which, whether the idea be old or new it matters little, so that the singer has a *spianato*[4] passage to bawl or sigh out, either *solus* or in unison with his comrades, a semblance of intensity and contrivance being given by a use of the orchestra, licentious enough to make Cimarosa and Paisiello (those colourists as tender but as consummate in their art as Watteau) turn in their graves.

Time may reconcile us to these strange principles: we may come to value music in proportion as all form and feature are effaced; and see, without a sigh, the Opera reduced to the shapeless recitative from whence it arose – with this difference, that whereas the voice was of old only supported by a *chitarra* or a *violone*, it will be smothered, under the new dispensation, by what the Germans call 'janissary music'.[5] Till, however, we reach this state of vitiated taste, we must conceive the ancient standards to be in the main, equitable, and try new productions thereby.

It is not many years since Sig. Verdi was in this country, among the myriad strangers who are attracted by 'the season', struggle vainly for a hearing, and retire unnoticed.[6] His first opera, if we mistake not, was *Oberto di San Bonifazio*, in which Mrs. Shaw made her appearance on the Italian stage.[7] He has since produced *Nabucodonosor*, *I Lombardi*, and *Ernani*, (the last, we presume, founded on Victor Hugo's tragedy), all of which are said to have succeeded; and selections from them are published here, comprising the portions thought most captivating and saleable. But we suspect that many of the pieces in the English editions have been transposed so as to bring them within the average compass of voice. For new melody we have searched in vain; nor have we even found any varieties of form, indicating an original fancy at work as characteristically as in one of Pacini's, or Mercadante's,[8] or Donizetti's, better *cavatinas*. All seems worn and hackneyed and unmeaning. The *andante mosso* to the 'gran scena', 'Lo vedremo' (*Ernani*), has some pretension to richness of accompaniment; but the repetition of the same phrase, bar after bar, betrays intrinsic poverty of resource. Hence, if effect there be, it must be monotonous, and *bizarre*. The *cabaletta* is but a feeble repetition of what Donizetti has done a hundred times, as in *Adelia*, *Robert Devereux*, not to cite his more popular operas. In 'Come rugiada', another *cavatina* from *Ernani*, we have a dilution of the *contralto rondo* in Pacini's *Saffo*. 'Ernani! Ernani! involami,' is a song of still greater executive pretension, written apparently for one of those *mezzo soprano* voices of extensive compass, which poor Malibran[9] brought into fashion. There is a good deal of what may be called pompous assurance, both in the *andantino*, and in the final movement, and an accomplished singer could doubtless work an *encore* with it.

Sig. Verdi's concerted music strikes us as a shade worthier and more individual than his songs. There are *intentions*, though the fillings-up be weak to puerility, in his duet for Ernani and Silva (*Ernani*, 2nd act), and the effect of the *longiura* chorus, is, probably, striking with the mass of voices and orchestra, though the unisons be surfeiting. These, by the way, first employed by Rossini in his *Gazza Ladra*, offer a rare expedient to the easily-contented and the ill-assured. To judge from the crudity of Sig. Verdi's harmonies and progressions, he belongs to the latter class, who 'think they are thinking.' And it may be questioned whether any of these conspiracy scenes, – Meyerbeer's thrilling 'Consecration of the swords'[10] not forgotten, – would have been written, had not the *maestro* of Pesaro showed the way in the second act of his *Guillaume Tell*. The only other piece from this opera before us calling for remark is the *terzetto finale*, 'Solingo errante misero,'[11] the middle movement, *a tre*, of which is capable of being rendered effective *in situation* on the stage; the *stretto* is the thousandth repetition of the *stretto* to Rossini's 'Crude sorte.'[12] We must note, too, that the progression of keys, in one movement, with a view to entireness in construction (a point till lately thought worthy of attention), is most curiously managed; unless some of the remarkable sequences are ascribable to transpositions on the part of the English publisher. Sig. Verdi shall have the full benefit of the doubt.

We cannot conclude these brief remarks, – incomplete for obvious reasons, as a judgment, – without saying, that flimsy as we fancy Sig. Verdi's science, and devoid as he seems to be of that fresh and sweet melody, which we shall never cease to relish and welcome, there is a certain aspiration in his works which deserves recognition, and may lead him to produce compositions which will command respect. At all extents, what we have *read* makes us curious to hear and see either *I Lombardi* or *Ernani* in Paris or London. *Nabucodonosor*, we suspect, is hardly presentable on this side of the water, on account of its story.[13]

1 To elicit applause.
2 Daniel François Esprit Auber, the composer of comic operas.
3 Wagner's operas were slow to make their way to England. *The Flying Dutchman* (1843) was not seen there until 1870, *Rienzi* (1842) not until 1879.
4 Smooth or even.
5 The Turkish band music imitated by European composers, as in Mozart's *Die Entführung aus dem Serail*.
6 I am not aware that Verdi visited England before 1846.

7 The English soprano Mary Shaw sang in the première of *Oberto, conte di San Bonifazio* at La Scala in 1839. *Ernani* (1844) was performed in London in 1845, *Nabucodonosor* or *Nabucco* (1842) and *I Lombardi alla prima crociata* (1843) in 1846.

8 Giovanni Pacini wrote some forty operas, most notably *Saffo* (1840). Saverio Mercadante was more prolific still.

9 María Malibran, the celebrated Spanish mezzo-soprano, died in 1836 as a result of a horse-riding accident.

10 In Act 4 of *Les Huguenots*.

11 The Act 2 chorus in Rossini's *Guillaume Tell* (1829), in which the assembled Swiss cantons vow to resist the Austrians.

12 Isabella's aria from *L'Italiana in Algieri*.

13 In England, the representation of biblical subjects was restricted to oratorio.

29

Heinrich Heine, 'Musical Season of 1844'

Augsburger allgemeine Zeitung (8 May 1844), from Oscar Sonneck, 'Heinrich Heine's Musical Feuilletons', *Musical Quarterly*, 8 (1922), trans. Frederick H. Martens

Liszt was at the height of his celebrity as a pianist when Heine (1797–1856) published this spirited satire on the virtuoso. (The article also takes swipes at the violinist Ole Bull and at Berlioz and Mendelssohn.) Heine was already well known as a poet when he began writing for the *Augsberger allgemeine Zeitung* in 1840. His literary brilliance and personal, conversational style of criticism soon attracted attention – and imitators.

... There has been no lack of concert-giving pianists this year, either. The Ides of March in particular were critical days in this connection. Everyone was thumping away and wanting to be heard, if only for appearances' sake, in order to be able to act like a great celebrity – on the other side of the Paris barriers. The odds and ends of *feuilleton* praise which the artists have begged or sneaked together, these disciples of art, in Germany especially, know how to exploit to advantage, and in the advertisements there we are told how that famous genius, the great Rudolf W., has arrived, the rival of Liszt and Thalberg, the hero of the keyboard who attracted such attention in Paris, and was even praised by Jules Janin, the critic.[1] Hosannah! Of course, anyone who has seen some poor ephemerid of this kind, and knows in addition the slight attention paid to far more important personages, finds the credulity of the public most entertaining, and the clumsy shamelessness of the virtuosos most disgusting. The evil is deeper-rooted, however, in the condition of our daily press, and this, again, is the result of conditions still more fatal.

I must hark back again and again to the fact that there are but three pianists: Chopin, the gracious tone-poet, who, unfortunately, has been very ill this winter and not much seen; then Thalberg, the gentleman of music, who, in the end, does not need to play piano at all, in order to be greeted everywhere as a pleasant sight, and who really seems to regard his talent as no more than an appanage; and finally, our Liszt, who, in spite of all his perversities and wounding angles, still remains our cherished Liszt, and at this moment is once more exciting the Paris world of beauty. Yes, he is here, the great agitator, our Franz Liszt, the wandering knight of all sorts of orders (with the exception of that of the French Legion of Honour, which Louis Philippe will give to no virtuosos). He, the Hohenzollern-Hechingen court-counsellor,[2] the doctor of philosophy, the thaumaturge doctor of music, the ever newly-risen Ratcatcher of Hameln, the new Faust, who is always followed by a poodle in the shape of Belloni,[3] the ennobled and nevertheless noble Liszt, he is here! He is here, the modern Amphion, who sets in movement the stones of the Cologne Minster with the sounds of his strings, so that they join themselves together, as once the walls of Thebes! He is here, the modern Homer, whom Germany, Hungary and France, the three greatest of countries, claim as their child, while only seven small provincial cities laid claim to the singer of the Iliad! He is here, the Attila, the scourge of God of all Erard pianos, which tremble at the mere rumour of his approach, and who once more start, bleed and whimper beneath his hand, so that the society for the prevention of cruelty to animals ought to take pity on them! He is here, the mad, handsome, ugly, mysterious, fatal, and at the same time very childlike child of his time, the gigantic dwarf, the raging Roland with the Hungarian sword of honour, the Franz Liszt who today is robustly healthy, and tomorrow once more ill, whose magic power conquers us, whose genius delights us, the genial fool whose madness turns our own sanity, and whom we are at all events doing the most loyal service in making public the great furore which he is exciting here! We establish without circumlocution the fact of his tremendous success; no matter how we may privately explain the fact and whether or no we accord or deny the celebrated virtuoso our personal applause. It can surely be a matter of indifference to him, since ours is but a single voice, and our authority with regard to tonal art of no special weight.

When formerly I heard of the fainting spells which broke out in Germany and specially in Berlin, when Liszt showed himself there, I shrugged my shoulders pityingly and thought: quiet sabbatarian Germany does not wish to lose the opportunity of getting the little necessary exercise permitted it. It wants to shake its drowsy limbs a bit, and my Abderites[4] on the Spree like to tickle themselves into an enthusiasm allowed them, one following the example of the other in declaiming: 'Armor, ruler of men and gods!' In their case, thought I, it is a matter of the spectacle for the spectacle's sake, regardless of what it may be called: Georg Herwegh, Saphir, Franz Liszt or Fanny Elssler.[5] When Herwegh is forbidden, they cling to Franz Liszt, who is unobjectionable and does not compromise. Thus I regarded, thus I explained this Lisztomania, and looked on it as a sign of the politically unfree conditions existing beyond the Rhine. Yet I was mistaken, after all, and I did not notice it until last week, at the Italian Opera House, where Liszt gave his first concert, and gave it before an assemblage which one might truly term the flower of local society. At any rate, they were wide-awake Parisians, people familiar with the greatest figures of the present, who, more or less, had shared in the life of the great drama of their own time, among them many invalids of all the arts, the most wearied of men in fact, and women who were also very weary, having danced the polka throughout the winter, a multitude of bored and busy minds. This was truly no Germanically sentimental, sentimentalizing Berlinate audience, before which Liszt played, quite alone, or rather, accompanied solely by his genius. And yet, how convulsively his mere appearance affected them! How boisterous was the applause which rang to meet him! Bouquets, too, were flung at his feet. It was an uplifting sight, to behold the triumphator letting the bunches of flowers rain down on him with entire self-possession, and finally, with a gracious smile, thrusting a red camellia, which he drew from one of the bouquets, into his buttonhole. And he did this in the presence of some young soldiers who had just come out of Africa,[6] where they had seen not flowers, but leaden bullets rain on them, and whose breasts were decorated with the red camellias of their own heroic blood, without anyone, here or there, paying any special attention to it. Strange, thought I, these Parisians, who have seen Napoleon, who had to win one battle after another in order to hold their attention! Now they are acclaiming our Franz Liszt. And what an acclaim it was! A veritable insanity, one unheard of in the annals of furore! What is the reason of this phenomenon? The solution of this question belongs to the domain of pathology rather than that of aesthetics. The electrical action of a demoniac nature on a closely crowded multitude, the infectious power of ecstasy, and, perhaps, the magnetism of music itself, this spiritual illness of the times, which vibrates in nearly all of us — these phenomena have never yet presented themselves to me in so clear and intimidating a manner as in Liszt's concert.

A physician, whose specialty is female diseases, and whom I asked to explain the magic our Liszt exerted upon his public, smiled in the strangest manner, and at the same time said all sorts of things about magnetism, galvanism, electricity, of the contagion of a close hall filled with countless wax lights and several hundred perfumed and perspiring human beings, of historical epilepsy, of the phenomenon of tickling, of musical cantherides, and other scabrous things, which, I believe, have reference to the mysteries of the *bona dea*.[7] Perhaps the solution of the question is not buried in such adventurous depths, but floats on a very prosaic surface. It seems to me at times that all this sorcery may be explained by the fact that no one on earth knows so well how to organize his successes, or rather their *mise en scène*, as our Franz Liszt. In this art he is a genius, a Philadelphia, a Bosco, a Houdin,[8] yes, a Meyerbeer! The most distinguished persons serve him gratis as his colleagues, and his hired enthusiasts are models of training. Popping champagne corks, and a reputation for prodigal generosity, trumpeted forth by the most reliable newspapers, lure recruits to him in every city. Nevertheless, it may be the case that our Franz Liszt is really by nature an easy spender, and free from miserliness where money is concerned — a shabby vice which sticks to many virtuosos, especially the Italians, and with which we even find the sweetly fluting Rubini[9] afflicted, regarding whose avarice a very amusing anecdote is related. The celebrated singer, so it seems, had undertaken a concert tour with Franz Liszt at joint expense, the profits of the concerts, which were to be given in various cities, to be divided. The great pianist, who carries the general *intendant* of his celebrity, the aforementioned Belloni, about with him everywhere, referred all business arrangements to him on this occasion. But when Signor Belloni, once he had concluded his business management, handed in his bill, Rubini noticed with horror that among the expenses in common a notable sum was set down for laurel wreaths, bouquets of flowers, laudatory poems, and various other ovational costs. The naive singer had imagined that these signs of approval had been flung at him because of his beautiful voice. He at once flew into a great rage, and absolutely would not pay for the bouquets, among which there may have been the most costly camellias. If I were a musician, this quarrel would offer me the best possible subject for a comic opera.

Yes, indeed, we must not examine too closely the homage which the famous virtuosos garner. After all, their day of vain celebrity is a very short one, and the hour soon strikes when the titan of tonal art may, perhaps, crumple into a town musician of very dwarfish stature, who, in the coffee-house which he frequents, tells the regular guests, on his word of honour, how bouquets of the most beautiful camellias were formerly flung at his feet, and how, once, two Hungarian countesses, in order to secure possession of his handkerchief, had cast themselves on the ground and fought until the blood ran. The day-long reputation of a virtuoso evaporates and dies away, empty, without a trace, like a camel's wind in the desert ...

1 Sigismond Thalberg and Franz Liszt were mostly friendly rivals. The drama critic Jules Janin was a contemporary of Castil-Blaze (see no. 27) on the *Journal des débats*.
2 In 1840 Liszt was appointed Grand Ducal Director of Music Extraordinary at Weimar.
3 Gaetano Belloni was Liszt's concert manager and confidant.
4 Simpletons: from the Greek Abdera, whose inhabitants were bywords for stupidity.
5 Georg Herwegh, the German revolutionary poet; Moritz Gottlieb Saphir, the critic and writer; and Fanny Elssler, the Austrian dancer known for her sensuality and energy. All were controversial figures.
6 In the early 1840s France was involved in a series of conflicts with local potentates in North Africa.
7 The Roman goddess of chastity and fertility, whose temple was associated with licentious behaviour.

8 The magicians Philadelphia, Bartolomeo Bosco and Jean Houdin.
9 Giovanni Battista Rubini, the Italian tenor.

30

John Sullivan Dwight, 'Mr. Fry and His Critics'

Dwight's Journal of Music (4 February 1854)

Arbiter of Boston's musical tastes for more than three decades, Dwight (1813–93) was America's first music critic of international stature. Conservative by nature, he took issue both with Wagner and Brahms and with American composers like William Henry Fry (see no. 35) who were struggling to establish a native musical identity. *Dwight's Journal of Music*, which he published from 1852 to 1881, filled his prescription for 'a great, many-sided, high-toned musical journal'. Dwight's remarks about Fry's *Santa Claus (Christmas Symphony)* reveal both his idealistic convictions and his opposition to cultural parochialism.

Not many of our readers, we are sure, will murmur at the space we give to-day to the very remarkable letter of Mr. Fry to the editor of the New York *Musical World and Times*, Mr. R. S. Willis.[1] The closely printed columns look quite formidable; but let the eye once light on any paragraph and you will certainly read on, and then go back and read the rest. We are only sorry to be obliged to make *any* (though comparatively slight) omissions, in order to furnish the gist of the whole at one reading. So pleasant a piece of most decided individuality has seldom turned up in the dry ways of musical literature, as this *Santa Claus* letter, whatever may be thought of *Santa Claus* itself. Whether Mr. Fry succeeds or not in vindicating the title of his so-called 'symphony' to be considered an important product of a new and earnest school of 'High Art,' in which he walks in no man's footsteps, but transcends the 'classics' as to all the real ends of Art; whether he succeeds or not in proving the love of Handel, Mozart and Beethoven sheer affectation, slavish idolatry, pedantry and 'old-fogyism,' and in demonstrating the huge strides by which 'Young America' has put all that far behind it: he certainly does write up his own artistic merit with a splendid audacity of disbelief in the world's musical authorities and models, with a refreshingly heroic and naive self-confidence, a glorious top-of-the-world sort of feeling, a smart, eccentric, spicy talent, an evident knowledge of the science, history and practice of his Art, and a wonderfully quick and quaint suggestiveness of thought, that must make this apology for *Santa Claus* against the classics, and for musical Young America against musical old Europe, a memorable document of the present queer stage in our musical history. It sums up and intensifies to an almost burning focus the arguments and aspirations of this would-be-all in music, as in all things, – this ambitious and irreverent young giant Jonathan. We think it ought to stand here in our columns as a part of the record of this strange early stage of musical development in our 'fast' country. And in this view we doubt not our friend Willis will look kindly on our thus transferring bodily so large an amount of matter from his columns to our own.

Besides, we had hoped and promised to say more of *Santa Claus*, after having owned ourselves amused and surprised by novel and striking instrumental effects in the one hearing that we had of it when Jullien's orchestra was here. But every thing is said, a hundred times better than we could say it, both from the composer's and the sober critic's point of view, in this rich correspondence we are copying. To Mr. Willis belonged of course the right and the delicate duty of replying to the letter; and he has done it with most admirable tact and temper, as we mean to let our readers see next week.

Like Mr. Willis, we confess that we had never dreamed of regarding *Santa Claus* as anything but an *extravaganza*. Like him, we admire the talent, the independence and the generous social qualities of William Henry Fry, and prize his friendship, while we dissent from his peculiar notions about Art, and while we are unconscious, so far, of having felt in any of his compositions that unmistakable magnetism of genius which should stamp his novel forms, or formlessness, as classical for times to come. Like him, too, we have necessarily, by the whole tone and spirit of our criticism, and our whole Art creed, implied or spoken, drawn down upon us the displeasure of this 'manifest destiny' native American, or anti-European party in music, which deems it an insult to suppose that anything attempted by an American, upon as great a scale, in composition, is not as worthy of attention and of fame as any great work of the greatest masters. It behoves us, therefore, in our own inability to take their point of view, to let the ablest advocates of this cause speak in our columns for themselves. And where both advocate and artist are united in one person, as in Mr. Fry; where, if preaching and prophecying and interpreting and arguing can possibly do the thing, he is so eminently the man to do it; where he *has* set about it with such thoroughness and vigor as in this letter; the least that we can do in justice to him and to his position (which we possibly do not appreciate), is to copy the letter for our readers.

But tell us, good friends, after all, are you not fighting a vague bugbear of your own erecting, under this name of 'classical'? Some time ago we indited an editorial (which we left half finished), in the hope of clearly settling what is meant, in the living and best sense of its every-day use, by this phrase 'classical music;' if we succeeded in proving anything it was its undefinableness. For instance, here is our friend Fry, who makes it to consist in one or both of two things: viz. 1. a respectable degree of age, and, 2. certain technical forms of structure, arbitrarily adopted by men like Bach or Mozart, and tamely and mechanically copied by their followers. Now where is the real lover of what in common parlance we call classical music, who will accept both or either of these definitions? Do we love the older music *because* it is old? No. Do we limit our admiration to the writers of any given period? By no means. Are not the warmest worshippers of Handel, Bach, Beethoven, just the very men who hail with most enthusiasm a Schumann and a Wagner, compared with whom, as innovators, (at all events the latter), Mr. Fry has certainly not gone any very alarming length. Mr. Fry cites the *Freyschütz* overture against the *classics*, Beethoven's symphonies and all; – but every classical music-lover includes that *in* the classics. To be sure, there has been some talk about a distinction between classical and romantic in music, as in literature; but the common use of the term classical – as when the Germanians, for instance, contrast a 'classical' with a 'light' or miscellaneous concert – covers both those kinds. Chopin, in his dreamiest reveries, following the freest play of fantasy, is quite as classical as Bach or Mozart now with the great mass of music-lovers whom Mr. Fry arraigns. Chopin, who is for the most part all fantasia, shares our enthusiasm with the great symphonists and fuguists. The overture to *Tannhauser* is newer and stranger, and not less romantic nor dramatic, than the *Freyschütz*; yet it has earned its place, by pretty general consent, in the most strictly classical programmes. And Mr. Fry and Mr. Bristow,[2] and 'Herr Löstiswitz' himself, whose programme rivals Fry's, are sure to be accepted just so soon as the world shall see that they have done what they themselves suppose they have: – just so soon as their audiences shall feel that there is genius, inspiration, beauty, poetry of music in their symphonies, at all proportioned to the audacity and oddness of their designs. Believe us, it is not a question of schools and authorities, of following or discarding models, whether a man shall be recognized as a great composer. It is simply a question of *genius*. And genius can be perennially fresh in old forms, or draw us intimately near to itself and make us feel at home with it in whatsoever new forms.

Why then is not friend Fry willing practically to submit the merit of the American symphonies to what he himself maintains to be the only true test? – namely, to time and the world's impression. Have they not an equal chance with every work of Art, which rests upon no previously earned *prestige* of authorship? Have they not all the chance that genius ever has, to work their way into recognition? Of course the bulk of our public concerts and musical entertainments must consist of pieces of a guaranteed excellence, of works that the world *knows* to be good, sure to give pleasure, sure to inspire and to reward attention. It will not do to invite the public to perpetual experimental feasts of possibilities; to assemble a concert audience, like a board of jurors, to listen to long lists of new works and award prizes. Yet if a work have genius in it, it will sooner or later make its mark upon the world. The chances now-a-days are that it will do it pretty soon, in spite of classical or of contemporary competition. This talk about pedantry, and blind reverence for the past, is very well and very brave. We all like it in the abstract. But whom does it hit? Does Mr. Fry believe that any set of musical pedants, purists and exclusives have the power in this country, or in any country at this age of the world, to make or damn his symphony? Pedants have little power over the world's likings. A musical pedant would think a dry, mechanical fugue-writer, provided he were only learned, and did all strictly according to the rules, as good as Bach. But it is the musical instinct of mankind, it is the feeling and poetic soul, in the most instances unlearned, that has kept Bach and dismissed the thousand and one mechanical fuguists to oblivion. Germany has produced thousands of symphonies as classical, according to Mr.

Fry's definition of the word, as Beeethoven or Haydn; but the appreciative music-lovers, learned or unlearned, professional or amateur, who love Beethoven's music, and do not love Fry's, have not been apt to recognize the classical affinity.

No. The value of a symphony is settled by the public, precisely as the value of a poem or a novel. A large class are captivated in either by superficial glitter, or feeble sentimentality, or high spiced novelty, or blood and thunder. A large class seek amusement and amusement only. Presently the opinion of the appreciative, serious, thinking minds is felt, and it is recognized that there is a vast difference between Tennyson or Wordsworth, and the magazine poetry that circulates so widely. Is this difference based, think you, upon the grammatical or rhythmical or logical construction of the poems? No, nor is it in the world's ultimate appreciation of musical poems, symphonies, &c. *Der Freyschütz* overture, to cite Mr. Fry's favorite, could never have been talked and argued into popular acceptance. It is of no use to tell us why we ought to like *Santa Claus*; the thing is to make us like it.

The letter opens many topics into which we canot enter. For instance, the question of 'the unities' and of 'imitative music,' which have found fitting treatment at the hands of Mr. Willis. What we are most anxious to state here as our conviction is, that there is no very general prejudice, (certainly none on our part) against American composers as such. Art soars above all narrow nationalities; and there is of course no inherent *a priori* reason, as a correspondent in another column says, why this age and this country may not produce works of Art, in every kind, as great or greater than the famous masterpieces of the world. The creative soul and genius of humanity undoubtedly are not exhausted; but progress, growth, continual upward aspiration and achievement, we believe as strenuously as any one, are still the law of human history. But who shall foretell the coming of a genius in the world? Who shall anticipate its hour and birth-place? What patriotic faith in our New World's great destiny can ever make us feel the new spell of genius, until that genius convert us to itself by its own proper magnetism? If a new Beethoven was born in America this very morning, is not the world as sure to hear from him and own him, as if he had sprung up under the guardianship of Liszt at Weimar, or of Hauptmann, Moscheles & Co., at Leipsic?[3]

Time will take care of all these questions. Meanwhile we conclude with assuring our correspondent, 'w,' that our few hasty words in anticipation of Fry's Christmas Symphony contained no 'covert sneer.'

1 Fry had written to protest Willis's cursory notice of *Santa Claus*, claiming that it was the largest unified composition on a single subject yet attempted by an American. The piece was performed in New York on Christmas Eve 1853 by an orchestra under the direction of Louis Jullien, the French conductor famous for his 'monster concerts for the masses'.
2 The composer George Bristow was Fry's ally in attempting to start an American school.
3 Moritz Hauptmann taught composition and Ignaz Moscheles piano at the Leipzig Conservatory, founded in 1842.

31

Abramo Basevi, 'Italy and Music'

Gazetta musicale di Firenze (25 October 1855)

In Italy as elsewhere, cultural and political nationalism marched hand in hand. Basevi (1818–85), Italy's first important critic, was infused with the idealism of the Risorgimento and played a prominent part in the movement to reform Italian music and musical taste. 'The spectator receives his critic's diploma at the door of the theatre, with his ticket,' he wrote. Basevi was a staunch, though not uncritical, admirer of Verdi, as this article shows. Compare Chorley's criticism (no. 28).

Once upon a time Italy, through Rome, her heart, imposed her laws upon the world. The valour of her sons made her the queen of peoples. When the Roman Empire fell, and with it material dominion, there remained to her the power of genius no less than that of arms.

And yet since man, by his nature, always tends to break the bonds which impede the free venting of his passions or which place an obstacle to the fulfilment of his intentions, the rulers' prudence ordained that the weight of the chains should be hardly noticeable. The same prudence knew how to make timely and just concessions to the spirit of the times, so that Roman supremacy endured until depravation, forgetfulness of their own dignity, and selfishness, in making the Romans less the masters of themselves, in the end reduced them to slaves of others.

So when Italy's genius succeeded the power of her arms in the dominion of the world, the peoples, who hate no less the yoke which is imposed on them by talent, did not cease their attempts at independence.

Italy saw many famous men perish in her bosom and others appear in the midst of other nations, which pitted genius against genius, as steel had been pitted against steel in other times, to liberate themselves.

Only in music did our fair nation manage to maintain her supremacy. Nevertheless, some people tried to emancipate themselves from us, and in part they succeeded. In a special way Germany, with the development she gave to instrumentalism and so-called dramatic music, set herself up as Italy's rival, wanted to share her conquests, and finally sought to invade us. France is the country where Italy and Germany share musical power.

Italian musical genius lies in melody. Instrumentalism and musical drama, partly accepted by Italian masters, are merely sensible concessions to prevent her from losing dominion in Germany and France.

In spite of these concessions, which were maintained conscientiously by the immense genius of Rossini as long as he lived for art,[1] not only are Germany and France drawing further and further away from us, but we are finally seeing attempts at independence in the nations which used to be considered the most barbarous, musically speaking. At the same time England and Spain are taking the initiative to found a national opera.

What is Italy doing in the meantime? Will she let this remaining prize slip out of her hands? Once this last fortress of music has been captured, nothing is left to us but the memory of past glories. But the memory of glory is its tomb, and the land of memories is a cemetery.

The great Rossini showed the road the Italians had to take to conserve their empire, and he wrote *Guillaume Tell*. It did not please the great man from Pesaro to continue to compose in this new manner, and he fell silent.

Now Verdi is the only one who is battling for this Italian supremacy and, having not been lucky in two attempts, today he runs the risk of a third: because a third attempt can be called the third manner adopted by the man from Busseto, first with the opera *La Traviata* and now with *I Vespri siciliani*.[2] Will he emerge victorious in the end? We must in any event be thankful to him for trying, since at this moment he alone holds the banner of Italian musical genius in his hands. Still, we do not believe that he has yet reached the goal, and we consider Verdi nothing but a master of transition. Perhaps he himself, being young, will create the true school demanded by the musical progress of the age.

Two extreme factions are found in Italy: one would have no attention paid to the present state of music, to new needs, and to the transformation of taste, in order to go back to Bellinian melodies in blessed peace; the other, renouncing Italy's musical nature, would destroy Italian melody in order to throw itself into the arms of foreign music. Neither one nor the other of these factions holds the key to the truth. One does not retreat in the fine arts, just as one does not retreat in politics, except to return to barbarities. No one deliberately renounces the genius of his own nation, except to create artificial things without soul or life.

There is a middle way, which on the one hand respects Italian melody, the true reason for our country's musical supremacy, while on the other hand profiting from other peoples' advances in instrumentalism and musical drama. This middle way we have called *Italo-German eclecticism.* Meyerbeer we consider to be representative of this beginning of modern art.

Convinced of this thought of ours, we now take the greatest satisfaction in seeing Meyerbeer's operas, which are becoming increasingly appreciated and prized from one end of the peninsula to the other, performed in the principal theatres before the most intelligent audiences. The music of the greatest Berlin master, because it is the daughter of Italy and of Germany, will bring immense advantage to Italy by demonstrating which road Italian genius should choose if it wants to maintain for ever this fair land of ours as a sovereign, and not as a vassal of other nations.

1 Rossini was still very much alive in 1855, the year he moved to Paris, though he had written no operas and very little other music since *Guillaume Tell* (1829).

2 Basevi was the first to divide Verdi's operas into four stylistic periods. *La Traviata* (1853) and *I Vespri siciliani* (1855) belonged to the third; the last, influenced by German music, started with *Simon Boccanegra* (1857).

32

James W. Davison, 'A Leonine Virtuoso'

Musical World (5 June 1858)

Chief critic of *The Times* of London from 1846 to 1879, Davison (1813–85) helped shape British musical taste at a time when the country's musical life was dominated by Italian opera and foreign virtuosos. Like Chorley (no. 28), he took a sceptical view of the new influences emanating from the Continent; and he shared Heine's low opinion of the virtuoso performer (no. 29). The reviews he wrote for *The Times* were sententious and somewhat stuffy; his writing for the *Musical Examiner* and *Musical World* attests to a lighter touch.

There is an evident and we believe insuperable antagonism between the modern style of pianoforte-playing, inculcated by the so-called 'virtuosi' (who might be more appropriately denominated 'viziosi'), and that which still enjoys the very modest title of 'legitimate.' The difference between the two is so marked that no one can possibly overlook it. It is the difference between the Ambigu-Comique[1] and the Théâtre-Français, the *Trovatore* and *Don Giovanni*, Mr. Disraeli, and Mr. Thackeray, Mr. Hicks and Mr. Macready.[2] It is the difference between tragedy and melodrama, common sense and bombast, poetry and rhodomontade. The question, however, is, can the two be reconciled? Can the professor of the one style either stoop or raise himself to the level of the other? In one respect we think *not*. We are quite sure that Mr. Disraeli is utterly incapable of writing a book like *The Newcombes*, and that Mr. Hicks could never have made even a tolerable Hamlet; but we are almost as certain that Mr. Macready, if inclined to amuse himself that way, could out-Hicks Hicks; while that Mr. Thackeray, when in the vein, can beat Mr. Disraeli on his own ground, is triumphantly shown in his *Codlingsby*, which we have always regarded as the literary masterpiece of the present Chancellor of the Exchequer.[3]

The same argument applies to the opposite schools of pianoforte-playing. The works of the fantasia-mongers are by no means impracticable to the fingers (the mind having nothing to say in the matter) of a pianist well 'up' in the compositions of the classical masters. But *vice versa* does not follow, as a matter of course. There have been numberless proofs to the contrary.

'Cette musique *naïve*' – exclaimed M. —t, fumbling over a prelude of Mendelssohn's – 'cette musique naïve, après tout, n'est pas *trop* facile. Fichtre!'[4] M. —t spoke from his heart, and very soon suiting the action to the word, abandoned the prelude, together with his intention of astonishing the English public after the special manner of '*virtuosi*' generally. He returned to his fantasias, and commended '*cette musique naïve*' to the prince of darkness. M. —d de —r, a very fire-eater among '*virtuosi*,' being invited to a musical party at the house of a distinguished amateur, since deceased, was assigned, for his share in the programme, one of the sonatas of Dussek.[5] Nevertheless, having laboured hard for more than a week, he gave it up in despair. 'This is not pianoforte music' ('Celle-ci n'est pas écrite pour le piano') – he insisted; and shutting up the book was speedily lost in arpeggios, chromatic scales ascending and descending, showers of octaves, and crossings of hands, thumbing the while some unhappy opera-tune, which had to make itself heard amidst all this smothering, smashing, and belabouring.[6] 'Voilà un morceau véritablement écrit pour piano!'[7] – said the *virtuoso*, after a last sweep from one extremity of the keyboard to the other, with both hands in contrary directions. The 'distinguished amateur,' however, was of a different opinion. He resided in Queen's-square, and preferred Bach's *perruque* to M. Liszt's *chevelure*[8] – the head-dress of modern virtuosity, the first duty of which is to ape the highly gifted man from the least healthy part of whose idiosyncrasy it sprang. The 'distinguished' amateur would not hear of anything being substituted for Dussek's sonata; and Sterndale Bennett,[9] or some other *non-virtuoso*, played it at sight.

There are those, however, among the 'virtuosi' who are more capable, if not more willing to play legitimate music as it should be played. Somebody asked Herr Castle – a devoted worshipper of Staudigl[10] the singer – whether Staudigl could speak Italian. 'I don't know, exactly' – replied Herr Castle – 'but he could if he would.' So the 'virtuosi' to whom we are now alluding, 'could' if they 'would.' But, alas! they won't. When they come across real music they are puzzled how to handle it. To bestow any amount of study upon it would be to step from a pedestal of their own imagining down to the standing point of their (presumed) inferiors. At first, it appears so easy, that they feel inclined to spread out the close harmonies into vaporous arpeggios, to double the passages in the bass, and to introduce subjects of their own – one for each thumb – with an eye (or rather a thumb) to richness and variety. A genuine 'virtuoso' (a 'lion' proper) cannot (or will not) understand twenty-four bars of pianoforte music in which the entire keyboard has not been once or twice galloped over. The *'jeu serré'* – where all the fingers are constantly employed (as in the gigues of Bach) – is as unwelcome to them as *'terre à terre'* dancing to the choreograph whose vocation is to cut capers half-way between floor and ceiling. They cannot (or will not) keep their fingers quiet. To 'virtuosi' repose is nauseous – unless it be the repose indispensable to a winded acrobat. Thus they do injustice to their own executive powers and to the music set before them – by obtruding the former and caricaturing the latter.

A remarkable instance in illustration of the point in hand occurred the other night, when a *'virtuoso'* of the first water had to do with a concerto by Mozart. We do not mean Sig. Andreoli, but a 'virtuoso' of such water that it is unnecessary to designate him by name.[11] A 'lion' in the most leonine sense of the term, he treated the concerto of Mozart just as the monarch of the forest, hungry and truculent, is in the habit of treating the unlucky beast that falls to his prey. He seized it, shook it, worried it, tore it in pieces, and then devoured it, limb by limb. Long intervals of roaring diversified his repast. These roarings were 'cadenzas.' After having swallowed as much of the concerto as extended to the *point d'orgue* of the first movement, his appetite being in some measure assuaged, the lion roared vociferously, and so long, that many adverse to Mr. Owen Jones's[12] idea of acoustics, admitted that, at all events, a 'lion' could be heard from the 'recess' in St. James's Hall. Having thus roared, our 'lion's' appetite revived, and he ate up the slow movement as if it had been the wing of a partridge. (Never did the slow movement so suddenly vanish.) Still ravenous, however, he pounced upon the finale – which having stripped to the *queue* (*'coda'*), he re-roared, as before. The *queue* was then disposed of, and nothing left of the concerto.

We remember, many years past, we used to go to Exeter Change,[13] to see the lions fed, watching the movements of those noble and voracious quadrupeds, and listening to their roar with rapt attention. All our early impressions were revived on the present occasion; and we made a solemn vow to attend whenever and wherever the same 'lion' should be advertised to devour another concerto. (He – the same 'lion' – is to feed upon Weber's *Concertstück* on Monday, in the Hanover-square Rooms. – *Printer's Devil*.)

On the other hand this 'lion,' like Staudigl the singer, 'could' speak Italian 'if he would' – in other words, 'roar you like any sucking-dove.' But it goes against the grain with him; and we are sorry for it, since he is no ordinary 'lion.'

1 The Ambigu-Comique was associated with comedies and vaudevilles, the Théâtre-Français with serious drama.
2 William Charles Macready, the actor, and William Robert Hicks, the humourist and popular storyteller.
3 Disraeli served as Chancellor of the Exchequer in 1858-9. His novel *Coningsby* (1844) depicted the conditions of the urban and rural poor. In 1847 Thackeray, author of *The Newcombes* (1853–5), wrote a series of satires of famous writers for *Punch* in which 'Codlingsby' appeared.
4 'This *naïve* music isn't easy, after all. What a devil!'
5 Op. 61. *The Elegy on the Death of Prince Ferdinand* (author's note). [The composer is Johann Ladislaus Dussek. – Ed.]
6 The drawing-room window was open. Mr. Thackeray was most likely passing near the house. At any rate, not long after, we read the famous description of 'Such a getting upstairs,' with variations (author's note).
7 'Here's a piece really written for the piano.'
8 Let it not be supposed that we include Friar Liszt among the 'virtuosi' proper. Heaven forbid we should hold him in such light esteem (author's note). [cf. Heine's view of Liszt (no. 29) – Ed.]
9 William Sterndale Bennett, the pianist and composer.
10 Joseph Staudigl, the Austrian bass, often sang in London in opera and oratorio.
11 The references are to the Italian pianist Carlo Andreoli and the Russian pianist Anton Rubinstein. Davison reviewed the latter's concert in *The Times* on 7 June 1858.
12 The architect of St James's Hall and author of *The Grammar of Ornament*.
13 Byron was among those who went to see the animals fed in the menagerie at Exeter Change on the Strand, which was demolished in 1829.

33

Hector Berlioz, 'Beethoven in the Ring of Saturn: Mediums'

Journal des débats (24 November 1860)

Berlioz (1803–69) is the paradigm of the nineteenth-century composer-critic. A brilliant and irreverent writer, he railed at France's conservative musical establishment, in particular at conductors and composers who presumed to 'improve' the music of others. The journalistic *feuilleton* reached supple perfection in his hands. A livelier critic than Fétis (see no. 24), and a more perceptive one than Castil-Blaze (no. 27), Berlioz was better known in his day as a writer than as a composer.

The musical world is in a tizzy at the moment; the whole philosophy of art seems to have been turned on its head. Just a few days ago it was the general belief that beauty in music, like mediocrity and plainness, was absolute – that is, that a piece which was beautiful or plain or mediocre for the self-anointed people of taste, connoisseurs, was equally beautiful, mediocre, or plain for everyone, and thus for people without taste and learning. From this comforting idea it followed that a masterpiece capable of bringing tears to the eyes of a resident of no. 58 rue de la Chaussée-d'Antin in Paris, or of boring or revolting him, must necessarily produce the same effect on a resident of Cochin-China, a Lapp, a pirate from Timor, a Turk or a dockhand in the rue des Mauvaises-Paroles.

When I say it was the general belief, I mean among scholars, savants and simpletons: for in these questions great and small minds find common ground and opposites attract. As for me, being neither a scholar, nor a savant, nor a simpleton, I've never quite known where I stand on these weighty and controversial issues. I believe that I used to have no beliefs; but now I'm sure I've made up my mind, and I believe in absolute beauty much less than in the unicorn's horn. I ask you, why not believe in the unicorn's horn? It has now been proven conclusively that unicorns exist in several parts of the Himalayas. Evryone knows about the adventure of M. Kingsdoom. The celebrated English traveller was amazed to meet one of these animals, which he believed to be fabulous (that's what you get for believing!), and his attentive gaze mortified the elegant quadruped. The unicorn, irritated, charged at him, pinned him against a tree, and left a long piece of horn in his chest as proof of the unicorn's existence. The unfortunate Englishman never got over it.

Now I must tell you why I've lately come to believe with certainty that I do not believe in absolute beauty in music. A revolution was due to take place – and actually has taken place – in philosophy since the marvellous discovery, first, of séance tables (in fir), and then of mediums, evocations of spirits, and spiritualist conversations. Music could not avoid being influenced by such a considerable fact and remain isolated from the spirit world: music, the science of the impalpable, the imponderable, the ungraspable. Many musicians have therefore made contact with the spirit world (as they ought to have done long ago). By means of a very reasonably priced fir table, on which one places one's hands and which, after several minutes of reflections (the *table*'s, that is), begins to raise one or two of its legs in a manner that Englishwomen, I regret to say, will find shockingly immodest, one manages not merely to evoke the spirit of a great composer, but even to enter into regular conversation with him, to compel him to answer all sorts of questions. What's more, if you go about it the right way, you can force the great master's spirit to dictate a new work, a whole composition emerging piping hot from his brain. As for the letters of the alphabet, it's understood that the table, in raising its legs and letting them fall back on to the floor, makes so many taps for a *do*, so many for a *re*, so many for a *fa*, so many for a quaver, so many for a semi-quaver, so many for a crotchet rest, so many for a quaver rest, etc., etc. I know what you're going to reply: 'It's understood, you say? Understood by whom? By the spirits, apparently. But before this understanding was reached, how did the first medium learn from the spirits that it was understood?' That I can't tell you; all I know is that it's certain. Anyway, in big questions like this, it's absolutely necessary to let oneself be guided by instinct, and above all not to quibble.

So therefore already (as the Russians say), at last the spirit of Beethoven, which lives in Saturn, was evoked. Since Mozart lived in Jupiter, as everyone knows, it seems the composer of *Fidelio* ought to have chosen the same star for his new abode; but it's no secret that Beethoven is a little wild and capricious; perhaps he even feels some unspoken antipathy toward Mozart. At all events, he lives in Saturn, or at least in its ring. And that is where, last Monday, a medium who is on excellent terms with the great man, and who isn't afraid of putting him out of sorts by asking him to come such a long way for nothing, placed his hands on the fir table to send to Beethoven, in the ring of Saturn, the command to come chat with him for a moment. At once the table began to make indecent movements, to lift its legs, and to reveal ... that the spirit was near. These poor spirits, you must admit, are quite obedient. During his earthly life, Beethoven wouldn't have gone as far out of his way as the Carinthian Gate in the imperial palace, if the emperor of Austria had bade him to visit, and now he leaves the ring of Saturn and interrupts his lofty meditations to obey the command – mark you, the *command* – of anyone who happens to own a fir table.

What a business death is, and how it changes your character! And how right Marmontel was to say, in his opera *Zémire et Azor*:[1]

Spirits, whom we are made to fear,

Are the best people in the world.

That's the way it is. I warned you that one mustn't quibble in questions like this.

Beethoven arrives and says by means of the feet of the table: 'Here I am!' The enchanted medium taps him on the stomach ...

'Come, now, you're talking nonsense.'

'Bah!'

'Oh, yes. Just now you spoke of the brain in connection with a spirit.Spirits aren't bodies.'

'No, no, but you know very well that they are half-bodies. This has been explained perfectly. Don't interrupt me with such worthless observations.'

'I continue my sad story.' The medium, who is a half-spirit himself, now makes a half-tap on Beethoven's half-stomach and, without further ado, begs the half-god to dictate a new sonata. Beethoven doesn't need to be asked twice, and soon the table begins to gambol ... The dictation is taken down. Having written the sonata, Beethoven returns to Saturn. The medium, surrounded by a dozen stupefied spectators, goes to the piano, plays the sonata and the stupefied spectators become confused listeners when they

recognize that the sonata is not a half-platitude but a whole plati-
tude, nonsense, stupidity.

Now how can we believe in absolute beauty? When Beethoven
went to live in a higher sphere, surely he could only have
improved himself; his genius must have grown, risen; and in dic-
tating a new sonata he must have wanted to give the denizens of
earth an idea of the new style he had adopted in his new abode, an
idea of his 'fourth period', an idea of the music played on the
Erards in the ring of Saturn. *Voilà*, this new style is exactly what
we lowly musicians of a lowly and sub-Saturnian world call dull,
silly, and intolerable. Far from sending us to seventh heaven, it
irritates and nauseates us ... Ah! it's enough to make one lose
one's mind, if such a thing were possible.

Hence one has to believe that since beauty and ugliness are not
absolute and universal, many products of the human spirit which
are admired on earth will be scorned in the spirit world. And I feel
justified in reaching the conclusion (which I have long suspected in
any case) that operas staged and applauded every day, even in theatres which modesty permits me to name, would be hissed on
Saturn, on Jupiter, on Mars, on Venus, on Pallas, on Sirius, on
Neptune, in the Big and Little Dippers, in the constellation of the
Charioteer, and that they are, in the end, merely infinite platitudes
for the infinite universe.

This isn't a very encouraging conviction as far as great producers
are concerned. Several of them have been stricken ill by this dis-
tressing discovery, and it's said they could well pass on to the spirit
state. Happily, it will be long.

1 Comédie-ballet (1771) with libretto by Jean François Marmontel and music by
Grétry.

34

Józef Sikorski, 'Music and Citizenship'

Ruch muzyczny, no. 45 (1860), trans. Mirka Zemanová

Sikorski (1813–96) was an early and energetic advocate of a Polish school of composition. He was already well known as a critic and a scholar of old Polish music when he founded the weekly *Ruch muzyczny*, the first Polish music periodical of consequence, in 1857. Here he pleads eloquently for an art rooted in the soil of society and valued equally with the more tangible accoutrements of civilization. For contrasting perspectives on the issue, see the articles by Stasov and Salazar (nos. 44 and 61).

... Art ought to be homegrown before it enters life. It ought to be homegrown even afterwards, so that it can hold its ground and at the same time run with life, so that it can be both the interpreter and the ennoblement of life. Then art is free to be cosmopolitan if it can, not forgetting the source from which it draws inspiration ... Hence, a painter of nationalist bent or a composer of songs conceived in a nationalist spirit is more popular than a painter who treats general historical or religious themes, or a composer who writes symphonies and operas for the entire world. The former show that they love humanity through their nation; the latter see their nation as part of humanity. The latter may be higher-minded, may burn with a more intense flame, but the former will be the first to win recognition. The influence of the former will be more beneficial and faster to spread, since it will be more direct. 'Art through and for life' is their slogan; their goal: vigorous promotion of national ideas and citizenship. The latter's slogan is 'Art for art's sake'; their goal: vigorous promotion of humanity and cosmopolitanism ...

It is understood that the arts are an expression of society: art expresses what society knows. Hence, if music talks nonsense, it is clear that the matters society uses it to express are not understood as they should be. Society is not all half-baked and superficial: even people who are sensible and profound run away from music or fail to see how it could be of use to them, thinking that music cannot teach what they crave to know ...

How can art which is imperfect be improved? How can art which is feeble be fortified? The only answer is to create a community of artists and artistry among the citizens ...

Those who would give pride of place to industry, trade and the physical and social sciences do so in vain. A nation breathing this atmosphere alone would wrongly believe itself to be on the path to perfection – if perfection is accessible to people. History teaches that a nation at the height of civilization has never renounced art. And rightly so, since it is mainly art which, through its monuments, gives testimony of peoples' lives, makes them into historical proofs and, in the absence of proofs, throws light on the times to which it belongs ...

Citizenship does not depend on slogans and wishing our fellow citizens well ... It depends on applying itself to the task which the nation deems most urgent. This does not mean that artists should abandon their keys, bows, notes and ideals, put on aprons and stand by a workbench, or perform some other tangible service for the nation, letting their home ground go to seed. But it does mean that they ought to act in a spirit of national direction, guided by a good heart and a sound mind ... Therefore we say to you, composer: if you desire to be a citizen of your nation, learn what to say and how to say it, without fooling either yourself or others (as often happens on account of music's inherent vagueness). And you, virtuoso, don't bring us in vain to concerts, which are merely a worn-out form of alms-collecting. We have heard many a better musician than you before. Stop twittering and squealing and flaunting your technique; fix your sights on the main goal of art. And you, teacher, don't deceive the young people and patrons. Don't instil bad taste in them because good taste is too hard to develop. Don't turn out puppets who are dependent on you for guidance. Scour the storehouse of knowledge for awareness and love of art, both for yourself and for your pupils, and don't run after fame and fortune. All of you, cast off the deceit you have nurtured in various ways. Learn, work and act, contemplating the country which yearns with all its might to rise up. May the tempting superficiality of art not infect the fruit of the serious effort of those who see clearly and far. May the spirit of your activity agree with their spirit; where they weep and work, you are not free to play and laze about. Be citizens, and you will be acknowledged ...

Artists, rouse the spirit inside yourselves! As children of a great father, as citizens, you have enough within yourselves to work with. Yet you have no idea how to use this material, nor do you consider how it ought to be used. For you are thinking about the worldly uses of art, and it is often only because of these that you become artists. To enter inspiration while lacking the capacity to seize it means to have no specialist and broad erudition (routine and learning are not the same thing), no constantly growing general education (refinement is not the same thing), no consciousness of the country's situation. It means not to support the country's ideas, to live like the birds in the sky, which neither plough nor sow yet crave to reap. That's not what it means to be an artist, a citizen of the world, except perhaps in the negative sense.

Likewise, that which creates the citizenry of artists also guides the citizens into artistry. When we talk about a citizen, we obviously don't mean an owner of goods and houses, nor do we think of him in a political sense. Our citizen is a man of the people who understands his nation and fulfils his duties in the spirit of the common good, with love for the vocation to which he has committed himself and in which he aspires to artistry. He cultivates his vocation as a way of repaying society for the debt which he contracted involuntarily at birth, but which became binding on him as soon as he acknowledged it …

Just because someone lives by the sweat of his brow, tilling the land; because he earns a good living by racking his brains managing the peasants on his estate or making the best machine; because he produces material objects instead of products of the spirit – does this give him a right to disregard the arts and sciences, which produce spirit and through it material objects? Because he has millions to spend, he thinks he's free to spurn the treasures of the national spirit, which can't be expressed in terms of jingling coins, and to measure their value in figures. 'Music, music! What childishness. Give us the plough, the oar, the hammer, the sword!' Bravo! Let us then cast away everything that is beautiful. Let us become the material objects themselves. Let us kill the spirit, since it's not crucial to the enhancement of our financial affairs. Well and good! But to what end do we crave this advancement? Economists are more cautious than aestheticians: they will not say that production must be never-ending in order to increase, since production is only a means to an end, the goal being the advancement of the spirit. But do the fine arts have any other goal? Is their goal not full of dignity, are they not themselves the direct product of spirit?

Agreed, the economists will say, but music is only a source of pleasant relaxation; it puts us to sleep and coddles us. It merely entertains, without teaching us to think. If this is indeed the case with our homegrown music, who is to blame? Not music itself, certainly. Rather, the blame lies with those who claim to be citizens but who neither have become acquainted with music, though they have learned to play an instrument, nor have enough culture or (let it be said) time to take an interest in aesthetics, even though it could be directly useful to them. An artist summons them to a serious concert, but they refuse to go because they have already heard him! He has published a composition for them, but they won't buy it, even though it is a trifle. The more serious an artist is, the more they avoid him; the more highly someone values art, the louder they laugh at him. They have no money to spend on art, preferring to squander it on cards, drink, spa vacations, women's clothes, racehorses, liveries, etc. Listening? Buying? That's boring, that's not entertaining, that's too learned, etc. If music is to be patronized, then a strange kind of music it must be – as if it suited them, the 'citizens of their country,' best. Having heard music – trumpets at the fair, a mazurka played for their children, a polonaise at the ball, an entrance march in the dining hall – and become convinced of its wonders, they marvel that there is room for anything else in our country! To the pub with it, to the kitchen! Where is your artistry, O citizens? Where is your understanding, O you women who direct the musicianship of our youth ... for drawing-room exhibitions? ...

Uttering this *cri de coeur* is like throwing peas against the wall, as we well know. For we share this view of the people's opinions and the state of our domestic musical affairs. Artists support music in a feeble, incompetent way, for they are not citizens; citizens support music in a feeble, incompetent way, for they are not artists. In other words, neither artists nor citizens are what they ought to be – they prefer to remain in separate camps. Nevertheless, one cannot tear asunder what nature has united; one cannot frustrate the rational faculties of the nation and make artists and citizens independent of each other. Let them all cultivate those faculties for their own profit as well as for that of their fellow citizens. Above all, let them be citizens of their own country ...

35

William Henry Fry, 'Academy of Music'

New York Daily Tribune (15 December 1862)

America's first distinguished composer-critic, Fry (1813–64) was music editor of the *New York Tribune* from 1852 until his death. His *Leonore* (1845), though musically derivative, is notable as the first grand opera by an American. Fry lobbied tirelessly for America's musical independence, a position which set him at odds with J. S. Dwight (see no. 30). This piece, written in the midst of the American Civil War, conveys the flavour of his passionate commitment.

The 'season' of Mr. Grau[1] concluded with a Benefit to Mr. Grau, in which the singers took a spontaneity part. It was all very pleasant and gracious and deserved. The bella, horrida bella, smashed the regular season. Mr. Ullman[2] with the contracts of the Titiens in his pocket-book – not to mention those of the Ristori[3] – gave up with their consent the musical and dramatic battle for the season; and doubtless having read 'The Legend of Montrose,'[4] he learned from the redoubtable Dugald Dalgetty that 'the great Gustavus gained his victories as much with the pickaxe and shovel as with the pike' – and, accordingly, Mr. Ullman threw up intrenchments and declined a contest this year. Thereupon Mr. Grau, with a different style of tactics, comes in and cries 'Guerrabella!' – which, for the benefit of others than Italian scholars it may be said, means Beautiful war! all in one word! Then he gives another *en avant* cry of (Mont) Morenci – an old chivalric shibboleth – and so with other musical war cries – and he takes the public by storm and wins the day. He has now retreated with Xenophon skill with his 10,000 troops to Philadelphia – including the goat – then and there to gain a new victory.

– There are two theories – always have been two – of life – of practical philosophy – those of the brace of Grecian philosophers – Heraclitus and Democritus – the one the Grinning, and the other, the Boo-Hooing Philosopher. The 'peoples' pays their 'monish' and takes their choice. While carnage rages, and death rides the hot blasts of war, we may weep – shut ourselves up o' nights, and deplore the folly, stupidity and crime which have led to the red wrath glowing around: – Or, we may say, – what's the use of sighing, to-morrow we may be dying – a remarkable truth in rhyme – and thereupon go to places of relaxation and amusement; where, bathed in the idealism of characterizations on the stage, with the soft suasions of the human voice divine, we may find comfort and pleasure in the marvellous exaltations of the music of the nineteenth century.

Music, by the way, was the last of the arts to be perfected and is the only romantic art left, for statues and temples were magnificently built 4,000 or 10,000 years ago, and in the very heart of what is called the dark ages was the miracle of grandeur in architecture – the Cologne Cathedral: and now the statue means nothing – it has lost the hallowed signification which it enjoyed when it petrified virtue, and courage, and genius, and divinity – and architecture, too, has no longer any holy significance, it being a mere matter of more or less square feet, and more or fewer bricks, slabs, and tiles. Now, the idea of a church is a cosy library-sort of an affair, with pews and carpets – anti-asthmatic and anti-consumptive, and very comfortable and agreeable. The place carries no more sublime inspiration with it than a drawing-room. The age is simply one of anti-vastness, as applied to churches; and the sanctity of symbolism is, every day, more and more merged into secular actualities. But the ancient Egyptian walked through the enormous avenues to the temples, flanked with gods of stone – whose strength and size defy the ravages of years – and felt himself in a divine presence. The statue and the temple – to his simple idea were heaven on earth. And the Greek, so particular in selecting the site, the shape, the statues, and the various decorations of his temple, was wafted up to the Glorious Apollo or the Thundering Jove, as he sought the sacred shrine. So, too, the Christian of the Middle-Ages, in entering the sublime Cathedrals, – whose marvellous grandeur cannot be fathomed by hearsay, but must be seen to be judged-of – was exalted by their physical vastness and harmonious forms and colors, up to the seventh heaven of the apostle. But all that has passed away – the statue and the building no longer breathe a super-mundane language, because of their beauty, proportion and vastness.

But music cannot be so cheapened, when on a pure grand scale.

With the advance of the epoch in mechanical means, it grows more and more into proportions which are heroic, romantic, – despite all the wonder-murdering tendencies of the age. So exalted has music become on a grand scale in England, above all other countries, that on a recent occasion five thousand performers – the body of singers being over four thousand, executed at the Sydenham Palace choral music, with an effect that all competent auditors and judges agree in saying was preternatural for its largeness, its immensity – and bore comparison musically with other performances, as does Niagara with an ordinary little waterfall. It was at turns as vast as the undying chorus of nature on the sea-side, or lashed itself into a hell of declamatory vehemence and force, too great almost for the nerves of the auditors – and yet it was not noise, not dishevelled sounds, but tones in sequence and in combination as exactly measured and poised as the mathematics of the spheres, and as true evidences of the majesty of the Creator.

1 The impresario Jacob Grau, whose nephew Maurice later produced opera at the Metropolitan in New York.
2 Bernard Ullman produced opera at the Academy of Music from 1857 to 1860. He moved to Europe shortly before Fry's article appeared.
3 The references are to the German soprano Therese Titiens (or Tietjens), who settled in England in 1858, and Adelaide Ristori, an Italian actress active in Paris.
4 The novel by Sir Walter Scott (1819). Captain Dugald Dalgetty is a loquacious pedant and soldier of fortune.

36

Arrigo Boito, 'Musical Chronicle'

Perseveranza (13 September 1863), from P. Nardi, ed.,
Arrigo Boito: Tutti gli scritti (Milan, 1942)

Although he composed two operas and other works, Boito (1842–1918) is best known today as a writer and librettist (most notably of Verdi's *Otello* and *Falstaff*). The bulk of his criticism dates from the 1860s, when as a young Turk fresh out of conservatory, he championed 'futurism' and lashed out at convention. This article explains the distinction between 'form' and 'formula' which underlay his philosophy of art. For another discussion of the subject, see no. 78.

Has anyone heard frogs croaking or wind blowing from the north? Has anyone seen swallows skimming along the ground or cats whirling gaily? Can anyone tell me, from these or other omens, whether the artistic atmosphere is about to turn into a nourishing downpour? Dry, asphyxiatingly dry, *secco ostinato*: this is the forecast we have been hearing for several years. Still, those timid souls who drown in a glass of water can abandon themselves to the fine weather and leave their umbrellas at home, since today too the atmosphere shows no inclination to change.

The Teatro della Scala has reopened: this is what makes me think of meteorology. It reopened with a nearly new opera by maestro Cagnoni: *Il Vecchio della montagna*.[1] And here the trouble begins, as usual, with the libretto.

Really, another fine subject ruined, another great swath of history wasted, or at least spoiled, by the shortsightedness of the man who has taken it upon himself to treat it. The assassins' origins, their bloody and powerful regime in the twelfth century, was a topic fit to make a poet's and a musician's head seethe. A story so splendid and dreadful that it borders on legend and which, at this distance in time, still appears to historians like a dimly remembered dream ...

But the man who had such poetry within his grasp saw fit to swap it for its weight in prose, saw fit to drug the public, not with the opium of Hassan but with rancid wine, and they are fed up, nauseated, disgusted with it. And this is the trouble: these melodrama-makers haven't a doubt in the world about the great role that has fallen to them today; not for a moment do they consider that the stalled engine of music awaits a jolt from them to make it run. They lie about idly, quite content with their easy profession, caring not a fig for art. Meanwhile, art is shrivelled up, wasting away, abandoned to the life of a roadside beggar, like a poor churchmouse. The subject is serious and more fitting now than ever – but let us proceed.

Human language has words and meanings which are easily confused and which, especially where aesthetics are concerned, it is useful to disentangle: two of these words are *form* and *formula*. The Latins, who knew a thing or two about it, made the second the diminutive of the first; but the Latins also knew how to speak *and* think more clearly than we do. *Form*, the extrinsic manifestation, the fine clay of art, has as much in common with *formula* as an ode of Horace has with Ruscelli's rhyming dictionary,[2] as the horns of Moses have with a donkey's ears. And what needs to be said at once is that, from the birth of melodrama in Italy right up to today, we have never had true melodramatic form but instead always the diminutive, *formula*. Born with Monteverdi, melodramatic formula passed to Peri, to Cesti, to Sacchini, to Paisiello, to Rossini, to Bellini, to Verdi, acquiring strength, development and variety as it passed from hand to hand (especially in these later masters), and yet *formula* it always remained, as *formula* it had been born. *Aria, rondo, cabaletta, stretta, ritornello, pezzo concertato*: all the names are there, in serried rows, to prove my point. The time to change style should be at hand; the form widely achieved by the other arts should likewise have developed in this studio of ours; it should be in the fullness of its manhood. Let our *praetexta* be cast off and replaced with a toga.[3] Let the name and shape be changed, and instead of saying *libretto*, that little word of conventional art, let us say and write *tragedy*, as the Greeks did.

All this hasty talk redounds to Signor Cagnoni's advantage and amply justifies him, because it naturally leads to the conclusion that it is impossible today to make music which is either beautiful or good, not just with a bad libretto but with any libretto. Cagnoni, in turn, to be helpful to us, redounds to our advantage and amply justifies that conclusion, since in truth his music is neither beautiful nor good. A bitter German composer, to whom the phrase *music of the future* is erroneously linked (a phrase that he never had any intention of spitting out), would call Cagnoni's music 'table music' and laugh heartily to hear it; and Horace, if he were alive, might exclaim, 'Nugaeque canorae!'[4] all over again, with his amiable irony of word and thought. We won't linger too long on the details, since it would be the same old anatomy lesson taught every month, every week, on the same old corpse – a most depressing lesson which by now everybody knows by heart.

There is certainly a strong tendency in this music – a tendency to make other people's things one's own. Nor is this anything to wonder at, since, just as gold is made of gold and books are made of books, so music is made of music, and everybody knows that masters are even more given to snatching than thieves. This sin may be widely overlooked, but another is much less forgivable, and we hardly know how to say it. With the present wondrous development of orchestration, our century's great conquest, it would be right to demand of everyone who possesses the material of art (and Cagnoni is among them) a younger, warmer style of instrumentation. The proper disposition of the four horns and the different *families* of the orchestra, the skilful use of the *quartet*[5] – this isn't everything; indeed, it's nothing. The orchestra is not a guitar, it is a soul, a palette, a drama, the chorus of Greek tragedy. Everybody knows it; and since everybody knows it, it should be shown that they do. The author of this chronicle remembers hearing Carafa,[6] two years ago, regret the demise of the old spinet, which once upon a time accompanied in the orchestra the ancient, ingenuous recitative; and he was lamenting with an air of real grief. So every age has its own opinions, its own likes. But today that famous master has very white hair; we, who have dark hair, think otherwise ...

On 31 August our conservatory of music[7] closed, after a year of valiant, courageous effort and robust experiments. There's a novelty for you – to see an academy (usually a reservoir of prejudices and fears) arising today with an independent school, a young style, an almost foolhardy cultivation of the most foolhardy things in art. A noble and highly laudable achievement, since, more than with any other art, the prejudices and fears of theory are detrimental to music ...

Finally, it is a beautiful sight to behold young people in a school staying young, without being forced to wear periwigs and spectacles: it is a peaceful sight. So much so that we are almost consumed with desire to strike out the unpleasant beginning of this chronicle, with its talk of drought and other nonsense; since, unless we are very much mistaken, we seem to have heard frogs croaking and wind blowing from the north. Certainly art is on the move: witness the confident stride of many young truths; witness the tired wavering of many old lies; witness the public's curious anticipation of an unknown something; witness, above all, the powerful reasoning of that aesthetic which true artists carry in their hearts and which is the master of art.

The development to which music is pointing today is based precisely on the most material of musical elements, the one which is most palpable to the coarse hands of the many (as we said): *form*. Thus, this development will be discovered and resisted, as no other has been up to now, perhaps. From the day when the work of our tonality was established and finished, from the first years of the seventeenth century to today, from Fra Pietro d'Uregna[8] to Meyerbeer, music has made continuous progress, now in one, now in another of its elements, with a circular and centrifugal motion (let the image pass through our minds) which gives it a resemblance to that spiral figure which rises, rises, and expands eternally, the sublime symbol of earthly civilizations. Certainly, more than any other art, music feels the inevitable fate of its elements, its *centre of gravity*; it feels this at every moment in tonality, in rhythm, in that heavy but necessary incarnation of the idea which is called *form*. To loosen the pull of this centre as much as possible, this is the great intention, the great and ceaseless operation of art.

Harmony developed magnificently in the sixteenth century; rhythm followed in the first half of the seventeenth; *form* (at that time *formula*) followed rhythm in the second half. The demands of art having been pacified for a brief period but then reawakened, a miraculous expansion of harmony took the field again in the eighteenth century and, as if by a geometric progression, the first half of the nineteenth century saw a vast, indeed almost undefeatable rhythmic progress, in which our greatest Italian masters have cooperated vigorously. And so, in order to fully confirm this artistic palingenesis, our half-century has predicted and marked what is to be done.

1 Antonio Cagnoni, whose *Vecchio della montagna* had its première in Turin in 1860.
2 Girolamo Ruscelli's *Rimario* (1559) went through many editions into the mid-nineteenth century.
3 The praetexta was the outer garment worn by free-born children in ancient Rome until they came of age and put on the toga.
4 'Sonorous trifles' (*Ars poetica*, 322).
5 i.e., the strings.
6 The composer Michele Carafa.
7 The Milan Conservatory, established in 1807.
8 A Spanish monk who wrote a treatise on music in 1620. He is identified as Piero d'Urena in Fétis's nineteenth-century *Biographie universelle*.

37

Bedřich Smetana, 'Public Musical Life in Prague: Opera'

Národní listy (People's Newspaper) (15 July 1864),
trans. Mirka Zemanová

As composer and critic, Smetana (1824–84) gave voice to the nationalist aspirations of the Czech people. When he became critic of the Prague daily newspaper *Národní listy* in 1864, the repertoire of the Provisional Theatre consisted largely of Italian opera. Smetana – who had already written his first opera, *The Brandenburgers in Bohemia*, though it wasn't produced until 1866 – fought to redress the balance in favour of his compatriots. For similar efforts on behalf of native opera in other countries, see nos. 26, 31 and 40.

In the previous article we showed how our Czech opera has so far made little effort to prove its worth as an artistic institution, aware of its lofty task.

Today we shall take the liberty of drawing its attention to this task, and at the same time of pointing out what we rightly expect from this operatic institution of ours, so that it can work and remain at the level of its well-earned reputation in the art of music.

Far from *any dreaming*, we protest beforehand against any reproach and insist on the most practical standpoint – that is, the status quo in which our stage finds itself at present. We shall, at the same time, thoroughly consider the practicalities and impracticalities of our demands, which we shall adapt to a state of affairs which, alas, cannot be changed for a long time yet.

Nurturing native music is the foremost and most beautiful task of our opera.

That this is its task – nay, its duty – cannot be doubted, and one would scarcely find anyone who would deny it, not excepting the opera's directorship. Nevertheless, how is the matter to be realized?

A year ago we would have got the directorship of our opera into trouble if we had asked such a question, but not today.

It is a well-known fact that operatic works by native musicians exist; indeed, there are so many of them that the repertoire could be

filled for several years. Why, we have heard excerpts from individual operas in a concert hall – from *Horymír's Leap*,[1] for example.
Why doesn't Horymír dare to attempt the leap from the Žofín Hall
to the nearby Provisional Theatre?[2] It is equally known, if we are
well informed, that *three new operas* have been submitted for the
Harrach competition.[3] Why does the opera's directorship not insist
that the results are, for its own benefit, finally published, since
works of competitors have been lying idle for an entire year, without anyone knowing anything about their fate?

Indeed, it would do no harm if the intendant's office would itself
take care of the matter. Or do people think that there is enough
time when the result is postponed somewhere *ad calendas graecas*?[4]
Or do they think that it is the duty of the composers to beg the
illustrious directorship to do them a favour and accept their works?
Which composer would himself make an offer for an acceptance of
his work? Should he not be afraid that this favour will be counted
as his real *wages*, if the opera is produced and remains in the repertoire? Here we come to a field which would lead us too far from
our aim – that is, *administrative matters* – but it is neither to our
taste at this time, nor do we have space for it. We offer only this
piece of advice to the directorship: it would be a bad misjudgment
to try to save money in obtaining new works, and an even worse
one to fail to remunerate native musicians.

Should the management of our opera have some influence on
native music, it would have to be exerted partly through *buying* of
works, partly through *benefit performances*, and partly through
royalties. And it is obvious that this influence must be attained,
since it is in the management's own interest. Another good means
would be for the directorship to take care of good librettos, which
it could obtain either through *competitions* or directly through an
arrangement with skilled poets. It could entrust the best of these
librettos to those composers in whom it had complete confidence
that they would create something worthwhile. Moreover, it is possible to realize other things that are not mentioned here, through
private discussions between composers and the directorship. But
good librettos are much harder to come by than good composers.

Should the illustrious directorship present *only two native operas*
by way of novelty, it would do justice to its duty and its artistic
diligence would be fully praised. The box office would certainly do

well at the same time, even if the novelties did not have enough life-force to remain in the repertoire. For the public always demands something new and would certainly come for the first two or three performances in sufficient numbers so that at least all the expenses could be covered. Besides, one must not forget that the public wants to educate itself, and our public in particular is always devoted, if the matter in question, as we have already said, is a good one.

The second task is not to neglect our older native composers. All foreign works must still be translated; why not translate works of our composers which were set to German texts? Why are there no performances of Škroup's *Columbus* (which, moreover, would be a novelty)? Why has Kittl's *Die Franzosen vor Nizza* been forgotten?[5] This opera is indeed better than many others which have lately been performed with tenacious obstinacy. And where are still other composers and their works?

Furthermore, it is time to acquaint ourselves with the operas of our tribal brothers, such as Glinka, Moniuszko, Rubinstein and others. *The Children of the Steppes*,[6] by the last-named composer, has been performed even in Vienna, and with much praise.

And now, to come to the most outstanding works by the classical and romantic composers, where are these? Where is Mozart's *Le Nozze di Figaro*, which was long ago translated into Czech and often performed at that time?[7] Where is *Don Giovanni*? Where is Beethoven's *Fidelio*?

Since Goethe's *Faust* has been performed on our stage, this same stage need not be afraid of great music dramas by German composers. Wagner, too, could be performed, if only there were an appropriate theatre! But there is time enough for that. It would indeed be comical to think that our opera should have done everything that we have stated briefly here. We only wanted to show how our directorship can exploit the enormous treasure of operatic literature by uniting artistic efforts with box office successes. Our Czech opera must start making a greater effort. Indeed, had it done only that much, it would have saved us from writing these lines – a Sisyphean labour, perhaps. But the entire nation must take care of the reputation of native opera, if those who should properly do so have not done so. And this is why we have registered here our wishes, our demands.

Once our repertoire is planned from an artistic point of view,

Italian operas – even warhorses like *Montecchi, Belisario, Lucia,*[8] and others – can still be given for those who long for them.

The final demand we must make of our opera is *conscientious, truthful performances, full of genuine artistic spirit.* Duty alone is not sufficient here, duty which reminds one more of a corporal's stick than of a baton. For this, inspiration is necessary. Operas must not be mere musical productions where one only sings for the sake of singing, where it is enough to follow the beat and not to falter, where the baton is always the main thing. Operatic performances must be elevated to the level of *drama*, during which we forget the external machinery.

Is all this of which we remind the reader in these lines impossible? On the contrary, this is the *only* way along which it is possible to reach the honour due to us, before the whole of Europe, as a nation of born musicians; the way which offers *greater benefits to every directorship* and reaps better rewards than the present stagnant, mechanical management.

1 *Jaromír, Duke of Bohemia*, by J. v. Mayr. Apparently the duke was originally called Horymír.
2 The hall of the Žofín Academy, where Smetana was a regular conductor. It was situated on an island in the Vltava River, opposite the Provisional (later National) Theatre.
3 A competition announced on 10 February 1861, the year before the Provisional Theatre was opened, by the Czech patriot Count Jan Harrach. Prizes were to be given for the best Czech historical and comic operas. The prize was finally awarded in 1866 to Smetana's *Brandenburgers in Bohemia*.
4 i.e., indefinitely.
5 *Columbus* (1855) is the most important opera of the Czech composer Frantisék Jan Škroup. Jan Bedřich Kittl wrote *Bianca und Giuseppe, oder Die Franzosen vor Nizza* (1848) to a libretto by Wagner.
6 Anton Rubinstein's *Die Kinder der Heide* (1861).
7 *Le Nozze di Figaro* was first heard in Prague in Italian in 1786, the year of its première, and was repeated the following year in Czech.
8 Bellini's *I Capuleti e i Montecchi* and Donizetti's *Belisario* and *Lucia di Lammermoor*.

38

Aleksandr Nikolayevich Serov, '*Ruslan* and the Ruslanists'

Muzyka i teatr (Music and Theatre) (1867), from G. N. Khubov, ed., *A. N. Serov: Izbrannye stati* (Moscow, 1950–), trans. Richard Miller

A born controversialist who cultivated eccentricity and polemics, Serov (1820–71) none the less took a more measured view of Glinka than his friend Odoyevsky (no. 26). His admiration for Wagner, however, was boundless, and it set Serov at odds with Slavophiles like Stasov (see no. 44). This often cited attack on the 'Ruslanists' is drawn from a series of articles that appeared in Serov's 'special-critical newspaper' *Muzyka i teatr*.

Art and its consciousness – that is, criticism – cannot slumber. The old axiom that art is constantly, ceaselessly transforming itself along with the life of the human species must not, it would seem, even for a second escape the attention of those who judge and write about art. Unfortunately, all too often the contrary occurs. The field of artistic criticism today, as in the past, overflows with various types of sectarians, old believers and schismatics. These people behave as though they have never heard of the aforementioned axiom, and concentrate all their sympathy and understanding on one style, one author, one work, raising the forms of *that* style, *that* author, *that* work to an immutable law and hurling fantastical invectives against artists and against critics who dare to look upon art differently, who dare to recognize in it not one but many roads, who dare to admire not one work but a great many, not exclusively by one artist, in one style, but by *all* who have achieved a clear and full embodiment of their ideals, *all* who, by that very embodiment (that is, the force of talent), play a paramount role in the history of the development of art.

At every step in the history of music criticism we find examples of zealous researchers and biographers who have taken as their hero some single great figure and then viewed all music through the prism of the work of their hero, without acknowledging any other ideal but *his* ideals, any beautiful forms except those created by *him*, and have with disdain and indignation turned away from *everything* in art that does not measure up. Where did these gentlemen get the idea that their measure is an immutable measure? And can there even be such a thing in art, and is it worth bothering about? ...

This exclusive fanaticism for one style, one artist, sometimes climbs to very great and, in reality, comical heights, especially when each of the warring sides hardly is aware of what it is fighting for ...

Musical taste, musical ideals and sympathy for them are in constant dependence on the epoch, the nationality of the artist and his critics, the degree of development of this or that branch of art and its interpretation under the influence of innumerable historical causes.

Another nationality, another age brings *another* phase of art, another critical view. One would think that there is nothing to argue about in this, but in practice, look how people argue! ...

Doesn't this eternal changeability, this eternal 'progress' first in one, then in another direction, tell us that the search for *one* absolutely highest artistic figure, who, without comparison, stands above all the rest, is a chimera either of unenlightened people or of the enlightened but stubborn and shortsighted? ...

Who is correct? Those who reserve a place of honour for Glinka among the other greats in music, or those who, having forgotten about Gluck, Mozart and Weber, on account of *Ruslan* pronounce Glinka the absolutely greatest operatic composer in the world and seat him directly beside Shakespeare? ...

In 1836, for the opening of the renovated Bolshoi Theatre, there appeared on the Petersburg scene, amid the foreign blossoms, between the mellifluous operas of Bellini and Rossini, alongside the grand but somewhat fraudulent eclecticism of Meyerbeer, an enormously honest opera, independently Slavic from start to finish, the first 'opera', in the present strict sense of the word – not a vaudevillean Singspiel but, as they then called it, a 'lyric' opera, equal in its execution to the big German and French operas of the most serious and careful style!

It is well known that the chronology of truly Russian operatic music, meaning a new artistic movement, a new school, begins with Glinka's *Ivan Susanin* ... But why list the beauties and charms of *Ivan Susanin*? What Russian who loves music does not already know those beauties?

Our task is somewhat different. We need to review the *weak* points in that opera, the *weak* points in Glinka as an artist, in order to be guided by these very results of observation when examining *Ruslan* ...

The general conclusion [of the review of *Ivan Susanin*] is not new – namely, that Glinka is much more of a *lyric* and *epic* writer in music than he is a *dramatist* ... Too often he entirely forgets about the scene, the theatre, and develops his own ideas simply musically, without concern for anything else, as if he were writing his music for a concert or just to have the score published (much as Byron, for example, did not write his dramas for the stage) ...

It should be noted that Glinka's shortcomings were 'historically' conditioned and even necessary. His calling was to cast opera-vaudeville into the shadows and create a Russian opera that from the point of view of musical execution was exemplary and mature, to create a new Russian-opera style that demanded skilled singers, to prove the possibility of the legitimate existence of an independent music built on native melodies and crafted on a par with the master-works of the West – to be for Russia, together with Gluck and Mozart and Weber. For this purpose the *musical* side was enough, and the scenic side could be relegated to second place. But only the stubborn, narrow-minded fanatics who don't understand anything about Glinka or the operatic ideal can, in our time, acknowledge this weak drama as the highest stage of operatic work ...

The whole life of an artist runs in an eternally unsatisfied striving toward something more and more clearly perceptible and neverthe-less eluding actual realization. Anyone who *stops*, rests on his lau-rels and settles into inactivity, has outlived his time in art and ceased to create the new – that is, has ceased to be an artist. For a strong creative genius every work, no matter how gigantic and powerful for others, is for himself no more than an experiment, a landmark he has passed along the way. The conclusion of one deeply pondered work opens up for the artist new horizons and, just as in nature, the higher the mountain, the broader the view from atop it, so in art, the higher the work, the more discoveries it brings to its creator, the more unencompassable the infinite horizons of art that open before his inner eyes.

A Russian artist, Glinka, having reached the height of his pow-ers in the development of his talent, having ascertained the factual possibility of writing Russian operas in a particular, unprecedented and most serious Russian musical style, immediately began to reach further, to push forward ... The forms, the colours he used in the first opera were for him extremely few. There lies hidden within him a wealth of individual and absolutely original orchestral coloration, a whole treasure of diamonds and pearls of harmony and melody in the most opulent and fantastical compositions. All this begged to see the light of day. The subject for such riches would have to be the most splendid and brilliant, varied to the point of capriciousness, motley in its designs, like the *Thousand and One Nights*; at the same time, it would be good to stay on native Russian soil ... And what could be better, we have our own sort of Sheherazade's stories, a magical poem with a national fairy-tale title, the fantastical, whimsical creation of the best of Russian poets – in a word, *Ruslan and Liudmila* by the great Pushkin – a poem that at the time, the end of the thirties, was still garnering praises.[1]

The author had very little with which to concern himself regarding the inner foundation of the subject, the *thread* on which he would string his pearls and diamonds. And it is *for that reason* that the opera bears within itself its own judgment. It is bereft of an inner, all-connecting, fecund idea, bereft of pathos (of any kind), and therefore cold, boring, dead; it creates no interest and conveys no sense of an integral whole. It comes out as a luxurious 'pattern', but a pattern is a far cry from a 'picture' ...

A serious approach to Pushkin's poem and its subject is absolutely impossible. But if one were to preserve Pushkin's half-ironic attitude toward the poem's heroes and their deeds, without chasing after local colour and Russian national character yet retaining the bright whimsy of the pictures and situations, one could turn the poem into a *ballet* or a *comic-fantastic* opera of the lightest, most playful style ... And yet the author or authors of the libretto (who? they are not named)[2] approached this subject from just such a *serious*, tragic perspective!!! ...

It remains for us to trace the opera scene by scene, in the next article, in order to see how much the great genius Glinka managed to conquer, or at least hide with miracles of music, the nonsense of his canvas. But here we must ask the reader: does that mean there is any possible *defence* of such nonsense! ...

One representative of the ardent Ruslanists laughs at the *logic that worked in my head*. My logic is before the readers. If such a critic as Belinsky,[3] who adored Pushkin, could in 1843 declare the poem *Ruslan* already *impossible to read with pleasure*, who do they take us for in 1866 and 1867 if they want to prove to us the harmoniousness and sense and absorbing interest in a long, five-act quasi-serious but magical (!) play, where (except for a few stanzas of verse) absolutely everything that constituted the charm of Pushkin's poem has been lost, and the absurdity of its canvas is set out for all to see, its poetic details exchanged for the unpoetic hash of the librettists, its merriment exchanged for insuperable boredom?

V. Stasov is surprised that I of all people should find '*both organic form* and sense even in such trivial, ordinary librettos as the libretto for *Ivan Susanin* and in such funny, clumsy, and stilted librettos as all the librettos for Wagner operas'. I suppose that no one will dispute that the libretto for Glinka's first opera is not among the finest of operatic texts in general. But everyone can see that it does have a unity and wholeness built on one main idea. It has interest of action, and its own 'pathos', and a great character, Susanin; the whole exudes Russian national character, and the epilogue plucks the strings of Russian historical life. In comparison with such elements even the poem *Ruslan* becomes a cipher, let alone the clumsy parody of the poem in the unfortunate libretto for the opera.

A parallel between the text of the opera *Ruslan* and the librettos of Wagner (!) could only occur to someone who has no conception of logical categories. One might compare subjects, however similar. Who, for instance (besides V. S[tasov]), would take it into his head to compare an ancient Chinese painting (without shadows, without perspective) and a painting by, say, Kaulbach?[4] In the one case a childlike inability, underdevelopment of thought and its expression, in the other an overabundance of thought and philosophy and therefore a certain heaviness of expression. It is clear that with anyone who does not understand such things, who does not recognize such *differences*, there is no sense arguing about art: it would be like discussing colours with a blind man ...

The preceding careful analysis of [the opera *Ruslan*] should convince every clear-thinking and dispassionate discussant of the matter that the very *construction* of the opera is burdened with inexcusable faults.

The comparison of this opera, in the light of its faults, with such famous torsos of world art as the Vatican's headless Hercules can only convince one that the panegyrist is likewise headless or at the least, to use the Russian expression, is without a czar in his head.

A defence of the disconnectedness of the opera by recourse to the artist's lyricism and the 'magical subject' also, as we have seen, does not stand up to criticism. Hence parallels between *Ruslan* and Byron's weak dramas and Schumann's entirely unsuccessful opera *Genoveva*⁵ are not complimentary to Glinka; on the contrary, they go to prove that it is impossible to equate him with Shakespeare.

That Glinka ranks first among Russian operatic composers is a settled question and is not open to debate. But the place that Glinka occupies on the general musical horizon is still to be determined: the panegyrics and advertisements of V. Stasov and company in this case do not help and only complicate matters, bringing before the public confused, untruthful and even absurd notions.

1 Pushkin's poem was published in the mid-1820s; Glinka's opera had its première at the St Petersburg Bolshoi in 1842.
2 Valerian Fyodorovich Shirkov, with contributions by other hands, including Glinka's.
3 Vissarion Grigoryevich Belinsky.
4 Friedrich Kaulbach, the German historical and portrait painter.
5 First staged in Leipzig in 1850.

39

Filippo Filippi, 'Wagner: Musical Voyage in the Land of the Future'

Perseveranza (19 June 1870), from *Musica e musicisti*
(Milan, 1876)

Italy's most influential critic in the late 1800s, Filippi (1830–87) was an ardent supporter of both Verdi and Wagner. In 1870 and again in 1876 he travelled to Germany to report on Wagner's music for the Milan periodical *La Perseveranza*, for which he wrote for the last twenty-five years of his life. Filippi saw Wagner and Verdi as building on the achievements of Meyerbeer and Rossini. Shaw (no. 50) offers a rather different assessment of Wagner's contribution to operatic history.

In Italy, where there is much prattle about music and everyone writes it, Wagner is dragged out for denigration at every opportunity, without the slightest understanding of the nature of his genius, of the public for which he writes, or of any of his artistic tendencies, and not even of one of his works in its entirety. I myself, with my detestable reputation for being not an apostle but an ogre of the future, have received that baptism, accompanied by the usual imprecations, merely on account of having shown my sincere admiration for several highly admirable fragments of Wagner, from which I deduced that a genius of this sort cannot be sneered at and ill-treated every day by those who neither know nor wish to know anything ...

Wagnerphobia reaches the level of paroxysm in certain people: they claim not only that his music (which they never understand) is the negation of art, of melody, of common sense, but also that listening to it is a veritable curse; and serious newspapers do not hesitate to proclaim that listening to a Wagner opera can cause jaundice, smallpox, cholera, and heaven knows how many other diseases! And that poor tenor who died while he was rehearsing some opera or another by Wagner is said to have died through the maleficent influence of the music of the future! Added to the virulent criticisms of the operas are the personal insinuations against Wagner, against his exclusiveness and his boundless egotism, which after all is true of all great geniuses ...

About Weimar I shall say nothing in this first letter, except that it seems to me to breathe an air of art and poetry which explains why it has been the preferred retreat of so many brilliant geniuses.[1] Before getting down to business, as they say, I must preface my account of the impressions Wagner's operas made on me with some of my ideas about the conditions and the present direction of art. It would be absurd indeed for me to have come here to study and possibly to decide for myself the question of the stageworthiness and viability of Wagner's operas, especially in Italy, were I not guided by a concept of art and of some of the new school's plans, without which one could neither gratuitously accept nor repudiate that extremely bold form of opera known by the vulgar and unjust name of 'music of the future'.

In music today, and especially in theatrical music, there is undeniably a marked tendency to escape from the fetters of convention and the colourless formulas which were the delight of another generation. It is undeniable that some Italian geniuses gave great splendour to that school, and that certain features in their works which are truly stamped with genius will remain immortal. But one cannot say that opera has made progress with the system of melody at any cost, of fixed forms, and of hasty workmanship; on the contrary, one can say that it has taken a perceptible step backward, especially from where it was left by the *cavaliere* Gluck and by Weber, the great innovators as regards dramatic expression and orchestration. The new school of Wagner takes music drama back to the original concept of Gluck (see the Dedicatory Epistle to *Alceste*),[2] and rightly so, since, if one accepts the fiction of expressing human passions with music, it is better to employ Gluck's and Wagner's approach than the one preferred, because it is easier, by fly-by-night composers who make the same cabaletta do double duty for Orestes' rage and for Enea's filial love.

Ignorance, sensualism and epicureanism have favoured the products of this school, which I venture to call transitional, especially in Italy, where at the theatre listening attentively is the last thing on people's minds, practically all their time being squandered on prattle or other worldly occupations, until the arrival of the tune, which tickles the ear and elicits smiles of bliss and pleasure. Because for many people – indeed, for the great majority – music is considered only in the guise of that fleeting and personal pleasure which is called 'tickling the ear'. Elevation of the spirit, noble and profound stirrings of the soul, feeling music with the heart but through the mind – this is a futile task ...

The whole blind, stubborn war that some people are waging against dramatic music, the very music that even Verdi has produced superlatively in his latest works, is summed up in this Aristotelian formula: 'Music is melody; the dramatic music of the future does not have melody; therefore it is not music.' It would take a volume to reply to this balderdash, there are so many objections to it. I will say here in brief, first of all, that music does not consist of melody alone, and especially that ultradramatic music, including that of the future, is anything but deprived of this essential element. If some follower of Wagner, without ideas and without genius, has found a way to write music without melody, so much the worse for him, for he will be repudiated by all schools, even that of the past more-than-perfect! This stubborn desire to

deny dramatic composers ideals or any melodic invention whatsoever is the most depressing disease of the partisans of melody at any
cost ...

The futurists – since one has to call them by that name – do not
flee from melody; on the contrary, they seek it out, and if they find
it, they are extremely pleased with it, as with a precious treasure. It
is common, vulgar melody from which they flee, the kind that some
people would enclose within eight or sixteen beats, under pain of
ostracism.

All too much of this last kind of melody has been used and
abused until now. It has been put to use as filler in operas whenever
genius was lacking or flagging. In the school of the past, these
melodic fillers belong to those short-lived operas made for the success of the moment. Few are the operas on which genius, embracing
a single synthesis, has lavished treasures of harmony and melody
even in the less important parts: these operas are called, by way of
example, *Guglielmo Tell*.[3]

In the operas of the new school, which subordinate everything
to drama, to the meaning of the word, and to the situations, filler
consists instead of a kind of ideal melody, recitative supported by
the instrumental forces, in which absent melody is replaced by a
powerful efficacy of expression, which cultured persons prefer to
the triviality of convention and formula. Reduced as art is today,
this second style is preferable to the old one, and with us the same
Verdi has proved it, employing it in many, if not all, parts of his
latest operas. There was an intermediate school, that of Meyerbeer
and Halévy, which tried to reconcile the two opposed tendencies.
It would almost have been preferable, if Wagner had said his last
word and if it had not been probable that *Roberto* and *Gli
Ugonotti*[4] would soon be surpassed, in the public taste, by
Lohengrin and *The Flying Dutchman*!

What remains to be done in Italy is to accord Wagner the same
hospitality that was accorded Meyerbeer, Halévy, Auber and a hundred others, at no expense whatever to the instinct and national
character of our music. Moreover, it is necessary to educate the
public, to make it patient and attentive, fully aware of the idea that
music is an art whose enjoyment and (especially) comprehension
develop with patience, overcoming their initial boredom, casting
prejudices aside, taking it seriously, as they do here in Germany,

where people enjoy what they listen to because they understand it, and because the public's education goes on everywhere – in the town square, in the homes, and in the theatres, with the hearing of great music, classical music, true music. Don't tell me that music is an art for the masses, for the people. No, sirs: music is for educated people, for those who, attending a drama in music, ought to understand and value all its historical and aesthetic motivations. What is *Guglielmo Tell* to someone who doesn't understand the Swiss revolution? What is *Gli Ugonotti* to someone who doesn't understand the Saint Bartholomew's Day Massacre?

There is music for the people, with its free and easy rhythms, its vulgar motives; and there is a way to make them enjoy it fully. The lyric theatre public is something else; if it doesn't know, if it doesn't understand, and if it then gets bored – the loss is its own. Boredom is a well-deserved punishment for all those who say they have heard *Jone, Ernani, Attila, L'Arco di Giovanna*, and *La Tenda di Beatrice!*[5] Music is an aristocratic art par excellence: to be among the few to enjoy it, when it is truly good, is neither a crime nor a great misfortune ...

1 Weimar was a centre of the *avant-garde* in the eras of Goethe and Liszt.
2 The classic statement of Gluck's reformist principles, published in 1769.
3 Rossini's *Guillaume Tell* (1829).
4 Meyerbeer's *Robert le diable* and *Les Huguenots*.
5 Errico Petrella's *Jone* (1858); Verdi's *Ernani* (1844), *Attila* (1846) and *Giovanna d'Arco* (1845); and Bellini's *Beatrice di Tenda* (1833).

<hr />

40

Antonio Peña y Goñi, 'Zubiaurre and His First Opera'

(11 April 1874), from *Impresiones musicales* (Madrid, 1878)

Peña y Goñi (1846–96) has been called the founder of modern Spanish music criticism. In the pages of *Imparcial*, the *Correspondencia musical*, and other periodicals, he discoursed on the virtues of *zarzuela* and native Spanish opera. A lively writer, as this article shows, he was fond of leavening his criticism with homely analogies from bullfighting and the game of pelota (see Pedrell's allusion to him in no. 55).

Some time ago a group of Spanish educators, second to none as lovers of their art and solicitous of its future, had a remarkable idea.

At no little sacrifice for most of them, they raised a considerable sum and hit upon the plan of holding a competition for Spain's young composers, in which cash prizes would be awarded to the authors of works worthy of that distinction in the judgment of a specially appointed jury of experts.

It was a bona fide musical event; everyone was incredulous. Various young, aspiring composers saw the sky as the limit. They could hardly believe their luck. Somebody had remembered Spanish musicians! It must be madness!

They hunted for librettos, found them, good or bad, and eagerly set to work. The jury was formed. Señores Eslava, Arrieta, Monasterio, Balart and Calahorra were appointed. The works were examined and the prizes awarded.

Two operas shared first prize. One of them bore the signature Valentín María Zubiaurre on the last page. It was entitled *Don Fernando el emplazado*.[1]

The press covered the affair in the gossip section. The public knew that there were prize-winning operas, sagely opined that the composers of said operas must have talent, and, content with that philosophical pronouncement, gave no more thought to operas or composers.

The prize-winning composers reaped the fruits of their labours, as well as sound advice from their respective teachers and sundry plaudits – however unlikely it seems – from their fellow composers. They took the operas in hand, carefully packed them up, tucked them under their arms, looked back and forth, up and down, and post-haste made a heroic resolution. They put the prizes in their pockets, kept the money and disappeared.

The next day, competition, jury, prizes, operas, composers – everything was forgotten. They had been a drop in the ocean. The drop was called politics, the ocean was called art. The drop had flooded the ocean, the dwarf had defeated the giant, nothingness had overwhelmed immensity. That's Spain for you!

Some years later, in 1870, a dozen people of good will, much faith and a great deal of enthusiasm noticed that there was no Spanish opera in Spain. What about making Spanish opera? they said to themselves. What will it take? An opera. Where do we go to find it?

What else do we need? Money. Who will provide it?

They turned to the composers who had won prizes in the competition, and operas were found. They turned to private individuals, and money was found. As for that last point, let's be fair: no one gave a thought to approaching the government.

The Centro Artístico y Literario: an eloquent demonstration of what faith, persistence and enthusiasm together can achieve! They wanted Spanish opera and they came up with opera by a Spaniard. They wanted the end and they got the beginning. They desired a building and they created its foundations.

A noble and fervent quest, with an impossible dream as its goal; a battle of pygmies who, cornered by superior forces, beat a retreat as glorious as the most signal victory.

The great, immense idea of Spanish opera overwhelmed them. They stood alone, absorbed in their own exertions; all gave orders and all obeyed. They had nothing to go by but a beacon, Spanish art; they had only one goal, Spanish opera ...

The glorious ensign planted by the desperate efforts of the Centro Artístico y Literario waved above the fortress, the artistic fortress which took in the first breath of an opera written in Spain and for Spain – a majestic enclosure in those momentous days, an august temple which sprinkled baptismal water upon the forehead of a new master ...

The Centro Artístico y Literario and the Alhambra Theatre: that is the story of Valentín María Zubiaurre's life, his whole history ...

The sincere, ardent, dispassionate enthusiasm of the public; the deaf, concentrated fury, the envy of the average musician – such were the fruits of *Don Fernando el emplazado*. A complete triumph, victory hands down ...

The first thrust had been made and the Centro's efforts had been crowned with complete success. But the success was meteoric. Lack of repertoire doomed the Centro, as it will surely doom every society formed with a similar goal. The public demanded sustenance and food ran out. Result: starvation, then death.

Let us take a critical look at Zubiaurre and *Don Fernando el emplazado*. Zubiaurre's opera is a mirror which faithfully reflects the composer's artistic physiognomy. Let us behold the mirror and see Zubiaurre. We face a difficult task. Let us be impartial ...

Zubiaurre requested an Italian libretto;[2] perhaps he mistrusted

Spanish singers and was forgetting the artists who had championed him. On the first count he was not mistaken; it was the latter who saved him.

The libretto arrived act by act and with long interruptions. Zubiaurre threw himself into it and set to work with a vengeance. The libretto was childishly ingenuous – a work worthy of Scribe, written for the *tenorino* Palermi.[3]

This Zubiaurre did not, could not see. He was blind: blind with longing, blind with impatience, blind with music. To tell the truth (since we promised to be impartial), he was mired in inexperience, imprisoned by his failure to consider the thousand and one obstacles that modern art throws in the path of a novice who lacks artistic culture.

Zubiaurre trusted totally in his instinct, and his instinct saved him. He knew little about the history of art and for this reason, perhaps, was ignorant of the dangers to which he was exposed. The bandage over his eyes encouraged his foolhardiness.

He unplugged the dike which had long held his musical impulses in check. He gave full rein to the ideas seething in his head, and from that powerful imagination, from that terrible longing, sprang a score full of life, full of warmth, impetuous, breathtaking, vigorous, rambling, interminable.

It was a flood, a genuine musical deluge, which blackened under promontories of ink and inundated millions of musical staffs.

Melodic ideas put down on paper, harmonic periods strewn like rubbish, endless codas and *ritornellos*, instrumental preludes vying with one another, instinctive dramatic warmth, uplifting romances, bellowing recitatives, worn-out ensemble pieces, full-throated choruses, Italian *fermatas*, German cadences, impassioned rhythms, orchestration by turns delicate and noisy, a surfeit of music: all this roils and boils convulsively in *Don Fernando el emplazado*. This is the opera.

The eager longing to compose, the mercurialness of the artist, a superior instinct which vacillates among various paths and forges through them all – Rossini and Donizetti, Meyerbeer and Gounod – the most enthusiastic eclecticism, the uncertainties of inexperience, the fire and fecklessness of youth, the potent seed, the manifest talent, perhaps a hint of genius: this too roils and boils convulsively in Zubiaurre. This is the composer of the opera.

Great virtues, great defects. So began the great masters; so has Zubiaurre begun. He knows what his virtues are; he also knows his defects. He is good-natured, accommodating, a stranger to envy, open to suggestions, modest, and mindful of the terrible difficulties of the art to which he has dedicated himself. His ingenuousness at times borders on innocence ...

1 In 1873 Valentín María de Zubiaurre (1837–1914) was the first recipient of a scholarship from the newly created Spanish Academy of Fine Arts in Rome. Two years later he became *maestro* to the royal chapel in Madrid. *Don Fernando el emplazado*, composed in 1869, shared first prize (with Barrera Gómez's *Atahualpa*) in a national contest to promote Spanish opera. It was first performed on 12 May 1871 at the Teatro de la Alhambra in Madrid.
2 According to *Grove*, *Don Fernando* was first performed in Spanish, but it was revived in Italian at the Teatro Real in 1874.
3 Eugène Scribe was known for his grandiose historical dramas. About Palermi I have been unable to discover anything except his first name, Ernesto.

41

Pyotr Ilich Tchaikovsky, 'Musical Chronicle: *Don Giovanni* and *Zora* at the Italian Opera'

Russkie vyedomosti (Russian Gazette) (16 January 1874), from *Muzykalno kriticheskie stati* (Leningrad, 1986), trans. Mirka Zemanová

Tchaikovsky (1840–93) practised criticism part-time in the early 1870s. His motivation seems to have been purely economic, and Max Graf dismisses his writing as 'narrow-minded' and of little value. Tchaikovsky was certainly not a great prose stylist, but he was an entertaining writer whose often trenchant observations and judgments are still worth attending to.

The repertory of the Italian Opera has recently been enlivened by two productions.[1] One occupies first place among the musico-lyrical works of all times and nations; the second represents a felicitous blending of the best qualities of a composer who is enjoying enormous popularity and at the same time considerable critical attention. The operas are Mozart's *Don Giovanni* and Rossini's *Moïse*, given here in Russia under the title *Zora*.[2]

I have already had occasion to talk in detail about *Don Giovanni*'s highly unsuccessful revival last season, and therefore I will not start enlarging now on the astounding beauty of this brilliant operatic work. The centenary of *Don Giovanni* is approaching, and yet in all the long period since its première there has not been a single opera which combined in equal measure a graceful, inspired melodic line with richness of harmonic accompaniment, and a deeply truthful musical characterization with rounded completeness of forms. The adepts of Wagnerism or our own home-bred operatic realists deny *Don Giovanni* its great historical importance because Mozart, as an artist of genius who never held back his musical inspiration for the sake of conventional concepts of dramatic truth, gave full scope to the organic development of his ideas into broad forms, independently of stage action. Nevertheless, this hundred-year-old opera holds its place, and even achieves growing success, on all the lyric stages of the civilized world. It is heard with complete aesthetic enjoyment of the kind which is never aroused to such a degree by the effects and thunderings of contemporary operas. It could be that Mozart's music is full of irresistible charm because he was a pure specimen of the spontaneously creating artist, untormented by reflection.

Reflection is death to inspiration. Look where contemporary composers' latest attempts to plant opera in the soil of the realistic reproduction of life have led – attempts which renounce traditional form in pursuit of the ghost of rationality and truth! Wagner, joining the fight against the abuses of vocal virtuosity, subjects the singer to the whole orchestral horde, which not only deprives the characters of their dominant role but also drowns them. Dargomyzhsky[3] goes even further: having determined to sacrifice musical beauty to poorly understood conditions of truthfulness of dramatic action, he not only takes away the singer's captivating quality but also deprives himself of the rich means of musical expressivity. His *Stone Guest*, whose subject is close to that of Mozart's *Don Giovanni*, is the pitiful fruit of a dry, purely rational process of invention which can only impart fatal melancholy to a listener who seeks in art not merely the narrow realization of truth, according to which a real apple looks better than a depicted one, but the higher artistic truth which springs from the mysterious depths of man's creative power and pours out into clear, intelligible, conventional forms. Only the self-satisfied, dilettantish stupidity of some unrecognized innovators, who take refuge in the *feuilletons* of the *St Petersburg Gazette*, can, with comic seriousness, allow them to proclaim that the last opera of the highly gifted Dargomyzhsky represents the 'new' opera and to put it on a par with the sublime achievements of the masters of the lyrico-dramatic art.

The music of *Don Giovanni* is an unbroken string of pearls of musical inspiration, such that everything written before and after this opera pales by comparison. From whatever angle one analyses this unique, inimitably beautiful opera, one can only be surprised by the magnitude of human genius and admire it. A lover of elegant *cantilena* stops at the marvellous first-act duet for Don Ottavio and Donna Anna, mourning the death of her father and already calling for vengeance; at the duet for Don Giovanni and Zerlina; at the arias of Donna Elvira, Zerlina and Donna Anna; at Don Giovanni's famous serenade. An admirer of musical declamation, which was brought to such remarkable perfection by Gluck, will find in Donna Anna's recitatives staggering pathos combined with bewitching beauty of harmony and modulation, a strength and power of tragic expressivity before which the beauty of Gluck's recitatives pales. Whether one turns one's attention to ensembles, to the large-scale development of the finales, to the instrumentation, to the art of writing vocal music while considering the affinities and conditions of practicality – or whether one studies the masterful musical characterization – to all of these demands *Don Giovanni* gives plenty of answers and will serve as the best model until art ceases to exist …

1 In the early 1800s St Petersburg had two opera houses, German and Russian, but the repertoire of both was dominated by French and Italian operas. The Maryinsky Theatre, built in 1860, became a focal point of Russian nationalism (Mussorgsky's *Boris Godunov* was staged there the month Tchaikovksy's article appeared), while Italian opera continued to hold sway at the Bolshoi.

2 Rossini's *Mosè in Egitto* (1818) was revised for the Paris Opéra in 1827 as *Moïse et Pharon*. St Petersburg first saw it in 1829 as *Pietro l'Eremita*; the second version was performed there in 1853 as *Zora*.

3 Aleksandr Dargomyzhsky's *The Stone Guest*, seen at the Maryinsky in 1872, was hailed as music of the future by Cui, Serov and others (see nos. 38 and 42). The libretto was based on a Pushkin text on the Don Juan theme.

42

César Cui, 'The New Russian School: *Boris Godunov*, Opera by M. Mussorgsky'

Revue et gazette musicale (18 January 1880)

Like Stasov (see no. 44), Cui (1835–1918) was a committed champion of Glinka and the Russian nationalist composers. From 1864 to 1900 he contributed incisive and often sharp-tongued articles to the *St Petersburg Gazette* and other periodicals. This piece – written for the French journal *Revue et gazette musicale* – was later published as part of a book comprising the first comprehensive survey of Russian music. Cui had disliked *Boris* at its first performance in 1874; here he expresses a more measured view of Mussorgsky's operatic 'realism'.

As can be judged from the précis of this work, there is no question here of a subject whose diverse parts, combined so as to make a suite with one part flowing from the last, respond as a whole to the ideas of strict dramatic unity. Each scene is independent; the characters, for the most part, make only brief appearances. The episodes seen to follow one another necessarily have a certain interconnectedness; all of them relate, more or less, to a general reality, a common plot; but the opera would not suffer if scenes were shifted around, or even if certain secondary episodes were substituted for others. This is related to the fact that *Boris Godunov*, strictly speaking, is neither a drama nor an opera, but rather a musical chronicle, in the manner of Shakespeare's dramatic chronicles. Each scene, taken separately, arouses serious interest, which is not, however, activated by the preceding ones and which stops abruptly, showing no sign of being united with the scene to follow. In this respect, the text of *Boris* has much in common with that of *Ruslan*.[1]

Whole pages of the text of *Boris* are written in prose; this process, demanding frequent changes of rhythm, can be truly useful to the musician in the crowd scenes, where phrase endings, exclamations coming from one side or another on different notes, ought necessarily to produce a movement which is uneven and, so to speak, entirely fortuitous. Besides, a whole libretto treated in such a way would perhaps be preferable to the seriousness of little, ludicrously rhymed verses which are built into many opera librettos; still, a total absence of sustained rhythm in a text meant for singing would be irksome for the composer, especially in the lyrical episodes, where a certain regularity in the melodic phrase structure is almost obligatory. In such a case, verse which is not rhymed, otherwise known as blank verse, is preferable to any other type of text. As far as the cadence or prosody of the verses is concerned, it must not be forgotten that we are dealing here with Russian verses, which are not only syllabic but also tonic. It is unquestionably necessary for the rhythm of the verses to undergo frequent modifications, according to the changes of situation, or else to make them correspond more closely to the inner meaning of the words.

M. Mussorgsky's melodic faculty is of great richness and remarkable abundance. The harmonies he finds are also nearly always very striking and new. And yet, strange though it may seem to say so, at times this nature so amply endowed seems not to be absolutely musical, or rather not to belong to the category of *sensitifs* in music. There are, indeed, very large gaps to be noted in his work, along with numerous virtues. The symphonic forms are completely foreign to M. Mussorgsky; he is hardly one to work out or develop musical situations. His modulation is excessively free and at times one would say that it behaves purely by chance; he does not know how to put deliberate continuity in the outline of the parts of a harmonized melody, and in his hands these parts often take on impossible appearances, contrary to nature, producing harmonies which go to rack and ruin and passages of intolerable harshness. Critical sense and instinct for beauty do not always reveal themselves to his intellect; his talent clothes the character in a surprising savagery, impatient of any restraint. Nevertheless, all of these impetuous mistakes, all of these disordered irruptions flow abundantly, with bounteous vigour, and give M. Mussorgsky a physiognomy which is utterly individual and original.

The author of *Boris Godunov* is above all a realist composer, with all the good and bad aspects of this novel and overly attractive tendency; but in music, even more than in the other arts, realism has limits which we must beware of exceeding, because the musical language, on account of its lack of defined meaning, is not well equipped to communicate it.

M. Mussorgsky is a past master in declamation; in this regard he takes first place after Dargomyzhsky;[2] but his undisciplined abuse of imitation unfortunately reveals too great an aptitude for seizing and rendering exterior effects at the expense of the musical meaning. The result is that beside one of the most admirable melodic recitatives he makes you listen to vocal inflexions which are, so to speak, mechanical, in which the accents and intonations are precisely observed but very little is to be seen in the music.

M. Mussorgsky's music is eminently expressive and descriptive; however, we have no scruples about stating that it relies much too freely on certain details which are completely secondary. Always adulterated by realism, it often abdicates any poetry, any musical charm, and then ends up in an effect of veritable repulsion, in which all things appear in a shocking nudity.

With all that, and thanks to the same tendency, M. Mussorgsky is not only an utterly independent and very original musician, but also one to whom it has been given to explore new, unknown shores of modern dramatic opera ...

The scene of Boris's death produces the most gripping effect. The religious chants, profoundly sad in their pomp and majesty and accompanied by the knell announcing the czar's impending death to the Muscovites; Boris's few phrases, cut short by death rattles; his last attempts to cling to life and the desperation of his final cry; the silent stupor of the Boyars arrayed around the dying man – in short, all the solemnity of such a moment has been painted by the musician with the colours of the most poignant truth; his orchestra, moreover, achieves a rare eloquence here. It remains to be known whether M. Mussorgsky would have done better not to try so hard to reproduce certain details of this scene with photographic precision, and especially to have composed a religious hymn of his own instead of using the one from the ordinary ritual. He was wrong not to pull back from the crudity of certain effects which should have been allowed to melt in the artistic crucible ...

From the sketch that we have tried to give, one is easily convinced that neither the spectator nor the auditor of M. Mussorgsky's work will be able to receive a whole, stable impression from it; the permanent realism of this very modern work, pushed to the point of ostentation, too often takes the place of what one should always look for in music: the expression of poetic beauty. Nevertheless, *Boris*

Godunov is a highly significant event in the artistic world; the sallies of powerful energy and proud originality must be admired. The passions of the Russian people, as well as the humour of which it is capable, are depicted with an artfulness and truthfulness of expression which cannot be praised too highly.

1 Glinka's *Ruslan and Liudmila*; cf. nos. 26, 38 and 44.
2 Aleksandr Dargomyzhsky, the composer of *The Stone Guest* and a proponent of dramatic realism.

43

Eduard Hanslick, 'Wagner Cult'

Neue freie Presse (September 1882), from *Aus dem Opernleben der Gegenwart* (Berlin, 1884), trans. John Gingerich

The titan of late nineteenth-century criticism, Hanslick (1825–1904) was in some respects an arbiter of taste in the mould of the previous century's dogmatic critics. Yet it was not erudition alone, but also the suppleness and wit of his writing, that won him both admiration (from Brahms and his circle) and scorn (from the Wagnerians). Shaw (see no. 50) argued the case for Wagner with similar élan. In his four decades at Vienna's *Neue freie Presse*, Hanslick established the critic as a personage of importance on the staff of the daily newspaper.

The veneration we accord a famous contemporary can be deserved, either wholly or in part, but nevertheless move us to protest the lack of proportion in its form and content. This is the case with the Wagner cult of our day. This cult, unparalleled in the history of the arts, strikes me as such a curious sign of the times that a closer, unprejudiced examination seems called for. We shall not consider Wagner's artistic work, nor touch upon his merits, but examine solely the conduct of his disciples, and even this only in so far as we possess literary evidence. The most relevant public document is without question the monthly publication edited by H. Wolzogen[1] under Wagner's personal aegis, which constitutes the official organ of all Wagner societies: the *Bayreuther Blätter*, now in its fifth year of publication. For a later age, which will look back on the Wagner epidemic of our time in tranquil judgment, yea, with incredulous astonishment, the *Bayreuther Blätter* will have considerable cultural-historical significance. The musician will find in it only very scanty and dubious instruction, for the *Bayreuther Blätter* is concerned with everything *but* Wagner's music. The future historian of German culture, on the other hand, will be able to establish authentically from the five volumes of this publication how severely the delirium tremens of the Wagner intoxication raged among us, and the excrescences it has left in the thinking and perceptions of the so-called learned ...

To his disciples, united, as is well known, through a large chain of 'Wagner societies' into one large congregation, Wagner is not just an all-surpassing master of music, but 'the master' pure and simple, the highest authority in all fields of knowledge, an educator and redeemer of humanity. Every pronouncement he makes on politics, philosophy, morals or religion counts as a major event, a revelation that must be obeyed like a religious commandment. The literal proof is in the *Bayreuther Blätter*, which we have studied with hot and tormented effort. The most important of these Wagnerian revelations, echoed and tirelessly interpreted by his disciples, concern, first, Schopenhauer's philosophy and its profound connection with Wagner's operas; second, the religious, social, and political regeneration of humanity and its salvation from our worthless culture; third, agitation against vivisection, which is indispensable for medical studies; fourth, and particularly amusing, vegetarian propaganda. Now these things undoubtedly have nothing whatever to do with dramatic and musical art. Wagner's personal attitude toward them is absolutely irrelevant to his artistic importance and to the musical world. But, as I've already said, the odd thing about that unbelievable curiosity known as the Wagner cult is that 'the master' is authoritative in all things. The true Wagnerian must not only be an unquestioning worshipper of every one of Wagner's verses and measures, he must also be a Schopenhauerian, a pessimist, a foe of vivisection, an anti-Semite, a vegetarian, a believing Christian and whatever else the 'master' prescribes.

I have already exposed (on the occasion of the *Nibelungen*)[2] the arrogant fraud the Wagnerians have perpetrated on Schopenhauer, whom they believe they alone understand, and I would refer the reader to my earlier essay. The wish I expressed there, that we might at long last be spared the supposedly profound application of Schopenhauer's categories and terminology to Wagner's operas, has not been fulfilled. The young gentlemen of the *Bayreuther Blätter* continue to bring Schopenhauer up at every opportunity, as if they were white-haired students of philosophy[3] ...

A healthy human intellect, which tells us not to consult a composer of operas for advice on philosophy and philosophical systems, will also teach us that physicians, authorities on physiology and pathology, should judge the necessity or indispensability of vivisection, rather than musicians. This is not true for Wagnerians. The 'master' has glibly damned vivisection, and immediately the *Bayreuther Blätter*, whose mission we had hitherto supposed to be connected to the study of the arts, begins to overflow with articles condemning vivisection as frivolous animal torture, and among other things fiercely reprimanding the Reichstag for not allowing an anti-vivisection petition on to its agenda ... Another of Wagner's private passions is at least partly related to this tender disposition toward the animal kingdom: his propaganda for vegetarian fare ... It's well known that tenderness toward animals, elevated to sentimentality, is often found in people who are by no means distinguished for exaggerated love of humanity. We know how tenderly Robespierre tended his pigeons. So Wagner declares an exclusive diet of plants to be indispensable to the reorganization of humanity, and behold! greens become an article of faith and partisanship among Wagnerians. Can anything be more comical than the editor's call to like-minded comrades, amidst the public announcements for *Parsifal*, to sign up early for the 'vegetarian table' at Bayreuth? ...

Many Wagner admirers who have at least kept their heads in the matter of nourishment will be reassured to find out – and this we have from a highly reliable source – that Wagner is only theoretically opposed to eating meat, and that he relishes his roast, along with the wine that is taboo to vegetarians. We never doubted it for a second. *Tannhäuser* was not composed on sour milk and beans, not even by a pious Knight of the Grail. The unity of theory and practice, of teaching and example, are well known to be matters of convenience for Wagner. The majority of his disciples gathered at Bayreuth preferred to follow the example rather than the teaching, and the 'vegetarian lunch' ended as sadly as the solemn assembly on

28 June of 'Bayreuth patrons', who gathered to found an endowment 'out of which shall be paid grants to deserving but impecunious visitors to the festivals'. Wagner himself had broached the idea and endorsed the proposed statute for the new endowment, which would 'achieve more sensibly and efficaciously what at present is thoughtlessly attempted by travel fellowships for prize-winning composers, fellowships that are ludicrously insufficient to support the required advanced studies in Rome or Paris'. After this 'noble' initiative, it seemed only natural to expect the 'noble' master – as the *Bayreuther Blätter* likes to call him – to kick off the new endowment with a sizeable contribution. But since his 'empathy born of compassion' never reaches his wallet, the Bayreuth patrons, who had already made sufficient sacrifices to the holy cause, decided that the master's example was the preferable course. Hugely compassionate for the unfortunates whose impecunious circumstances would deny them access to Bayreuth's healing grace, the patrons dispersed with their pockets buttoned tight.

The tendency of the Wagner school to consider their master merely incidentally as the greatest poet and composer, and to present him primarily as a prophet bringing wisdom and salvation to humanity, has reached its apex in recent years. Two of Wagner's essays, 'Religion and Art' and 'Know Thyself,'[4] have unleashed a delirium of admiration in the Wagner camp and are constantly being put forward as dogma, interpreted and preached in the *Bayreuther Blätter*. These pamphlets, which agitate in a pompously oracular style for the protection of animals and the persecution of Jews, have been amply discussed and dismissed; we will not discuss them further at this point. True friends would have urgently warned Wagner not to publish them – but a god has no friends, only worshippers ...

From these few examples the reader will have surmised that a tone of affected piety, a Christian, religious tone, has recently made its presence felt in the Wagner *Blätter* and continues to intensify. The ageing Wagner has given the cue with the 'sigh which once we perceived on the cross at Golgotha, and which now issues from our own soul', and immediately we see the youngsters parrot and pray along ...

And music? we hear the reader asking impatiently. Does music no longer play any part in Wagner's newspaper? A very subordinate one in any case. Since Wagner spoke those ironic, haughty words: 'I am no musician,' and simultaneously assured us that he would prefer to see our entire musical life disappear from the face of the earth sooner rather than later – since then it must seem utterly inappropriate for Wagnerians to make much of a fuss about music ...

I have saved the greatest edification for last. Mr Joseph Rubinstein,[5] the same who made a name for himself by belittling Robert Schumann, published an essay entitled 'Symphony and Drama' in the *Bayreuther Blätter* which concludes: 'If with regard to post-Beethovenian attempts in the genre of the absolute symphony one has to consider that the last real symphonist was carried to the grave with Beethoven, one must admit that every important musical property of this genre celebrates its resurrection in the music drama, and in such a real sense that these properties appear here for the first time in a completely spotless, as it were transcendent, form.' The symphonies of Schubert, Mendelssohn, Schumann, Brahms – all superfluous and decadent. After Beethoven, the only symphonist is Richard Wagner. The orchestral accompaniment of *Tristan* and the *Nibelungen* completely and transcendently replaces the symphony, which was buried with Beethoven.

We would accord the *Bayreuther Blätter* too much honour or too much importance were we to deem it the sole literary clinic of the Wagner paroxysm. Countless, often quite remarkable, books and brochures exhibit an acute form of the *Blätter*'s disease. We now invite the unprejudiced reader to review the positions himself and to judge whether or not the current idolization of Wagner, in its form and content, should be counted among the epidemic mental illnesses.

1 Hans Wolzogen edited the *Bayreuther Blätter* from 1877 until shortly before his death in 1931.
2 *Musikalische Stationen* (Berlin, 1880), p. 258 (author's note).
3 Wagner was profoundly influenced by Schopenhauer's aesthetic and by his philosophy of pessimism.
4 *Religion und Kunst* (1880) and *Erkenne dich selbst* (1881).
5 The Russian pianist.

44

Vladimir Vasilyevich Stasov, 'Twenty-five Years of Russian Art: Our Music'

Vestnik Evropy (European Journal) (October 1883), from *V. V. Stasov: Selected Essays on Music* (London, 1968), trans. Florence Jonas

No Russian critic was more closely identified with the nationalist school than Stasov (1824–1906). It was he who coined the sobriquet 'Mighty Handful' to describe Balakirev and his circle. In his writings on both art and music, Stasov rejected traditional criteria of beauty and symmetry in favour of the realism exemplified by Mussorgsky (see Cui's review, no. 42). His feuds with Serov (no. 38) were famous. Glazunov wrote a piece in his memory.

Half a century ago the Russians firmly believed that they had already achieved their own national, truly Russian music. The reason for this was that they had a 'national anthem', which had been written on commission by Lvov and was being assiduously disseminated, and also Verstovsky's opera *Askold's Tomb*,[1] whose quasi-gypsy, quasi-popular, melodies (such as 'In the Famous City of Slavyansk' and 'The Goblets Pass Round the Table') excited many listeners. But the belief that these constituted a national music was only an illusion. Neither the anthem nor the opera had any national character, and despite the expectations of the authorities and the public, they did not give rise to any national music or school of composition whatsoever. Both authors were too lacking in national feeling to have initiated such a school; what is more, judging from their compositions, both were completely untalented musicians. The new music and new national school were brought into being not by official prompting or the public's crass taste and enthusiasms; they were born out of the innermost need of the times. Our music followed the same path in the thirties that our literature had during the first quarter of the present century with Krylov, Pushkin and Griboyedov,[2] a path which none of our other arts had as yet embarked on.

At the beginning of the thirties, Glinka went to Italy as if it were a treasure house of the classics from which he might derive all manner of inspiration, enlightenment and learning. He did not find these things there, however. Something totally unexpected happened to him instead. He brought back from Italy, not what he had gone there for, but something entirely different – the idea of a national art, of a Russian music. As he attended the Italian theatres and concert halls, listened to Italian music and famous Italian singers, he suddenly came to feel that this was not what he or his people wanted. He realized that the Italians are one kind of people and we Russians another; that what suits and satisfies them does not suit us. This sudden questioning, this moment of uncertainty about what he had till then so firmly believed in, was the decisive moment in the history of Russian music. Then, for the first time, our music entered upon a genuine, full life of its own. Glinka thought that he was creating only a Russian opera, but he was mistaken. He was laying the foundations of Russian music, of a whole school of Russian music, of a whole new system. In the fifty years that have elapsed since then, our national school has grown and flourished, and has brought forth works of singular beauty, genius, and power ...

What, then, were the forces that produced the special features of our school, the factors that determined its unique development and character?

A primary factor was open-mindedness – the absence of preconceptions and blind faith. Since its very inception, with Glinka, the Russian school has been marked by complete independence in its views and attitudes towards the music of the past. It has never accepted without question the judgments of 'recognized authorities', but has insisted upon verifying everything for itself, on determining for itself whether or not a composer is great and his works important. While such independence of thought is found all too rarely among European musicians even today, it was still rarer fifty years ago. Only a handful of them – men like Schumann, for example – dared to apply their own critical judgment to the established idols. Most of the musicians in the West blindly accept all the opinions of the authorities and share all the tastes and prejudices of the crowd. The new Russian musicians, on the other hand, are dreadfully 'irreverent'. They view traditional attitudes with scepticism and will not value anything they are supposed to until they themselves are persuaded of its worth ...

Further, none of our great musicians, from Glinka on, have ever put much faith in academic training. They have never regarded it with the servility and superstitious awe with which it is regarded even nowadays in many parts of Europe. It would be ridiculous to deny the value of learning in any field, including music, but the new Russian musicians, unfettered by Europe's age-old scholastic tradition, look learning boldly in the eye. They respect it, they avail themselves of its blessings, but they do not exaggerate its importance or genuflect before it. They reject the notion that learning must necessarily be dry and pedantic. They refuse to have anything to do with the academic capers to which thousands of people in Europe attach so much importance. They do not believe that it is necessary to vegetate dutifully for years and years over erudition's ritualistic mysteries ...

Another important distinguishing feature of our school is its constant search for national character. This began with Glinka and has continued uninterruptedly until the present time. No such striving is to be found in any other European school of composition. The historical and cultural conditions of other peoples have been such that folk song – that expression of the simple, spontaneous musicality of the people – has long since all but disappeared in most civilized countries. In the nineteenth century who knows or ever hears French, German, Italian, or English folk songs? There were such songs, of course, and they were once widely sung, but they were mowed down by the levelling scythe of European culture, which is so inimical to all folk art and customs, and nowadays it requires the efforts of musical archaeologists and curious travellers to unearth remnants of them in remote corners of the provinces. In our country it is a completely different matter. Folk songs are heard everywhere even today. Every *muzhik* [peasant], carpenter, bricklayer, doorkeeper, cabman; every peasant woman, laundry-maid and cook, every nurse and wet-nurse – all bring the folk songs of their villages with them to Petersburg, Moscow, to each and every city, and we hear them the whole year round. We are constantly surrounded by them. Every working man and woman in Russia sings endlessly while working, just as their ancestors did a thousand years ago. The Russian soldier goes into battle with a folk song on his lips. This being the case, every musically gifted Russian is surrounded, from the day of his birth, by a truly national music. Moreover, it so happens that almost all of the most important Russian composers – Glinka, Dargomyzhsky, Mussorgsky, Balakirev and Rimsky-Korsakov – were born, not in the capitals, but in provincial towns or on their fathers' estates and they spent all their early years there. The others also spent much of their youth in the provinces, in frequent and close contact with folk songs and folk-singing. Their earliest and most deep-seated musical impressions were derived from folk song. The fact that we were so long in producing an art music of our own was due solely to the unfavourable conditions of Russian life in the eighteenth and nineteenth centuries, when everything national was trampled in the mud. Nevertheless, the need for a national music was so basic and widespread that even during the time of Catherine the Great, a time of courtiers and powdered wigs, one of our composers after another tried to incorporate folk melodies into his poor operas which were patterned on the poor European operas of the day. This is precisely what Verstovsky did later on. Of course, in such cases the folk material appeared in the most unfortunate form, but still it was there, and this, in itself, testified to a need which did not exist among other peoples. No sooner did the times begin to change, however, no sooner did the Russian folk become a topic of discussion in life and literature, no sooner was interest in them rekindled, than gifted people appeared who wanted to create music in the national idioms that were dearest and most congenial to them. No doubt European composers (at least the most gifted of them) would have followed the same path as ours did, beginning with Glinka, but such a path was no longer open to them. Proof of this is the eagerness with which they have always seized upon the folk material of other peoples, even in fragmentary form. We have only to recall, for example, Beethoven's attempts to use Russian folk themes, Schubert's to use Slovak, and Liszt's to use Hungarian. Yet they did not create Russian, Slovak or Hungarian music. For music does not consist of themes alone. To be national, to express the spirit and soul of a people, it must be rooted in the people's life. And neither Beethoven, Schubert nor Liszt immersed himself in the life of the people. They simply took the beautiful gems, the fresh, ever-new and sparkling creations which had been preserved by one or another people, and mounted them in the setting of European art music. They never immersed themselves in the world from which these exquisite fragments came; they only chanced upon them, toyed with them, admired their beauty, and displayed them, brilliantly illumined by their own talent. The situation of the Russian composers was entirely different. They were not guests, they were 'at home' in the world in which our folk melodies, indeed all Slavic melodies, originated, and therefore they were able to use them freely, to present them in their true colouring, flavour and character. Today Glinka's achievement is universally known and recognized. He blazed a new trail; he created a national opera in a manner not to be found anywhere else in Europe. His successors followed in his footsteps, guided by his brilliant example and initiative.

Along with the Russian folk-song element there is another which distinguishes the new Russian school of composition. This is the Oriental element. Nowhere in Europe does it play such a prominent role as it does in the works of our composers. At one time or another every truly talented European architect, sculptor and painter has tried to reproduce the unique forms of the East. Thus far only the musicians have lagged far behind their fellow artists. Mozart, Beethoven, Weber and certain others, who wrote pieces 'alla turca,' made a few attempts to incorporate something Eastern, but their efforts only demonstrated their interest in this element. They were never really successful. Félicien David, who lived in the East,[3] introduced several *truly* Eastern melodies into his symphonic ode *Le Désert*, but he had little talent and produced nothing of importance. It was a completely different matter with the new Russian musicians. Some of them visited the East (both Glinka and Balakirev spent some time in the Caucasus), and although the others never actually went there they were exposed to Eastern influences all their lives, and therefore were able to reproduce them vividly and clearly. They shared the interest which Russians in general have in everything Eastern. This is hardly surprising, since so much of the East has always been an integral part of Russian life and has given it such a special, distinctive colouring ...

Finally, there is one other feature which strongly characterizes the Russian school of music – that is, its strong predilection for 'programme music' ... Virtually all Russian symphonic music is programmatic, as the following account will show. It is quite clear that the propensity for this kind of music is much stronger in our country than almost anywhere else in Europe.

These, then, are the principal characteristics of the Russian school of music. In noting them, I have not meant to suggest that our school is superior to other European schools – that would be stupid and ridiculous. Each nation has its own great men and its own great achievements. It is only that I felt it necessary to define the special features of our school's character and tendencies which, of course, are very interesting and important ...

1 Aleksei Verstovsky's opera had its première in St Petersburg in 1835.
2 The fabulist Ivan Krylov, the poet Aleksandr Pushkin, and the statesman and poet Aleksandr Griboyedov were leading figures in Russian literature in the early 1800s.
3 David spent two years in the Near East in the early 1830s. *Le Désert* was first performed in Paris in 1844.

45

Hugo Wolf, 'Haydn's *Creation*'

Wiener Salonblatt (15 November 1885), from *The Music Criticisms of Hugo Wolf* (New York, 1978), trans. Henry Pleasants

Wolf (1860–1903) was virtually unknown when he began writing criticism for the *Wiener Salonblatt*, a weekly paper popular with the Viennese aristocracy, in 1884. His intemperate attacks on philistinism and conservatism – which earned him the enmity of Hanslick (see no. 43) – and his equally passionate defence of Wagner, Liszt, Berlioz and Bruckner won Wolf a notoriety which did no harm to his composing career. This is his contribution to the debate on 'programme' music.

The Creation by Haydn. What a spirit of childlike faith speaks from the heavenly pure tones of Haydn's music! Sheer nature, artlessness, perception, and sensitivity! It is the mark of his greatness as an artist that when we hear his music we are utterly unaware of the art, and yet what a variety of musical structures encloses his charming tonal pictures!

His extraordinarily keen artistic perception is most conspicuously evident in the field of tone painting, much cultivated in recent times, and now falling into disrepute. And, indeed, we would shudder at the very thought of what a modern composer might do in the handling – or mishandling – of a subject offering such opportunities for tone painting as *The Creation* or *The Seasons*. There would be so much depiction that we would hear no music. If a modern composer wished, for example, to illustrate chaos, it is certain that we would encounter no triad, unless possibly an augmented one. It would probably fall to a perfect fifth to defray the musical expenses of such a vision.

(If we could suppose that the good Lord had consecutive fifths ringing in his ears at his first glimpse of chaos, then it would follow that justified self-defence rather than wantonness or malice, as some philosophers have suggested, prompted his desperate decision, in the ridiculously short span of seven days, to inflict so much evil upon the world. An ordinary piece of cotton wool, to be sure, could have rendered the same service, but there were no trees at that time, nor plantation owners. The cotton wool industry still dreamt peacefully in the womb of chaos, and Jaeger shirts rightly were still a chimera. O, happy days of chaos!)

Still, one could live with this diabolical expressive device if only that had been the end of it, for today dissonances and shrill instrumental effects fall like hail about our ears, and the orchestra moans and groans until one is ready to believe that chaos has become a wild beast with a toothache. If a composer's intention was, indeed, to portray the tumbling about of contentious air currents, or the hissing ascent of a fiery rocket, or some other natural phenomenon, his motives may have been of the best, but he has achieved nothing, and we retain, moreover, a very low opinion of his good intentions.

To such extremes can confusion go, however, when tone painting is so dominated by the purely external, that from all the atmospheric no atmosphere emerges, no mood, and from all the characterization no character. There is always the occasional detail, but never an effective whole. How different was Haydn's procedure. Just look at chaos in his *Creation*. The very first measures, with the muted violins, awoke in us the sensation of being in the presence of a mysterious something. A magician, he evokes the sombre picture of chaos. Gray fogbanks roll slowly on in disordered masses, illuminated by iridescent lights. Listen! What manner of voices were those, cries of distress and despair, gently solemn strains? They intertwine, dissolve, melt away. Another apparition emerges from the darkness, radiant in magical beauty. The soul thrills at the sight of this enchanting phantom. With serene movement it pursues its course. It drifts upward. The atmosphere is suffused with deep red. It falters, falls – a flash of lightning out of the black abyss – and the apparition has vanished. Seas of mist again envelop the richly coloured scene. The tone poet has awakened from his dream.

That is, to be sure, a pitiful sketch compared with the fantastic world conjured up by the tone poet in his prophetic vision. But had Haydn wished to turn into music exactly what he had seen, one may assume with reasonable certainty that his chaos would have remained the more unintelligble in just the same degree that it speaks the more intelligibly to us now. Why? Because the composer has given us not his vision, but rather the impression made by the vision upon his musical sensibility[1] …

1 Compare Rousseau's famous lines, cited by Castil-Blaze (no. 27).

46

Leoš Janáček, [*Carmen* and *The Bridegrooms*]

Hudebni listy (15 January 1887), from *Janáček's Uncollected Essays on Music* (London, 1989), trans. Mirka Zemanová

Like Smetana (see no. 37), Janáček (1854–1928) fought a lifelong battle to establish an indigenous Czech music. In 1884 he became editor of the journal *Hudebni listy*, published by the Beseda choral society, but his progressive views offended many of the society's members and he relinquished the post after four years. This brief review illustrates his outspoken, telegraphic style.

Carmen with Miss Wollnerova! The low and the middle registers of a contralto stand out so much because of their fullness and sweetness that it is difficult for a soprano to compete. Since the part of Carmen is largely placed in this most effective compass of the contralto or, if you like, mezzo-soprano, even celebrated singers avoid Carmen. Miss Wollnerova, however, commands a sonorous organ precisely in the range b–a', and sings the high notes with natural ease. And because she devotes much care to details, and working out the acting, the success was certainly greater than with the previous cast. We do not deny, however, the 'glowing fire' in the acting and singing of the engaging Miss Maxantova.

Have you ever fixed your eyes on the sunset, burning with a thousand colours? Have you ever trembled with awe at the strength and grandeur of a storm? Have you never been dazzled by the distinctness, clarity and purpose of every fold in the shape of a beautiful statue?

These qualities are the reason why they make such an indelible impression.

When musical works distinguish themselves through such qualities, they do not fade from memory. If, at the time of hearing, they stand out because of their originality, they will imprint themselves on the memory with particular strength, since the agitation in our soul in this case is especially lively. Original music refreshes us, warms us; originality in beautiful forms victoriously forces a path for itself.

The theatre bill for 8 January of this year reads:

An original novelty

First time

The Bridegrooms

A comic opera, etc., music by

Karel Kovařovic[1]

(Given at the National Theatre, Prague, with brilliant success.)

'Which tune has stuck in your mind?' ' – ' 'Which motif, at least?' ' – ' 'In what way is this opera dramatic?' 'I would not say "an opera, music by", but "with music accompanying a comedy by Machaček, etc."'

'The libretto and the music are independent of each other. Write a new operetta to the former, and for music – a drama of a sort, full of awful gloom, desperate cries, a drama stuck through with daggers.'

Hence this strange phenomenon: Machaček's (rather than Kovařovic's) *Bridegrooms* makes you break into laughter several times.

'Musical talent is borne out in the overture, and the undulations of chords and keys: this is what will properly deafen you.'

1 Karel Kovařovic, composer of *The Bridegrooms* (1884), became opera conductor at the National Theatre in 1900. Three years later the theatre turned down Janáček's *Jenufa*, possibly as a result of this scathing review.

47

Camille Bellaigue, 'Boredom in Music'

Revue des deux mondes (28 April 1888), from *L'Année musicale, Octobre 1887 à Octobre 1888* (Paris, 1889)

Bellaigue (1858–1930) had a distinguished career as critic for the *Revue des deux mondes* from 1885 until shortly before his death. Although he was generally conservative and opposed Wagner and Debussy, Bellaigue's magisterial judgments carried great authority. Max Graf regarded him as an exponent of the French academic style. This article, by contrast, shows him in a whimsical and irreverent mood.

We talk about religion, nature and love in music. Why not talk about boredom? Not the boredom music expresses, but the boredom it inspires. Music is one of the most frequent and dreaded sources of boredom, one of the most active agents of that state of the soul which, depending on the causes that produce it and the natures that experience it, manifests itself in melancholy, sadness and dejection, or in nervous illnesses, irritation, despair and frenzy.

Nothing is more boring than boring music, that's for sure. In the first place, art, being a luxury, does not and must not tolerate mediocrity. Unlike the lawyer, doctor or notary, the artist can't excuse himself on the grounds that his services are necessary. Notaries, for example, can be quite stupid (I'm even told that a few are) because the world positively needs them, imbeciles or not. On the other hand, nothing in the world is less indispensable than mediocre artists.

That's not all: of all the arts, music is the most capable of boring, because music is noise and disagreeable noise is an odious thing. At least the other arts are silent. Besides, you can put down a volume of poetry or turn your eyes away from a statue or a picture, but you can't escape music. A concert or opera piece, a singer, a pianist thrust themselves upon you. To a certain extent, music compels attention; sometimes it won't even let you sleep. No art yields such delights as well as such torments ...

At the end of a Parisian winter, you understand what boredom in music is and how to measure it! Like a far-away mist, it drifts down on to many of the pieces you've heard. Impartial, eclectic, it is associated with music of the most disparate schools. There is German boredom, big, pedantic and pretentious; Italian boredom, better behaved but coarse and vulgar; and French boredom, small, shabby and bourgeois. There are the boredom of the dead and the boredom of the living, the boredom of the theatre and the boredom of concerts, public boredom and private boredom, boredom by orchestral music and boredom by chamber music, boredom by works and boredom by men, by music and by musicians. Ah, it would take more than an article or two to do justice to the subject; it would take a treatise, an encyclopedia ... Some musicians are boring all the time, some are merely boring occasionally (they are the very great ones). No musicians, however, are never boring.

Of all the third-rate composers, the most boring may well be Hummel,[1] the master of what is called, in a deceptive euphemism, 'well-made' music. One day, after Hummel had been improvising for a quarter of an hour, someone asked bluntly: 'Now then, when are you going to begin?' He never should have begun. Hummel's is an extreme version of classic boredom: serious, honourable boredom. Hummel had everything the great masters had – everything except genius. No one could go on as long as he could without saying anything; no one could beat him at making symmetrical compositions of empty, pointless formulas: pianistic flourishes, scales in thirds and sixths, decorously insipid variations. Hummel was a poet without ideas, though he had beautiful handwriting.

After him comes a musician who was at least second-rate; a few men and all women even say he's first-rate: Chopin. He was the musician of the piano *par excellence*; therein lie both his originality and his inferiority. It's impossible to write with impunity for an instrument like the piano without lapsing into a mechanical display of technique. Chopin is a melancholy dreamer, a marvellous improviser, the most sentimental of composers. He gave poetry to the dry sonorities of the piano, mellowness to the classic phrase. He came up with a few melodies that were admirable and many that were charming. But listen to some of his works, especially the E minor Concerto, which M. Planté[2] played so artfully at the Conservatoire on Holy Thursday: it's enough to make you weep with boredom. Let's not talk about the orchestra – Chopin never came to terms with it – but the piano itself! He takes an elegant or touching phrase and then proceeds to drown it in a flood of notes. What useless babbling, what intolerable festooning of every melody with trills, *grupetti*, scales, ornaments of every kind. Chopin couldn't say anything the way everyone else did. He had to add a gewgaw or a grace note before or after every phrase, every note. Every bar of his music stumbles and stammers. This elegiac Slav would have bedecked the Venus de Milo with pompoms ...

The greatest of the great musicians, the one without whom music would not exist, the founder, the patriarch, the father, the Abraham, the Noah, the Adam of music – Johann Sebastian Bach – may be the most boring of them all. Handel only comes in second place. If Bach's were the only music in the world, I would admire it deeply and study it assiduously, but I'd hardly love it. If there were no other concerts besides the Rhine Festivals, where the oratorios by the master of Eisenach are played each and every year, I'd never go to a concert.

Bach's massive *oeuvre* is the foundation, the cornerstone of all music; all the rest is built upon it and could not have been built without it. But are the foundations the most beautiful part of a building? Bach is the great original. When he appeared, music had yet to be made; he made it. The notes were scarcely acquainted with one another; it was he, I tell you, who made them acquainted. He introduced them to one another, in so many ways that all at once harmony was created, and today you can scarcely find any combinations that the wise old man didn't find ...

Yet when rejoicing and emotion, not work and exercise, are what you need, read a Bach suite, that is, a prelude, an allemande, one or two courantes, plus some bourrées, gigues and sarabandes. Read one of his concertos, especially the concerto for three pianos (frightful trinity!). Read (I shudder at my blasphemy) the *Saint Matthew Passion*! For ten minutes you are astounded; after fifteen you are enraged. Even so does the traveller, in a gallery surrounded by Cranachs, van Eycks and Memlings, yearn for Rubens's *Descent from the Cross*.

How many times, in the bosom of one of these massive oratorios, of these choruses or double choruses with orchestra and organs, crushed by the relentless, four-square rhythms, lost in that sonorous algebra, in that living geometry, smothered in the folds of those interminable fugues – how many times have you wished to close your ears to these prodigious combinations and listen to the quiet lyricism of the Andante of Mozart's Clarinet Quintet, or to the Allegretto of his A major Symphony. Bach never – almost never – wrote tunes like these. Conversely, Beethoven and Mozart almost never wrote his beloved fugues; when they did write them, it was a mistake. In Mozart's Requiem and Beethoven's Mass in D, the academic passages are far from being the most touching ...

Fugue, alas, is not the only source of musical boredom. There exists, from the hand of a master who was great in another way than Bach, the greatest of all masters, one of the greatest of all men, not a symphony but part of a symphony which we have heard ten, fifteen times, always with respect, with good will – and always with boredom. It is ... well, yes, one must have the courage of one's convictions, be they right or wrong; one must speak up, albeit like Balaam's ass.³ It is ... the finale of the *Choral* Symphony.⁴

Horror! you say. *That* finale! But it's the starting point, the dawn of music, of true music, music of the future; it's the beginning. Perhaps – but the beginning of the end ...

To conclude this litany of aesthetic scandal, must I name the great man (a very great man, to be sure: so don't stone me to death!) who may have done the most to push back the frontiers of boredom in music, who opened immense new horizons; the master, the pope – the intolerant, fanatical pope – the grand inquisitor of boredom?

Whether you admire or detest him, Wagner does nothing by halves. And Wagner's boredom has a special something: it is aggressive and wicked. Here is boredom which doesn't let you sleep, which makes you suffer almost physically, which enervates, irritates, drives you crazy ...

What's more, Wagner isn't just boring; he can be ludicrous – ludicrous in the German manner. His childishness is colossal, his humour ponderous. Oh, the role of Mime in the tetralogy: fine words from a frightful hunchback, insipid contortions of a foetus of the North! Oh, the aquarium of *Rheingold*, the virginal naiveté of Siegfried, a baby-faced colossus who dances with bears and fights with smoking dragons! Oh, Beckmesser's shouts in the fault-finding machine in the first act of *Meistersinger*!⁵ And family life in the Gibichungs' palace! And Wotan's conversations with Erda, and the trio of Norns winding the rope of destinies, and Fasolt and Fafner, and the evaluation of the goddess Freia, and Fricka's goat-drawn carriage – carnival mythology, Mardi Gras Olympus! And the unbearable leitmotivs, music by the kilometre, acts lasting two hours, that frightful drivel, that heaviness, the slowness which drives you to despair and exasperation! And the dismay, or rather the irritation, to think that the creator of so much nonsense is also the creator of so many marvels!

Boredom of originals and progressives, boredom of cantatas, oratorios, concertos and fugues, boredom of long-hairs and low-brows, boredom of classics and romantics, boredom of the dead whom we have just examined and of the living whom we are going to examine now – assemble, all of you, and you won't come close to this boredom! ...

1 The pianist and composer Johann Nepomuk Hummel.
2 The pianist Francis Planté.
3 The biblical donkey who rebuked his master for cursing the Israelites.
4 The Finale of Beethoven's Ninth was a perennial bone of contention, as we have seen (e.g., no. 21).
5 In the contest, Beckmesser sits behind a screen and tallies the singers' mistakes. The shouts are his protests at Walther's performance.

48

Willy (Henry Gauthier-Villars), ['A Mishmash of Eroticism and Prayer']

Art et critique (2 February 1890), from *Lettres de l'ouvreuse* (Paris, 1890)

One of the outstanding literary music critics of the nineteenth century was Henry Gauthier-Villars, known as Willy (1859–1931), whose sparkling wit and irreverence capture the spirit of the *Belle Epoque*. Much of his criticism was couched in the form of letters to the editor of *Art et critique*, which he signed 'a worker of the Cirque d'Eté'. Of his alter ego, Willy wrote: 'In music, he posseses only deliciously vague notions and conscientiously flies into ecstasy over modulations which exist only inside his skull.' In 1893 he married the writer Colette, and it has been claimed that she and others ghost-wrote many of his articles.

Jules Massenet[1] is the flavour of the week. Our subscribers have just been served up a 'selection' from *Esclarmonde*. The young member of the Institut[2] hasn't always been so popular with the boss. A trilogy *(ohne Vorabend)*[3] could be written about Jules's relationship with ... (I still can't call him Arthur!)[4] – with the boss, if you like. Day one: a photograph of Jules, hung in the master's office and inscribed with a flattering dedication. Day two: the reign of Wagner and d'Indy; Massenet bitter: 'When it comes to French musicians, Lamoureux only plays the ones who make German music.' Day three: *Le Dernier Sommeil de la Vierge,*[5] ecstatically conducted by Lamoureux, who was kicking Marty[6] around as he waited. It was a fine spring morning ... (Hartmann,[7] editor).

I won't pretend to teach you *Esclarmonde*, monsieur le Directeur. If I know any more about it than our performance revealed, I owe it to a nice, indiscreet companion – from the Opéra Comique. It's a kind of musical Bottin,[8] a *History of the Century* in which all the Gervexes[9] of harmony seem to have had a hand, an end-of-year review for some higher Cluny, where all the masters are represented, from Meyerbeer to Wagner, from Gounod to Massenet himself (for that clever fellow excels in the art of warming up his own leftovers). It's rampant eclecticism, impartiality to the nth degree in style and formulas.

Inside, mark you, there's a devil of a talent, a disconcerting facility and ease. And allusions running full throttle. In *Le Roi de Lahore*, that old softy Massenet orchestrated the beautiful classic 'Champagne is the wine of women, Clicquot the wine of loves'. This time he's conscientiously robbed great Richard's wine cellars. There are enough leitmotivs to put you off the system for good! No sooner have they left than they return, undistortable, incompressible, unbreakable. You want to call in the exterminator.

What a strange musician he is, this Wagner for courtesans, this boudoir mystic, who takes a sweet and awe-inspiring subject and turns it into the boring, false, unseemly *Marie Magdeleine*, with the connivance of Gallet, the male midwife![10] And yet, how talented he is, the sly old fox! How many truly welcome pages there are in *Le Roi de Lahore* and in *Esclarmonde* itself! Now and then subtle harmonies make exquisite dissonances; now and then, for a few bars, a felicitous melodic idea takes shape. But it's not for this that he's loved, not for this that so many lovely hands make their gloves snap with applause and so many fair and noble gentlewomen compose operas under his name. He's loved because his music has the vicious sentimentality which pleases our *demi-mondaines* (and even, Jodelet[11] would say, our real *mondaines*); because it has poetic charm, the ambiguous religiosity which teases the public's impotence. Women cherish Massenet's signature as they do Redfern's in a related order of ideas. This mishmash of ladybirds and chapels, of worldliness and illusion, of eroticism and prayer, enchants the smart young things of the Third Republic. His orchestration offers the same studied *mélange* of apples and oranges. Born of the unnatural marriage of a cello and a bass drum, it squanders its energies on romances on the A string – when it doesn't end in an unspeakable racket.

And yet, one must be grateful to Jules for having composed *Esclarmonde*, after the abominations of *Hérodiade* and *Le Cid*. Moreover, one must set aside certain artistic aversions, enter into the composer's mind, and understand that this academician is practically *alone* – you understand – in clearly grasping the evolution of the public, following it and, when necessary, giving it a nudge. Wonderfully adaptable, he constructs his works in such a way as to offer something to please the imbeciles and something to hold the attention of the fastidious, if only momentarily. He knows his Wagner; to a certain extent, he makes the masses ready for it. At least he'll never be trapped in musical obscurity, in the dead-ends that lure artists who are too naive and shallow. Amidst countless platitudes, he has written *Le Roi de Lahore*, *Manon*, *Esclarmonde*, which mark three stages. Let us be on guard!

Let me mention in passing an excellent performance of the trio of the young Ishmaelites in *L'Enfance du Christ* by Berlioz. What a chaste and sweet melody! Berlioz, eager to write a 'song of the hearth' in which childhood's virginal peacefulness would piously shine in all its ancient simplicity, chose light, pure timbres, devoid of passionate colour, white, airy, ingenuous – those of the flute and harp. Are these not, moreover, the true instruments of yore? That touching passage, full of tender genius, charmed me deliciously; it was done to a tee, but I couldn't help thinking that Hennebains, Lafleurance and Franck were a little long in the tooth for young Ishmaelites.

A thousand stars were shining in the firmament of the concert-hall promenade; but, not to keep tiring you with the same names, I'll tell you about the Châtelet, where my little companion says she saw bald-pated Albert Bataille,[12] the fickle *figariste*, who praises *Lohengrin* and *Meistersinger* and despises the *Ring of the Nibelung*; Mariotti, gloomy cellist; Adrien Remacle, athletic and Apollonian ... Mme Krauss[13] [sic] sang Hatred's marvellous aria from *Armide* ... Oh! the man from Reyssouze,[14] that you weren't there to strew flowers on your beautiful ruin! You know, her voice gets shakier every day, but even so she has style, and that's rare. Edouard's[15] horns weren't brassy enough and the attacks weren't incisive enough ... but what music! I'd trade M. Gounod for the simple minor second in the violins at the heart-rending words: 'Sauve-moi de l'Amour!'

Several people were stricken by a sudden outbreak of cholera and had to be carried out during the concert. M. Pasteur, summoned hastily, discovered the microbe in the folds of a concerto by Godard,[16] brusquely projected into the hall by the violinist Johannès Wolff. The victims' condition offers little hope.

1 Although he is remembered today chiefly for *Werther* and *Manon*, Massenet was second only to Gounod in popularity in late nineteenth-century France. Among his other operas are *Esclarmonde* (1889), *Le Roi de Lahore* (1877), *Hérodiade* (1881) and *Le Cid* (1885).

2 The Institut Nationale de Musique.

3 'Without a preliminary evening,' as Wagner called *Das Rheingold*.

4 To understand this aside, the reader is informed that the director of the Nouveaux Concerts had expressed the desire no longer to be designated by his baptismal name (author's note). [An oblique reference to Charles Lamoureux, who founded the Société des Nouveaux Concerts in 1881. – Ed.]

5 A popular orchestral piece from Massenet's 'sacred legend' *La Vierge*.

6 Georges Marty, conductor and composer of, among other things, *Matinée de printemps* (Spring morning).

7 Georges Hartmann, the librettist of Massenet's *Werther* and *Hérodiade*.

8 An annual of current events.

9 Henri Gervex, the impressionist painter.

10 Louis Gallet, the librettist of Massenet's oratorio *Marie Magdeleine* (1873).

11 The comic actor Julien Bedeau, known as Jodelet, was a member of Molière's troupe.

12 Albert Bataille was law correspondent of the newspaper *Le Figaro*.

13 Gabrielle Krause, the Austrian soprano.

14 Lully, presumably.

15 Edouard Colonne, conductor and founder of the Concert National.

16 The *Concerto romantique* for violin and orchestra by Benjamin Godard, best known for the Berceuse from his opera *Jocelyn*.

49

Paul Dukas, 'The Debussy Quartet'

Revue des deux mondes (May 1894), from *Les Ecrits de Paul Dukas sur la musique* (Paris, 1948)

Dukas (1865–1935) is best known today for his opera *Ariane et Barbe-Bleue* and his orchestral tour de force *The Sorcerer's Apprentice*. His writing about music, most of which dates from the 1890s, shows that he was a perceptive and fair-minded critic as well. Dismissive of Wagner's many imitators, and wary of Strauss's programmatic innovations, he was an early champion of Debussy. This article casts a rather new light on the much-discussed issue of 'absolute' music.

The chamber music performance given the other day by M. de Guarniéri, with the assistance of MM. Henri Falke, Lammers, Ruffin and Kerrion, ranked among the most interesting of the season. Besides the quintet by César Franck, destined to be a classic, and a sonata for cello and piano by M. Edvard Grieg, we heard a quartet by M. C.-A. Debussy which, among recent works of this genre, is certainly one of the most deserving of capturing the attention of connoisseurs ...

The general observations we made some time ago about the symphony are equally applicable to the quartet and to pure music of every sort. The dramatic tendencies music has evinced since Beethoven's day are undeniable, it's true; but once again we say that it would be excessively pedantic, when contemplating a strong or simply attractive work from the hand of an original artist, to cling to the theoretical viewpoint that Wagner once adopted, for reasons both temperamental and strategic, and to repeat, more or less blindly, things he declared merely in order to shore up his convictions as a musical dramatist. Whatever people say, think, or write, some artists will always be more exclusively musicians than others. It must be admitted that if one of these artists, motivated by a sincere impulse alien to systematic thinking, writes an original work, it's both absurd and mean-spirited to condemn it in the name of an abstract principle. This principle is already sufficiently condemned by the very *existence* of the work it proscribes.

M. Debussy, one of the most richly endowed and original artists of the new musical generation, unquestionably belongs to the class of composers who see music not as a means but as an end, and who consider it less as a catalyst of expression than as expression itself. It's a lyric, in the full sense of the word. If he is setting a fixed text, he doesn't so much try to make it the master of his thought as to note down, in a kind of personal paraphrase, the musical impressions suggested by his reading of the poem. Given his particular spiritual make-up, one imagines that M. Debussy came to pure music quite naturally after composing several collections of delectably beautiful songs and a highly original poem for soloists, chorus and orchestra on Dante Gabriel Rossetti's *Demoiselle élue* – in spite of the operatic training inflicted uniformly on all aspirants to the Rome Prize at his alma mater, the Conservatoire.

A three-part fantasy for piano and orchestra and the quartet about which we are going to speak are the first fruits of the new direction his ideas have taken.

M. Debussy's quartet is a work in which intensity of colouring at first seems to predominate over expression, strictly speaking. But that's only an illusion. By our own definition of M. Debussy's temperament, he intends to convey musical sentiments and nothing else, unlike many composers, for whom music is only a more vehement way of expressing general impressions and thoughts. A superficial listener might be led to believe that M. Debussy's music means nothing, but in this he would be extraordinarily mistaken. For if one finds in the quartet in question neither the incisive accents nor the quasi-dramatic development sections which are so common with other composers and which bear out Wagner's theory, if the meaning of M. Debussy's work is purely musical, does that make it devoid of meaning? It does – if one concedes that tremolos and diminished sevenths have a monopoly on expression. But not if one thinks, on the contrary, that instrumental music is an end in itself and that, far from trying to invest itself with a meaning that's more or less foreign, it must move us without straying from its own domain. We know that this was Mozart's professed opinion.[1] For him, music always had to remain music, whatever it intended to express. Recently the Russian school has adopted the same principle. M. Debussy, paradoxical though our claim may seem to him, in this respect appears to us to belong to the school of Mozart. He belongs to it to the same extent as Weber, Chopin and Schumann belonged to it, and in general all the masters who regard the exaggerated dramatization of music with something like horror. Beethoven's progeny are a different kettle of fish: most of them have shown the opposite tendency. Uneasy with pure music that lacks precise meaning, they have always tried to pin down the sense of the symphonic works they admired. Berlioz and Wagner, for instance.

M. Debussy's quartet bears the stamp of his style. Everything is clear and cleanly laid out, despite great freedom of form. The melodic essence is concentrated but richly flavourful, imbuing the harmonic tissue with a penetrating and original poetry. The harmony is never harsh or austere, despite some very bold strokes. M. Debussy takes particular delight in rich sequences of chords, in dissonances without crudity, more harmonious in their intricacies than consonances themselves. On them his melody treads as if on a sumptuous carpet with sophisticated patterns and exotic colours from which all shrill and discordant tones have been banished.

A single theme serves as the basis of all the work's movements. Some of its transformations are particularly captivating in their unexpected grace – for example, the one in the middle of the Scherzo (this movement is merely an ingenious variation of the main theme). Nothing could be more charming than the expressive return of the rhythmic theme accompanied by the gentle sighing of the passagework in the second violin and viola, and by the cello's pizzicati. If we had to name our favourites among the four movements, we would choose the first piece and the Andante, music of truly exquisite poetry and supreme delicacy of thought ...

---

1 See, e.g., Mozart's oft-quoted letter to his father of 13 October 1781, in which he writes that 'in an opera the poetry must be altogether the obedient daughter of the music'.

50

George Bernard Shaw, [Wagner as a Dramatic Poet]

World (17 January 1894)

Although his career as a professional musical journalist covered less than five years, Shaw (1856–1950) is generally regarded as one of the greatest critics in the English language. Of his contemporaries, perhaps only Hanslick (see no. 43) was his peer in terms of authority and influence; but Shaw's combination of musical knowledge, literary virtuosity and tweakish impudence was unique. This view of Wagner's operatic 'reforms' shows him in characteristically lively and combative form.

It is not often that one comes across a reasonable book about music, much less an entertaining one. Still, I confess to having held out with satisfaction to the end of M. Georges Noufflard's Richard Wagner d'après lui-même (Paris, Fischbacher, 2 vols., at 3.50 fr. apiece). Noufflard is so exceedingly French a Frenchman that he writes a preface to explain that though he admires Wagner, still Alsace and Lorraine must be given back; and when he records an experiment of his hero's in teetotalism, he naively adds, 'What is still more surprising is that this unnatural regime, instead of making Wagner ill, operated exactly as he had expected.' More Parisian than this an author can hardly be; and yet Noufflard always understands the Prussian composer's position, and generally agrees with him, though, being racially out of sympathy with him, he never entirely comprehends him. He is remarkably free from the stock vulgarities of French operatic culture: for instance, he washes his hands of Meyerbeer most fastidiously; and he puts Gluck, the hero of French musical classicism, most accurately in his true place.

And here let me give a piece of advice to readers of books about Wagner. Whenever you come to a statement that Wagner was an operatic reformer, and that in this capacity he was merely following in the footsteps of Gluck, who had anticipated some of his most important proposals, you may put your book in the waste-paper basket, as far as Wagner is concerned, with absolute confidence. Gluck was an opera composer who said to his contemporaries:

'Gentlemen, let us compose our operas more rationally. An opera is not a stage concert, as most of you seem to think. Let us give up our habit of sacrificing our common sense to the vanity of our singers, and let us compose and orchestrate our airs, our duets, our recitatives, and our sinfonias in such a way that they shall always be appropriate to the dramatic situation given to us by the librettist.' And having given this excellent advice, he proceeded to shew how it could be followed. How well he did this we can judge, in spite of our scandalous ignorance of Gluck, from Orfeo, with which Giulia Ravogli has made us familiar lately.

When Wagner came on the scene, exactly a hundred years later, he found that the reform movement begun by Gluck had been carried to the utmost limits of possibility by Spontini, who told him flatly that after La Vestale, etc., there was nothing operatic left to be done.[1] Wagner quite agreed with him, and never had the smallest intention of beginning the reform of opera over again at the very moment when it had just been finished. On the contrary, he took the fully reformed opera, with all its improvements, and asked the nineteenth century to look calmly at it and say whether all this patchwork of stage effects on a purely musical form had really done anything for it but expose the absurd unreality of its pretence to be a form of drama, and whether, in fact, Rossini had not shewn sound common sense in virtually throwing over that pretence and, like Gluck's Italian contemporaries, treating an opera as a stage concert. The nineteenth century took a long time to make up its mind on the question, which it was at first perfectly incapable of understanding. Verdi and Gounod kept on trying to get beyond Spontini on operatic lines, without the least success, except on the purely musical side; and Gounod never gave up the attempt, though Verdi did.

Meanwhile, however, Wagner, to shew what he meant, abandoned operatic composition altogether, and took to writing dramatic poems, and using all the resources of orchestral harmony and vocal tone to give them the utmost reality and intensity of expression, thereby producing the new art form which he called 'music-drama,' which is no more 'reformed opera' than a cathedral is a reformed stone quarry. The whole secret of the amazing futility of the first attempts at Wagner criticism is the mistaking of this new form for an improved pattern of the old one. Once you conceive

Wagner as the patentee of certain novel features in operas and librettos, you can demolish him point by point with impeccable logic, and without the least misgiving that you are publicly making a ludicrous exhibition of yourself.

The process is fatally easy, and consists mainly in shewing that the pretended novelties of reformed opera are no novelties at all. The 'leading motives,' regarded as operatic melodies recurring in connection with the entry of a certain character, are as old as opera itself; the instrumentation, regarded merely as instrumentation, is no better than Mozart's and much more expensive; whereas of those features that really tax the invention of the operatic composer, the airs, the duos, the quartets, the cabalettas to display the virtuosity of the trained Italian singer, the dances, the marches, the choruses, and so on, there is a deadly dearth, their place being taken by – of all things – an interminable dull recitative.

The plain conclusion follows that Wagner was a barren rascal whose whole reputation rested on a shop-ballad, O star of eve, and a march which he accidentally squeezed out when composing his interminable Tannhäuser. And so you go on, wading with fatuous self-satisfaction deeper and deeper into a morass of elaborately rea- soned and highly conscientious error. You need fear nothing of this sort from Noufflard. He knows perfectly well the difference between music-drama and opera; and the result is that he not only does not tumble into blind hero-worship of Wagner, but is able to criticize him – a thing the blunderers never could do. Some of his criticisms: for example, his observation that in Wagner's earlier work the melody is by no means so original as Weber's, are indis- putable – indeed he might have said Meyerbeer or anybody else; for Wagner's melody was never original at all in that sense, any more than Giotto's figures are picturesque or Shakespear's lines elegant.

But I entirely – though quite respectfully – dissent from Noufflard's suggestion that in composing Tristan Wagner turned his back on the theoretic basis of Siegfried, and returned to 'absolute music.' It is true, as Noufflard points out, that in Tristan, and even in Der Ring itself, Wagner sometimes got so rapt from the objective drama that he got away from the words too, and in Tristan came to writing music without coherent words at all. But wordless music is not absolute music. Absolute music is the purely decorative sound pattern: tone poetry is the musical expression of poetic feeling. When Tristan gives musical expression to an excess of feeling for which he can find no coherent words, he is no more uttering absolute music than the shepherd who carries on the drama at one of its most deeply felt passages by playing on his pipe.

Wagner regarded all Beethoven's important instrumental works as tone poems; and he himself, though he wrote so much for the orchestra alone in the course of his music-dramas, never wrote, or could write, a note of absolute music. The fact is, there is a great deal of feeling, highly poetic and highly dramatic, which cannot be expressed by mere words – because words are the counters of thinking, not of feeling – but which can be supremely expressed by music. The poet tries to make words serve his purpose by arranging them musically, but is hampered by the certainty of becoming absurd if he does not make his musically arranged words mean something to the intellect as well as to the feeling.

For example, the unfortunate Shakespear could not make Juliet say:

O Romeo, Romeo, Romeo, Romeo, Romeo;

and so on for twenty lines. He had to make her, in an extremity of unnaturalness, begin to argue the case in a sort of amatory legal fashion, thus:

O Romeo, Romeo, wherefore art thou Romeo?

Deny thy father and refuse thy name,

Or, if thou wilt not, etc., etc., etc.

It is verbally decorative, but it is not love. And again:

Parting is such sweet sorrow

That I shall say good-night till it be morrow;

which is a most ingenious conceit, but one which a woman would no more utter at such a moment than she would prove the rope ladder to be the shortest way out because any two sides of a triangle are together greater than the third.

Now these difficulties do not exist for the tone poet. He can make Isolde say nothing but 'Tristan, Tristan, Tristan, Tristan, Tristan,' and Tristan nothing but 'Isolde, Isolde, Isolde, Isolde,

Isolde,' to their hearts' content without creating the smallest demand for more definite explanations; and as for the number of times a tenor and soprano can repeat 'Addio, addio, addio,' there is no limit to it. There is a great deal of this reduction of speech to mere ejaculation in Wagner; and it is a reduction directly pointed to in those very pages of Opera and Drama which seem to make the words all-important by putting the poem in the first place as the seed of the whole music-drama, and yet make a clean sweep of nine-tenths of the dictionary by insisting that it is only the language of feeling that craves for musical expression, or even is susceptible of it.

Nay, you may not only reduce the words to pure ejaculation, you may substitute mere roulade vocalization, or even balderdash, for them, provided the music sustains the feeling which is the real subject of the drama, as has been proved by many pages of genuinely dramatic music, both in opera and elsewhere, which either have no words at all, or else belie them. It is only when a thought interpenetrated with intense feeling has to be expressed, as in the Ode to Joy in the Ninth Symphony, that coherent words must come with the music. You have such words in Tristan; you have also ejaculations void of thought, though full of feeling; and you have plenty of instrumental music with no words at all. But you have no 'absolute' music, and no 'opera.'

Nothing in the world convinces you more of the fact that a dramatic poem cannot possibly take the form of an opera libretto than listening to Tristan and comparing it with, say, Gounod's Romeo and Juliet. I submit, then, to Noufflard (whose two volumes I none the less cordially recommend to all amateurs who can appreciate a thinker) that the contradictions into which Wagner has fallen in this matter are merely such verbal ones as are inevitable from the imperfection of language as an instrument for conveying ideas; and that the progress from Der fliegende Holländer to Parsifal takes a perfectly straight line ahead in theory as well as in artistic execution ...

1 Wagner presented Gabriele Spontini's *La Vestale* at Dresden in 1844 and invited the composer to conduct.

51

William Foster Apthorp, 'Canons'

From *By the Way* (Boston, 1898)

A native of Boston, Apthorp (1848–1913) was a contributor to *Dwight's Journal of Music*, music editor of the *Atlantic Monthly*, and critic for the *Boston Transcript*. His urbane criticisms represent a transition between the pontifical style of Dwight (see no. 30) and others and the lively subjectivism of the French critics and Phillip Hale (no. 57). The programme notes Apthorp wrote for the Boston Symphony are notable for their lightly worn learning. This essay echoes Berlioz's views (see no. 33) on the dissolution of the old canons of beauty.

We all have heard of the canons of Art; though exactly what they are is not so easy to discover. They would seem to be rather fragile things, for Art itself has progressed through the ages at the expense of an enormous breakage of them. You can track the march of an art through time by the shattered canons in its path, as you can that of a picnic party through the woods by the broken egg-shells. Yet every single one of these demolished canons was once held sacred, held to be a thing infrangible, good for a safe voyage through eternity. At the least crack in any one of them a terrific outcry was raised, summoning all hearts of oak to rally round the legitimist banner, for Art was in danger; just as we hear the dread news that the Country is in peril from our every-year's national Tungenagemot. But *Ars longa, canones breves*; Art still lives and mocks at danger, in spite of her broken canons.

Yet, may it not be said, on the other hand, that an art without canons, an absolutely lawless art, must be no art at all? Where there are no laws, one would think that only one of two things can exist: either autocracy or anarchy. To the autocratic pitch, to the point of unquestioning obedience to the dictates of a single, irresponsible ruler, no art has ever yet brought it; perhaps also, never quite to the anarchic pitch. One concludes, therefore, that Art can not but obey some laws, – often of the unformulated, unwritten sort, – and that to discover these laws, and formulate them distinctly would be a

not undesirable performance. But this discovery has had its difficulties. Probably no single entire law of Art has ever yet been fully discovered, but only parts and portions of laws. The formulating these
parts and portions, too, the reducing them to ostensible rules and
canons, has been done, for the most part, with a wisdom that saw
no farther than its own nose. Rules have been made to fit isolated
cases, and then proclaimed as valid for all cases and all time – with
the results we know. No man has yet had the penetration of insight,
the scope of vision, to see enough of a law of Art to be able to
express it in a rule fit to oulive the ages and be more perennial than
bronze. One may even expect that such penetration and scope of
vision will be refused to man, to the end of time.

Yet, amid this continual breaking of canons – partial formulations
of laws, pretending to completeness; temporary makeshifts, claiming to be everlasting, – it is to be noted how many rules, as yet
unbroken, gain weight and authority by insensibly establishing
themselves as conventions. The half-conscious plebiscitum of artists
decrees that the truth contained in them is worth recognizing; and,
from being partial, perhaps tyrannical, expressions of laws, they
become willingly accepted conventions, conformity to which soon
grows to be a matter of habit. In this condition, they exert their
most potent, also their most beneficent sway. Convention is not to
be rashly undervalued; without it, we should all be in but ill ease.
Our very language is nothing more than a long-inherited convention; there must needs be something conventional in the expressive
methods of Art, or people would not understand them.

There are no relations in life in which at least something has not
to be taken for granted; and the art which can take a widely recognized convention for granted is in the safest condition. It is only
when conventions cease to answer to the needs of the times, cease to
be true expressions of the general feeling, that they become irksome,
and the few advanced leaders cry for their abolition; only when the
canon that has become conventional can no longer be believed in,
and the place of belief is usurped by cant. But, abolish the worn-out
convention as you will, it must be replaced by another, which other,
too, will be based on a canon whose truth may be as largely alloyed
with falsehood as the old one. Only, the truth it contains will be
better adapted to the needs of the age; it will more exactly express
the feeling of the artistic world at large, and correspond more

adequately to its demands. But note this: as the power of pure faith wanes in the world, and the craving for investigation, reasoning, and the exercise of judgment waxes loud, the authority of the new canon will be but feeble, till it can embody itself in a new recognized convention. The condition of Art meanwhile – between the death of the old convention and the establishment and recognition of the new – will seem to the thoughtless very like one of anarchy. A simple canon, no matter how well formulated, can exert little sway nowadays over the doings of men; it must first prove its viability before the world will accept it. And, where there is no rule, it seems as if nothing but anarchy can be. Yet, to my mind, this supposed condition of anarchy does not really exist.

Remember that analogies are ever liable to limp a little; you can find hardly one that stands and walks squarely on both feet. When we speak of anarchy in Art, it is only by analogy with anarchy in the State. And I here use the word 'anarchy' in its current sense, not only of a state of no recognized rule, but of a state of no-rule which, from being such, is intrinsically and admittedly hurtful to mankind. Its badness lies in its practical workings more than in any theoretical considerations. Anarchy in the State virtually means far more than there being no recognized laws, no recognized government, and every man ruling himself; this is what it means theoretically, but practically it means every man not only ruling himself, but trying to rule all his fellows into the bargain, and make the whole world walk his gait. But there is little of this in the so-called anarchic periods of an art. The artist does, in any case, what he pleases: in times when convention holds sway, he does it conventionally; when convention is dead, he does it unconventionally, but suits himself all the same. His innovations hurt no one, and there is little recalcitration, save from the critics; and, whew! who cares a rap for them? Possibly the 'passionate press-agent'; and his regard for them is of a somewhat mixed quality. Here the theoretical and practical sides of anarchy coincide; but so innocuous a state of anarchy as that is hardly worthy the name!

The important gist of the matter is, after all, this: the new canon – whether before or after its embodying itself in a recognized convention – will in all probability be no more complete, universal, nor lasting an expression of a law of Art than the old one it has displaced; it will probably be quite as partial and temporary. More than this, the old convention, which had ceased to be adequate to the needs of the times, was probably not inadequate all over and all through; it had become irksome in some ways, enough so to make men clamour for its abolition; but, in abolishing it, at least something good and viable was lost, something the loss of which the world can not endure forever. It is likely, too, that this lost something will not be contained in the new convention; so that this one also will have to be abolished in time, that the loss may be made good. In its progress, Art is ever thus dropping stitches, which it will in time have to go back and take up again. No convention, no matter how superannuated and effete, no matter how unfit for the world's complete adherence, is wholly and irredeemably bad; if it were so, it could never have been good; for, change as he may, the human animal remains always the same at bottom. It is by – perhaps unavoidably – abolishing the good with the bad in an effete convention that we prevent the new, fresh convention being altogether excellent. It is only more adequate to our present needs than the old one; that is all we can truly say in its favour, and that is enough. It furnishes the most convenient channel for the art-workers of the day to let their inspiration flow through, affords them the fittest form in which to embody it. So soon as they begin to feel that, in losing something in the old convention, they have lost something of intrinsic, permanent value, they will not be slow in going back to take up the dropped stitch again. You may trust them for that.

No doubt, the great art-workers, who are really the principal abolishers and promulgators of conventions in Art, do not always act with impeccable prudence nor the longest foresight. But Art is a field where feeling and enthusiasm – and their almost inevitable concomitant, sharpness of temper – have more to say than reason and circumspection. The original artist is so overjoyed to be rid of the harassing old, and be on with the welcome new, that he wishes the old good riddance forever and aye without compunction. Perhaps also it is true that, in Art, no man can acquire sufficient force of energy to rise to the pitch of kicking out the old, and embracing the new, unless he has a somewhat exaggerated, morbid, undiscriminating yearning for the one and hatred of the other. Something of the insanity of a fixed idea may be needful for the purpose. Few men advocate a revolution against what they deem merely inconvenient; man gets to the pitch of revolt only against what he has found intolerable. So the art-worker abolishes, not what he finds merely useless, but what he can no longer by any means endure. Then, to be sure, he abolishes it, root and branch; probably to be followed by another who will in time lovingly examine the old ploughed-up roots, to see if there be no green shoots sprouting from them; in which examination he is more than likely to be successful.

PART III

The Twentieth Century

52

John F. Runciman, 'English Music in the Nineteenth Century'

Saturday Review (13 January 1900)

The dawn of the twentieth century elicited both prophecies of a brave new world and post mortems for the passing age. Runciman (1866–1916) was one of the most independent-minded British critics of the day. A lively and often contentious writer, at his best he was in a class with Berlioz (see no. 33), Shaw (no. 50), and Max Beerbohm (his colleague on the *Saturday Review*). This scathing assessment of English music exemplifies his intemperate iconoclasm.

Although it now seems a long time ago, I distinctly remember meditating one evening towards the end of the last century on the craze for 'something new' which was doing all it could to ruin all the arts and had already all but ruined music in England. Even at that time it was possible to see how our composers were divided, roughly, into two sets: those who wrote by rule, Academically, trying to do again what had been done superbly before, and those younger men who did not seek with all their strength to express something that they had felt deeply, but strove simply and solely to do the accursed 'something new.' Now that we are (as I believe) plunged into a new time and can calmly survey the men and their works of the dead nineteenth century, it seems to me more obvious than ever that the something new notion was, and for that matter is, the worst enemy we could possibly have. It produced the Academics as well as the young men who wrote consecutive fifths under the erroneous impression that consecutive fifths had not been written before and that it was a noble and highly original thing to write them. At any rate, both the Academics and the young men were possessed by the same notion, and whether it was best to go on trying to produce the something new out of nothing, or to give the game up forthwith and go on trying to do the old thing again, was simply a matter of taste or of training. Often a man's taste changed, so that the rash, daring, youthful experimenter became the dry, if learned, contrapuntal Sir Hubert Parry[1] in middle age. The young Mr. Parry never learnt the grand secret for the middle-aged Sir Hubert to forget: the secret that before you can say something new you must have in you something new to say, and that in any case there is only one safe plan, to go on trying to utter in the clearest, most effective way possible things you have genuinely and deeply felt, leaving it to be decided hereafter whether the things you have felt were original things. For if a man has anything original in him it can be levered out by industry: the original man in fact cannot help being original any more than, as Mozart said, he can help the shape of his nose; but no amount of industry, or daring attempts to do the things most people wisely abstain from doing, will produce anything original from an unoriginal mind or from no mind at all. This, of course, is a truism; but it has been forgotten by all English composers and a great many foreign ones during the latter half of the nineteenth century.

The something new of Wagner, of Schumann when he hailed the appearance of that false light of morning, Brahms,[2] of Beethoven when he announced on a day his determination to take 'the new road,' was quite a different matter from the mere craze for a true or bogus individuality. With Wagner the new form built itself round the new content that his imagination had already vaguely shaped: he had felt the new thing and only needed to create the music that expressed it. Beethoven, too, had already felt the new thing for the expression of which the new musical form was an absolute necessity. Schumann's only mistake was in thinking that Brahms had the new stuff in him and that time (and industry) would bring it out. In addition, Wagner, Beethoven, even Brahms, had a keen sense of beauty: their something new was to be a beautiful expression of the new thing that had been experienced. This, I repeat, is altogether different from a desire to make something, lovely or unlovely, pregnant or meaningless, which shall be different from anything done before – it is as different as is the music of Wagner and Beethoven from Dvořák's or the music of Richard Strauss, or from the music of our dullest or boldest men. And our musicians have never even taken the trouble to put themselves in the way of getting a new content into their minds. They have rigorously shut themselves off from any chance of getting new impressions, new thoughts, new emotions; they have lived lives of arithmetic and small-talk, paying no heed to all that was going on in the practical world, or literature, or painting, or, for that matter, in the degenerate drama of the century. I am sorry to have to say that the English musicians of to-day remind me chiefly of a pack of querulous, gossiping, afternoon-tea old ladies. They have no higher ambition than to make money, to be applauded at a country festival, to become conductor of a festival or the Philharmonic Society.[3] To gain the lowly objects of their ambition they intrigue against each other and grow to hate each other; and, without a noble aspiration in them, their vanity makes them so restlessly sensitive to criticism that they become furious when they are reminded that their aspirations are not noble. There are a few exceptions, naturally – thank heaven that one can say naturally! – but those of my readers who know of the intrigues that have disgraced the musical life of England during the past few months, that have even led one popular musician to resign a festival conductorship,[4] will not wonder any more than I do why we produce no great music. Our men have nothing to say – such men have never anything good to say: the really great men are not pettish, querulous, vain, and given to intrigue – and I go so far as to question whether they could say it if they had.

For this is the worst part of the case of our English musicians: that the majority of them have no command of modern technique. Of course Fritz Delius has, and Marshall-Hall; but the technique of Mackenzie, Stanford, Parry and their pupils is already old-fashioned, has already served its purpose and died the death.[5] Now if a country cannot produce great artists, it can at least do something by building up or continuing a technique for the big man to use when he arrives. We call Bach the composer of the B minor Mass, Handel the composer of the 'Messiah,' Beethoven of the C minor symphony and Wagner of 'Tristan;' but in truth hundreds of small men – most of them utterly forgotten – had a share in those works; for if none of the small men had genius to compose any one of the works, or anything so great, neither a Bach nor a Handel, a Beethoven nor a Wagner, could have invented in one lifetime the means of constructing the works by which they live and have their fame. A language in which one's landlord or the Government may be effectively abused cannot be invented by one man or indeed by any number of men in one generation; and how much more difficult is it to invent a language flexible enough, strong and sensitive enough, for the B minor Mass and 'Tristan' or any of the great things that came between them! It is by helping in the building up of the language of music that the small men help; and if our small men would only be honest with themselves they would see that their true function is not to re-write badly the fine oratorios and masses, but to make themselves masters, or at least schoolmasters, of the newest technique, and so hand on something which will be serviceable, and to the glory of England, when a divinely gifted one at last comes this way.

Meantime, it must be owned that the history of English music in the nineteenth century is a blank page. Whether that page will be covered with some one's gorgeous handwriting during the twentieth century is a thing that no man can tell. I have given up looking, like Robert Schumann, for a musical Prophet. This looking for the one shining, original man is only one manifestation of the desire for something new. Rather I wish that our men would go ahead in a more business-like way, learning all that their young German contemporaries know, and either writing no music at all or simply turning out the best that is in them. I have a suspicion that if they did that, and gave up all their petty squabblings, the right man would come sooner than we expect him – like a thief in the night, perhaps. In that case, I fear, the Academics would send the police after him.

1 Parry, director of the Royal College of Music and professor of music at Oxford, epitomized the establishment composer.
2 The reference is to Schumann's famous article 'New Paths,' published in the *Neue Zeitschrift für Musik* on 28 October 1853.
3 Founded in 1813 to provide Londoners with regular concerts of orchestral music.
4 In 1899 Sir Arthur Sullivan was forced to resign from the conductorship of the Leeds Festival. The festival committee was reportedly concerned about his failing health and unhappy with his lacklustre image on the podium.
5 Frederick Delius had settled in France in 1888, George Marshall-Hall in Australia in 1890. Alexander Mackenzie was principal of the Royal College of Music; Charles Villiers Stanford was professor of music both there and at Cambridge.

53

Claude Debussy, 'Conversation with Monsieur Croche'

Revue blanche (1 July 1901), from F. Lesure, ed., *Monsieur Croche
et autres écrits* (Paris, 1971)

Like many of his fellow composers, Debussy (1862–1918) took up criticism
partly in order to promote the progressive ideas expressed in his music.
Unlike such composer-critics as Berlioz and Thomson, however, Debussy
was never a professional critic, and his writings appeared sporadically in
various journals. This article, introducing his fictional alter ego Monsieur
Croche (Mr Quaver), marks his debut as a journalist. The combative,
impressionistic tone is characteristic.

It was a lovely evening and I had decided to do nothing. (To put it
politely, let's say I was dreaming.) To tell the truth, it was not one
of those commendable moments that one speaks of later with emotion as having set the stage for the Future. No, it was just one of
those unpretentious moments when one is completely free to do as
one likes.

And what was I dreaming about? Putting my thoughts in order?
Finishing some pieces? Questions prompted by childish egotism, by
a need to divest oneself at any price of an idea that one has lived
with for too long. And all this a poor way of hiding the foolish
obsession to be seen as superior to other people. Being superior to
other people has never taken much of an effort, provided it isn't
combined with a high-minded desire to be superior to oneself. The
latter takes a very special alchemy and demands that one make a
sacrificial offering of one's own precious little personality – which is
a hard thing to maintain and accomplishes absolutely nothing.
Besides, currying universal favour means wasting a considerable
amount of time in constantly proving one's worthiness and tirelessly promoting oneself. The only reward is the right to belong to that
pack of famous men whose names are bandied about to revive flagging conversations about art. But I wouldn't want to belabour the
point, lest I discourage anyone.

It was still a lovely evening but, as you can probably tell, I wasn't happy with myself. I was losing my bearings and drowning in a morass of the most irritating generalizations.

Precisely at that moment my doorbell rang and I made the acquaintance of M. Croche. To recount in detail all the incidents, both natural and preposterous, that attended his arrival at my house would encumber this interesting narrative to no avail.

M. Croche was a short, wizened man whose gestures were obviously tailored for holding up his end of metaphysical discussions. You can place him physically by relation to the likes of Tom Lane, the jockey, and M. Thiers.[1] Overall, his manner gave the impression of a freshly honed knife. He spoke very softly and never laughed. Sometimes he underlined his words with a silent smile that started at his nose and wrinkled his whole face, like a smooth pool into which a pebble has been thrown. It was long and intolerable.

At once he aroused my curiosity with his peculiar views on music. He talked about an orchestral score as if it were a painting, using words that were hardly ever technical but none the less uncommon; they had a dull, slightly worn elegance that seemed to resonate like old medals. I remember the parallel he drew between Beethoven's orchestra, which for him was represented by a black-and-white formula, resulting in an exquisite range of greys, and Wagner's, a sort of multicoloured putty, spread almost uniformly, in which he told me he could no longer distinguish the sound of a violin from that of a trombone.

Since his intolerable smile was especially obvious when he spoke about music, I suddenly took it into my head to ask him his profession. He replied in a voice that silenced any attempt at criticism: 'Antidilettante'. He went on in a monotonous, exasperated tone: 'Have you noticed the hostility of a concert-hall audience? Have you studied those faces, ashen with boredom, indifference, and even stupidity? Never do they partake of the pure dramas played out in the symphonic conflict. Never do they glimpse the possibility of reaching the summit of the musical edifice and imbibing the atmosphere of perfect beauty. These people, monsieur, always seem like guests who are more or less well bred. They patiently submit to the boring task at hand, and if they don't leave, it's because they must be seen going out; otherwise, why would they come? You must admit that this is the sort of thing that would make one allergic to music for ever.' When I protested that I had witnessed and even taken part in quite respectable demonstrations of enthusiasm, he replied: 'You are very much mistaken. If you showed that much enthusiasm, it was because secretly you hoped that one day people would do you the same honour! Surely you know that a genuine impression of beauty produces only silence. When you witness the daily enchantment of a sunset, have you ever thought of clapping? You must admit that its effect is somewhat less predictable than your little musical stories in sound. What's more, it makes you feel so insignificant that you can't partake of it body and soul. But before a so-called work of art you find your voice and gush over it in classic jargon.' I didn't dare tell him how close I was to his opinion – nothing kills conversation like agreement. I preferred to ask him if he was a musician. Raising his head abruptly, he said: 'Monsieur, I dislike specialists. For me, to specialize is to contract the boundaries of one's universe. One becomes like those old horses of bygone days who used to work the merry-go-rounds and died to the familiar sounds of the *Marche lorraine*! Even so, I know all the music there is to know and nothing has stayed with me except the special pride of being immune to any sort of surprise. Two bars give me the key to a symphony or any other piece of music.

'Just think: if a few great men demonstrably possess a "stubborn determination" to break new ground, this is not true of many others, who just as stubbornly revisit the sites of their past successes. I couldn't care less about that sort of ability. We call them "masters"! If we're not careful, that will become just a polite way of getting rid of them or excusing them for treating us to the same manoeuvre time after time. In a word, I'm trying to forget music, because it keeps me from hearing music that I don't know or that I will know tomorrow. Why be attached to something that one knows too well?'

When I mentioned the most famous of our contemporaries, he became more assertive than ever.

'You have a tendency to exaggerate events that would have seemed natural, for example, in Bach's day. You speak to me of M. Paul Dukas's sonata. No doubt he's one of your friends – and a music critic to boot.[2] Reason enough to speak well of him. Nevertheless, you've been outdone in the praise department. M. Pierre Lalo,[3] in a *feuilleton* in *Le Temps* devoted exclusively to this sonata, in one breath compares it favourably to the sonatas of

Schumann and Chopin. To be sure, Chopin's highly strung character was poorly suited to the patience required to concoct a sonata; he wrote elaborate "sketches" instead. All the same, one can state that he had a special way of handling this form, to say nothing of his delectable musical inventions. He was liberal with his ideas, often cashing them in without demanding a 100 per cent return – which is the brightest glory of some of our masters.

'Naturally, M. Pierre Lalo doesn't neglect to evoke the great shade of Beethoven in connection with the sonata of your friend Dukas. In his shoes, I would have been only moderately flattered! Beethoven's sonatas are very badly written for the piano; the last ones, especially, are more like orchestral transcriptions. The third hand that Beethoven surely intended (at least I hope he did) is often missing. It would have been better to leave Schumann and Chopin out of it. They really wrote for the piano, and if that seems faint praise to M. Pierre Lalo, at least he can be grateful to them for having paved the way for the perfection represented by a Dukas – and a few others.'

These last words were uttered by M. Croche with icy imperturbability: you could accept them or toss them out the window. I was too interested to respond and let him go on. There was a long silence, during which the only sign of life was the smoke of his cigar, whose blue spiral he watched curiously as it wafted up. He seemed to be contemplating curious contortions, bold systems, perhaps. His silence was disconcerting and a little scary. He began again: 'Music is the sum of scattered forces: in theory, you could make a song out of them. I prefer the few notes of an Egyptian shepherd's flute. He is at one with the landscape and hears harmonies unknown to your treatises. Musicians only hear music written by practised hands, never the music written in nature's script. To see the sunrise is more profitable than listening to the *Pastoral* Symphony. What's the use of your nearly incomprehensible art? Shouldn't you suppress its parasitical complications, which make music seem as ingenious as the lock of a strongbox? You stamp your feet because you know nothing but music and obey its barbarous and unknown laws. People lavish praise on you, but you are merely smart alecks, a cross between a monkey and a housekeeper.'

I ventured to tell him that some poets and painters (with great difficulty I thought of a few musicians as well) had tried to shake off the dust of tradition, but for their pains they were only labelled 'Symbolists' or 'Impressionists' – convenient terms of abuse for one's fellows. 'Only journalists and professionals use those labels,' M. Croche went on without faltering. 'They're of no importance at all. Any imbecile can make fun of a pretty idea while it's in the formative stage. You can be sure that there is more potential for beauty in men who have been made fun of than in those who flock like docile sheep to the slaughterhouse which a clearsighted fate has readied for them.

'Remain unique ... unblemished! Society's enthusiasm spoils an artist for me; I'm always afraid that he will end up being nothing but the expression of society.

'Discipline must be sought in freedom, not in the formulas of a decrepit philosophy fit only for the feebleminded. Listen to no one's advice except that of the wind, which tells us the story of the world.'

At that moment M. Croche appeared to light up. I seemed to see inside him, and his words fell on my ears like a strange music. I don't know how to translate their special eloquence into words. Maybe this will do:

'Do you know of any experience more beautiful than chancing to decipher the secrets of a man who has remained unknown for centuries? But to have been one of those very men – that is the only glory worth winning.'

Daylight was breaking. M. Croche was visibly tired and went away. I accompanied him as far as the door on the landing. He no more thought of shaking my hand than I dreamt of thanking him. For a long time I heard the sound of his steps fading away as he descended floor by floor. I dare not hope ever to see him again.

P.S. The Société des Concerts du Conservatoire recently had a chance to appoint M. André Messager as its conductor. Naturally they passed it up. The subscribers to this music hall for the feebleminded can continue their sleep.

1 Adolphe Thiers, the historian, premier and later president of France in the mid-1800s.
2 Dukas was one of Debussy's early supporters; see his review of the String Quartet (no. 49). The reference is to Dukas's Piano Sonata, first performed on 10 May 1901.
3 Pierre Lalo, son of the composer Edouard, was highly critical of Debussy.

54

Silvio Benco, 'The Post-Wagnerians'

Piccolo della sera (2 December 1906), from *Scritti musicali*
(Milan, 1974)

Journalist, novelist and historian, Benco (1874–1949) was editor of the
Independente and later of the *Piccolo della sera*, both in Trieste. Like
Basevi (see no. 31), he was deeply concerned with Italian culture and wrote
about Verdi with special insight. But like Filippi (no. 39), he was also
drawn to Wagner and attuned to the seismic shift in musical taste and
styles that followed Wagner's death.

In dismissing Ferruccio Benvenuto Busoni's *Turandot*[1] so coldly
and with such a sternly judgmental scowl, was the public asking
too much, in its heart of hearts, of a contemporary of Richard
Strauss to give them music of Beethoven?

Certainly, from the very first drumrolls, artless and sinister, the
strident cacchinations of the little instruments twisted into a grim
joke, it was clear that the public, with its smile of implacable judgment, was dead set against forgiving the composer for his lack of
respect for the seriousness of life and the august traditions of art.

Now life is certainly very serious, but it is not all serious. The
man who wants seriousness in everything wilfully shuts himself off
from many of life's sensations. It will appear to him a heavy and
oppressive thing, impervious to childhood games, to the temperament of the witty man, to the originalities and whims of the ironic
artist. He will measure genius by the profundity of the end product, but he will not know how to measure it by the deft sharpness
of the comic remark. He will find a five-act tragedy in free verse
magnificent, but he will not know how to find insight and grace in
a light-hearted marionette comedy. He will be an incomplete man,
cut off from part of existence: wishing to find Beethoven in Richard
Strauss and Dante Alighieri in Heine, he will become a poor judge
of Strauss and Heine.

In every work of art, impressions ought to be sought from the
standpoint of the author's intentions. Otherwise, judgment will

wander on to roads that lead far away from the work itself. The more cultured a public is, the more broadly it conceives the intentions of a greater number and variety of artists, and the readier it is to perceive them. Before a highly cultured public, no work of art needs commentators; each work speaks for itself and mounts its own defence. But when the public, through its virginal smile of derision, shows itself inexperienced in a new cultural ambience with which a new work of art is in tune, and when that work does not – cannot – speak to the public's imagination in any language, then it is necessary to take up the pen and explain.

Today there is no one in the public who does not pay attention to the art of Richard Wagner. Dish up a Wagnerian and [the public] will recognize the master's tragic orchestral fingerprints, and understand the disciple as well. But confronted with a post-Wagnerian, a musician who was born after the period when Bayreuth was the source of all light and who has the soul and impressions of a new artistic generation, the public will be less able to find its way around in his music. Wagner sprang forth in full romantic effervescence and, with his incomparable energies, transmitted the afflatus of grandiose dramaticality which was central to that era. Today the public is thoroughly permeated by this afflatus. But after romanticism other things came into the human soul: naturalism, with its finely pointed analyses and its dissections of surroundings; pictorial impressionism, with its rapidity of vision in the blaze of light; as well as the artistic phenomenon which was called 'decadence' and whose fundamental note seems to me to be the superimposition of all the arts, so that a romance imitates a symphony, the theatrical scene imitates a painting, and the painting resembles a musical score ...

We know full well – or at least it has always been presumed up to now – that music by itself is incapable of expressing anything concrete. This was the gist of Hanslick's criticism of Wagner,[2] who seemed to him the most incorrigible proponent of the contrary viewpoint. But if Wagner himself had scrutinized his scores, he might have despaired of having expressed anything that was incapable of conveying more than one meaning. To a listener unfamiliar with *Siegfried*, the divine, sparkling arcs of sound heard subtly and penetratingly at the hero's death in *Götterdämmerung*, which speak so celestially of Brünnhilde's awakening, may well seem to express the dissolution of life, the torment of the soul breathing its last. Hitherto, the firm link between reality and music was presumed to have been traceable only via the word. Wagner was indeed a dramatic poet, and he spoke; on the stage, the descriptive elements of his polyphony are dependent on the logic of gesture and word.

Now the post-Wagnerians, harkening to their own inmost impressions, seem firmly determined to violate these musical boundaries in order to transmit their impressions via the orchestra. Thanks to the value of sounds, they want to be understood without speaking. They believe deeply in disposing the instruments in their orchestra with a sense of harmonic intervals such as gives rise in the listener to the sensation of an atmosphere, a mass of air formed by the music. They believe deeply in instrumental timbres and their associations giving rise to a thought, an idea, an image. Finally, they believe that a melody filtered through this harmonic air, through the voices of such suggestive instruments, takes on a colour of truth and poetry, as if one were listening to it in its natural ambience.

This is not altogether new. The bewitching melody of *Carmen* sounds more terrible when it is superimposed on the materiality of the taps echoing from a distant camp and when confusion grips the heart of the soldier whose sense of duty wrestles with the eroticism that is undermining it. In Saint-Saëns's *Suite algérienne* we have seen colours and images arrange themselves and form small pictures within the smooth, mellifluous and bold harmonies of the French style. But above all in Germany the experiment of representational music quickens the hearts of the modern sound-psychologists: and from an Italian living in Germany came that exotic and pictorial and comic *Turandot*, against which we are up in arms on account of our habitual ideas about colour, form, and the destiny of music, without quite asking ourselves whether at the present musical time a Chinese fable ought to be told some other way.

But why tell Chinese fables? That too is a question. The world could get along even without China. Who knows?

1 Busoni published an orchestral suite from his incidental music to Gozzi's *commedia dell'arte* in 1904. The operatic version was first performed in 1917.

2 Wagner's ideal of music drama was antithetical to Hanslick's belief in musical absolutism. For Hanslick's views on the 'Wagner cult', see no. 43.

55

Felipe Pedrell, 'Snobs'

(15 June 1906), from *Musicalerías* (Valencia, 1908)

Like Peña y Goñi (see no. 40), Pedrell (1841–1922) took a keen interest in the creation of Spanish opera. As writer, composer, musicologist and teacher (Falla, Granados, and Albéniz were among his pupils), he worked tirelessly to foster a national musical consciousness. His writing appeared both in scholarly journals and in newspapers like the *Diario de Barcelona*. His lighter journalistic touch is evident in this mock-scientific analysis of 'snobbism' – a phenomenon discussed by many critics of the time.

For my friend X.

Do you mean to tell me that you haven't figured out what a snob is, even after reading every page of that delicious satire *Vanity Fair* by the English humourist? And you want me to *explain* it to you – poor fellow! – when the hallmark of the snob is not to be aware that he is one, or to believe in a vague sort of way that everybody is a snob? What's more, you want me to enlighten you scientifically, by axioms and propositions, the way the old Spaniard taught the art of playing castanets? What is a snob, scientifically speaking? Here's the lesson straight from the horse's mouth, just as a friend of mine who is a qualified micrologist taught it to me. Listen and learn.

A snob in isolation poses no threat to anyone, but he is dreadful when he comes out in force. The monad *Snob*, examined under the most powerful microscope and analysed with all the most up-to-date means, exhibits a frustrating neutrality, with no fixed vibrating point, no special affinity, no resultant of interior forces. The snob *per se* exists only in seclusion, so to speak, or in a test tube, and for that reason is totally impotent. To create a snobbic culture which shows some symptoms of direction, it's necessary to cluster four or five snobs around a snob of superior vitality, or around a conducting agent of a different species. Do you begin to get the picture?

In the first case, the culture medium is short-lived and not very productive. It's snobbism aborted and failed, which neither pricks nor cuts: a collective aspiration which falls kerplunk as soon as it encounters an obstacle. In the second case – well, that's a more serious affair. Do you know whom the Holy Books called clever? Well, let's call the conducting agent clever. He's a devil, with tail and everything (if it disgusts you, take it away from him), who knows how to put human stupidity to work for him. The devilishly clever man is the man – even the superman – who is eager to attain a noble and lofty goal and understands that, in order to reach it, it's useful to gather forces, group them, and point them in one direction, using them like a battering ram to break through ... snow, or the 'obstacle' of a common goal. In art, believe me, my friend, the forces which that clever man, that charming, clever man, can marshal to his advantage constitute the legion of snobs. And so they break down into distinct species, an infinity of species: the *Sn. politicus*, the *Sn. scientificus*, the *Sn. censorius* ...

The variety *Sn. artisticus* is most amusing: a harmless enough monad, glittering with multiple colours: a species which owes its existence to the sex which men – presumptuous ones! – call ... to paraphrase Shakespeare: 'Frailty, thy name is snob.' Precisely on account of the sexual predominance of the species, the lab medium of the *Sn. artisticus* produces exceptionally fruitful results when it is prepared and handled by an expert.

Wagnerism, which pitted a healthy, synthetic, profound poetry against ignorant and mocking philistinism, owes its victory to the recruitment by strong and clever spirits – remember Mendès, Schuré, Gautier[1] and the rest – of snobbish forces massed, mobilized, aroused and launched against Meyerbeer's peanut-brittle citadel and Gounod's confectionery outpost (where tasty bonbons were sold just the same). The variety *Snob artisticus iracundus* provoked fights between Schumannists and Mendelssohnists. It turned that unstable fellow Nietzsche one day against Wagner (whom he adored the day before) and the next day against Brahms (who was the utter antithesis of an impersonal, peripheral figure, a master copyist). Lined up against the musical uncertainty which at present reigns in Germany, you have a champion team of snobs in formation, ready to follow Strauss in his now-multiple evolutions, from *Don Juan* to the *Sinfonia domestica*, without caring a whit about dispelling the shadow that hangs – still! – over the pure music of Obermann, Bruckner, Reger, Mahler ...

The rediscovery of the polyphonic classics of the sixteenth century, which has taught moderns music we didn't know, and the renaissance of Bach, Monteverdi and Carissimi have been welcome, logical, just and timely, thanks to the zeal of a well-focused snobbism. And though the results have been somewhat mixed when we've been asked to swallow the gilded pill of the Perosis and the *veristas* of today's Italian opera, the lump can be pardoned for the whack on the head.[2]

In these fertile lands of ours, snobs of the most varied species are cultivated: the *Sn. artisticus aerarius*, who expounds on everything from the ups and downs of the stock market to the art of cooking and eating *garbanzos*; the *Sn. artis antistes*, who raves about the tenor and is spellbound by virtuosity; the *Sn. melifluus vel melosus*, who hasn't got beyond the 'Spirto gentil';[3] the *Sn. artisticus tumultuosus*, who pretends to understand the last page of Naharro[4] without having deciphered the first ones. The latter species of snob grows his hair out to cover his bald spot; he smokes a pipe, spits through his teeth, and wears the filthy, foul-smelling clothes that were fashionable last year in Batignoles.[5] Oh, he's an awful snob, but of the most amusing kind. There are also the *Sn. artisticus perparvus*, who rolls his eyes at the fatuousness of everything he hears; the *Sn. artisticus balatro*, who is as like Don Ramon de la Cruz[6] as two peas in a pod, condemned to be content for ever with two pesetas …

But the most typical variety of our snobbism is the *Sn. censorius petulans*, whose only way of criticizing art is to heckle – as potent and persuasive a form of criticism as ever there was. Next door, in the Country of Daydreams, the *censor taurinus* practises the curious sport of heckling. In one and the same person he combines the functions of music critic, bullfighting critic and even *pelota* critic (a triple threat). Peña y Goñi[7] drew the strength of his conviction from that promiscuity of natural dispositions which ranged with impunity over bulls, *pelotas* and music, mixing the Lame Person of Cirauqui with Frascuelo and Patti.[8] Mariano de Cavia was mixed up in that double critical game in his early days, as are Muñoz, Millán and other musical-bullfighter censors today.[9] What, you don't see what *bandilleras* have to do with solmization or veronicas with counterpoint? If you want to know, Unamuno at the University of Salamanca, the *Sn. homunculus*, will tell you.[10]

Nevertheless, the snob has one reassuring and redeeming quality. In a hospitable culture, it can sometimes divest itself of the empty-headedness and irresolution which it tolerates in its natural state. Thanks to prolonged contact with a pure and genuine artistic medium, it suddenly casts off its chrysalis's or neophyte's shell, and there it is – transformed into Everyman, capable of discerning and thinking for himself, with no one to give him the pseudo-discernment to distinguish good from bad; ready to applaud without his neighbour's consent or to heckle without relying on the clique. So when the work of the *snob listo* is finished, he no longer leads a bunch of innocently ignorant snobs: it's an armada, a new and strange armada of salvation, of disciplined soldiers and well-trained combatants, experienced and loyal, which he deploys to defend his ideas, to see that they prevail, and to hold the positions they have conquered.

My friend, the erstwhile specialist micrographer, sums up the axioms and propositions about the snob with the following comparison: 'A magnificent automobile – eight cylinders, sixty horsepower – this is what snobs are. If you want your snobbism to be poorly steered, entrust the automobile to a reckless driver, a daredevil or an ignoramus, and he'll play foolish games with it. If you want your snobbism to be well steered, entrust the automobile to an intelligent chauffeur and he'll use it to take you on a tour of the most interesting countries in the world. If he really sets his mind to it, he may even discover new horizons.'

So make use of that formidable but blind energy. Channel it. Set it on track for the glory of ... art or whatever you want. Use it, yes, but don't forget that when it comes to snobbism, those native glittering colours, resistant to all spectroscopy, make it difficult, if not impossible, ever to know what map to follow.

---

1 Catulle Mendès, Edouard Schuré and Judith Gautier were prominent Wagnerites.
2 'Se le puede perdonar el bollo por el coscorrón': i.e., one has to take the good with the bad.
3 The popular aria from Donizetti's *La Favorita*.
4 Bartolomé de Torres Naharro, the sixteenth-century dramatic poet, considered the founder of Spanish theatre.
5 A district of Paris.
6 An eighteenth-century Spanish dramatist known for his short, comic sketches of low-life.
7 Peña y Goñi often laced his criticism with metaphors from bullfighting and sports.
8 Frascuelo (Salvador Sánchez Povedano) was a well-known bullfighter, Adelina Patti an opera singer. Cirauqui is a town in the province of Navarro, but I have been unable to decipher this allusion.

9 Mariano de Cavia was a journalist and critic who often wrote about bullfighting. Pascual Millán wrote a history of the sport, while the novelist Eugenio Muñoz bitterly attacked it.

10 Miguel de Unamuno, the philosopher, poet, playwright and novelist, was rector at the University of Salamanca.

56

Edward H. Krehbiel, 'The *Salome* of Wilde and Strauss'

New York Tribune (23 January 1907)

Critic of the *New York Tribune* for more than four decades, Krehbiel (1854–1923) was a towering figure in American musical journalism. A confirmed Wagnerite, he welcomed Brahms, Tchaikovsky, Dvořák and other moderns, but drew the line at Stravinsky, Schoenberg and Prokofiev. His ambivalence about Richard Strauss – whose *Salome* caused a sensation in America as in Europe – did not blind him to the composer's musical genius. For a less nuanced view of Strauss, see no. 63.

A reviewer ought to be equipped with a dual nature, both intellectual and moral, in order to pronounce fully and fairly upon the qualities of the drama by Oscar Wilde and Richard Strauss, which received its first American representation at the Metropolitan Opera House last night. He should be an embodied conscience stung into righteous fury by the moral stench with which *Salome* fills the nostrils of humanity, but, though it make him retch, he should be sufficiently judicial in his temperament calmly to look at the drama in all its aspects and determine whether or not as a whole it is an instructive note on the life and culture of the times and whether or not this exudation from the diseased and polluted will and imagination of the authors marks a real advance in artistic expression, irrespective of its contents or their fitness for dramatic representation ...

Several attempts have been made to habilitate Oscar Wilde's drama on the New York stage, and they have failed. If it succeeds now, it will be because a larger public has discovered that the music which has been consorted with the old pictures, actions and words has added to them an element either of charm or expressive potentiality hitherto felt to be lacking. Is that true? Has a rock of offence been removed? Has a mephitic odor been changed to a sweet savor by the subtle alchemy of the musical composer? Has a drama ten times as abhorrent, bestial, repellent and loathsome as that which handles the same subject, and which called forth denunciation from Mr. Winter in yesterday's issue of this journal, been changed into a thing of delectability by the potent agency of music? It used to be said that things too silly to be spoken might be sung; is it also true that things too vile, too foul, too nauseating for contemplation may be seen, so they be insidiously and wickedly glorified by the musician's art? As a rule, plays have not been improved by being turned into operas. Always their dramatic movement has been interrupted, their emotional current clogged, their poetry emasculated by the transformation. Things are better now than they were in the long ago, when music took no part at all in dramatic action, but waited for a mood which it had power to publish and celebrate; but music has acquired its new power only by an abnegation of its better part, by assuming new functions and asking a revaluation of its elements on a new aesthetic basis. Mr. Strauss does not call *Salome* an opera; he does not call it a lyric drama, or a musical drama, or a melodrama (which is what it is), or even a drama with music. He calls it simply a drama. If put to it he would probably not call the extravagantly complex and sumptuous tonal integument with which he has clothed it music, except in parts, and then with the understanding that the word be received with a new significance. In *Salome* music is largely a decorative element, like the scene, like the costumes. It creates atmosphere, like the affected stylism of much of Oscar Wilde's text, with the Oriental imagery borrowed from 'The Song of Solomon,' diluted and sophisticated; it gives emotional significance to situations, helping the facial play of Salome and her gestures to proclaim the workings of her mind, when speech has deserted her; it is at its best as the adjunct and inspiration of the lascivious dance. In the last two instances, however, it reverts to the purpose and also the manner (with a difference) which have always obtained, and becomes music in the purer sense. Then the would-be dramatist is swallowed up in the symphonist, and Strauss is again the master magician who can juggle with our senses and our reason and make his instrumental voices body forth 'the forms of things unknown.'

It would be wholly justifiable to characterize *Salome* as a symphonic poem for which the play supplies the programme. The parallelism of which we hear between Strauss and Wagner exists only in part – only in the application of the principle of characterization by means of musical symbols as typical phrases. Otherwise the men work on diametrically opposite lines. With all his musical affluence, Wagner aimed, at least, to make his orchestra only the bearer and servant of the dramatic word. Nothing can be plainer (it did not need that he should himself have confessed it) than that Strauss looks upon the words as necessary evils. His vocal parts are not song, except for brief, intensified spaces at long intervals. They are declamation. The song-voice is used, one is prone to think, only because by means of it the words can be made to be heard above the orchestra. Song, in the old acceptance of the word, implies beauty of tone and justness of intonation. It is amazing how indifferent the listener is to both vocal quality and intervallic accuracy in 'Salome.' Wilde's stylistic efforts are lost in the flood of instrumental sound; only the mood which they were designed to produce remains. Jochanaan sings phrases, which are frequently tuneful, and when they are not denunciatory are set in harmonies agreeable to the ear. But by reason of that fact Jochanaan comes perilously near being an old fashioned operatic figure – an ascetic Marcel,[1] with little else to differentiate him from his Meyerbeerian prototype than his 'raiment of camel's hair and a leathern girdle about his loins,' and an inflated phrase which must serve for the tunes sung by the rugged Huguenot soldier. Strauss characterizes by his vocal manner as well as by his themes and their instrumental treatment; but for his success he relies at least as much upon the performer as upon the musical text. A voice and style like Mr. Van Rooy's[2] give an uplift, a prophetic breadth, dignity and impressiveness to the utterances of Jochanaan which are paralleled only by the imposing instrumental apparatus employed in proclaiming the phrase invented to clothe his pronouncements. Six horns, used as Strauss knows how to use them, are a good substratum of the arch-colorist. The nervous staccato chatter of Herod is certainly characteristic of this neurasthenic. This specimen from the pathological museum of Messrs. Wilde and Strauss appears in a state which causes alarm lest his internal mechanism fly asunder and scatter his corporeal parts about the scene, and the crepitating volubility with which Strauss endows him is a marvellously ingenious conceit; but it leans heavily for its effect, we fear, on the amazing skill of Mr. Burrian,[3] not only in cackling out the words synchronously with the orchestral part, but in emotionally coloring them and blending them in a unity with his facial expression and his perturbed bodily movements. Salome[4] sings, often in the explosive style of Wagner's Kundry, sometimes with something like fluent continuity, but from her song has been withheld all the symmetrical and graceful contours comprehended in the concept of melody. Hers are the superheated phrases invented to give expression to her passion, and out of them she must construct the vocal accompaniment to the instrumental song, which reaches its culmination in the scene which, instead of receiving a tonal beatification, as it does, ought to be relegated to the silence and darkness of the deepest dungeon of a madhouse or a hospital.

Here is a matter, of the profoundest aesthetical and ethical significance, which might as well be disposed of now, so far as this discussion is concerned, regardless of the symmetrical continuity of the argument. There is a vast deal of ugly music in *Salome* – music that offends the ear and rasps the nerves like fiddlestrings played on by a coarse file. We have taken occasion in a criticism of Strauss's *Symphonia Domestica* to point out that a large latitude must be allowed to the dramatic composer which must be denied to the symphonist. Consort a dramatic or even a lyric text with music and all manner of tonal devices may derive explanation, if not justification, from the words. But in purely instrumental music the arbitrary purposes of a composer cannot replace the significance which must lie in the music itself – that is, in its emotional and aesthetic content. It does not lie in intellectual content, for thought to become articulate demands speech. The champions of Richard Strauss have defended ugliness in his last symphony, the work which immediately preceeded *Salome*, and his symphonic poems on the score that music must be an expression of truth, and truth is not always beautiful. In a happier day than this it was believed that the true and the beautiful were bound together in angelic wedlock and that all art found its highest mission in giving them expression. But the drama has been led through devious paths into the charnel house, and in *Salome* we must needs listen to the echoes of its dazed and drunken footfalls. The maxim 'Truth before convention' asserts its validity and demands recognition under the guise of 'characteristic beauty.' We may refuse to admit that ugliness is entitled to be raised to a valid principle in music dissociated from words or stage pictures, on the ground that thereby it contravenes and contradicts its own nature; but we may no longer do so when it surrenders its function as an expression of the beautiful and becomes merely an illustrative element, an aid to dramatic expression. What shall be said, then, when music adorns itself with its loveliest attributes and lends them to the apotheosis of that which is indescribably, yes, inconceivably, gross and abominable? Music cannot lie. Not even the genius of Richard Strauss can make it discriminate in its soaring ecstasy between a vile object and a good. There are three supremely beautiful musical moments in *Salome*. Two of them are purely instrumental, though they illustrate dramatic incidents; the third is predominantly instrumental, though it has an accompaniment of word and action. The first is an intermezzo in which all action ceases except that which plays in the bestially perverted heart and mind of Salome. A baffled amorous hunger changes to a desire for revenge. The second is the music of the dance. The third is the marvellous finale, in which an impulse which can only be conceived as rising from the uttermost pit of degradation is beatified. Crouching over the disseevered head of the prophet, Salome addresses it in terms of reproach, of grief, of endearment and longing, and finally kisses the bloody lips and presses her teeth into the gelid flesh. It is incredible that an artist should ever have conceived such a scene for public presentation. In all the centuries in which the story of the dance before Herod has fascinated sculptors, painters and poets, in spite of the accretions of lustful incident upon the simple Biblical story, it remained for a poet of our day to conceive this horror and a musician of our day to put forth his highest powers in its celebration …

The orchestra paints incessantly; moods that are prevalent for a moment do not suffice the eager illustrator. The passing word seizes his fancy. Herod describes the jewels which he promises to give to Salome so she relieve him of his oath, and the music of the orchestra glints and glistens with a hundred prismatic tints. Salome wheedles the young Syrian to bring forth the prophet, and her cry, 'Thou wilt do this thing for me,' is carried to his love-mad brain by a voluptuous glissando of the harp which is as irresistible as her glance and smile. But the voluptuous music is no more striking than the tragic.

Strauss strikes off the head of Jochanaan with more thundrous noise upon the kettle-drums than Wagner uses when Fafner pounds the life out of Fasolt with his gigantic stave; but there is nothing in all of Wagner's tragic pages to compare in tenseness of feeling with the moment of suspense while Salome is peering into the cistern and marvelling that she hears no sound of a death struggle. At this moment there comes an uncanny sound from the orchestra that is positively bloodcurdling. The multitude of instruments are silent – all but the string basses. Some of them maintain a tremolo on the deep E flat. Suddenly there comes a short, high B flat. Again and again with more rapid iteration. Such a voice was never heard in the orchestra before. What Strauss designed it to express does not matter. It accomplishes a fearful accentuation of the awful situation ... This is but one of a hundred new and strange devices with which the score of *Salome* has enriched instrumental music ...

1 The serious and abstemious servant in Meyerbeer's *Les Huguenots*.
2 Anton Van Rooy, the Dutch bass-baritone known for his Wagnerian roles.
3 Carl Burrian, the Bohemian tenor.
4 Portrayed by Olive Fremstad in a celebrated performance. Later in this article, Krehbiel describes her as 'a sleek tigress, with seduction speaking in every pore, gesture, look and utterance'.

57

Phillip Hale, 'Debussy's *Pelléas* Stirs up Critics'
Boston Herald (23 February 1908)

Hale (1854–1934) carried on the tradition that Dwight (see no. 30) had started in Boston. But the overtly personal tone of his criticism contrasted with his predecessor's Olympian objectivity. Music and drama critic of the *Boston Herald* for three decades, Hale is best known for his elegant programme notes for the Boston Symphony Orchestra. He was one of the first American critics to recognize Debussy's genius. Compare this review of *Pelléas et Mélisande*, which New York's Metropolitan Opera presented on 19 February 1908, with Dukas's earlier appreciation of the composer (no. 49).

... It has been said that this lyric drama is tapestry with music, Many things have been said about Debussy's opera, many foolish things as well as wise, and this is no more foolish than other epigrams suggested by the play. It is true that Debussy has given sonorous life to these characters. Henri Ghéon[1] well said that the important thing in the opera house is 'not the idea, which is antimusical in principle unless it becomes a sentiment or a sensation'; the important things are 'the sentiment and the sensation themselves,' and Debussy puts them in a close relationship so that they soon become one and the same thing; with the same succession of chords or same orchestral pattern he invokes the one or the other for a common impression; the depth of the castle vaults and the anxiety of Golaud, 'all the air of the whole sea' and the youthful intoxication of Pelléas, the freshness of the fountain and the unconsciousness of lovers – these sing with one voice and that is emotional. The passion of the characters and the atmosphere which they breathe are musically and scenically only one, and from the beginning to the end of the drama the characters breathe 'the atmosphere of their passion.' The 'picturesque' and the 'human' cannot be separated here as in this or that romantic drama.

Mallarmé condemned the inclusion in verse of anything, but 'for example, the horror of the forest, or the silent thunder afloat in the leaves; not the intrinsic, dense wood of the trees.' There are thousands who see in a forest only cordwood or material for paper. To them *Pelléas and Mélisande* will be tiresome foolishness.

There are others who will have much to say about the 'lack of dramatic interest.' They would like to see the characters 'doing something.' They will miss the prima donna with her eagerly awaited grand aria; the baritone with his fortissimo climax; the tenor with his brilliant assortment of notes above the staff; the material and soaring orchestra. Even in conventional opera the beauty of the nuance escapes them.

How can Debussy's lyric drama become popular? ...

Pelléas and Mélisande will suffer in two ways: from the invincible ignorance of philistines and from the hysteria of faddists.

Many years ago Jean Philippe Rameau declared: 'To enjoy fully the effects of music, it is necessary to be in a state of complete self-abandonment.' There are many that have ears and will not hear, because they, deliberately prejudiced and fanatical, will hear only music to which they have long been accustomed. The history of opera abounds in proofs of this. Debussy is only one of a long line of composers misunderstood, abused, maltreated. Monteverde, Gluck, Rossini, Verdi, Wagner – each one in turn was anti-Christ in music. They that were the last to accept Wagner are now the most bigoted in their admiration of him. He said the last word. Anyone coming after him must be an imitator. If they hear an English horn in a recently composed opera, they say significantly, *Tristan*. Their only enjoyment in listening to new operatic music is to hear echoes of Wagner's music dramas. But there are anticipations of *Tristan* in the introduction to Beethoven's *Pathetic* sonata, as Mr. Huneker[2] said to me a few days ago.

There are few works of art from the time when there was an art of any kind down to the present day that are so wholly original in form and expression of beauty as is the *Pelléas and Mélisande* of Claude Debussy.

The probability is that Beckmesser himself was finally converted and actually succeeded in singing freer songs than those approved by the obdurately conservative mastersingers. The fanatical admirers of Wagner, amusingly fanatical at this late day when Wagner himself must be ranked among the conservatives, when many of his pages must be characterized as 'old hat,' may at last see a new light and show the seal of the late convert. The hysterial faddists are more dangerous foes to Debussy, dangerous even when they do not attempt to imitate him, to 'debussyize' in music.

These faddists are found, of course, in their perfection in Paris. The late Jean Lorraine[3] wrote a bitter article about them and named them 'pelléastres.' He described them as they appear at the Opéra Comique with long hair carefully arranged over the forehead, with their coats with velvet collars and slightly puffed sleeves. They all have fine hands and they wear precious rings of Egypt or Byzantium. The 'pelléastres' are of families that are in fashionable society.

In the large cities of our own country the majority of the musical faddists are women. They decree suddenly that this or that composer must be in fashion. They crowd the hall or parlor where some one lectures on the chosen composer and 'explains' his work. Already there are lecturers on Debussy. Already has the Baedeker for *Pelléas and Mélisande* been published. Yet never was there an opera less in need of explanation, of guide book.

And there are some who are mightily concerned about the 'symbolism' of this lyric drama. Where is the kingdom of Allemonde? What is the esoteric significance of the word? Why did not Pelléas go to see his sick friend? Who are the three asleep in the grotto? Why did not Mélisande tell Golaud where she lost her ring? What is the symbolism of Mélisande's golden crown? The scene in which little Yniold endeavors to lift the rock and then wonders at the actions of the sheep is omitted in the performance at New York, or these questioners would be at their wit's end.

If the beauty of either Maeterlinck's or Debussy's work rested solely on symbolism it would be only specious and short lived. Gérard de Nerval[4] 'knew that the whole mystery of beauty can never be comprehended by the crowd, and that while clearness is a virtue of style, perfect explicitness is not a necessary virtue.' But he did not insist on symbolism alone.

Debussy's music has no existence apart from Maeterlinck's drama. It has no life in the arrangement for voice and piano. It is purely orchestral, and its purpose is to supply the emotional atmosphere in which the stage characters live, which the spectator must breathe ...

1 The French dramatist, critic and essayist.
2 The critic James Gibbons Huneker (see no. 62).
3 The French novelist and Symbolist poet, who died in 1906.
4 Nerval's own writing was, of course, tinged with insanity.

58

Julius Korngold, [Mahler's Ninth Symphony]

Neue freie Presse (27 June 1912), from M. Wagner, ed., *Geschichte der Österreichischen Musikkritik in Beispielen*
(Tutzing, 1979)

Korngold (1860–1945) was critic of Vienna's respected *Neue freie Presse* for more than three decades. Although his writing lacked the magisterial authority of his predecessor, Hanslick (see no. 43), he was one of the most influential musical journalists of his day. His mixed review of the première of Mahler's Ninth Symphony echoes the critical reactions to Beethoven's

Ninth (see no. 21). Korngold's son, Erich Wolfgang, was a child prodigy composer; both emigrated to the United States early in the Nazi era and ended their careers in Hollywood.

Today the first and only new work of the festival week was heard. Dead masters alone are played and commemorated. To score a success with a new work, a composer must be fresh in the ground. Such was Mahler's fate: the laurel tree is growing lushly over his early grave.[1] The programme highlighted the significant relationship between his Ninth – a posthumous work, like Bruckner's – and the works of Bruckner and Beethoven. To draw comparisons between Bruckner and Beethoven would be in poor taste (and unacceptable in any case). But can a composer who goes ahead with a ninth symphony help bearing the works of his predecessors in mind? Even for a more naive artist than Mahler, not to do so would have been difficult. Ever since Beethoven, certain ideas have become attached to a ninth symphony. People expect a culmination, a solemn singularity from the music, a metaphysical confession of faith from the musician. Perhaps this is precisely why a man of Mahler's paradoxical spirit, having dealt with enough metaphysical needs in his preceding works, decided to dispense with examinations of the riddle of the universe in a ninth symphony.

Bruckner instinctively wrote his Ninth in D minor, the Beethoven key. He needed to keep faith only with himself, to remain Brucknerian in his solemnity and the earnestness of the prayer in which he joins his hands in this last work in a spirit of resignation. In so doing he quite unintentionally avoided the sphere of Beethoven's creation. I have already disclosed that Mahler did not remain undetached with respect to the key of his symphony. 'The main theme actually came to me in D, not in minor but in major,' he asserted. None the less, what followed was minor enough – spiritual minor. Mahler sought to turn as far away from the tonal realms of the two Ninths as from their form. All the same, it happened that his symphony ended in an Adagio, just like Bruckner's, and that in this symphony too, at least in its most important parts, the deeply moved soul, addressing the final questions of existence, sang out, softly this time, in a humble dirge. A ninth will always be a ninth, after all ...

The Adagio at the close: no novelty, by the way, in Mahler's symphony cycle. The Third displayed the same order of move-ments, which is also found in Tchaikovsky of course.[2] Only in Mahler's Third does the Adagio, with its ardent yearning of the heaven-seeking heart, seem to bring the psychological course to an urgent concluding climax, as in the Ninth. Here the preceding mid-dle movements – a Scherzo that strings *ländler* together like the waltzes in the Scherzo of the Fifth Symphony, and a burlesque Rondo – in no way reveal spiritual tensions that call for a reconcil-ing finale in an Adagio mood. Formally, the last movement should follow immediately after the first; they belong together spiritually. The two middle movements are out of place psychologically and, I hasten to add, out of keeping with the much deeper and purer mood of the outer movements ...

The moods, the melodic turns of the first movement, do they not seem remarkably familiar? They are Mahlerian, eminently Mahlerian, to be sure. But their colours are unmistakably those of the *Kindertotenlieder*. Thus did Mahler sing the lullaby to the dead child, a melody of bleeding heart-wounds and at the same time the tenderest transfiguration, perhaps the most beautiful and the most touching the composer devised. He sang the mystical Nietzsche song in the Third Symphony in a similar tone – and here as there, the key is D major. Has not some experience of the composer sought musical form in this symphony? There is probably no need for the hint given by a passage marked 'Like a heavy conductus' – a conductus of another sort than the sarcastic-realistic one in the Fifth Symphony. The *Kindertotenlieder* were copied down as if out of a dull premonition, but Mahler's Ninth Symphony falls in a year which followed the dreadful one that robbed the artist of a beloved child.[3]

The deep harp-tones with which the movement begins sound like the peal of bells. Is a tender babe not being borne to church? From the delicately singing main theme full of moving, lyric beauty, there emerges a child's face in gracious innocence. And what follows appears to be dedicated to the destiny of this creature, seems to tell of the awakening child's soul, of the father's love, as it does of despairing father's grief, of the hard-won consolation never to be forgotten ... The musical development goes hand in hand with the psychological, programmatic development. The bell motive is hair-raisingly present when the dead one is being carried to the grave, and its first five measured notes, on the same pitch, are transformed into the heavy clods that fall on a coffin. With that begins the recapitulation, both masterful and stirring, which condenses the material. Wonderfully delicate is the finale, with expansions and fragmentations of the motive, dying out at last in flutes and violins. The whole movement has an individual language, Mahler's sweetest and most individual: lyricism. He is one of the most important and loveliest of the masters, one, certainly, who has lived life as inwardly as possible.

The two middle movements are on a much lower level musically. They lapse, if we may so express it, into the style of a bloated serenade. The rollicking high spirits of the second movement's *ländler*-potpourri turn out to be not really symphonic, despite all their harmonic, contrapuntal, and orchestral finery. The composer's effusive spirit clashes with the inflexible, rhythmic dance scheme – and the clash goes on too long. In the third movement, designated 'Rondo-Burleske', he gives vent to a defiant gallows humour. The piece suffers from hypertrophy of fugue-loving counterpoint, which implants itself loudly in the winds. It also suffers from the themes themselves, which don't carry their fair weight, despite clever distortions of normal voice-leading: hoarse hurrahs, grotesquely contorted body-leaps. Even so, the movement flows with dazzling brio. Does it not seem to point to Reger's influence? The satanic grimaces in the clarinets, in the middle of the D major central section, and the ensuing harp *glissando* certainly bear Mahler's stamp; but so does the more beautiful, quiet beginning of this section in the trumpets. The closing Adagio stands out afresh. It really does have the manner and mood of Bruckner's last Adagio ...

To sum up briefly: the exquisite, valuable prize of this last symphony of Mahler's is its first movement; the last movement is a beautiful bonus. In the middle movements his inventiveness flags, as one can see unmistakably in their forced frenzy. If our interpretation is correct, the work would be truest to his ideas – or at least remain the truest in its effect – if it went out into the world as a two-movement symphony. Doesn't a last, posthumous symphony have the right to be a torso? Some 'unfinished' symphonies are finished ...

1 Mahler died in 1911. The Ninth Symphony, written in 1908–9, was first performed on 26 June 1912.

2 Tchaikovsky's *Pathétique* Symphony also closes with an Andante.
3 Mahler's daugher Maria died of scarlet fever in 1907.

59

William J. Henderson, 'The Function of Musical Criticism'

Musical Quarterly, vol. 1 (1915)

Henderson (1855–1937) was the undisputed dean of American critics in the early 1900s. His career at the *New York Times* and *New York Sun* spanned five decades. Notoriously unsympathetic to contemporary music, he none the less hailed Wagner and wrote with special sensitivity about a wide range of opera and vocal music. This article, which appeared in the inaugural issue of America's first important musicological journal, is a classic statement of the principles of journalistic criticism. Compare it with Rochlitz's essay (no. 17).

In the age of analysis and introspection we probe all things. If we are disposed but little to philosophical contemplation and much to the materialistic scrutiny of physical science, our results are perhaps none the less valuable. Sooner or later the supremacy of the inductive method of reasoning is bound to enforce itself, and upon the observation of our patiently acquired array of cold fact we are incited to rear an edifice of codified law. That in the end we subject the very process itself to the operation of its own methods is inevitable. Criticism must above all things be self-critical, lest it mistake its own purpose.

In the popular mind criticism occupies a vague position and enjoys a very tenuous respect. It is judged not by ultimate, but by immediate results. The dramatic critic goes to the first performance of a new play, writes a comment perhaps none too favorable for the next morning's journal, and on the third night the theatre is full. *Ergo* the critic has failed and the worthlessness of his office is once more happily demonstrated. The music critic declares that the creations of Richard Strauss are not of the order of genuine art. Straightway they are performed all over the world and applauded rapturously. Once more the inefficiency of criticism is proved ...

As known and understood in this country musical criticism is a department in the complicated service of the daily newspaper. The critic, harnessed to the chariot of the press, is no brother of Pegasus, but rather of the more humble steed that draws the early milk wagon to the consumer's door. He is but a polite newsmonger, permitted in the routine of his day to make his bow before you and say: 'Yesterday Mistress Farrar was in prodigious spirit and her song was vastly diverting' or 'Were you at Mr. Kneisel's concert of chamber music last night? I do assure it was admirably prepared. My Lady Smith and Lord Jones applauded right heartily.' And this is criticism as the man in the street knows it. Small wonder that he discredits it.

But even when it rises to clearer heights and attempts a wide survey of a new composition, a survey in which the discernment of the operation of the artist mind behind the work must surely be sought, even here the restrictions of the professional gossip are not to be removed. But by taking thought and stemming opposition with a heart of controversy some may contrive to rise above the conventions of the newspaper and compel the reader to think of something larger than the mere personal triumph of the artist or the possible popularity of the new opera.

Whether these critics have formulated a theory of their art or not, their practise thrusts forward certain features which furnish a basis for definition. The daily occupations of musical criticism are indeed manifold; but as it is deducible from the methods of the best commentators on both sides of the western ocean, its ultimate function is to measure musical art by the standard of the thought of its time.

This is not a simple postulate; it is rather a summary of basic laws. But it sets forth a vital principal [sic] which must govern all critical commentary worthy of esteem. The commentator who carries the art work away into the seclusion of his own spiritual paradise, and, shut out from the raging of the heathen or the confusion of jarring sects, seeks to saturate his soul with its meaning as a purely monastic creation, serves no real end. He may glorify his own ego and indirectly pander to the vanity of the artist, but he is out of tune with the world and ciphers in the computation of humanity. He may preen himself upon the chastity of his thoroughly dispassionate speculation, but he is one of the futilities …

This brings us to the necessity of considering what must precede in the criticizing mind the measurement of the art work by the standard of its time. Since the creation places itself always in front of the creator, since only from it can we eventually deduce our understanding of him, it follows that criticism finds itself first of all in the presence of a tangible embodiment of an intangible conception, and that its first effort is to recognize the art work as the adequate presentation or realization of an art ideal.

There has never been any period in the devlopment of the art of music when this portion of the function of criticism was of more importance than it is at this moment. For it is obvious that criticism to-day cannot confine itself to the brilliancy of the technical achievement nor even to the absolute beauty of the music as such, because the composer of to-day refuses to write music dissociated from some ideal lying outside the art itself. His incessant effort is to raise or lower music to the estate of a representative art. Herein he seeks to evade the responsibility which should stand always before him of worshipping his art for its own sake.

Music is the most complete and self reliant of the arts. It has no utilitarian purpose, like architecture; it never, like literature, becomes a treasure chest for the archives of history. Despite Wagner's exhilarating interpretation of the Seventh Symphony [of Beethoven] as 'the apotheosis of the dance,' that composition remains an absolute symphony in A major, capable of resting wholly upon its own musical beauty. A suite by Bach can live a thing of beauty and a joy forever, even while it calmly defies every attempt to create for it any foundation outside its own thematic materials. Mozart's concertos and the symphonies of Brahms belong in this same class. All their eloquence consists in lofty song. They tell no stories; they paint no pictures; they make no futile essays at preaching philosophies.

The critic who sets himself to the estimate of such music thinks only of music, that unapproachable art in which the form and the substance are wed in perfect union. But when he scrutinizes the music of the contemporaneous period, he finds an art ideal wholly different. He is compelled to accept, as it were, a double standard. He must first consider whether the art ideal which is to receive tangible expression is in itself beautiful and indeed musical at all, and second whether the expression constitutes an artistic product. And in bending his mind to this second consideration, he is inevitably forced back to the primal condition of the tone art. He must ask himself whether the thing is beautiful as a musical composition regardless of its relation to the extraneous thoughts which the composer's title or programme seeks to associate with it ...

Music, like the other arts, addresses itself to some one – not exclusively to its own maker, nor yet to a few kindred souls. Art which cannot reach a public is without life. It is futile for the composer or the poet to sit like Prentice's[1] Napoleon 'wrapped in the solitude of his own originality.' Yet there is after all no great difficulty in discovering the line of demarcation between the man who follows and the man who leads the public. The former prostrates himself at the feet of his audience; the latter preaches from the pulpit of art with irresistible eloquence. In considering the product of the man whose eyes are ever fixed on the altar of art and who perhaps demands readier sympathy than the public can give, the position of criticism may become unassailable, or at any rate tremendously helpful. Is it Music? Not, is it the kind of music Beethoven or Mozart or Tschaikowsky wrote; but is it music, founded imperishably on the immutable laws of art? That is the test, and whether he shelters himself behind the classic ramparts of the old masters or storms the strange harmonic heights held by the Schoenbergs and the Debussys, by this test every master must stand or fall ...

The man and the music, the music and the man: these stand and fall together and thus the magic spell of human interest attaches itself to every page of score.

It is at this point, too, that we are confronted by the demand of the interpretative artist. Of this any one who places the function of criticism upon a high plane would wish to say very little. The consideration of the performer is the least important office of real criticism; but unfortunately it is the one on which the public lays the largest attention. You may write many pages assailing the fame of Beethoven and no one will take issue with you; but expose the paltry pretenses of some third rate opera singer and the vials of wrath are opened ...

To return then to the loftier duty, that of studying the originating soul and its product, we must once more lay emphasis on the asseveration that the ultimate function of criticism is the discernment and appreciation of the art work in its relation to the spirit of its time. What, then, becomes of immortal fame? Well, in the first place it is extremely doubtful that such a thing exists. Certainly musical art is so young that no one dare predict the indestructibility of any creation brought forth up to the present. But granting that immortality can be attained, one thing is perfectly certain, and that is that it is never gained by deliberately setting out in pursuit of it. The man who enslaves himself to so vague an object cannot become free, and only a free mind can create great things.

But he who is aflame with the thought of his own time and who is urged night and day by irresistible forces to strive for its expression, he is the man upon whom the world will in the end bestow the title of master. Large or small in type his work may be; that matters not. The Providence of art watches the fall of the sparrow, too. A pretentious epic sinks into obscurity and a three-stanza lyric goes singing itself down the pathways of the centuries. A folk song, bred in the puissant loins of unconscious parenthood, marches in the highways and trumpets the thought of a people and an epoch. Where is the composer who can imprison the mood of such a song? For him the laurel and the glory ...

But perchance this is the point at which we may pause for a moment to inquire whether the composers of our own day do not suffer from the utter want of a point of view. Or shall we not possibly be forced to declare that some of them profit by it? Have we some composers who suffer from intellectual asceticism, who are unconsciously living outside of the world about them? Or have we others who, incapable of understanding and expressing the spirit of their own time, are nevertheless governed by its less ennobling impulses? The study of one's own time, as already intimated, is a large undertaking, and a small mind is sure to seize on the smallest matters. On the other hand it should be candidly acknowledged that the majority of composers are not essaying such large creations that they can be expected to walk hand in hand with Shakespeare, Michel Angelo, or Schubert. The majority cannot be expected to do more than strike notes which fully harmonize with their time. The musican who does this is not to be put aside as unworthy of exhaustive critical consideration. He may not excite transports, but he will assuredly arouse interest.

It will be urged, and with reason, that the appreciation of a man's work as an embodiment of the spirit of his age is almost impossible to his contemporaries. We do not grasp the meaning of our own time, but are we entirely ignorant of it? Is it not the duty of criticism to look beyond the confines of the art of which it treats? There cannot be any man who has earnestly practised the calling of music critic and who has not arrived at the conviction that nothing human is foreign to him. The more he knows about things outside of music the better qualified he is to discern the significance of a musical art work. And the broader his vision, the higher his point of view, the more will he enter into the spirit of his time.

It is not essential that he should seek to fix the final standing of an art work according to his own conception of his period. Perspectives of all types, and particularly the historical, alter views. But criticism is in duty bound to stand upon the firm foundation of historical scholarship to rear thereupon an edifice of comment which shall command a clear perspective. If there is probability that contemporaneous criticism may err as to the place of Reger or Debussy in the art world, it is less likely to blunder about the position of Mozart or Donizetti ...

The true desideratum, after all, is not the infallibility of criticism. The acquisition of a ready made opinion is sought only by the intellectually incapable or indolent. A real man prefers to think for himself; and the best criticism is that which compels him to do so. Therefore what we should value most in critical commentary is its point of view, its endeavor to attain an altitude from which the whole breadth of the subject may be surveyed. Unfortunately this type of criticism, like the art with which it will be obliged to concern itself, will not command the attention of a large public. It will perforce address itself to the society of the intellectual, and its dearest hope should be to raise music to that station beside literature and painting which that society habitually neglects to give to it.

Despite its wide activity the art of music is still in need of propaganda and of explication. Halting, inadequate, often blundering as it must ever be, critical discussion is still the foremost agent in bringing to the general public a perception of the nature of musical art and of the ends sought by composers. This is none the less true because the major part of the criticism which reaches the public eye is a mere record of the doings of performers. Admitting that such critical commentary is nothing more than the ephemeral record of the passing incident, we shall find that by sheer force of accretion even this increases the general stock of appreciation of that which lies behind the performance. Meanwhile the broader outlooks of such masters of critical practice as Rolland, Dent, Newman[2] and their compeers must inevitably lead men toward a discernment of the organization of musical art.

1 George Denison Prentice, a popular nineteenth-century American poet and newspaper paragrapher.
2 Romain Rolland, Edward J. Dent and Ernest Newman (see no. 72).

60

Zoltán Kodály, 'On the Occasion of the Première of *Bluebeard's Castle*'

Nyugat, vol. 11 (1918), from *The Selected Writings of Zoltán Kodály* (London, 1974), trans. Lili Halápy and Fred Macnicol

The composer and music educator Kodály (1882–1967) turned his hand to music criticism in Budapest for a brief period after the First World War, and continued to write throughout his life. Like his forerunner Mihály Mosonyi, Kodály strove to define and create an identifiably Hungarian musical idiom and culture. This discussion of the musical qualities of the Hungarian language echoes sentiments expressed by eighteenth- and nineteenth-century critics; see, for example, nos. 1, 8, 9, 26, 37, 40 and 48.

Today neither the public nor the critics see Bartók's music as the castle with seven locked doors which it appeared to be ten years ago,[1] but even now there are few who have been able to follow him on the road from searching, based on older foundations, to his own discovery. Even his opponents to date reluctantly recognize the richness of his inventive capacity, the individual colour of his orchestra, the simultaneous birth of colour and thought, the strictly organic interrelationship between his ideas. No one has succeeded in categorizing him into either of the branches of 'modern music,' neither into the motley style of the old–new mixture, nor into the anarchy–chaos of half-talents and pseudo-talents.

His completely individual combination of ancient primitiveness with the most developed culture makes his musical individuality stand quite apart. His music is a single-material, self-contained, unified organism, virtually without any trace of borrowing or imitation. He too has his ancestors, but the connection is not apparent in externals; the spirit of all great music of the past lives in him, all that is not bound to time, all that is permanently valid. But for average musical culture what is most difficult to approach in him is what developed from his connection with folk music.

More recently it has become customary to regard folk art as the incomplete survival of the older stages of art. Even if there is much of this among it, this does not wholly exhaust it. Its true value lies in what it has preserved from ancient music and that to which it gives an inspiring example – an expression of feeling which is free of all formal pattern, not limited by formal schemes, and for this reason of extreme intensity; it is the free, direct speech of the soul. Those who do not know this folk music – and how many do know it? – will not be able to recognize it in Bartók either; they will only feel some great peculiarity, for this is precisely what has no analogy either in art music or in Hungarian music so far.

The first musical efforts of the forties in the nineteenth century saw the bloodless song literature of the beginning of the century and gypsy dance music as their direct predecessors, and joined forces with them. Whatever got into this development here and there from below, from the more ancient layers, like sporadic rocks in a waste of rushes, led to freshly prospering Hungarian music which precisely through its more ancient and original side was able once again to grasp the broken thread of tradition.[2]

I do not believe that this music is 'felt' to be Hungarian by those who think the style of the few hundred songs written around 1850 to be the only Hungarian style. This semi-dilettante literature is not entirely worthless for what it is, but it shows such a superficial Hungarian quality and smells so much of the public house, and so many associations of the wind-and-gypsies atmosphere cling to it, that it had to remain outside the gates of higher art.

From the new Hungarian music flows the pure clean air of another Hungarian quality with deeper, everlasting roots, like that of the Szekely pine forests where something was forced into hiding, something which remained of a life-current of monumental strength, something which had once embraced a whole country. The buds of this grew large, as with Bartók's music, providing volcanic work of a quite extraordinary creative strength developing into a spiritual language of infinite expressive force, but also having firm construction. Today we can search in vain for something comparable. This is no longer the sentimental revelry of the Bach-period gentry, nor the rousing alarm of Kossuth, nor the sorrowing of the *kuruc* insurrectionists.[3] In short, it is not just one part of Hungary but everything together: a multi-layered, deeply tragic world-Hungary containing within it the self-consciousness of the conquerors of the country and the wild energy of the will to live in the face of present wretchedness. This sort of music is really in its element when it is in association with drama. It was quite ready for it. It was only in the development of the vocal element that it proved necessary to tread an unbeaten track.

As until recently the great majority of our traditional operatic repertoire consisted of works translated from foreign languages, these developed a peculiar kind of musical declamation which even composers of original operas were latterly not very capable of avoiding. It became almost a general rule that in this declamation the stresses of language and music should always be at war with each other. Usually the music won, and for two generations the audience (mainly aristocracy and German-speaking bourgeoisie) put up with this murdering of the Hungarian language, their linguistic instinct making no protest against it. In the last few years some new artistic translations brought a considerable improvement. But even the best translation is still a translation. It can follow only imperfectly the melodic line born for another language. And possibly even the opera public of today does not fully appreciate that the Hungarian language is not only standing on its own two feet, but setting off under its own steam and even trying to fly.

Bartók set out to liberate the language, intensifying natural inflections into music, thus contributing a great deal to the evolution of a Hungarian recitative style. This is the first work on the Hungarian operatic stage in which the singing is consistent from beginning to end, speaking to us in an uninterrupted Hungarian way.

This kind of composition, in which every word and phrase gains a cutting plasticity, illuminates even the tiniest linguistic unevennesses in the text. That such things might exist in Balázs's text would be serious cause for complaint, but even strict critics do not mention it. Virtually unanimous condemnation of such unevenness – without any justification here, it is true – creates the impression that as far as opera libretti are concerned we are faced with very exacting demands. Nevertheless, our writers do not consider the libretto to be a serous genre, forgetting that in the golden ages of opera even the text was always the work of a professional. For this reason it is a striking phenomenon when an opera text stems from a real writer or even a dramatist. For this reason special praise is due to Béla Balázs, who did not grudge writing one of his most beautiful and poetic concepts in the form of an opera libretto, thus contributing to the birth of a magnificent work. His text 'without events' is not indeed an integral part of any customary operatic scheme. But as the old tale is unfolded and the eternally unsolved man–woman problem is displayed before us, the listener is transfixed by tragic tension from the first word to the last. Its outline quality, the way the bringing to life of the contours is entrusted to the music, make it possible to weld it together organically with the music. Neither the drama nor the music is compelled to deny its own separate existence, and yet they are able to merge into a greater unity. This unity is not disturbed but rather enhanced by the symphonic construction in the music: the curve of the drama and the parallel curve of the music reinforce each other in a powerful double rainbow.

The constructive strength of the music asserts itself even better if we hear *The Wooden Prince* [4] after it. This dance-play balances the disconsolate adagio of the opera with a playful, animated allegro contrast. The two together merge into one, like two movements of a giant symphony. And let those who consider atonality to be Bartók's principal achievement notice in the end that both of these works have a recapitulating basic key, like any Mozart opera …

1 *Bluebeard's Castle*, written in 1911, was first produced by the Budapest Opera on 24 May 1918. In the opera the 'seven locked doors' open on to Bluebeard's past.
2 The early 1800s saw a spate of folk-like art songs in Hungary based on traditional *verbunkos*, *csárdás*, etc., as well as operas on Hungarian themes.
3 Louis Kossuth was a hero of the Hungarian Revolution of 1848 and later president of the Hungarian republic. The Bach period is named for Alexander Bach, who, as head of the post-revolutionary government, personified the oppressive rule of the Habsburgs.
4 Bartók's ballet of 1917, for which Balázs also wrote the scenario.

61

Adolfo Salazar, '*Goyescas* and "Local Colour"'

From *Andromeda: Bocetos de critica y estetica musical* (Mexico, 1921)

A prolific and wide-ranging writer, Salazar (1890–1958) served as critic of the Madrid daily *El Sol* from 1918 until the outbreak of the Spanish Civil War, when he moved to Mexico. Despite his early enthusiasm for Falla and his life-long advocacy of other Spanish and Latin American composers, Salazar's cosmopolitan outlook set him apart from Pedrell (see no. 55) and other exponents of musical nationalism (see nos. 31, 34, 35, 37, 40 and 44).

A New York critic – I don't know his name – who reviewed the première of *Goyescas*[1] in the *New York Glass* on 29 January 1916, made a digression concerning the work's 'local colour' which filled me with perplexity. The critic began by saying that he had never been to Spain, but that Chabrier's *Rhapsodie espanole*, Debussy's *Ibéria*, Laparra's *Habanera*, and Zandonai's *Conchita*[2] had given him a sensation of colour that *Goyescas*, which Granados presented as 'the real thing' compared to Bizet's tambourine-Spanishness, had failed to achieve.

Works by composers of such disparate tendencies are capable of producing in a foreign listener a sensation which is related to his *a priori* concept of Spanishness. Isn't this strange? How can works which are so diverse arouse this feeling? One might reasonably suppose, first of all, that the foreign criterion of Spanishness is inseparable from an insipid Andalusianism which lends itself readily to export – and which has not victimized foreigners alone. The greatest following for this sort of Italianizing Spanishness is found among ourselves. Granados may have been right to consider *Carmen* a model of debased Spanishness, but are the majority of our own 'Fantasías españolas', 'Serenatas españolas', 'Potpourris españoles' and so forth any better than that celebrated work? Certainly, the methods of that kind of Spanish music are no more sophisticated than Bizet's ...

Bizet found his melodic ingredients in the collections of popular songs which a Catalan editor obtained for him;[3] then he stewed them up into a tasty compote. Are the aromas of our whole repertoire from the end of the last century any more penetratingly Spanish than that? Luckily, let us hasten to say, we are beginning to catch a whiff of them. Some windows have opened in the old stage set, letting in a warm, springlike breeze laden with subtle promises. A few golden rays of early-morning sun pierce the moth-eaten curtain. The artificial lantern so well suited to bright colours and to tin pales before the splendours of the new light, and the deathly pallor of a decrepit art gives way to the rich palette of an artistic springtime.

But no more digressions: let's stick to facts. A swarm of young artists is now at work, filling its honeycombs with the pollen of the flowers of the fields. In different ways and with different tendencies, they follow the great teachings of [Felipe] Pedrell, [Manuel de] Falla, [Bartolomeo] Pérez Casas, [Oscar] Esplá, [Joaqín] Turina, [Rogelio del] Villar, and [Jésus] Guridi, drawing inspirations from the fountain of the people and bringing them to them life – whether lasting or ephemeral, only time will tell.

This brings me to the nub of my investigation: would any of these young composers produce a sensation of local colour in the New York critic, who holds his *idea* about Spain without having stepped off Fifth Avenue?

My main doubts are these: that it has repeatedly been demonstrated that works based on *clearly* Spanish themes are as likely as not to give a foreigner the idea of Russian, French, Scandinavian or Bohemian music, just as the reverse is also certain. Will the technique be adopted by our composers? If so, I don't understand why Debussy or Chabrier give a foreigner a sensation of Spanishness, and why certain Russian and Bohemian music gives us the sensation of Spanish music. The reason must lie, then, in the vitality of the theme, or rather in the fact that the *theme* manages to arouse in the listener the concept he has already labelled, which is no more deep-rooted or valid than a (nearly always overly hasty and banal) first impression.

We may lament the concept of Spanishness professed by the aforementioned critic, but is it any less sensible than our concept of, for example, Russian music, which is nothing but the Orientalism of *Sheherazade* or *Prince Igor*?[4] This brings up the vexed question of *nationalism*, about which not even your fiercest partisans can agree. [Nicolai] Medtner or Stravinsky may protest against those who deny the Russian character of their music, just as Granados, Villar or Guridi may against the New York critic. In my opinion, the truth is that the common, vicious concept of nationalism is an *error by extension*: that is, the overly hasty cataloguing of a national spirit under the heading of a single regional aspect. Beyond the Pyrenees Spain is nothing more than Andalusia or the *jota*, just as for us there is nothing more to Russia than its Asiatic East. What's more, this is true even for ourselves. A given set of Castilian songs, a given Basque or Levantine opera in a strictly folkloric vein, risks boring us in light of our inability to perceive the gradations of 'local colour' clearly enough, just as a Frenchman is unable to perceive them in a given opera from another Spanish region. I speak of cases that are in everyone's memory, without blaming anyone – or rather, blaming only those who are excessively preoccupied with making 'local colour' or coming across it. None other is the deplorable cause of that trashy Andalusianism to which I alluded before, a transgression committed for the sufficient reason of flattering that sinful taste.

A path to redemption has now opened up after Pedrell, with the above-mentioned composers: Albéniz first of all, creating a deeply felt Spanish music which couldn't possibly be Frenchified;[5] then Falla and Turina, sensing their region and placing little importance on the Madrilenian, *café chantant* concept of Andalusia; then Esplá, steeping his creative inspiration in the Levantine atmosphere, even though no one recognizes it; likewise with Villar, whose fine Castilian feeling was once derided as Scandinavian;[6] so too Pérez Casas, whose admirable feeling for the music of the Levant could put one in mind of a Levant beyond the Mediterranean ... So all our great young musicians, and so too that beloved and hapless Granados who, like a true artist, was above banal conventions, too prone to superficial criticism or facile pleasure.

1 The Metropolitan Opera in New York gave the première of Enrique Granados's opera *Goyescas* on 28 January 1916. Returning to Europe shortly afterwards, the composer was killed when a German submarine torpedoed his ship.
2 The references are to Chabrier's *España*, one of Debussy's three *Images*, and operas by Raoul Laparra and Riccardo Zandonai.
3 Several melodies in *Carmen* are based on folk material, which Bizet may have

gleaned from a collection of Spanish folk songs entitled *Echos d'Espagne* at the Bibliothèque National.

4 Rimsky-Korsakov's symphonic suite and the opera by Borodin.

5 The Spanish composer Isaac Albéniz spent most of his career in France.

6 Villar was known as the 'Spanish Grieg'.

62

James Gibbons Huneker, 'The Music of Yesterday?'

From *Variations* (New York, 1921)

Among critics of America's 'Golden Age', none was a more polished literary stylist than Huneker (1857–1921). Most of his essays on music, art, literature and other topics were collected in books. Sympathetic to Richard Strauss and other moderns, Huneker here expresses a healthy scepticism about 'progress' and a typically American sense of immersion in the present. Fétis and Shaw had interesting things to say on the subject as well; see nos. 24 and 50.

Notwithstanding the fact that he played the flute and ranked Rossini above Wagner, Arthur Schopenhauer said some notable things about music. Here is a wise observation of his: 'Art is ever on the quest, a quest and a divine adventure;' although this restless search for the new often ends in plain reaction, progress may be crabwise and still be progress. We fear 'progress,' as usually understood, is a glittering 'general idea' that blinds many to the truth. Reform in art is like reform in politics. You can't reform the St. Matthew Passion music or the fifth symphony. Is Parsifal a reformation of Gluck? This talk of reforms is confusing the historic with the aesthetic. Art is a tricksy quantity and, like quicksilver, is ever mobile. As in all genuine revolutions, the personal equation counts the heaviest, so in dealing with the conditions of music at the present time we ought to study the temperament of our music-makers and let prophecy sulk in its tent as it may.

One thing is certain: The old tonal order has changed forever; there are plenty of signs and wonders in the musical firmament to prove this. Moussorgsky preceded Debussy in his use of whole-tone harmonies, and a contemporary of Debussy and an equally gifted musician, Charles Martin Loeffler, was experimenting before Debussy in a dark but delectable harmonic region. The tyranny of the diatonic and chromatic scales, the tiresome revolution of the major and minor modes, the critical Canutes who sit at the edge of the musical sea and say to the modern waves, 'Thus far and no further!' and then hastily abandon their thrones and rush to safety, else to be overwhelmed – all these are of the past, whether in art, literature, music, or – let Nietzsche speak – in ethics. Even philosophy has changed its garb and logic is 'a dodge,' as Prof. Jowett[1] used to say. Every stronghold is being assailed, from the 'divine' rights of property to the common chord of C major.

If Ruskin had written music-criticism he might have amplified the connotations of his famous phrase, the 'pathetic fallacy,' for we consider it a pathetic fallacy (though not in the Ruskinian sense) in criticism to be overshadowed by the fear that, because some of our predecessors misjudged Wagner, Manet and Ibsen, we should be too tender in our judgments of our contemporaries. Here is 'the pathos of distance' run to seed. The music of to-day may be the music of to-morrow, but if not, what then? It may satisfy the emotional needs of the moment, yet become a stale formula to-morrow. What does that prove? Though Bach and Beethoven built their work on the broad bases of eternity – employing that tremendous term in a limited sense; no art is 'eternal' – nevertheless, one may enjoy the men whose music is of slight texture and 'modern.' Nor is this a plea for mediocrity. Mediocrity we shall always have with us; mediocrity is mankind in the normal, and normal man demands of art what he can read without running, hear without thinking. Every century produces artists who are forgotten in a generation, though they fill the ear for a time with their clever production. This has led to another general idea, that of transition, of intermediate types. But after critical perspective has been attained, it will be seen that the majority of composers fall into this category of the transitional; not a consoling notion, but an unavoidable conclusion. Richard Wagner had his epigones. And so had Haydn, Mozart, Beethoven. Mendelssohn was a feminine variation of Bach, and after Schumann followed Brahms – Brahms, who threatens to rival his great exemplar. Yet I can recall the incredulous smiles when, twenty-five years ago, I called the Brahms compositions 'The Music of the Future.'

The Wagner–Liszt tradition of music-drama and the symphonic

poem have been continued with personal modifications by Richard Strauss. Max Reger pinned his faith to Brahms and absolute music, though not without an individual variation. In considering his Sinfonietta, the Serenade, the Hiller Variations, the Prologue to a Tragedy, the Lustspiel overture, the two concertos respectively for pianoforte and violin, we are struck not so much by the masterly handling of old forms as by the stark, emotional content of these compositions. It is an error to dismiss his music as merely academic. He began as a Brahmsianer, but he did not succeed, as did his master, in fusing form and theme. There is a Dionysian strain in him that too often is in jarring discord with the intellectual structure of his work. The furor teutonicus in conflict with the scholar. Yet at one period Reger was considered the rival of Strauss, though that day has long passed. Arnold Schoenberg now divides the throne. And there are many other claimants – [Emil] Rezniček, [Eugène] d'Albert, Ernst Boehe, Walter Braunfels, Max Schillings, Hans Pfitzner, [Friedrich] Klose, [Carl] Ehrenberg, [Heinrich] Noren, Franz Schreker, and the younger choir whose doings are analyzed weekly by clever Cezar Searchinger in the pages of the *Musical Courier*. Their name is legion. They enter the lists sounding golden trumpets of self-praise and are usually forgotten after a solitary performance of their huge machines, whether opera or symphony. Size seems to be the prime requisite. Write a music-drama that consumes three nights in its performance, a symphony that takes a hundred men, with a chorus of a thousand, to play and sing. Behold! You are a modern among moderns. But your name is as mud the following year. Exceptions are Mahler and Bruckner, yet I have my suspicions that when the zeal of William Mengelberg[2] has abated, then the Mahler craze will go the way of all flesh, despite the fact that he has composed some thrilling pages. Otherwise, his symphonic structures are too mastodonic to endure; like those of Berlioz, they are top-heavy with ennui, and many chambers are empty of significant ideas or vital emotions. Musical intellectualism at its extreme Kamchatska.

Our personal preferences incline us to the new French music. To be sure, substance is often lacking, but you are not oppressed by the abomination of desolation which lurks in the merely huge, by what Mr. Finck[3] calls Jumboism in music. The formal clarity, the charming color sense, the sprightly, even joyful, spirit, combined with an audacious roving among revolutionary ideas, all endear these youngsters to us. Debussy is their artistic sire, Ravel their stepfather, and if d'Indy does not fall into this category, being a descendant of Franck, he is none the less admirable as a musician. Stravinsky outpoints them all in the imprevu, as does the incredible Prokofieff – a man to be carefully estimated, one who thus far hasn't put his best foot foremost in America.[4] The Richard Strauss case is no longer a moot one. He has in all probability given his best work, and superlative work it is, despite its slag, scoria, rubble, and refuse. He is the chief of a school, a position from which he can never be dislodged, and when history sifts the pretensions of all the second and third rate men of his generation, his figure will be found standing close to Wagner's and Berlioz's and Liszt's. An epigone? Yes. But an epigone of individual genius.

With Arnold Schoenberg freedom in modulation is not only permissible but an iron rule; he is obsessed by the theory of overtones, and his music is not only planned horizontally and vertically but in a circular fashion. There is in his philosophy no such thing as consonance or dissonance, only perfect ear training. (We quote from his Harmony; a Bible for Supermen.) He writes: 'Harmonie fremde Tone gibt es also nicht' – and a sly dig at old-timers – 'sondern nur dem Harmonie-system fremde.'[5] After carefully listening to his 'chaos' a certain order disengages itself; his madness is methodical. For one thing, he abuses the interval of the fourth and he enjoys juggling with the chord of the ninth. Vagabond harmonies in which remotest keys lovingly hold hands do not dissipate the sensation of a central tonality somewhere – the cellar, on the roof, in the gutter, up above in the sky so high. The inner ear tells you that his D minor quartet is really thought, though not altogether played, in that key. As for form, you must not expect it from a man who has declared: 'I decide my form during composition only through feeling,' a procedure which in other composers' works might be called improvisation. Every chord is the outcome of an emotion, the emotion aroused by the poem or idea which gives birth to the composition. Such antique things as the cyclic form or community of themes are not to be found in Schoenberg's bright lexicon of anarchy. He boils down the classic sonata form to one movement and begins developing his theme as soon as it is announced. We should be grateful that he announces it at all; themeless music is the rage at present.

So, as it may be seen, the new dogmatism is more dogmatic than the old. The absence of rule in Schoenberg is an inflexible, cast-iron law of necessity as tyrannical as the Socialism that has replaced Czarism with a more oppressive autocracy, the rule of the unwashed, many-headed monster. Better one tyrant than a million. There is no music of yesterday or tomorrow. There is only the music of Now.

1 Benjamin Jowett, the renowned British classical scholar.
2 Willem Mengelberg, the Dutch conductor of the Concertgebouw Orchestra, was a champion of Mahler.
3 The American critic Henry T. Finck.
4 Prokofiev came to the United States in 1918, at the age of twenty-seven.
5 'There are, then, no nonharmonic tones, no tones foreign to harmony, but merely tones foreign to the harmonic system' (*Harmonielehre* [1911]; trans. Roy E. Carter as *The Theory of Harmony* [Berkeley, Calif., 1978], p. 321).

63

Max Brod, 'On Vítězslav Novák's Storm'

From *Prager Sternenhimmel* (1923; reprinted Vienna, 1966)

A distinguished novelist and poet, Brod (1884–1968) is best known to musicians for his widely performed German translations of Janáček's *Jenůfa* and other operas. An eloquent advocate of Czech music and musicians, Brod wrote criticism in German for the *Prager Tageblatt* and later for newspapers in Palestine and Israel. This comparison of Novák – whose reputation was eclipsed by Janáček's after the First World War – and Strauss 'the musical tourist' echoes discussions of programme music by critics like Castil-Blaze, Dwight and Wolf (see nos. 27, 30 and 45).

What is truly wretched about Richard Strauss's *Alpine Symphony*? People compare it with another musical journey, namely, Berlioz's *Harold in Italy*. At the centre of the Berlioz stands the sensitive soul, expressed through melodic peaks and the dark velvet of Paganini's viola; but at the centre of the Strauss stands – a tourist. The tourist must have everything: waterfall, alpine pasture, meadow, glacier, dangerous places, two minutes of ecstasy and five minutes of melancholy, storm, and mist – in short, everything Baedeker says there is to see and hear in the Alps. The soul, on the other hand, is content with four sections, arbitrarily chosen but at least filled to bursting with the most intense life. Richard Strauss the musical tourist strings together his geographical inspirations (which are pretty in spots). They are unalloyed realism; no self stands behind them to colour the changing landscape. On the contrary, the self is so transparently impersonal, so exclusively focused on 'impressionism', that every two or three minutes by the metronome it takes on a different hue, like a chameleon. In Berlioz the landscapes are nothing but his self; they are colour and long-breathed melody of his boundless, yearning heart; in a word, they are music.

So too do Novák's musical landscapes rise to soulful heights, not to the materialistic theme rattled off in the programme. His *In the Tatra Mountains*, its summit bathed in a glass-harmonica atmosphere, towers above Strauss's cardboard panorama of the Alps. But above all towers his masterpiece, sea-voyage and shipwreck, drunkenness and loves, a veritable oratorio of passion: his masterpiece *The Storm*. Let me tell you about it! First I want to say that Novák and Suk are, after Janáček, today's representative Czech composers, as Smetana and Dvořák were in their time (much less justifiably in the latter's case); and that it is incomprehensible that this *Storm* has still never been performed in German!!

The Storm. After a tale by Svatopluk Čech, from the decades when Lord Byron's fashion reigned. First some maiden from storm-lashed shore is sending her prayer over the dark Slavic-Illyrian south sea: '*Ave, stella maris*, deliver my beloved!' ... For we are far away on the ship, somewhere outdoors; its decks echo with song. Overhead, in the crow's nest, rolls the soprano voice of the sailor boy, who fears not the maternal wave and whose face fronts the driving wind. On the top deck the folk song of the working sailors is heard, while to one side the young sailor yearns for the maiden, whose greetings he seems to sense over hundreds of watery leagues. And in the bowels of the ship, in the bottom cabin, the black slave (a king in Sudan, he was sold into bondage) stares at his white mistress, whom he loves ... New waves of music, typhoon and revolt on deck, long-rolling disaster upon white crests of foam: the ship is wrecked. Captain, drunken workers, blackamoor, and princess, all go down; only the soprano once again flings its merry 'la-la-la' into the air from the top of the wreck. For the sea is closing round, subsiding. Somewhere on the coast pirates are fishing for the young sailor's engagement ring, and from the band emerges the sacred chorus: *Stella maris* ...

Can one guess how the composer has transformed this poem, forging the sea's ceaseless roaring in the ear and endless yearning into a unity? No one can imagine the sound of the menacing trumpets, the deep-snorting horns, and the voices calling wordlessly behind the scenes. Above all, no one can imagine the relentless, ever-mounting urging, the urgent pursuit of the basic motif 'Oh Star of the World-Sea', the *cantilena* and its restless variations. This urging – I feel it, and therein I feel Novák's greatness, therein above all – must, yes, *must* lead to the shipwreck, and with a necessity quite different from what the poem alone demands. From the pure aesthetic-plastic *post hoc* of the model, the composer has made an ethical *propter hoc*. Perhaps this does not lend itself to explanation in words, but the music says it as clearly as could be: This ship, in whose bowels the mistreated, needle-pierced black slave sits – this ship of human outrage, of human wrong-doing and wrong-suffering – does not sink by accident. It must be wrecked; it cannot bear on its sorrow-gnawed planks the sailor's pure, elated, youthful love and his innocent joy. This ship simply casts off the unjust and drowns itself, the good with the bad, for we are all guilty in tragic complicity.

That, my friends, is the storm! No touristic panorama of the sea, with beating waves and setting sun, but the storm in the soul, urgings, despair, sins, and in the end – who has not felt it today more deeply than ever? – hope tender but firm.

64

Emile Vuillermoz, 'Arnold Schönberg, *Pierrot lunaire*'

From *Musiques d'aujourd'hui* (Paris, 1923)

The French tradition of fine critical writing was carried on in the early twentieth century by Vuillermoz (1878–1960), critic of *L'Excelsior, Le Temps* and other journals. Bernard Gavoty, one of the best French critics of the postwar period, praised him for 'giving each of his articles a tone, colour, and variety that put one in mind of the shimmerings of orchestration'. Vuillermoz's catholic taste enabled him to see the links between composers as seemingly disparate as Schönberg and Debussy. For another view of Schönberg, see no. 86.

Arnold Schönberg's name is well known to our musicians – much better known than his music. Some years before the war people were already beginning to drop his name casually in discussions of aesthetics in the intimacy of clubs and literary groups. Whenever some young composer, French or foreign, showed a penchant for a harsh, disjointed, violent, dissonant style, it was said knowingly, 'He owes a lot to Schönberg.' For many ordinary people, the sprinters in the race toward dissonance lined up like this: Wagner, the former grand champion, had been overtaken by Debussy; Debussy had been outdistanced by Ravel; Ravel had been ditched by Stravinsky; and far beyond Stravinsky, way down yonder toward the Prater, madly galloped that phantom-racer, Arnold Schönberg.

This simplistic athletic image of the contemporary-music movement was – and still is – the only ranking system many music lovers required. It was convenient and all the more secure in that it was unverifiable, Schönberg's works being completely unknown in France.

True, a few people in the know spoke of a sextet, *Verklärte Nacht*; of a symphonic poem, *Pelléas et Mélisande*; of a certain *Gurrelieder* for chorus and orchestra; and of a String Quartet. But people who had read these scores or had gone out of their way to hear them found nothing in them as terrifying as they had been led to believe. Schönberg's style was linked to the Mahler tradition, though it showed greater freedom and inquisitiveness and a few somewhat bolder harmonic experiments. The author of such music simply couldn't have any active influence on the young post-Debussyians of 1912 who were liberally ascribed to him as pupils.

Nevertheless, oddly enough, the legend of Schönberg the revolutionary was merely a promise; it was going to become a reality. The apparition of *Pierrot lunaire* ten years ago suddenly revealed a new force emerging in modern aesthetics.[1] A disturbing phenomenon, apparently bred by spontaneous generation, confronted us. Strange stories were told about the insurmountable difficulties of this work, written in an unknown musical language. And on the eve of the war the late musicologist Jules Ecorcheville, eager to shed light on this historic moment, negotiated with the first interpreters of this mysterious score with an eye to its immediate performance in Paris.

That performance was to be postponed for eight years. It was given only last season, in an atmosphere of bewildered admiration. The score has been edited. No longer does the 'Schönberg case' belong to myth and legend; it can be studied dispassionately. It is a matter of keen aesthetic and historical interest which merits our closest attention ...

For some time we have been hearing frequent reports of harmonic or orchestral *coups d'état*, and we have lost count of the young composers who have been glibly presented to us as Lenins or Trotskys of the semiquaver. We are even a little blasé about bomb threats which turn out to be duds and about the earnest bolshevism of upstanding shopkeepers clenching paper knives between their teeth. But in Arnold Schönberg we have an authentic rebel who doesn't make fancy speeches or use big words, but instead turns our artistic institutions upside-down and proposes a new declaration of the rights of man and musician. And his message will be deeply disturbing to everyone who loves music without preconceptions ...

In the present state of musical scholarship and terminology, the style of *Pierrot lunaire* nearly defies analysis. Our harmonic, tonal and contrapuntal system explains very little in this composition, which unfolds carefreely, which is supple and spare, which reveals a paradise on earth and seems oblivious to the possibility that music and musicians ever could have existed before.

So refined is Schönberg's music that he appears to be totally ignorant of classical syntax. It's disconcerting to read his score: the writing seems utterly incoherent. Here is a passage based on the alternating or simultaneous use of two keys by tones which share the musical scale. Is this a system? Hardly – twenty measures later the point will be moot. Phrases are superimposed in canon: here one part chases another, an octave below and a single note behind; there the interval of imitation is a minor second, and three notes separate the parts. The resulting counterpoint is wild and artless and full of rude shocks. Clumsiness? Not a bit of it. These two patterns which wind and intertwine are delicious, provided your overly sophisticated ear can forget the old rules of the game and simply follow the graceful twists of two delicate arabesques which pursue but never catch up with each other. Here are impeccably dressed chords which seem to introduce themselves politely by their Christian names. Wrong: these phantom-chords have neither title, nor rank, nor profession, nor social function. They are homeless creatures passing between two arpeggio fragments, sucked into the cosmic vortex of this new-born universe of sound which holds the dust of the old, dead suns in its field of gravity. They are the pulverized debris of a world, just as in certain cubist paintings an eye, a foot, a hand, vestiges of a vanished humanity, are scattered to the four corners of the canvas by some mysterious explosion ...

Some of these tableaux are stark and harrowing because the subject demands it, but others are strangely seductive to the ear, caressing to the point of sweetness – sweetness obtained by means wholly unforeseen but absolutely irresistible. The transparency, the purity, the pearly light of certain descriptions of the moon strike the listener with singular force. One is bathed in silvery reflections, in cold light and trembling pallors, as if immersed in Debussy's rich and trembling impressionist orchestra; and yet no more than two or three instruments are gesturing capriciously, with studied awkwardness, and meekly falling silent after raising their voices for fifteen measures. Sometimes a single timbre suffices to create the atmosphere. In 'Lune malade', the solo flute, curling itself around the voice, opens infinite vistas on to a landscape of melancholy.

The nature of this concentrated, compressed, essential art is to generate the maximum of suggestive force with the minimum of material means, to obtain a hitherto unknown intensity of colouring, and to make us completely oblivious to the quality and quantity of technical resources employed to that end. The sense of proportion is so right that one feels the same sensation of strength in the presence of that bass clarinet, flute and viola as if one were listening to a Richard Strauss orchestration. And the prodigious variety of accents and colours which the composer draws from that strange little harmonium boggles the imagination.

But an even more gripping novelty awaits us. In *Pierrot lunaire* Arnold Schönberg wanted to renew and enrich the technique of the human voice. His audacity will certainly elicit universal reproaches from indignant voice teachers. You must admit it's a bold scheme. This is how it's carried out:

Schönberg wanted to entrust a 'spoken melody' to the singer. See how carefully and strictly he has notated the barring, the rhythm, and the melody of the vocal part, leaving nothing to chance ... A note will be a note, and the interpreter must respect its rhythmic value and intonation. But the voice will, so to speak, forget wind instrument technique in order to learn that of stringed instruments. Instead of producing each sound solidly in its pure form, like an organ pipe which mechanically calibrates a degree of the scale at the touch of a key, the singer will create notes in the manner of the harpist who, having set the string in motion, lets the sound drown, dissolve, and melt into the vibrating waves which he has set in motion and which are going to disappear on the horizon, far from their point of departure. Scarcely has the note been attacked when it must evaporate, decay, spread high or low, in a supple trajectory of flight. In her throat the singer has a keyboard of bronze or crystal bells which ring true but changeably, their peal dying away in a perpetual *glissando*.

Let us not talk about paradox, eccentricity or presumption. In fact, it would be very easy to parody and ridicule this delicate and sensitive technique with absurd *ports de voix* – a temptation which practical jokers won't resist for long. But remember the sneers elicited twenty-five years ago by the *Chansons de Bilitis*, when Debussy declared his intention of following the subtle, understated inflections of the French language more closely in his vocal writing. People made fun of that gloomy, monotonous psalmody and refused to find any melody in it at all.

Who would dare to make such a claim today? Henceforth a slight ripple of sound will convey to our refined ears all the nuances of expression that once had to be hammered home for effect. Schönberg has merely taken the experiment one step further, but he has done so in the spirit of the German language and of his special form of verbal gymnastics, with its practised high jumps, leaps, running jumps, pull-ups and splits. It would be foolish to introduce this sort of exercise in France; it's unwise and illogical enough to have applied it to performances of the French translation of *Pierrot lunaire*, where the show of respect for a missing tonic accent becomes a game devoid of interest. But our musicians aren't likely to remain indifferent to this endeavour. Following Schönberg's example, but paying closer attention to the emotive content of the word, they will wish to make the human cry more malleable and plastic, to refine its vibrations, to make it more trembling, quaking and shivering, to open it up to the nuances of murmuring, sobbing, cooing and sighing – nuances which are so poignant, so expressive, and, at heart, so musical .

In the chaos of today's aesthetic aspirations, Arnold Schönberg offers a precise and objective realization of a new ideal. The gist of it is somewhat disquieting and the formula can be disastrous in other hands than his. But hearing *Pierrot lunaire* offers such convincing proof that we are in the company of a born musician, a master of the sound-world, a magician of the note, that one could not long refuse to follow such a sure guide in boldly exploring the virgin forests of our art.

Where this new orientation will lead is very difficult to predict. But after the debauchery of the orchestral and harmonic riches of the last generation, one can perceive a tendency toward simplicity, spareness and technical humility. In France this ideal has given rise to a good deal of literature but not of music. Abroad it seems to be producing more interesting results. Artists of very different races and cultures are meeting at the same crossroads of thought and sensibility. The haunting and evocative experiments of a Schönberg are not, at bottom, very different from those of the young Catalan Federico Mompou, whose artless compositions of notes, at once naive and mysterious, open up in us a whole world of dreams.

The music of our most modern visionaries has already ceased to cater to the needs of our eyes; nor does it any longer show much concern about satisfying the scruples of our ears: its sole ambition, it seems, is to administer a direct shock to the hidden depths of our subconscious by a technique in which intuition plays a decisive role. In this new era, evidently, a musician will not receive permission to write unless he has genius – an agreeable prospect. But what will become of our poor ears if, perchance – anything can happen! – a certain number of composers who are in too much of a hurry decide to forgo that permission? ...

1 The première of *Pierrot lunaire* created a furore in Berlin in 1912.

65

Adolf Weissmann, 'Race and Modernity'

Modern Music (February 1924)

Weissmann (1873–1929) was one of Berlin's leading critics in the first three decades of the century. Graf compared him to Bellaigue, Huneker and Newman (see nos. 47, 62 and 72) as a writer of grace and imagination. In this article, which opened the maiden issue of the influential American journal *Modern Music*, he attempts to distinguish between 'racial feeling' and 'nationalism'. Boschot (no. 71) took a less charitable view of the Germanic spirit.

Modern music has drawn upon itself the charge of being a world-vernacular, a sort of musical 'Volapük'[1] without differentiating characteristics and, through this uniformity, of departing essentially and to its own prejudice from earlier music.

Superficially this reproach seems to rest on some foundation. It must be admitted that tendencies alien to the art, while not exactly removing all its distinctive features, have considerably weakened it. The commercial exploitation of music, intimately connected with the modern facility of travel, has effected a lasting process of reciprocal influence between nations, which gives a special emphasis to the relation between the concepts of 'mode' and 'modern'.

Then the war, re-directing the intercourse of nations, created a new idea of the 'modern'. For although it was deadly to artistic life, it made extensive use of art as a source of political propaganda. In the new sense, Germany appeared absolutely sterile, while France, Russia and England were acclaimed as modern.

Although international artistic relations have not yet been entirely restored, a lively exchange is now taking place in the world of art, which has doubtless sharpened the feeling for differences in music. The 'national' concept has been blurred by the misrepresentation of this idea in politics, and has of course still less import in art. But although in contemporary art a common feeling can be perceived, racial color is nevertheless apparent, indeed must be, or this art would be lifeless.

For Germany it was particularly difficult in 1900 to feel at home in the accepted world-view of modernity. This concept bore the stamp of Debussy. The essential modern element for which he struggled, and which was designated by his literary interpreters as 'impressionism', was the enrichment of sonority (tonality) through the loosening of tone-matter. It was the outcome of a basic concept fundamentally different from that of the German. In 'Debussyism' there is poetic feeling and sensibility, nothing of the ponderous or speculative.

Debussy, with the formal lightness that is in the very nature of French tradition, had risen from a melodious sweetness reminiscent of Massenet, and a Grieg-like landscape coloring, to his masterpiece *Pelléas and Mélisande*, a tender, poetic renunciation of the tangible world. In German music, on the other hand, the tendency was definitely to retain firm hold on actuality, a mood that gained triumphant expression in Richard Strauss.

At this time Debussy tempted many Germans to imitation; but it was possible for them merely to repeat the gesture, not to express creatively the spirit of impressionism. But the spirit was essential, and its expression so intimately related to the personality of Debussy, that even his own compatriots could but achieve imitation. To be sure, they succeeded in mastering his style whereas German impressionism betrayed obvious effort through its heavy movement.

However, Debussy, and even Ravel, who at the same time and later continued the struggle for modernity, achieving the expression of a clear-seeing spiritual personality, are now no longer modern. They have become the classics of modernity.

For the moment the world of music is under the spell of two men – Schönberg and Stravinsky. Even here race has accentuated diversity. To Stravinsky may be accorded the western domain, to Schönberg the remaining countries.

Schönberg, who is rooted in chamber music, in which field the most important utterance must be conceded his, draws with dialectic vigor and passionate feeling, with even more of the first than of the second – the final consequences of the Germanic music-civilization. It must be pointed out, however, that the dialectic sharpness which transformed this former Wagnerian into the reformer of music, rests on Jewish race feeling, which fused with the characteristic impulse of German music to form a new sonorous tissue.

This mingling process, that is, the racial penetration of German music, has provoked the great crisis through which we are passing. Atonality and linear counterpoint are the external characteristics of this new music. The animating spirit, however, is, or rather tends to be, the traditional one – the spirit that moved Bach and ultimately Beethoven. Dialectic rigor may have cramped this force, but undoubtedly something genuine, definitely and characteristically German is apparent in this music, and the way is open for a truly creative spirit, which, disregarding dialectic, shall seize and utilize this stimulus. We need, as Busoni understands the situation, something akin to a Mozart.[2]

The appearance of a Paul Hindemith in Germany, who, despite Schönberg, once again creates opus after opus out of a true musical impulse, demonstrates more clearly than Ernest Krenek, who pursues the path of the linear with cerebral force and relentless strength of will, that the world must judge Schönberg as a means toward an end and not an end in himself. His contempt for all that is consonant would of necessity lead to sterility. The German impulse must not be diluted into a paper music.

Fundamentally racial also is the influence of Stravinsky, on whom we have fixed as the impelling force in Western music. It is characteristic that the element which we call atonal, while automatically entering the Western world, should make its appearance there with different effect. Whereas the Germanic, or the music world dominated by Germanic influences, tends to throw off an academic heritage and struggles to create a new form from a new content, we see the new form rising in the West with ease and a certain inevitability.

One might say that the Western world is guided on the one hand by the feeling for sonority, and on the other by the instinct for the folk-psyche. Debussy was a fulfilment. What could follow? Moussorgsky, the Russian visionary, something of folk-mentality. Contact between the French and Russian mind was of long standing. The French folk-spirit was not potent enough of itself to create a new music. Salvation came from Russia. Through continued contact with Paris, and collaboration with the Russian ballet, Stravinsky paved the way for that music which we recognize as a synthesis of barbaric folk-feeling and the highest refinement, which finds its supreme expression in the *Sacre du printemps*.

Stravinsky's rhythm, his new tonality, have penetrated the world which is nearest him racially. The young Arthur Honegger, a Francis Poulenc, an Arthur Bliss may show us on what fertile field his inspiration has fallen.

It is race which colors modernity. But racial mixtures now appear, to open up new possibilities. In music, blood and not mind is the ultimate determinant.

1 An early 'universal' language, invented in the nineteenth century.
2 For example, at the beginning of *Von der Einheit der Musik* (On the Oneness of Music), Busoni wrote: 'This Oneness, which I advance as a first principle, exists already and is sustained almost uninterruptedly in the works of Bach and Mozart; these two are still the strongest and most enduring musical personalities in our present-day art of music ... ' (trans. Rosamund Ley).

66

Boris de Schloezer, 'A Proletarian Music'

Revue musicale (1 November 1924)

Most Russians who emigrated to the West in the wake of the Bolshevik Revolution retained close personal and intellectual ties to their homeland. Schloezer (1881–1969), who pursued his career as a critic in Paris, took a sceptical but not unsympathetic view of the revolutionaries' early efforts to create a genuinely 'proletarian' art. For other perspectives on the place of music in twentieth-century Russian and Soviet culture, see the essays by Sollertinsky and Ivashkin (nos. 77 and 99).

Whatever political views we hold, whatever judgments we make about the events in Russia and the men who seem to be directing them, that country is now unquestionably the laboratory for the greatest social experiment ever conceived and carried out by man ...

This experiment is being pursued more or less systematically in every area of social life. Naturally, what interests us in particular is the musical sphere: the efforts to make a new musical culture, a proletarian musical culture, take root in Russia.

Virtually all regimes have attempted, often successfully, to make art serve social and political ends and to regulate artistic life.

Sometimes the attempts are fairly brutal, employing police measures, and sometimes they are discreet and devious, using art as a vehicle for education and propaganda, protecting certain schools and tendencies, and even trying to establish a certain aesthetic ideal. What distinguishes the Soviet authorities' activity in this area is, first, its scale and second, above all, its consistency, boldness of conception, the simplicity and apparent clarity of the ideology, and the enthusiasm – the almost religious fanaticism – which animates that activity.

Social life being considered exclusively under the aspect of the class struggle, art, in the Bolshevik (or, in more general terms, Marxist) view, always mirrors the social structure more or less directly. It expresses the needs, tastes, aspirations and ideas of the ruling classes and contributes to the enslavement of the exploited classes. An art which once was aristocratic and feudal gave way to a bourgeois art – that of present-day Western Europe. But in Russia a new art is to arise, a proletarian art, the product of the proletarian revolution of October 1917. It will reflect the new social order dominated by the proletariat, the morals of that class, and the bulk of its ideas, philosophical, aesthetic and otherwise.

From the Bolshevik point of view, the revolution of 1917 is distinguished from all of its predecessors – from the bourgeois revolution of 1789, for example – in that Communism ultimately establishes a regime which makes class struggle impossible and creates a perfectly harmonious social order. But that is the future; in the present, the proletariat institutes its dictatorship in order to attain this far-off goal. In the midst of a bourgeois universe, Russia is a military camp and its art, the art of this transitional period, must be a combat weapon; all of its specifically proletarian qualities must be underscored, exaggerated, to make it an instrument of intellectual and moral liberation for the working and peasant classes.

On the one hand, this is a matter of democratizing art, particularly music, of helping to disseminate aesthetic values, of putting artworks within reach of the people, of getting on with the artistic education of the masses of workers and peasants. On the other hand, it is a matter of giving birth to a new art, rather like gardeners who produce new varieties of vegetables and fruits by giving them suitable temperatures and special fertilizers.

During the early years of the revolution, the overriding concern was to put art within reach of the people. Concerts and free shows multiplied all over – in schools, factories, military camps, proletarian clubs, etc. The efforts of the Soviet authorities were energetically supported and even instigated by the artists themselves, who, apart from loftier considerations (the new public could be very appreciative at times), saw that the Soviet programme offered them many tangible advantages. They threw themselves *en masse* into the various organizations hastily created by the Bolsheviks, and the greatest names of the Russian stage and concert hall could be seen taking part in 'platoon concerts' for a piece of bread or a sack of potatoes, before an audience of sailors or workers.

After two or three years of this, it became apparent that the goals the Bolshevik leaders had set for themselves could not be achieved merely by democratizing art. Artists were constantly obliged to play down to the public, who walked out as soon as they were fed anything at all refined. Then again, once the civil war was over and the regime was firmly established both outside and inside the country, the Communists, who had destroyed so much, could begin to rebuild. It is this 'constructive period' which we are now witnessing, in the economic as well as the artistic domain.

It is no longer a matter of making music *ad usum populi* and tossing scraps of bourgeois music to the people, but of awakening the latent artistic powers of the masses and creating an art for and by the people – an art opposed in form and spirit to the bourgeois art of Western Europe and pre-revolutionary Russia ... If one accepts the premises of the Bolsheviks, they cannot logically admit an art which claims to be apolitical: music which is not proletarian or revolutionary must inevitably be bourgeois or reactionary.

But what is a revolutionary music?

I have just read a new journal, *La Culture musicale*, published in Moscow.[1] It brings together some of the top names in Russian music criticism, such as Igor Glebov, Leonid Sabaneyev, and a few others[2] ... [In his article 'Modern Art,'] Sabaneyev defends the thesis of the musicians who, while accepting that Russian music must be proletarian and revolutionary, insist on the value of bourgeois musical culture and on the necessity of using its resources.

The art of a revoltionary era such as ours, he writes, does not necessarily limit itself to revolutionary subjects, celebrating barricades, the Red Army, factory work, etc. Music is a self-contained universe of sound, and every modification can be explained in technical terms. To social changes and upheavals, music responds by changing its sonorous content and its form.

Sabaneyev's article is clearly directed against those – and they are numerous – who accuse Russian musicians of not being sufficiently 'of the present', of not expressing in their works the new emotions and ideas born of the revolution. If one looks at this from the Marxist point of view, he replies, one perceives the naiveté of these accusations, 'which, in the final analysis, are merely the manifestation of a bourgeois ideology'.

Music being a certain kind of production, 'here, as in every area, we are concerned that the proletariat has at its disposal as perfect a production as possible ... In music we must achieve progress analogous to that brought about in agriculture by replacing outmoded tools with tractors and farm machines ... And so it is not a question of adapting a revolutionary text to some piece of music or another, as is too often the case. That sort of thing can have propaganda value, but it does not constitute the modern, revolutionary music to which we aspire ... ' Western modern art is in an advanced state of decay; it is the music of a dying world. But Russian composers must profit by the technical discoveries of their bourgeois colleagues; it would be a crime not to use them. In this *Fabrikat* (Sabaneyev insists on using the industrial and commercial vocabulary of the Bolsheviks), there are harmful elements which must be eliminated; but there are others which should be adopted ...

But Sabaneyev does not eliminate the individual factor, nor does he deny the role of the creative personality. Evidently, he considers the development of a new proletarian musical culture a complex natural process which can be assisted and hastened, but not regulated at will. His industrial vocabulary notwithstanding, he knows very well that a symphony is not an automobile – unlike the writers of the *Renouveau musical*, whose audacity is matched only by their ignorance and naiveté.

Their lack of understanding of European musical life is complete. They don't even wish to become acquainted with it, for they hold it in profound contempt as the product of a civilization which is rotten to the core. Naturally, everything to them seems simple and clear-cut when it comes to creating a revolutionary art. It must be an optimistic, vigorous, joyous art; Communist Russia has no room for sadness, discouragement or tragic feeling. And one of these young writers (I expect they are very young) takes pity on Tchaikovsky and especially on Scriabin for having been unable to witness the Soviets' triumph. Scriabin was highly gifted, but he was one of the bourgeoisie's many victims, for he took refuge in mysticism to escape the ugliness of the bourgeois regime.[3]

However odd it may seem at first, it's Beethoven whom all of these musical revolutionaries dream about when they develop their ideas about proletarian art. One of them writes that the definitive form of this art is found in the Beethovenian symphony. In their eyes, Beethoven is the musician of the French Revolution; in Marxist aesthetics, he is the poet of the Third Estate. Another thing that draws them to the composer of the Ninth Symphony is his humanitarian optimism, and one of the studies in the *Renouveau musical* is devoted to Beethovenian joy. Bach too has a place of honour in this ranking, which can be explained only by their complete ignorance of his religious music; for the religious spirit is the true *bête noire* of the *Renouveau musical*, as it is of all Bolshevik publications.

Naturally, one might ask whether the new proletarian music actually exists in any form, albeit only embryonic, outside the writings of its theorists.

The critics of the *Renouveau musical* warmly extol certain composers who have emerged from the people, former workers such as Vassiliev-Buglay[4] and others. I have seen some of their works: marches, revolutionary hymns, lyrical and satirical songs – music of utter insignificance. Russian themes, mostly popular (sometimes even religious songs), are cleverly harmonized according to elementary rules. Change the words and these revolutionary hymns would be perfectly appropriate for some 'bourgeois' ceremony, such as the inauguration of a mayor or a ministerial reception.

As for the art Sabaneyev dreams about, an art intrinsically revolutionary in technique and sound, we find no trace of it in the works of the Russian musicians in Russia who merely imitate Scriabin, Medtner or Tchaikovsky. To find that art, you must come to Paris, Vienna, Berlin. Reality is not always logical, and the examples of the French Revolution and Beethoven, the German, should make the

Bolshevik theorists somewhat cautious in their judgments and predictions.

1 The Russian title was *Muzikalnaya kultura*. It commenced – and ceased – publication in 1924. I have been unable to trace the *Renouveau musical*, which Schloezer mentions below.
2 Igor Glebov was the pen name of Boris Asafyev (see no. 67). Sabaneyev wrote for many Russian and foreign periodicals and was music editor of both *Pravda* and *Izvestia* in the early 1920s. He emigrated in 1926 and eventually settled in France.
3 Schloezer was a close friend of Scriabin.
4 Dmitri Vassiliev-Buglay was known for his patriotic ballads and choruses to revolutionary texts.

67

Boris Asafyev, 'Prokofiev's Third Piano Concerto'

(1925), from *Izbrannye trudy*, vol. 5 (Moscow, 1952–7), trans.
Anthony Phillips

Asafyev (1884–1949) was one of the leading musical figures in early Soviet Russia. Both his music and his criticism (which he published under the pseudonym Igor Glebov) reflect his abiding concern for the development of a Russian identity in music – a concern he shared with critics such as Stasov (see no. 44). This article represents an attempt to reclaim Prokofiev, who had left Russia for the West in 1918, as a true son of the Soviet Union.

Prokofiev's concerto[1] is a deeply Russian work; its essence can be understood only if we are prepared to cast off the conventional academic criteria to which Western European scholasticism has accustomed us. The form and construction of the musical texture, the functional significance of each element in the organization of the 'aural argument,' even the character of the piano passagework – everything is subordinated to the idea of the indivisible supremacy of the tonic, the fundamental key-note, as the *epicentre* of movement in any and all directions, the point of arrival and departure, the one and only stable point of reference. The tonic here is not merely the cadence that closes, *winds up* the activity of a particular section of the music. No, its role is *propellant*; it stimulates and sets in motion. However paradoxical, however at odds with the

'Tristanesque' notion and imperative that only by avoiding the tonic can melodic tension be continuously maintained,[2] it is precisely the supremacy of the tonic that here gives birth to a healthy, natural sensation of dynamic movement, free from any hint of stasis or sclerosis. There is a simple reason for this: instead of gravitating towards the bass, all the consonant elements gravitate to the centre and concentrate within that central line on a fundamental point. From this line and from this point, as from a *cantus firmus*[3] (but of course in a dynamic context), there radiate both longitudinally and latitudinally harmonic blocks, formations of secondary, ornamental figurations, contrapuntal material of a more or less independent nature, and, finally, what might be called 'coloratura,' that is to say, the elaborate virtuoso passagework of the concerto part. Underpinning all these elements are slow-moving bass lines, in which predominate progressions in fifths and tonic-dominant relationships, derived ostinato-like from folk instruments ...

The texture of the Third Concerto rests on an intuitive premise: *melos* is the basis of the musical dynamic. No trivial tunefulness this, derived from a tonic-dominant harmonic formula, but the tightly coiled germ of song-melody itself, from which sprang all the great musical culture of the East, the culture which impregnated the Mediterranean coast and the plains of Eastern Europe. Perhaps the time has now come when the art of Western European music must return to the dawn of its history and once again refresh itself at the springs of *melos*? In Russia there is today but one composer who alone has seen and, thanks to his profound artistic insight, been able to grasp the process that is in train. Many Russo-European musicians from the heights of their majesty have been inclined to overlook the 'boorish pranks' of Kastalsky,[4] the *narodnik*[5] with his idealization of the common people. It has always seemed to me that people – especially musicians – are afraid of anything that forces them to widen their horizons: they declare one system of musical thought to be almighty while denying to others the right even to exist. Therefore they failed to understand and support Kastalsky's quest: for a framework of Russian diatonic harmony – in essence not Russian at all but drawn from primordial human experience – whose sources would be the structure and dynamic of the *znammeny raspev*[6] and folk song. It is now time to look seriously at Kastalsky's work. When we do, we shall see that his ideas are coming to the fore among many musicians and researchers, indeed among all who seek a way out of the impasse of over-refined emotionalism and subjectivism.

However complete a European Prokofiev may feel himself to be, in his art he proceeds with sure-footed, undeviating, perhaps instinctive steadfastness towards the goal of asserting the primordial *melos*-based seeds of form. It is significant that he is insistently drawn to pronounce and glorify C major as the harmonic bedrock and self-sufficient domain, not just as one tonality among others. No less significant is the affecting care and bold relief with which he molds the melodic contours. But most important of all is the originality of his diatonic-harmonic language, with its characteristic shifts from one tonic arena to another, sometimes without intermediate steps, sometimes with the help of specific devices recalling the kind of *portamento* and *glissando* found in folk song and folk instrumental music. This is the reason why Prokofiev's Third Concerto sounds so extraordinarily free and effortless, so Russian, although there are no actual folk melodies, no deliberate stylization, no folkloric subtleties, no modish invocations of everyday life. This sincere and simply written work is profoundly in tune with the times. Prokofiev is alien to the West. And if this concerto is nevertheless accepted there, it is ultimately because, not understanding its essence, people are none the less drawn to this music in the same way as they are drawn to the music of Mussorgsky, sensing in it a spring of living water.

And certainly, as far as the purity and artlessness of this spring are concerned, Prokofiev's creative work, founded on the diatonic and the *melos*, is stronger and fresher than Stravinsky's. Stravinsky's music, basically instrumental in character, is infected by the poison, inherent in its instrumental origin, of unsupported chromaticism and a tendency towards mechanical, soulless sound-spinning. In this respect Stravinsky's and Prokofiev's creative geniuses are at opposite poles. Stravinsky's instinctive awareness of the danger of instrumentalism, teetering on the brink of the precipice (*L'Histoire du soldat*),[7] leads him to make a sudden sharp leap into the sphere of the *melos*: the brilliantly contrived *Noces* is the result of just such a violent essay. Prokofiev, by contrast, usually saturates his instrumental textures with elements of song but, fearful of lagging behind fashionable trends, sometimes yields to the onslaught of a terrible foe – the soulless demon of sarcasm – and with a tragic failure of will is led to create hideous images and masks as graphic as any of Gogol's imaginings from the time when the writer had lost all faith in the value of art.

It would seem that in Prokofiev's music the sunnier aspect will prevail over the delusions of the West to the extent that the elements intuitively revealed in the Third Concerto are aroused in his creative consciousness. It is noteworthy that the basic material of this composition becomes more clearly delineated in character as it moves from beginning to close. It progresses from contemplative folk-song melody through decoratively figured passagework and the archaically harmonious main theme, through the fanciful twists and turns of the first movement's second subject and the veiled chromaticism of the second movement (theme–variation–theme), to the precise, uncompromisingly masculine lineaments of the main theme of the third and final movement, in which for the first time the elements of the symphonic finale that we discern scattered throughout the creative output of Borodin, Mussorgsky and Balakirev find their finished and most perfect (in the sense of economy and dynamic) expression. For this reason it will be interesting to become acquainted with Prokofiev's recently completed symphony.[8] Will he find a path to the long-desired goal, the synthesis, the Russian symphony free of the subjective and the emotional – that very symphony which will successfully collectivize the musical instincts of the multitude of different tribes now in the process of assuming their identity in sound, the symphony which eluded Glinka and was dreamt of in vain by that most exceptionally gifted of Russian failures, Balakirev?

1 The most popular of Prokofiev's piano concertos, the Third was written in the West in 1921. Muscovites heard it for the first time in 1925.
2 Wagner's concept of continuous modulation, of avoiding the feeling of rest associated with a traditional tonal centre or tonic, is exemplified by the famous chord in *Tristan und Isolde*.
3 Many composers have used a plainsong, or *cantus firmus*, as the foundation of more elaborate compositions.
4 The composer and choral conductor Aleksandr Kastalsky, whose music combined modern elements with ancient church modes.
5 A member of a late nineteenth-century movement to improve the lives of the Russian peasantry.
6 Liturgical chants of the ancient Russian Orthodox church.

7 Barilli (see no. 69) describes *L'Histoire du soldat* in remarkably similar terms.
8 The Second Symphony.

68

Hans Heinz Stuckenschmidt, 'The Mechanization of Music'

Pult und Taktstock, no. 1 (1925)

Technology has played an increasingly important role in music in the twentieth century. This famous article by Stuckenschmidt (1901–88), Germany's best-known critic of recent years, reflects a widespread view in the 1920s and 1930s that electronically assisted or generated music was the wave of the future. In retrospect, of course, the 'mechanization' of music has been a mixed blessing, as Adorno pointed out (see no. 76). For other perspectives on technology and music, see nos. 82, 88, 95 and 97.

The problems of the orchestra and futile attempts to solve them fill today's music journals. Practically everything written on the subject springs from two points of view:

  1 the artistic
  2 the economic.

There is no longer any question that large symphony and opera orchestras must either be cut down in size (which is tantamount to disbanding them) or lead parasitical lives, i.e. exist at state or private expense.

The heavy demands that the newer music since Beethoven, Berlioz and Wagner make on the quantitative structure of the orchestra are no longer commensurate with the public's interest and ability to pay.

Large-scale public philanthropy, like that of the petty princes of yore, now occurs only sporadically. The energy of a music-loving Croesus can be compared with the well-known drops on the proverbial hot stone.

Result: in a few years the large symphony orchestra as a public institution will have ceased to exist. Wagner operas, Strauss symphonies, etc., will be available only on the radio to the mortal who doesn't have the advantage of living in a big city.

From an artistic viewpoint, this reflection opens up still more painful prospects.

For the use of gigantic orchestral forces did not prevent modern composers from continually ratcheting up the average technical demands they made on the individual musician. (It may be noted that the works of Wagner and Schönberg were long held to be unperformable.) Not only was the very foundation of instrumental technique changed, but in our progressive age we have considerably higher expectations in regard to intonation, ensemble, virtuosity, etc., than before.

Today it may already be considered unacceptable to assemble a good orchestra from artists who are merely first-class musically and technically, virtuosos of their instruments. The 'good artisan' is no longer enough.

The composer's intuition may be starting to lead beyond the limits of humanly possible technique ...

Like every man, the human interpreter is subject to the limitations and imperfections of his body and soul.

Strength and memory are relative things. The virtuoso suffers from a favourable or unfavourable disposition.

The human sense of tempo is never absolute. The best musician is demonstrably incapable of adhering to a mathematically exact tempo; today he will make a piece ten seconds shorter than it was yesterday.

In traditional analysis, music actually has no tempo. The question of time has still never been taken into account in music theory.

The argument that 'these slight deviations constitute the genius of the conductors' and virtuosos' interpretations' appears to us to be of a purely sentimental nature. Our opinion of the role of interpreters differs sharply from the generally accepted one.

The reproductive artist should merely be a custodian of the wish the composer has expressed (hitherto inadequately, of course) through his notation. His identity, his feeling of the moment, his private attitudes are in the highest degree synonymous with the essence of the artwork. The more 'objective' the interpreter, the better the interpretation. (Busoni shocked many people late in his life with the 'cold objectivity' of his playing.)[1]

Our age's growing need for precision and clarity illuminates ever more the true inability of humans to be considered as interpreters of artworks ...

People have reflected on the means of accurately establishing the tempo of a piece of music, terms like andante, allegro and presto being too absurdly informal to describe it.

These considerations led to the first use of a machine in music: the metronome.

The speed of an adjustable pendulum, furnished with a numbered scale, is an absolute measure of a tone's duration.

Oddly enough, the idea of mechanizing all the other musical elements – that is, of entrusting the interpretation of a piece of music entirely to a machine – didn't occur to people until much later. The first mechanical piano was built not to satisfy a need for playing music exactly, but to have an apparatus to provide music at any time, without requiring human effort.[2]

Today for the first time today we are beginning to grasp the value machines will have for the development of music.

Two groups of mechanical instruments are to be distinguished:

1 devices which reproduce the sounds of real musical instruments by mechanical means, and so substitute directly for the hands and the mouth of the interpreter

2 apparatuses in which the sound itself is produced in some other way than by playing on an instrument.

To the first group belong electronic pianos, orchestrions[3] and barrel-organs. They operate on the same acoustical principles as the piano with respect to the orchestra.

In the second group we count the phonograph and the gramophone, which are similar in principle.[4] Here the sound originates from a needle set in motion by sound-wave modulations in a groove, which in turn make a sounding membrane vibrate.

In manufacturing matrixes for both kinds of mechanical instruments, the preferred system has the advantage of convincing sceptics of the truly perfect possibilities of machines: for instance, a good pianist has been asked to play a piece while at the same time his playing is automatically recorded on a roll by means of a relief-script which is definite and extremely precise, and which preserves every nuance of touch, dynamics, and pedalling.

So faithful is the reproduction that even the best musician can't tell whether the pianist himself or the mechanical instrument is playing (as we have proven by experiment!).

Certainly, these methods have other advantages as well: in the future, a master's playing will no longer die with him, and the after-world will braid wreaths for the interpreter (as it has for the mime since the discovery of film-making).

But the essential significance of these machines lies in the possibility of writing authentically for them.

That is, with a little practice one can compose this relief-script directly on the machine, as used to be done with notes, with every conceivable refinement and with mathematically established tempi, dynamic markings and phrasings.

Thus today the problem of authentic notation has indisputably already been solved by music machines; only a little effort is needed to explore and learn the script in detail. Several composers are doing it – in fifty years this knowledge will be part of elementary musical education.[5]

By the way, this system is often applied to the orchestrion and the barrel-organ.

Naturally, it is conceivable to build a gigantic orchestrion including all the instruments and sounds of the orchestra. It would also solve the problem of orchestra music, but in a very complicated and costly way. Building such an apparatus, which would have to include some thirty violins, twenty violas, and an equal number of cellos, etc., would consume a fortune – a fortune, to be sure, which in a few years would be recouped by savings in musicians' pay.

The possibility of composing authentically on gramophone records opens up considerably richer prospects.

The improvements of the gramophone, on which people have been working feverishly for years, have made it into an instrument which already today produces a sound that is quite pure and free of ambient noise.

In the foreseeable future, it will be possible to construct an apparatus whose sound, in terms of purity and fullness, will be fully comparable to that of a real orchestra.

Inscribing music on a gramophone record has an apparently insurmountable disadvantage: the script is microscopically small. Only with the help of powerful eyeglasses is it possible to study the character of the script and the design of its features.

This study is considerably more complicated than that of the relief-script for an electronic piano. Timbres, pitches and dynamics are indicated by small variations in the grooves.

Thus it is a question of making possible a significant enlargement of this soundwave-writing ...

The authentic gramophone has the great advantage over the mechanical piano and the orchestrion of assembling all conceivable timbres into one extremely simple and small apparatus.

For the composer of the future, it will contain inspirations which are plainly unforeseeable.

The number of timbres is infinite. Each instrumental sound can be given as much scope as desired.

The differentiations of pitch are infinite. Quarter- and eighth-tones can be intoned with mathematical purity.

The multiplicity of sounds will make the old orchestra seem quite primitive.

No longer will there be deficiencies in the ensemble: no late entries, no 'coughing' horn players, no broken strings, no out-of-tune tympani, no mistakes in interpretation.

The form of the artwork is fixed on the disk for all time with mathematical precision.

Some more possiblities for all kinds of mechanical instruments:

Speeds can be increased beyond the limits set by human technique. Semi-quaver passages in the tempo $\quarternote$ = 208 will be easy to perform.

With the electronic piano all tones, for example, can be struck simultaneously.

The strength of sound is limitless.

The most complicated rhythms can be synchronized. This is no longer utopian. For years notable musicians have concerned themselves with the problem of mechanization.

Arnold Schönberg favours these ideas.

Igor Stravinsky has written pieces for the electronic piano.

I myself have made the basic experiments on the gramophone (at the same time as George Antheil in Paris).[6]

Sentimental resistance won't be able to hamper the development of music.

The role of the interpreter belongs to the past.

1 Ferruccio Busoni, the pianist and composer, was one of the forefathers of the 'New Objectivity' (*Neue Sachlichkeit*) movement in German music and art.

2 The earliest player pianos were developed in the 1890s. By the second decade of the 1900s several competing player-piano mechanisms were being produced by firms such as Welte-Mignon, Duo-Art and Ampico. As Stuckenschmidt notes below, some of these systems were capable of reproducing the pianist's touch with extraordinary fidelity.

3 A generic name for instruments intended to mimic the sound of an orchestra. The prototype was developed in 1779 by Georg Joseph Vogler (see no. 12).

4 The original phonographs played cylinders, while gramophones played discs.

5 Percy Grainger and other composers were experimenting with electronic tone-generators and similar machines early in the twentieth century.

6 Stravinsky's Study for player piano dates from 1917. Antheil's *Ballet mécanique* (1923–5) was originally intended for sixteen player pianos.

69

Bruno Barilli, 'Stravinsky'

Tevere (7 April 1925), from *Il Sorcio nel violino* (Rome, 1982)

A brilliant and idiosyncratic writer, Barilli (1880–1952) was one of Italy's foremost critics in the interwar period. He took a keen interest in Verdi and eighteenth-century Italian opera, which he often compared favourably to the music of his contemporaries. This irreverent view of Stravinsky as an *enfant terrible* contrasts with Schuh's soberly respectful appreciation (no. 87).

For people like us, accustomed to Stravinsky's eccentric abundance, the music of *L'Histoire du soldat*[1] could at first glance constitute an extremely meagre Lenten surprise.

Indeed, to hear it for the first time is to remain perplexed and entangled in the most bizarre contrarieties.

The listener ought to feel uneasy, prey to fugitive fears, like the unwitting accomplice of a cruel scientific hoax who is dragged behind the green curtain to peek at the body of the woman he loves and adores, treacherously pierced by X-rays.

Stravinsky we always keep in the sights of our telescope, like an inhabitant of the moon who interests us.

We know that he won't be able to go back and we follow him persistently, no matter how far he pulls away.

But when he goes about the countryside and tries to disappear, hiding among the brilliant clouds of the dead planet or curling up inside phosphorous-filled crevices, then to find him and run him down truly requires the vigilance and eyes of Argus.

Stravinsky's music is always theatre. A galvanized, shrill theatre, at the highest pitch of desperation and hilarity.

He does not, however, wish to make the mountains move, and he neglects, rejects and ignores the large, lumbering public.

Noble and aristocratic prophet of destruction, Stravinsky seeks the most intelligent and cerebral follower with the most sentimental stratagem. First he conquers him, then, as if to put him to the test, he does everything he can to leave him in the lurch at the earliest opportunity. And still one must admit that he does not mean to disturb decent people.

This Russian, you would say, being unable to compete with Mozart or Scarlatti, hates music and authors, and detests and harasses the instruments as well, and bowed instruments most fiercely of all.

No matter. As long as our patience lasts, we will follow him out of curiosity and inclination, because, among today's madding and disaffected crowd who today have lost the key and rhythm of tradition, he is still the most sincere, the most precise, and the most fantastical of all.

In the past he used to draw deeply on the virginal and indolent reserves of Slavic and Asiatic folklore. And he knew how to make use of savagery with an irresistible insolence.

Then a wind, of fabulous speed, a wind bounding forth from the world's eastern gorges, seemed to uproot everything, to lift it up and carry it away into the future. Nothing like this had ever been seen or heard before from Stravinsky.

Nevertheless, that drawn-out blast, sinister and full of a tremendous rhythm, gradually faltered and broke up into whirlwinds and whirlpools, dying down breathlessly and splitting up here and there into aerial games, absentminded, very light and ironic.

The despotic Russian had pitched his tent at the base of the Eiffel Tower, and little by little his tempestuous force found expression under the influence of style, and a new spiritual mechanism arose within him. His recent essays are tantamount to a little treatise on elegant anarchy.[2]

Now Stravinsky is shedding all the heavy tools of his trade; he dismisses the large orchestra, obliterates the harmony which is form in music, and destroys the tonalities which serve as its balance wheels.

He hangs his best ideas on the line to dry up, invents an irritating instrumental shorthand, suggestive rather than descriptive, and sketches chords with a cacophonous reticence full of verve. In short, he transforms pure air into carbonic acid and spitefully sets up on his fingertips a precarious and frail gear which, laboriously turning, with the *tics* of an old man who has been poisoned, ever so slowly produces a spiritous and subtle and very potent poison which causes insanity.

Several of the episodes by Stravinsky executed last Saturday at the Teatro Odescalchi by the corporation of new musics we find integrated with much greater power and clarity in the same author's previous compositions. One example shall stand for all: *Petrushka*.

Everyone knows how energetically Stravinsky handles musical *calembours* [puns]. The language of this *détraqué* [deranged] pole-vaulter and tightrope-walker is riddled with anachronisms. The shining cheats of cocaine are mixed with the exceptional and unseemly rashes that poorly digested onion causes.

Here his music becomes a stingy, arid material, flecked with precious excrements.

In this bold *Histoire du soldat* the weak-kneed parts are satirically balanced like marionettes over the void.

Defying the danger of falling together, the voices trip or prop each other up with a grotesque fraternity.

Much could still be said about it, bad and good, in an effort to hit the mark. But in conclusion we will add that last Saturday, on the seven memorable instruments pilloried and martyred by the abstrusenesses of the music, as if on an epic-sized group of conquered people marching in a curving line, we seemed to descry Igor Stravinsky's sleeping genius awakening hallucinated and falling back to sleep, changing position with childlike motions, full of an obscure and extraordinary innocence ...

1 First performed in Lausanne in 1918, *L'Histoire du soldat* had its Italian première in Rome in 1925.

2 Stravinsky's first major success outside Russia was *The Firebird*, which Diaghilev commissioned for the Ballets Russes' Paris season in 1910.

70

Willem Pijper, 'Neo-classicism'

(1926), from *De Quinten-cirkel: Opstellen over muziek*
(Amsterdam, 1929), trans. Jaap Schröder

Pijper (1894–1947), Holland's leading composer in the first half of the twentieth century, served as music critic of the *Utrecht Dagblad* from 1918 to 1923, and from 1926 to 1929 coedited the journal *De Muziek*. His writing, like his music, bears the stamp of a wide-ranging and venturesome intellect. This article reflects his disdain for superficiality and easy solutions; for other perspectives on the issue, see the essays by Hába, Adorno, Hahn and Porter (nos. 75, 76, 85 and 100).

European Western music was never simple; nor were Western thinking and life in Europe. It would be wrong to believe that all those complications of life, those thought-systems, are phenomena of our time only.

In musical matters: the polyphonic era (the 'Netherlands school') reflects a national mentality, rooted in a certain period of history, which is more complex than, for instance, the psychic disposition connected with the experiments of Alois Hába (quarter-tone music) or Ferruccio Busoni (*Essay on a New Musical Aesthetic*).[1]

Compared to the psychic dispositions of other, non-European populations, the combined results of Western European thinking are of a frightening complexity. It is enough to make a comparative judgment between the amount of brainwork involved in the construction of a Bosch magnet and in the thought process that gave birth to the writings of Confucius. I don't say that humanity is better off with Bosch magnets than with systems of cosmogony – I only give an indication.

One has to distinguish between apparent and real simplicity (or complexity). Apparently, a painting by van der Leck or Mondrian[2] is simpler than the *Anatomy Lesson* (Rembrandt). Apparently, [Strauss's] *Also sprach Zarathustra* is more complex than Ravel's *La Valse*. But in fact, both Monteverdi's *Orfeo* and Satie's *Socrate* are more complex than an Indonesian *lagoe*,[3] which, if we try to capture it in musical notation, turns out to look so unapproachable that it drives European instrumentalists to despair.

The 'stillness' of pieces like *Socrate*, like *Les Cinq Doits* of Stravinsky, the simplification in Mondrian's paintings, is but semblance. So many currents have collided here that the result was all but a full stop, a monody, one monochrome dimension. Underneath that stillness, behind that motionlessness, there is turbulence. Sometimes quite intense, sometimes hardly noticeable. In theory there is the possibility that all the currents find themselves – for a few moments – in absolute but precarious balance. The result at that point is: nothing. Nirvana is not exactly the frame of mind which has inspired the great monuments of human thinking. In practice, I don't believe we will ever encounter examples of this kind. We can go further and point out that the most inspired artworks have usually been created by the most unbalanced talents, the most singleminded characters. Has any composer expressed the longings and stammerings of a sublime and chaste eroticism in a more moving way than the schizophrenic neurotic Berlioz in his *Romeo*? Has any composer created a more passionate-sounding heroism, full of half-divine power, than the hypomaniac Richard Wagner? Baudelaire, Oscar Wilde, Verlaine, Tchaikovsky and dozens of other great artists led lives dominated by unhealable afflictions. Brahms was a hypochondriac, Hugo Wolf died from paralysis. All these were important artists who were unable to find a socially acceptable balance between their own affects, as well as between these affects and the accepted rules of society.

From the age of puberty, the human spirit searches for a *modus vivendi*. Some talented people throw themselves at a particular moment into a process of sublimation with all the energy at their disposal (Stravinsky, after about 1915); others take refuge in sterility.

Generally, the longed-for compromise remains out of reach. If the artistic potential has enough power, artworks will continue to be created and the (a-)social life goes on as before. If the creative impulse is strong *and* the correcting imperatives have much strength as well, then a life-or-death battle ensues, often enough followed by the elimination of the battling individual (Mozart, Schubert, in a certain sense also Beethoven, Mendelssohn, Weber, Lekeu).[4] In the case of less potential, the process is less dramatic, more superficial, and the resulting scars are fewer and hardly visible. Of course, one won't find any figures of historical importance in this category, but it is possible to study this phenomenon in many individuals of our own age. When an artist, a composer, changes course spontaneously, apparently without a motive, there is always an underlying conflict which has become acute. A man like Erik Satie, even though he was a relatively weak power field, was the perfect illustration of these phenomena. In the last years of his long life, he had reached a degree of austerity, soberness – which was not at all Athenian, by the way⁵ – with which he infected a long phalanx of young musicians. People like Auric, Poulenc and Durey were only too eager to follow Satie's recipe, and they wrote their music from the start in the infantile idiom which had found in Jean Cocteau, in those days, a not-too-inept advocate. They immediately came up to the level of their predecessor and within a few months surpassed him. At that point, true to his own tradition, Satie changed course abruptly and took in tow the Ecole d'Arcueil.⁶

But Auric and Poulenc forgot one thing – and, judging from their most recent works, they still have not understood it: namely, that Satie's primitivism was the result of very complex thought processes. *Their* simplifications were first of all imitations, the imitations became mannerisms, and now they are mystifications. 'Quod licet Jovi non licet bovi.'⁷ Since Jupiter-Satie's ruminations had been at one point obviously a serious matter in bovine fashion, it is difficult to accuse the epigones of following this divine example so blindly and deafly, the more so because their epigonism corresponded so well to their character.

However, all this is no reason for us to abandon our critical position. For a composer who is part of our modern culture, who is intimately connected with contemporary life and its manifestations, who is familiar with the preceding eras of civilization, it is impossible to express himself, his individuality, with the means of our grandparents. The time-clock of culture does not suddenly reverse itself; the results of so many centuries of European musical awareness can't crystallize anno 1926 in the sounds of 'Maman, dites-moi' or *La Prière d'une vierge*.

There have always been quasi-progressive, pedantic, non-original characters. And it has almost always been impossible for any person of the same generation to gauge or even guess accurately. In the eyes of his own time and of his own country, Bach was not at all the great and representative personality. Beethoven could not compete with Clementi, nor Berlioz with Félicien David. Therefore, the phenomenon in itself should not upset us.

But from time to time it seems necessary to oppose the latest tendencies and slogans.

1 The Czech composer Hába (see no. 75) was known for his microtonal music. Busoni's *Entwurf einer neuen Aesthetik der Tonkunst*, published in 1907, was a manifesto of musical modernism.
2 Barth Anthony van der Leck and Piet Mondrian were associated with the abstract De Stijl group.
3 Malay for 'melody'. Recordings of Indonesian music were readily available in Europe in the 1920s.
4 Guillaume Lekeu, the Belgian composer, died at the age of twenty-four.
5 An allusion to Satie's cantata *Socrate*.
6 The 'school' formed by Satie's followers, including Milhaud, Sauget and Desormière.
7 'What is permitted to Jupiter is not permitted to the cow.'

71

Adolphe Boschot, 'Pan-Germanism and *Der Rosenkavalier*'

Echo de Paris (10 February 1927), from *Le Mystère musical*
(Paris, 1929)

Equal parts poet and critic, Boschot (1871–1955) led the revival of interest in France in the music of Mozart and Berlioz. Believing that all music should be held to a single standard of beauty, he reacted coolly to the iconoclastic experiments of the French *avant-gardists* known as Les Six and opposed what he saw as a noxious spirit of nationalism emanating chiefly from Germany. For contrasting views, see Krehbiel's review of *Salome* (no. 56) and Benco's essay on the post-Wagnerians (no. 54).

Music it is; but it goes beyond music and raises a question or two.

As for the piece itself, what a disappointment! What a flop! Or perhaps I should say, how flat it falls!

Why?

Because the music is tediously dense, massive and gloomy – and because the libretto is implausible, dull, crammed with episodes and sometimes offensive.

If the authors were unknowns or beginners, one could offer them anodyne compliments – not that anyone would be fooled. But the two authors, the librettist M. Hofmannsthal and the musician, deserve special consideration. The composer, in particular, is the most famous and capable of the post-Wagnerian kapellmeisters, the author of well-known symphonic poems, and also of *Salome*, *Elektra* ... It is M. Richard Strauss. We owe him the truth.

Here it is, then, as we see it, in all candour and without any malice.

Without malice, we say, because such a disclaimer is necessary. For many years, indeed since before the war, we have been writing in this space that the art of Dr Richard Strauss was an *expression of the pan-Germanist spirit*. Such an art is not merely German, it's Kraut. There's simply no other word for it. We mean no harm, but facts are facts, and the word *Kraut* corresponds to a reality which is, alas, all too clear.

Before 1914, when we had occasion to speak of M. Richard Strauss's music and observed that it was animated by the pan-Germanist spirit, newspapers on the other side of the Rhine replied that we were 'sehr amusant'. That response was followed by other events, beginning in 1914, events which affected not only us but the entire world. Although they seemed to die down with the armistice of 1918, they are merely asleep, waiting to break out again. For the pan-Germanist spirit is still alive and speaks in certain kinds of music.

At the heart of a Europe yearning for peace, there is still, beyond the Rhine, a stubborn will bent on aggression. It is a barbarous, proud and pedantic mentality, the drunkenness of the *miles gloriosus*, of the upstart of finance and industry, of the *kolossal* superman, of the conqueror who would enslave the universe, seize all 'human material', and put it to work for the expansion of the Middle European Company.

What did the taste-makers who followed and commented on Wagner declare, and with good reason? Music, they said, is a profound expression of the man; it suggests the inner mystery, the *en-soi* of human beings ... So, just as 'Young Russian' music expresses the Bolshevik folly, Dr Richard Strauss's music is the expression of the menacing bombast of the pan-Germanists. We said this in print as early as 1910 – you can go back and read it in our volume *Chez les musiciens* (first series) – and events have proven us right. Would that we had been mistaken, for less blood would have been spilled.

Today, without malice or weakness, we will again do our duty as a French critic, confronted by a work imbued with the spirit that would suppress or enslave the Latin peoples. And, as we did more than once in the trenches, we will say to our sleeping neighbour: 'Wake up, the Krauts are here! Put on your mask – it's poison gas' ...

What is there to say about the music that isn't already common knowledge? M. Richard Strauss is not an unknown; the piece staged at the Opéra is some fifteen years old, and more than one theatre has already staged it abroad.[1]

The composer is indisputably a virtuoso of orchestration. He handles sound-material masterfully: his art is born under the star of Wagner.

On the other hand, what are his ideas worth? What is the personal touch, the profound originality, the creative *en-soi* to which these works bear witness? ... The verdict has been in for a long time: beneath the wonderful artifice, there is next to nothing. It reminds you of an enormous and sumptuously dressed balloon.

You can point to more than one successful passage in the piece, notably the trio of the third act, which demonstrates the power of fine writing: it achieves beauty and emotion through nothing but richness and sureness of style. Descended from the famous quintet of *Die Meistersinger*, it would suffice to place M. Richard Strauss in the first rank of Wagnerian epigones.

Because his mastery has long been recognized, it must be said that Strauss is an ill-fated master. Despite some dazzling successes, he threatens to overwhelm the music with the luxuriance of the sound-material: he smothers his Muse under crushing Teutonic ornaments.

In *Rosenkavalier*, such excess runs less risk of proving fatal, for *Rosenkavalier* is a marvel of boredom.

The boredom flows from the libretto, in which implausible episodes pile up for four well-nigh interminable hours.

The boredom flows from the music, in which the coarsest and most dramatic forces strive to be gay and light. The wit is hammered home by blasts of trombones and tetralogical tubas.[2] How far away this is from the eighteenth century that this opera wishes to evoke! Valhalla's bluffs masquerading as rococo consoles; 'pebble-work' made with boulders ... It's true that everywhere you turn Viennese waltzes are setting their sticky languors twirling: *Schokolade* and *Delikatessen* mingle with fits of lyricism, or rather of hysteria, borrowed from *Tristan* and *Salome* ... On and on this goes, hour after hour, inexhaustibly. And amidst the heavy Bachian counterpoint and long scholastic pedals, the music moves with feet of lead ... It's a *kolossal* marvel of pedantry and boredom.

When you've sat through four hours of this, you're really done for.

1 *Der Rosenkavalier*, which had its première in Munich in 1911, was performed in French at the Opéra in February 1927.
2 An allusion to Wagner's *Ring* tetralogy.

72

Ernest Newman, 'A "Physiology" of Criticism'

Sunday Times (16 December 1928)

The most influential British critic of the century, Newman (1865–1959) began his career at the *Manchester Guardian* in 1905 and retired from the *Sunday Times* fifty-three years later. Like Castil-Blaze in the nineteenth century and Henderson in the twentieth (see nos. 27 and 59), he tried to find a firmer and more broadly meaningful basis for judging music than the subjective impressions of the individual critic. The system of 'musical physiology' that he outlines in this article left a lasting mark on younger critics like Porter (see no. 100).

Any attempt to give a scientific basis to musical criticism, or even the suggestion that such a thing may some day be possible, is sure to be greeted by the confraternity with loud jeers. Then is the voice of the amateur and the dilettante once more heard in the land: criticism, we are told, is merely a matter of personal reaction to the work of art, and as no two temperaments are alike, no two reactions can be alike. All the critic has to do is to describe how the work has affected *him*, and leave the reader to agree with him or not, as he chooses.

In a sense this is true; the personal equation does come into play in our judgments of art. But so far from this plain and obvious statement representing the last word in criticism, it really represents hardly the first. The public quite rightly mistrusts 'the critics' because they all say different things about the same work; and I confess that I have great sympathy with the public on this point. If 'criticism' means merely your telling other people the effect the work of art has had on you, I cannot see that they can be expected to be vastly interested in that. And for my own part I long ago gave up reading that kind of criticism. I want a form of criticism that will tell me more about the object criticized and less about the critic ...

We might begin with small things; and I venture to suggest that before we indulge as we do in the higher flights of musical psychology we ought to work out some sort of a system of musical physiology. Let the poetic fancy play at will on the musical material offered by a composer's work, and we get a species of writing that is very readable and superficially plausible, but has often the minimum of relation to the facts.

A typical specimen of this kind of writing is the much-praised *Beethoven* of Paul Bekker,[1] that has been hailed in some quarters as the best of all books on Beethoven, but that, from the strictly musical point of view, I myself would regard as one of the worst – that is to say, one of the least *musical*, from a musician's point of view. Bekker reads things into Beethoven's music that are not to be found in the music, while the procedures in the music upon which he bases his poetic fancies are susceptible of much simpler explanations along purely musical lines. This is a typical case of a critic indulging in the psychology of a musical subject before he has mastered its physiology. But it is a form of indulgence that virtually all critics permit themselves, for it is easier to give the fancy its rein than to sit down to the patient discovery of facts.

Let me make clear to the reader, by a specific instance, what I mean by a physiology of musical criticism. The other evening Casals[2] took the andante con moto of Schubert's C major symphony at such a speed that to many of us it seemed all con moto and no andante; allegro molto would have been the proper marking for such a pace. Who is to say that Casals was wrong, however? If we tell him that our feeling of the music is against such a tempo, he would reply that that is how *he* feels it, and his feeling is as good as ours. If we want to *prove* him wrong, we must have recourse not merely to feelings, but to matters that are capable of proof.

I believe it possible, by careful analysis, to establish in each composer's work a physiology of style that is the basis of his psychology. I have suggested the title 'finger-prints' for the elements in a composer's style that are purely personal to him. In *The Unconscious Beethoven*³ I tried to establish one of these finger-prints – an ascending figure of three adjacent notes – but, judging from the reviewers' comments, with small success. Indeed, most reviewers missed the point completely. One or two sagely remarked that they could produce passages from Beethoven in which three *descending* notes occurred. This, truly, was an epoch-making revelation; the discovery that notes sometimes go down as well as up is one that ought to immortalize the name of the genius who first hit upon it. The point was, however, not that Beethoven was the only composer who ever wrote three ascending notes in conjunct motion – which would be a nonsensical thing to assert – but that he is the only composer in whom you will find such a sequence of three notes used with such frequency, always at the same equivalent point in the melody, and always as the obvious expression of a certain state of mind. The three-note sequence, I contend, is a veritable Beethoven finger-print, because it is not found in any other composer.

I have worked for some years at this subject, in connection with other composers besides Beethoven, and I have come to the conclusion that, stylistically, each of them proceeds unconsciously on a few basic formulae, and the mystery is how, out of these, he should have been able to evolve so infinite a world of expression. Always when he is in a certin mood or wishes to produce a certain effect he is found unconsciously turning to the melodic and rhythmic formula that, for him, is inseparably associated with that mood or that effect. The formula takes so many outward shapes that we may listen to him all our lives and not suspect the existence of it; but once we become aware of it we find it underlying all the superficial modifications it undergoes in this work or that.

Knowledge of this kind of the elements of a composer's style is not merely interesting from the scientific-analytic point of view. It is not a mere curiosity: it has a practical aesthetic value. For while on the one hand we see a certain mood always realized through a certain formula, on the other hand whenever we meet with the formula we are entitled to infer the mood.

Now suppose we had worked out in this way the constituent elements of Schubert's style – not at all a difficult task. Suppose we had found that, in the bulk of his work, a certain technical procedure was always unconsciously employed when Schubert wished to express a certain mood. If, then, we found the same formula in a work that, through the lack of more precise directions on his part, different conductors look at from different points of view, should we not be justified in saying 'Here is the formula that we know to have been used again and again by Schubert for a particular emotional purpose: is it not a fair inference, then, that when he uses it here his purpose was the same as in the other cases, and therefore the work is to be taken at a certain tempo and in a certain mood, and no other?'

The same problem is raised (and could be solved in the same way) by the repeated hammering notes in the finale of the symphony. To one conductor they mean one thing, to another, another, and to a third, nothing at all. But a scientific analysis of Schubert's style would show quite definitely what they mean. Apart, then, from all questions of 'criticism', I would urge that on the practical aesthetic side alone a good deal would be achieved if for a few years writers upon music would abandon their too easy psychological methods – which mean, in the last resort, only saying the first thing that comes into your head – and devote themselves to establishing a preliminary physiology of each of the great composer's styles.

1 Bekker was a leading critic in Berlin and Frankfurt.
2 In 1919 the cellist Pablo Casals founded a workers' orchestra in Barcelona and began a second career as a conductor.
3 Published in 1927.

73

Léo-Pol Morin, 'In Search of Genius'

From *Papiers de musique* (Montreal, 1930)

Like many French-Canadian musicians, Morin (1892–1941) studied in Paris and thereafter divided his time between France and his native Quebec. As critic and pianist, he was known as an astute interpreter of French music.

He also championed Canadian composers, though, as this essay shows, he believed that his compatriots had a long way to go before they could be said to have created a Canadian school of composition. Dwight (see no. 30) expressed similar sentiments about American composers in the nineteenth century.

Canadian music can't be talked about as seriously as European music, for example, or even American music, which is already alive and kicking. Properly speaking, there is no more a Canadian music, in the most objective and specific sense, than there is a Canadian language. Canadians' French or English is recognizable from a certain turn of phrase, from certain archaisms or from their accent. But Canadian music still has no distinctiveness, either melodic or harmonic. No doubt, just as we speak French or English rather than Canadian, sweet echoes of France or other places can be heard in our music; but its vocabulary is extremely limited and it has yet to acquire the easy manner of a language which is natural and ... exuberant.

Consequently, talking about it becomes difficult – no less difficult than trying to define the characteristics of something which, by common consent, hasn't officially come into existence yet in our country. But don't worry: I have no intention of seeing the spectre of Canadian music lurking behind every piece. Some pessimists even doubt that Canadian music can ever exist, but they are no more to be taken seriously than the overly optimistic types who lump everything together and naively believe that Canadian music has been around for a long time. I'm no believer in spontaneous creation, and I know that music is begotten too. And I like to think that just talking about Canadian music gives it reasons for existing.

Instead of music solemnly labelled Canadian, we have Canadian musicians (whose music is not Negro, for all our mania for imitation). So this music can be stamped 'Made in Canada' without having a strictly indigenous character. Music made by Canadians of French extraction, educated in France, will be French; music by people of English extraction, educated in the British Isles or in Germany, will be Anglo-German. Even the music of people who have never been abroad will share these characteristics, so true is it that our two cultures walk side-by-side without mixing and, alas, without complementing each other.

But if some musicians in our country have devoted themselves to a profession as paradoxical as composing, none seems to have achieved – among the general public, or even among a group of insiders – the prestige and influence which are the trademarks of strong personalities. No name has aroused instant admiration in Canada, let alone around the world. Guillaume Couture,[1] whose influence as a professor was so constructive, is the exception that proves the rule.

If our composers have lacked this prestige, it's not simply because they lacked authority and personality, nor because their works were weak: it's also because of the public's ignorance of what music and composition are. The composer's profession is not officially recognized in our country. No such anomaly was foreseen in Canada's future, and for some time its very existence was denied. For a good many composers – you know what artists are like! – seem to produce music the way the apple tree produces apples; whence it follows that writing music is not just another profession. Indeed, to read the works of some composers, it's reasonable to think that this profession actually isn't one at all, or that it's a profession in its infancy. But the amateurs' poverty of invention is no argument against the work of genuine composers, against those who have something to say and who have learned the craft they need to express themselves.

Besides, haven't our composers sometimes had the weakness of lacking genius? One doesn't necessarily say 'composer' and 'genius' in the same breath. And if Claude Debussy and Gabriel Marie, Maurice Ravel and the composer of *La Prière d'une vierge*,[2] for example, are on the same plane in the minds of many people, nothing prevents us from seeing the enormous gap between them. But it would be bad form to churlishly reproach our composers for having lacked genius! That imponderable quality can't be bought. What's more, our composers have lived in such paradoxical and exceptional conditions that even if their works had contained the spark of genius, they would have been no better appreciated and no more enduring. So long as composing is not accepted as an intellectual activity, it will remain a risky venture – unless genius is in command …

This lack of genius casts a harsh and revealing light on the state of our music, past as well as present. No longer can we ignore the fact that if Canadian music doesn't exist, it's because no composer has been equal to the task of creating it. We may still be a long way from such a harvest, and until then composition will remain the least of our concerns.

People never tire of repeating that the conditions of life in our country have never been hospitable to great works of music. In the first place, they used to say, we hardly have enough bread to feed ourselves. We've heard all that before. But it's 1930, and now we have not only bread but also the automatic telephone, the telegraph, the car, the radio, the airplane, a thousand marvellous machines we can use, besides institutions to match, etc. ... And all this in cities which are modern – naturally – and furnished with all the latest comforts, the world's finest streetcars, and impressive buildings that proliferate by the day. Modern life, genius, bread: could it be that there is something fundamentally incompatible among these words and things?

One knows of impoverished countries where a taste for beauty exists, where music is part of life. But they are ancient countries with ancient customs. We are a new country without ancient customs, where the artistic professions are often likened to manias that can hardly be condoned and should not be given too much encouragement. Even though we know it's a romantic misconception, don't we believe that genius always will out, in spite of everything, if a man has any fire in his belly? Consequently, although physical conditions here have long been hostile to musical creation, couldn't a musician endowed with creative imagination have left at least one beautiful page, one personal page, even if it were just a melody, one page recognizable the way a human figure is recognizable? But the famous manuscripts of all the famous archives hold no surprises, judging – as is right, moreover – by the published pages, which are certainly among the good ones. But in all of this – say, up to the 1914 war, to give the youngest musicians time to 'prove' themselves completely – there is nothing which informed and impartial judges could admire, much less envy.

Would we pride ourselves on having so far failed to build anything but wooden shacks to house our commerce, industry and various other institutions? What would we think of the diligence as a mode of cross-country transport? Instead, the world's finest ships visit our magnificently equipped ports, where luxurious, 'modern' (and how!) trains wait to whisk travellers from coast to coast without delay. If we would no longer put up with such poverty in our physical lives, why should we find it normal, excusable and natural in our spiritual lives? It's time we understood that in the realm of the spirit – I should say in the realm of the fine arts, and particularly of music – our culture has not kept pace with our material prowess. Recognizing this would already be the mark of a more vigorous awareness.

1 Couture, who died in 1915, was a prominent composer in Montreal. Morin considered him the first great Canadian musician.
2 Marie, a minor French composer, died in 1928. *La Prière d'une vierge* was a popular salon piano piece of the time.

74

Elmer Diktonius, 'Sibelius'

From *Opus 12: Musik* (Helsinki, 1933), trans. George C. Schoolfield

Diktonius (1896–1961) has been called the Finnish George Bernard Shaw (see no. 50). One of Scandinavia's most distinguished men of letters, he contributed regular music criticism (in Swedish) to the newspaper *Arbetarbladet*, the journal *Nya Argus*, and other publications in the 1920s and 1930s. Much of it was devoted to Finnish composers, in particular Sibelius, who, at the time the articles that formed the basis for this essay appeared, was just beginning to win widespread acceptance abroad. For a comparable view from America, see no. 79.

When now, after this symphonic junket, we devote several pages for variety's sake to modern Finnish music and Sibelius in particular, we must confess in the name of truth that our obvious enthusiasm for the master and his accomplishments is not terribly old. During the period when we were radical, pure and simple, and worshipped nothing but wild gods, we had a little difficulty in appreciating the tack he took after his Fourth Symphony; quiet waters were not precisely our liquor during those days – harsher drinks were needed to awaken our sympathy.

But time passes, and man lives himself asunder – and it can be very good indeed to catch your breath for a while and pour oil on the troubled waters. And besides, in his latest works Sibelius once again approaches the same ideals which made the earth around the Fourth so full of possibilities, to be sure coming from another direction now and with the screws given another turn, but going in the same direction, toward the same goal. Thus the Seventh Symphony has become our favourite, after the Fourth, and in its turn it waits jealously for the announced arrival of the Eighth.

Very well: all this ought to be reflected in the following, for which a short investigation of Cecil Gray's Sibelius book[1] is best suited as an introduction ...

Thus far our words about the English destroyer's cruise in Sibelian waters. Next follows our own target practice in the same channels – short and snappy, as is our wont. But cannoneers: let it ring out like a royal salute!

En saga

Sibelius's *Saga* contains the material of folk-epic in romantic disguise. What it tells is as simple as a folk song, as gloomy as the forest primeval, and as splendid as the princess and half the kingdom.

Spring Song

Sibelius's *Spring Song* is a depiction, pressed together out of green moss but seemingly made of bronze stained with verdigris, of the pre-spring of the North, its leisurely arrival and its slow advance. The melody, taking its own sweet time, lumbers along like a bear just emerged from its winter lair – it raises up on its haunches, it stretches, it sniffs the air in every direction – little by little nature awakens too, pants with full lungs in the accompanying crescendi of the background, becomes the ringing jubilation of a set of bells, light itself grown triumphant. A parade piece for the strings in particular – the strings indeed, in their full length.

The Dryad

– a freshly fluttering leaf from the forest.

Symphony I

A work of youth, but a uniquely manly and mature specimen of its kind, where not only the lion's claws appear, but where its roars resound too, and its tail whisks the ground. (A sequel follows in connection with Kajanus's[2] jubilee concert!)

II

It begins in nature and rises, by way of an individual's struggles, to something that is sublimely religious. A swan, but a swan with the noble airs of a beast of prey: with the beak of the eagle, the claws of the griffon.

IV

In music history, the Fourth Symphony could be called the 'bark-bread' symphony.[3] It is woefully poor, as far as external effects are concerned, all its movements – even the scherzo, with its bosky good nature – lie brooding upon moods of the wilderness; it sounds as though it had been written by a barefoot boy come from somewhere around Kuusamo.[4] Although it is not based on either national melodies or harmonies, it is the most Finnish composition we know, universal, without the put-on *Kaleva* airs of would-be 'true Finnishness'[5] – it is a musical counterpart to Aleksis Kivi's international home-baked discoveries.[6] This spiritual Finnishness is so strong in it that only a dyed-in-the-wool, all-knowing lover of this hard people and meagre land can fully appreciate the inexpressibly precious worth of the wildernesses-heart.

But there are also other paths leading to this cobblestone, for it approaches absolute music in the greatest measure ever to be vouchsafed a work by human hands, it speaks the same primal language as the best of the music written by the man on the mount – Father Bach, grey and mighty. Here, melody, harmony or instrumentation count no longer: one voice and one ear: that is all. It is so simple! And therefore it has naturally turned out to be so obscure to those who analyse God in accordance with the catechism. But it is our firm belief that this piece of bark-bread will be chewed by many generations of man.

Still IV

I wonder if, little by little, it hasn't become high time to shake the commonly held opinion that Sibelius's Fourth Symphony is something incomprehensible or, put as gently as possible, something that can be absorbed only with reluctant effort and slogging pain? To be sure, this symphony is no rose garden with lilies of the valley and neatly raked paths, but neither is it a desert where one trudges, burning with thirst, until one falls – it is a piece of absolute music framed by Finnish nature: people ought to be able to stand that! People ought to be able to admire it, love it, discover that it is unique. And perhaps people have already done just that, paying no heed to the warning signals and barriers set up by the critics and the analysts. For an incomprehensible work, an indigestible symphony could not be performed over and over, here and elsewhere, if it did not achieve a sympathetic public response. And, as a matter of fact, things have come to a point where among the seven the Fourth is the one most gladly heard again.

In its case, one need not, indeed one may not think of anything – it thinks for itself, it ponders but smiles a little too, it is absentminded, it looks to nature for the answer to riddles, it has its own brand of quiet humour and its stern philosophy; if it gives rise to literary associations, they are with Kivi and Sillanpää.[7] How the gold deep within it shines up through the sparse, plain orchestration; what life-saving value this piece of bark-bread possesses, what rich poverty in times when art all too often has become a cheap luxury! A country, a people are found in this juniper-music,[8] sixty thousand lakes, autumnal-grey and in some strange way a greeting from Bach. One may not, one ought not think, and least of all indulge in fantasies.

V

Instead, it seems to us that the Fifth, despite its festival splendour, lacks firm contours, unified shapes that stay in the mind's eye – but perhaps that was because of the performance, which on this occasion was not at Professor Kajanus's customary level of Sibelian performance. And the Violin Concerto – played by Anja Ignatius-Lagus[9] in an altogether respectable way, but without the fiery downward glance this demanding task requires – was perhaps not the right link, either, between the Fourth's mysteries and the clear sunlight of the Fifth: the rather run-of-the-mill concerto-style of the solo piece's third movement came as too much of a distraction. One of the master's earlier symphonic poems, for example, would have been a better choice.

VI

The more often one hears Sibelius's Sixth, the more carefully one weighs one's words: it has an evanescent quality to it that escapes definition. Mostly, it is an affair between the strings and the woodwinds, and thus easily takes on a religious, organ-like sound, but there is religion, too, in a motionless forest and in a calm stretch of water, grey with autumn, and God alone knows which religion is better – nature's blind reverence or man's conscious invocation. Georg Schnéevoigt[10] took the enigmatic work at a somewhat faster tempo than usual, which by no means hindered us in getting a view of the whole. But we saw merely what we heard – and were perplexed.

VII, VI and III

In 1492, Columbus discovered America; in 1931 America discovered Sibelius, the leading symphonist of our time. 'The biggest in the world' is often 'the latest'[11] as well; since the discovery concerned the master's Fourth Symphony – the 'bark-bread' symphony, the great watershed of style in Sibelius's production – forgiveness lies close at hand.

A reflection from this remarkable event, so important for the whole of our musical life, fell on the season's last symphony concert, spreading a jubilant patina over the programme, the auditorium and the performers, a patina that took solid form in the spontaneous ovations and fanfares with which the public and the orchestra paid homage to the master's unfailing comrade-at-arms, Professor Kajanus, who went into the breach for him yet again with a combative spirit and the certainty of victory. Three symphonies were put on display this time, VII, VI and III: a gorgeous cortège, cleverly planned, beginning with the compactness of strength and ending with a broad idyll – but it is strange, for the rest, that the Third Symphony's inexhaustible wealth of melody did not capture the public as quickly as its two predecessors on the programme. Perhaps one misses the expressive passion that sizzles in their nostrils. However, explosive servings of that material are to be found in the Seventh, which, in our opinion, despite the head-shakings of the aesthetes, has an excellent chance of winning the public in short order. Its form, gentle sirs, the lucid agility of its whole layout! The Sixth is fair, too, but somewhat pale – yet not like the daughter of a respectable family, instead like Silja in Sillanpää's novel.[12]

Tapiola and VII

It is difficult to say which of these works deserves priority. They are actually quite closely related, written during the same creative period (opus 105 and opus 112). Much brighter in mood than the 'bark-bread' symphony, but like it pictures of nature, interrupted by the confessions and hymns of the human heart. In Tapiola, the listener is captivated by a mad run of the strings, in the symphony the brasses erect a copper tower of huge strength. The orchestration is sumptuous, neither too clever nor too brilliant, but with a shining objectivity – spreading lights and shades over the whole like sun in a forest. Light-footed string passages, rhythmically spiced, alternating with the monotonous brooding of the woodwinds – taken all in all, happiness and brooding and a trembling intensity which scarcely hints at any senile slackening on our glorious master's part ...

Like a majuscule in gold, twined about with laurel, the memory of the splendid special concert may shine here, by means of which our city orchestra and the elite public of the nation's capital paid tribute, a couple of years ago, to the 'grand old man' of our musical life, Prof. Robert Kajanus ...

We guess that the performance of Sibelius's First Symphony on this occasion must have awakened treasured memories in the minds of those who had the privilege of being present when Finnish music, with Kajanus as its great captain and Sibelius as its standard bearer, set out to conquer the world.[13] But we also have a feeling that this youthful masterpiece, this eagle's flight in early morning, has very seldom or perhaps never gotten such a fiery and deeply tender performance as it did on the unforgettable evening of 2 December 1931 – that its content, nobly powerful and boldly confident despite its dark background, has scarcely ever emerged before in such a sharp and transfigured light as it did on that occasion. This symphony is a Viking ship, rushing forward, manned by a crew Finnish to the core, defying time even in the tiniest details of its orchestration, where mayhap the intended effect escaped the young composer but where his psychology of instrumentation, intuitive even then, never failed – : a mountain, a fountain, a fir tree, supple but hard enough to withstand lightning itself. The old truth about Sibelius as the most remarkable symphonist of our age is gradually beginning to dawn on the sluggish-minded world, and verily: none of the heroes of symphonic form – not even Beethoven – has had such a grandiose and overpowering debut.

1 The first major study of Sibelius in English, published in 1931.
2 The conductor Robert Kajanus was the leading Finnish exponent of Sibelius's music. Kajanus is the central figure in Akseli Gallen-Kallela's well-known oil painting *Symposion* (1894), where he is flanked, to his left, by the young Sibelius, and to

the right by a collapsed figure, his head on the table, and the painter himself: all the participants in the symposium are somewhat the worse for wear.

3 In the Finnish countryside, bread was made from tree bark during the country's repeated famines.

4 Kuusamo is a region in north-eastern Ostrobothnia, not far below the Arctic Circle; it is known for the wildness and beauty of its landscape.

5 By 'true Finnishness' (*äktfinskthet*), Diktonius refers to the Finnish supernational-istic movement which wished to reduce or eliminate the rights of the country's Swedish-speaking minority. Completely bilingual himself, Diktonius made relent-less fun of the programmes and excesses of the movement's linguistic (and ethnic) zealots.

6 Kivi (1834–70) was the father of modern Finnish-language literature. Diktonius admired his work, translating some of his poems and his novel, *Seitsemän veljestä* (Seven Brothers) into Swedish.

7 Frans-Eemil Sillanpää (1888–1964), the Finnish novelist and winner of the Nobel Prize for Literature in 1939.

8 A popular (and self-flattering) appellation for the Finnish people was 'the juniper folk', as hardy as the bush itself.

9 Anja Ignatius had an extensive concert career, as soloist and first violinist of the Helsinki Quartet. Later she taught at the Sibelius Academy.

10 Schnéevoigt was the founder, in 1912, of the Helsinki Symphony Orchestra, later combined with Kajanus's Helsinki City Orchestra. Subsequently he played a large role – not least as an interpreter of Sibelius – with orchestras in Stockholm, Malmö, Los Angeles and, at the end of his career, Helsinki again.

11 In the original these phrases are in English. Diktonius may have been thinking of Olin Downes's feature article on Sibelius's place in contemporary music, which appeared in the *New York Times* on 22 March 1931. More likely, however, Diktonius is engaging in typical exaggeration or inaccuracy for effect. By 1931, according to a survey made by Lawrence Gilman, there had been 265 performances of Sibelius's compositions by major American orchestras. The first American per-formance of the Fourth had been by the New York Symphony Society under Walter Damrosch on 2 March 1913; in June the next year Sibelius received an honorary doctorate from Yale University.

12 The heroine of Sillanpää's perhaps best-known novel, *Nuorena nukkunut* (1931; translated into English as *The Maid Silja* and, more accurately, as *Fallen Asleep While Young*). Diktonius named his daughter after Sillanpää's protagonist.

13 Diktonius is referring to the appearance of the Helsinki City Orchestra, conduct-ed principally by Kajanus and with compositions by Sibelius, at the Finnish Pavilion of the Paris Exposition in 1900.

75

Alois Hába, 'What would Leoš Janáček Do if He Were still among Us'?

Klíč (1 August 1933), trans. Mirka Zemanová

Composer, teacher, theorist and sometime critic, Hába (1893–1973) was a leading voice of the Czech *avant-garde* between the wars. Persecuted for his progressive artistic tendencies (notably his experiments with microtonal music), he came to be revered under the Communists as an outstanding Czech original. His emphasis on the composer's social responsibilities was shared by many other twentieth-century critics, not only Marxists; see nos. 66, 67, 76, 77, 80, 93, 94 and 99.

What would Leoš Janáček do if he were still among us?[1] Would he rest? Would he not be interested in the creative as well as the existential problems of the younger generation? Would he remain silent on seeing the various evils in our musical life?

Those who knew Janáček also know that he, with his artistic authority, would back up new endeavours and that he would fight alongside us. But he is no longer with us.

Let us ask a few counter-questions of ourselves who are alive: are we not too forgetful of Janáček? Do we realize that it was necessary to enforce a greater part of his work tenaciously in our musical life? Do we make an appropriate effort, through our personal and artistic authority, to make Janáček's work understood and valid? Do we fulfil the duty of each younger generation toward an important artistic phenomenon, who left his work in this country at a stage when it still had not become an emotional property of the public at large?

We are Janáček's debtors all the more, since in our own bad times we gain from Janáček's personality a constant, living inner support by bearing in mind the essential features of his character: a keen interest in life; sharp perception and clear judgment; tolerance toward people but no compromise in matters of ideas and art; perseverance and tenacity in realizing his creative intentions; a sense of pithy and concise musical expression; an obstinate endeavour to express matters in his novel way; and inner creative vigilance protecting him from musical banality.

Flirting with banality in concert and operatic works has become fashionable of late, and some 'smart' composers speculate in it with an eye on worldly success, as well as money.[2] Musical banality rages like an epidemic in operas, cantatas, operettas and concert works, in sound film, jazz hits and 'popular songs' of all types. It threatens to infect concert and operatic output even more. Production and reproduction of musical banality is supported by world capital, which has escaped from the realm of human spirit and human ethics. Today musical banality stifles whole nations and prepares them for indifference – toward the raging of war. Musical banality is more pernicious than nicotine and alcohol: at any rate, it likes best to have them both as bedfellows!

It is imperative to step up the fight against musical banality. In this way we shall help to vindicate Janáček's pure and noble music; and conversely, more frequent performances of Janáček's operatic and concert works are the best weapon against the spread of musical banality. Janáček's music, pure and in a healthy national spirit, is necessary for our public, particularly for our youth, as a model for the struggle for a purer, better, nobler, new human socialist order.

1 Janáček (see no. 46) died in 1928. See also Brod's review of *The Storm* (no. 63) by Novák, who was one of Hába's teachers.
2 Pijper (no. 70) has more to say about the anti-romantic reaction and vogue for simplicity after the First World War. Schloezer (no. 66) discusses the Soviets' efforts to create a music for the masses.

76

Theodor Adorno, 'Background Music'

Vossische Zeitung (31 January 1934), trans. John Gingerich

A brilliant student of the relation between music and society, Adorno (1903–69) applied the concepts of Marx and Freud to his analyses of the modern 'culture industry'. He was known as a principled advocate of *avant-garde* music (Schoenberg in particular) and a penetrating critic of popular culture. Adorno's longer essays on musical aesthetics, sociology and philosophy are standard texts; this characteristically sophisticated piece is an example of his less widely known musical journalism.

There is no longer any place for music in our immediate, day-to-day life. Any individual who wants to sing out loud on the street would risk being arrested for disturbing the peace; anyone humming silently to himself, withdrawn from the outside world, can run into a car at any moment. And those three college-age *Wandervögel*[1] on the square who sing to out-of-tune guitar chords as if they were travelling players, how sadly self-conscious they appear. Only political action, perhaps, is capable of revealing the manifest reality of song for a few short hours. We are a long way from Naples, not only in space but also in time. If there all speech still swings into song, if the fruitseller sings hymns in front of the heathen altar-wagon from which he dispenses his wares, here the street vendors have long since turned into revolving billboards. Whoever wants music must step out of the sphere of immediate life (which as such no longer exists) and purchase that lost immediacy with a ticket to the opera or a concert.

Nevertheless, that immediacy is not utterly destroyed. To be sure, barrel-organs and court musicians are archaic relics; they have their own law and their own history running athwart society, which discounts their obscure existence. The islands of domestic music lie close enough to the shimmering polar ice of conscious artistic practice. What remains is banished itself, pressed to the margins of existence: music as background. Since the demise of the silent film and its comforting accomplice, the movie orchestra, background music has become the music of coffee houses, or, as one cultishly likes to say, *cafés chantants*. It has survived the radio, even without outside support: locales with live music are certainly more crowded than those with a mere loudspeaker. The listener pays no money for it; the cost is almost imperceptibly included in the price of the coffee, chocolate and vermouth. If he notices it at all, he feels sophisticated, like a visitor to a fine establishment. Music is an integral part; though banished from the street, this art is not being made somewhere far away but rather accompanies the patrons of the café: drinkers restoring themselves after a tiring day, businessmen making deals, newspaper readers – flirters, too, if they still exist.

Above all, background music means you don't have to listen. No silence surrounds and insulates it; it seeps into the hum of conversation. If an unfortunate tenor trumpets his Italian *canzonettas*, he's deemed an intruder. Silence lasts only the few seconds until the next order is placed. Here, art lovers who shush their neighbours mercilessly reveal themselves as comical.

When the music is soft, it wants to disappear completely. The clatter of spoons and cups becomes perceptible, blending with the glockenspiel and perhaps the upper register of the piano; the cello's phrases sink down, lost. When it's loud, the music shoots up like a rocket, making sparkling arcs over the listeners, until they sit solitary once again in grey clouds of cigarette smoke. This is not a public: almost no one ever comments on the quality of the music. Nor are they musically attuned: the music scarcely touches their inner emotions. Instead, it's an objective process which goes on between and above them. The coldness that separates one table from the next, the distance between the young man and the unknown girl across from him, waiting to take offence at his glances – this estrangement is certainly not transcended by the music but captured and frozen. The man definitely won't dare to address the girl here, in this expensive fun spot. Coldness, desire, the strangeness of proximity – with an abrupt gesture the music transposes them to the stars, like abandoned Ariadne's name. Even those who are spoken to need take no notice. As soon as things get too loud, they withdraw their bodies from the astral proceedings, crying, 'Bill, please!' and striking their spoons on their wine glasses. But that, of course, is the sound of café music.

Has anyone ever eavesdropped on this sound? Connoisseurs claim to be able to distinguish between Parisian orchestration, salon orchestration and a number of others. The differences are quite internal. The sound is a common one: Hindemith fittingly commemorated it in his first *Kammermusik* written for Donaueschingen.[2] It has nothing to do with the orchestra: the infinite choir of strings, the colours of the winds, the resonance of the brass – all are missing. It must be chamber music then, one thinks – but the impossibility of this notion instantly becomes apparent. There is none of the intertwined play of instruments stepping in and out of prominence. Only the top voice has 'melody': the soloist presents himself as a 'stand-up violinist'.[3] The piano is not scored like a chamber music piano; it is the 'conductor', with foundation and harmony, perhaps the last descendant of the realized thoroughbass in European music. There is something splendidly shabby about this cosmetic sound. It's as colourful as tinsel but falls apart in the hands. It pretends to be an orchestra but takes its direction from the piano. Hardly anywhere else is the challenge to do justice to the 'material' as thoughtlessly flouted today as it is here. Like a *Stefanie-Gavotte*,[4] it affects the refinements of chamber music (but represents the 'stand-up violinist,' since the pizzicati[5] are inaudible). Nowhere has music become quite as illusory as in the café. But in illusion it is preserved. It probably must be emancipated in this fashion from all human earnestness and all genuine artistic form, if it is to be tolerated by humans amidst their daily activities without shocking them. But its illusion shines out to them – nay, it illuminates them. It doesn't change them but it changes their image; it becomes brighter, sharper, more contoured. If café music becomes silent, it sounds as if a miserly waiter had extinguished a few electric bulbs. Background music is a source of acoustic light.

The correct technical word for the fake, illusory aspect of background music is 'arrangement'. No original compositions are played, no piece as it was conceived. Everything is arranged for salon orchestra, which changes and distorts it. What was meant to be large becomes blandly intimate; what was tender becomes bloated with tremolo and vibrato. The works suffer decay, and decadent works, by once famous and then fallen masters, are the right ones for background music. The question is whether decay will prevail. Ruined works go mute; here they sound again – not in their original forms, of course, but the ruins are reshaped into a second, strangely transparent form. The piano doesn't simply replace the missing horns; the former fullness has become shabby and has therefore been entrusted to the piano. It is not the principal violin who makes a noble melody ordinary with his soloistic aggressiveness; rather, the melody has lost its nobility and therefore resigns itself to the care of the stand-up violinist. The truly noble will shine like a star out of the background: we hear it as music.

But otherwise the café arranges bouquets of dead flowers. The joins between the layers of brittle sound are not securely closed. They are permeated by the mysterious, allegorical illusion that arises whenever fragments from the past coalesce into an unstable surface. What pertains to the vertical sonority is no less pertinent to the horizontal, to the flow of time. Cafés are the place of potpourris formed from the fragments of a work, from the most beloved melodies. But they rouse the ruins to a second shadow-life. If our art music persists in the comforting realm of Orpheus, its echo from Euridice's region of sorrow resounds here. The sparkle is subterranean. This music can remain unnoticed because it is unreal. The shadow cast over it is not black but lighter, like frosted glass. You can listen, vaguely, through this music, over into the next room. That is why it shines.

One might suppose that background music, unnoticed music, would be no different from accompaniment: like good ballet music in contrast to pantomimes, which provides rhythm, colour and sonority and saves the melody for the dance up on the stage. Not so. Since the melodies perambulate around the café as ghosts, no disturbance by them need be feared, be they ever so present; because they are quoted from the unconscious memory of the listeners, not presented to them. The greater the ecstasies, the more perfectly rest the souls of those over whom they vanish in a flurry. There are masters – truly masters – whose greatness is fully revealed only by this strange displacement of passionate illusion into the cold comfort of reality. Puccini is the most prominent of these; one might believe that *Bohème*, *Butterfly* and *Tosca* were conceived with imaginary potpourris in mind, potpourris that arise once the last tear elicited by operatic catastrophes has trickled away. But Grieg, too, with pieces such as 'To Spring', is not to be despised. Tchaikovsky is well suited; Mignon and Marguerite, of course; Carmen mocks all ghostliness. Before Schubert, café music becomes blasphemous. Strange, too, that the new dances don't fit; their function is too fresh to fade into the background already. Best are the melodies with great, unbroken arcs, like Rodolfo's and Butterfly's arias. Whoever glances up, disconcerted, startled out of conversation or thought, is transformed into Georg Heym's[6] suburban dwarf: 'He looks up to the green dome of sky, where soundless meteors travel far.'

---

1 Members of a German back-to-nature movement; something of a cross between Scouts and hippies.
2 A major German festival of contemporary music.
3 i.e., like a violinist in a café.
4 Evidently, a popular salon piece.

5 Notes produced by plucking the string with the finger.
6 The Expressionist poet, known for his apocalyptic visions. I have been unable to locate the source of this quotation.

77

Ivan Sollertinsky, '*Lady Macbeth of Mtsensk District*'

Rabochii i teatr (The Worker and the Theatre), no. 4 (1934),
from M. Druskin, ed., *I. Sollertinsky: Kriticheskiye stati*
(Leningrad, 1963), trans. Mirka Zemanová

Sollertinsky (1902–44) was the leading Soviet music and theatre critic of the 1920s and 1930s. A close friend of Shostakovich, he was sympathetic to Mahler and Schoenberg but not to Stravinsky. While recognizing the composer's 'obligation to work with Soviet themes', Sollertinsky distanced himself from the anti-intellectual tenets of 'socialist realism'. He never muted his admiration for Shostakovich, even after *Lady Macbeth* was officially condemned in *Pravda* in 1936 as 'a bedlam of noise'.

Nineteenth-century Russian literature knows titles of analogous type: Turgenev's 'Hamlet of Shchigri District', Leskov's 'Lady Macbeth of Mtsensk District'.[1] All these stories and novellas, and those similar to them, are concerned with heroes whose psychology and fate remind one in many ways of the tragic fate of Shakespeare's magnificent characters. The 'district' principle entails an adjustment: the Russian counterparts are usually smaller, greyer and uglier than the Shakespearean prototypes; they are humdrum, provincial, gloomy, 'swallowed up in their surroundings', as if walled in a prison cell of the native, pre-Revolutionary, remote way of life. And when, in a fit of despair, they begin to 'rebel', their 'protest' finds an outlet in a series of wild, cruel, and often useless acts.

In Shakespeare, the imperious and ambitious Lady Macbeth puts a dagger into the trembling hand of her vacillating husband, inciting him to regicide: the stimulus for her behaviour is an almost maniacal desire for the throne. In Leskov, the distinguished merchant's wife, Katerina Lvovna Ismailova, kills her father-in-law, her husband, and the totally guiltless boy Fedya so that no one can hinder her happiness with the steward Sergei, to whom she is drawn by an unbridled, animal-like passion.

Leskov condemns his heroine perhaps even more severely than the moralist Tolstoy condemns Anna Karenina: 'Vengeance is mine; I will repay.'[2] According to Leskov, Katerina Ismailova is, despite the wholeness of her character, organically depraved by nature, a 'born criminal' (in the spirit of the now-fashionable theories of the Italian bourgeois criminologist Cesare Lombroso).[3] And Sergei's betrayal with the prostitute Sonyetka is nothing but moral vengeance, an act of higher justice.

This moralizing point of view in Leskov, glorifying the age-old purity of the ancient, patriarchal Russian mores, advocating humility, diligence and a religion of small deeds, understandably proved unacceptable to the great Soviet artist. Except for Leskov's plot and the characters' names, Dmitri Shostakovich radically rebuilds a general concept in his new opera.[4] The conception of the roles is changed: the victims become executioners and the murderer becomes a victim.

Shostakovich's rehabilitation of *Katerina Ismailova* is not realized through idealistic absolution, nor under the intellectual slogan 'There are no guilty in this world.' On the contrary, Shostakovich pinpoints the culprits of Katerina's downfall and destruction: the home-building structure of the family[5] and the merchant way of life behind which, under the mask of conservative views and patriarchalism, are hidden boundless petty tyranny, cynical dissoluteness, cruelty and bestial depravity. The culprit is – to put it concretely – her drunken rapist of a father-in-law, Boris Timofeyevich; it is the dissolute servants, and amidst them the common daredevil with a dashing part in his hair, greased with lamp oil, an ingratiating seducer with a 'sensitive' soul – the steward Sergei.

Against this background unfolds the action of this 'tragic satire' by Shostakovich, unique in the history of Russian opera.

The grandiose mastery of the score of Shostakovich's *Lady Macbeth*, its tragic pathos and accusatory power – these have already been truly evaluated in the Soviet press. It is possible to claim with complete responsibility that not since [Tchaikovsky's] *The Queen of Spades* has a work of the scale and depth of *Lady Macbeth* appeared in the history of the Russian musical theatre …

In itself, the principle of alternating tragic and grotesque scenes is not new. However, the very choice of material, subject to the design now on the tragic, now on the grotesque plane, is highly original in Shostakovich.

The grotesque in *Lady Macbeth* characterizes a way of life. It is in a grotesque manner that the drunken priest – the jester, the 'soul of the society' – is outlined. The masterly *fugato* of the guests, praising the bridegroom and the bride with songs, is on a predominantly grotesque plane. Grotesque, too, is the scene with the teacher in the police station (taken from Saltykov-Schedrin),[6] who dares to investigate 'whether a frog has a soul' and satisfies himself that 'it does' but that 'it is small and not immortal'. This grotesque element is necessary for Shostakovich to be able to show the small scale of the district's merchant world and, above all, to deprive this world of all shades of idyllic, complacent good nature, patriarchal sedateness, durability, immobility. In other words, it is necessary to avoid the idealization of the old times, which almost manifests itself even in [the work of] such an authoritative denouncer of the 'dark czarism' as Ostrovsky,[7] let alone in Russian classic opera.

It would be unthinkable to talk, in *Lady Macbeth*, in the language of [Rimsky-Korsakov's] *The Snow Maiden*, *The Czar's Bride*, or even [Mussorgsky's] *Khovanshchina*. Something essential would be missing – the irreconcilable hatred for the past which characterizes Shostakovich's work from first bar to last. A unique image in *Lady Macbeth*, to a certain degree going back to nineteenth-century Russian opera, is that of the 'shabby little peasant' in whom there is a little of the Idiot from *Boris* and even of Grishka Kutyerma.[8] However, he is portrayed in Shostakovich in a simpler and plainer manner: without any symphonic witticisms, without 'theomachy' and 'satanism'. And all the other characters are conceived and realized differently from the traditional types of Russian folk opera.

In general, one encounters pure ethnography in Shostakovich only once, and this on an ironical level: in Katerina Lvovna's hypocritical lamentations over the corpse of Boris Timofeyevich, whom she herself has sent to kingdom come. Completely devoid of any ethnographic stylization is the chorus of the servants seeing the young master off – an animated scherzo in a mazurka tempo, not without a shade of mocking toadying. Any stylization – whether high-amorous or parodic – would only impede the pace of dramatic events. Shostakovich does the opposite: where the action accelerates toward a catastrophe, he boldly introduces symphonic entr'actes, built on swift movement and contemporary dance rhythms ... These symphonic entr'actes make the action powerfully dynamic, giving it an extremely sharp, tense, nervous, spasmodic character.

The part of the heroine, wholly lyrical, deeply melodious, towers above all – from the sincere song in Act 1 to the terrible tale of the 'black forest lake', rising like a mirage from Katerina's sick, hallucinatory fantasy at the penal halting-place in Siberia. In the last act Shostakovich, it seems to us, even thickens the sombre atmosphere too much: the scene in which the female convicts mock the deceived and persecuted Katerina is painted in physically almost unbearable colours, arousing a frenzied, hysterical reaction. The final catastrophe is portrayed in an unusually laconic manner. The opera concludes with a melancholy, rather melodramatic song of the shackled prisoners, continuing their sorrowful journey in the impenetrable mist of the snowy Siberian night.

Shostakovich's opera is an enormous contribution to Soviet musical culture. Its staggering intonational realism, the broad scope of its historical theme, the scale of the satirical unmaskings, and its tragic sweep, more Shakespearean than Leskovian – all this makes *Lady Macbeth* a first-class work in the most serious sense. The issues of craft, dramatic expression, and qualitative value of the music – these Shostakovich raises, in *Lady Macbeth*, on to a plane unprecedented in Soviet music.

But the deserved success of *Lady Macbeth* puts Shostakovich himself under considerable obligation to continue his creative search of the musically realistic style, to widen his genres and themes. It puts him under an obligation to work with Soviet themes, for, no matter how exalted *Lady Macbeth* is, Shostakovich's third opera has to be even more significant, and deeper still. Only such aspirations can and must we demand from leading composers of the Soviet Union.

1 Turgenev's story appears in *A Sportsman's Sketches* (1852). Nikolai Leskov's 'Lady Macbeth' was written in 1865.
2 The biblical epigraph to *Anna Karenina*, Romans 12:19.
3 Lombroso, who died in 1909, argued that degeneracy and other hereditary factors determined criminality.

4 *Lady Macbeth* was first produced in Leningrad on 22 January 1934 and repeated later that year in Moscow under the title *Katerina Ismailova*. Public and critical reaction was favourable, but the depiction of adultery, murder and suicide in a merchant home under the czars offended Soviet officialdom. Pilloried in *Pravda* in 1936, Shostakovich was restored to favour by his Fifth Symphony the following year.

5. i.e., the puritanical domestic arrangements.

6 Mikhail Saltykov-Schedrin, the nineteenth-century Russian satirist.

7 The playwright Aleksandr Ostrovsky.

8 The peasant who betrays Kitezh to the Tatars in Rimsky-Korsakov's *The Legend of the Invisible City of Kitezh and the Maiden Fevroniya*.

78

Wilhelm Peterson-Berger, 'On Musical Form'

Dagens Nyheter (31 July 1936), from *Från utsiktornet: Essayer om musik och annat* (Östersund, 1951), trans. George C. Schoolfield

Peterson-Berger (1867–1942), critic of the prestigious *Dagens Nyheter* in Stockholm between 1896 and 1930, was one of the major figures of Sweden's national-romantic movement. A prolific composer, he was strongly indebted to Wagner and Grieg, and he opposed excessive formalism, whether in contemporary music or in the works of Liszt. For another perspective on the issue, see Boito's discussion of form and formalism (no. 36).

On 31 July 1886, the most outstanding apostle and supporter of Wagner's art and of 'the new German style' taken large, Franz Liszt, passed away in Bayreuth, in the midst of the Festspiele ... Throughout Europe, Franz Liszt still had a large band of devoted admirers, attracted principally by his piano playing and the lessons he gave, and his very presence at the Festspiele was an endorsement. People knew, of course, that he was also a composer and a conductor, but the importance attached to these activities was surely secondary to the image, persisting still, of the world-famous piano virtuoso,[1] a situation that has frequently been repeated in the musical life of Western Europe.

However, with Liszt's death a palpable change occurred. Not only were his remarkable accomplishments during his twelve years as Kapellmeister in Weimar generally recognized; the selflessness and energy of his labours for Wagner's art and for the concept of

Bayreuth began to be understood as well, and indeed a unified opinion emerged concerning Liszt's rank as an important composer ... What most fascinated experts and initiated laymen was the new form Liszt was thought to have discovered, as he himself believed, a form regarded as liberating wordless instrumental music of a serious nature from what was assumed to be the stiff, contrastive scheme of the symphony, assigning to a literary programme – a poem in verse or prose – the determination of the music's arrangement and the treatment of the musical motifs and melodies; these corresponded to the literary ideas.[2] Actually, Liszt had taken over this idea from Berlioz; but a richer gift, a more stimulating milieu, and more fortunate external circumstances enabled Liszt to fulfil Berlioz's initiative in a far clearer, more complete and more convincing fashion. The twelve symphonic poems were performed with ever greater frequency, and during the 1880s and 1890s could be found on almost every respectable symphonic programme. The listeners were inspired by the 'literary' programme, or perhaps simply by the spirit of the times, to find the symphonic poems and their music vital, or at least captivating, until ...

Yes, things went the way they always do, only a little faster than usual. This music, like all other, was worn out by repetition. Quite simply, it bore repetition less well than many other, older pieces – Beethoven's for example. Even today, one or another of these anaemic, over-emotional tone poems turns up on a programme as it were by necessity, presumably for lack of stronger numbers. And, considering the museum-like quality concert life has now acquired everywhere, there is really nothing ill to be said about it. Some reason can always exist for attempting to clarify the formal concepts of the musical art once more, concepts which constantly show a remarkable tendency to become blurred or confused.

Otherwise, Liszt himself, by means of a series of instrumental works without programmes, the rhapsodies and, above all, the two piano concertos, has cast quite an excellent light – albeit perhaps unconsciously and unintentionally – on the problem of form for which he thought he had been chosen to provide a new solution. But whether one takes these pieces or some other older or more recent examples as a measure and point of departure for the investigation of the problem, one is forced to arrive at the discovery that the problem quite simply – does not exist. The reason is that people persist in talking about form when they mean content.

The form of music is most fittingly compared with a vessel – for example, a vase into which I pour a liquid. The difference consists merely in the fact that the vessel belongs to the realm of space, in which it must have a firm consistency and a certain degree of practical shape, and so has to be made of a more or less precious material, with lines that are more or less appealing to the eye – all of which gives it an aesthetic value of its own, quite without any connection to the nature of the liquid it contains. The form of music, which exists only in time, can only have an influence through temporal proportions, which for the rest can be imagined to be liberated or abstracted from the content only with difficulty, and quite without arriving at any helpful result. The simplest melody can prove this to us. In more complicated pieces of instrumental music, such as symphonic music, where various moods, as they are characterized and individualized, may replace and influence one another with a certain psychological necessity, the question of form – that is, the problem of the proportions of time – still remains the same, save that it is seen, so to speak, through a magnifying glass. The only thing that requires special attention during the process of magnification is the psychological factor, by which it is determined how the repetitions of something already said shall be presented again, or masked, or avoided altogether. (The practice, generally followed nowadays, of not repeating the exposition of an allegro in a symphony, even though a *da capo*[3] is clearly marked, is a psychological procedure of this sort, whose motivation is plain as day.)

Thus musical form has no aesthetic value of its own and cannot be enjoyed if separated from its content, while a silver tankard has the same beauty, whether it be filled with a fine or a sour wine. The music might perhaps be compared to a wine which pours its own glass, light and transparent or heavy and murky, around itself in the very moment when it streams forth from the instruments, in which case the most transparent form is the best, since it reveals the most of the content.

As a matter of fact, I have not infrequently been forced to think these thoughts, and each time I do, I have the sense that they are all too self-evident to merit being put down on paper and imparted to others. But then, a while ago, I got a clipping from a Danish newspaper where, under the heading 'Living music – museum music', one P. Hamburger, M.A., closely examined the crisis presently pre-vailing in our European musical life. For several years, I have made myself a spokesman of a number of the thoughts to which he gives voice in the article, particularly those concerning classical music and its relationship to the public of today. But when he enters the realm of cures for the crisis, he falls into a treacherous trap: he demands new 'forms'. No symphonies! He seems not to under-stand that if a symphony is boring, this is due not to its form but rather to its content. In its totality, of course, the form can now and then be too long drawn out and tiring; unfortunately, that is often the case with both certain classical and certain romantic-modernistic works. But there is nothing theoretical that keeps a composer from writing short symphonies or symphonies of middle length in forms which can be varied in a thousand different ways, all of which are good, save for the tiresome ones, that is, those which lack inven-tion. Calling for new *forms* in music in our time is like complaining about getting our milk served in pitchers very much like those the ones used five hundred or two thousand years ago, or demanding that champagne bottles, starting tomorrow, have an altogether new shape. It is not the bottles that matter.

Liszt, who attended so many champagne parties himself (until he was ordained as an abbé), believed that higher laws of form pre-vailed in the sublime world of music. He was mistaken. But his mistake gave rise to thoughts and debates, and caused a great inten-sification of musical life, albeit not comparable to the one his cele-brated son-in-law [Wagner] called forth with *his* music dramas. They too contain formal mistakes, but in the midst of these mistakes a strong and burning music flourishes even today, music which keeps them alive. Unfortunately, the same cannot be claimed for the compositions of the father-in-law, in which he likewise wished to be a breaker of new ground, a pathfinder. Here he thought too little about the true content and too much about the supposed one, the task of which it was to create the new form. But, in and of itself, the task was a matter of no importance and worthless – the mistake con-sisted in regarding it as important and valuable.

1 Compare Heine's comments (no. 29).
2 For other views on programme music, see the articles by Schumann, Castil-Blaze, Wolf, Dukas and Brod (nos. 25, 27, 45, 49 and 63).
3 A repeat 'from the beginning' of the piece or movement.

79

Olin Downes, 'On Misreading Meanings into Sibelius'
New York Times (24 October 1937)

Downes (1886–1955) had a long and influential career as critic of the *Boston Post* and the *New York Times*. Most of his writing has retained its freshness, especially the articles introducing Americans to music of contemporary European composers and to indigenous jazz. Along with Newman in England and Diktonius in Finland (see nos. 72 and 74), Downes was an early and effective advocate of Sibelius.

A voice, gently admonitory, raises itself from the pages of a recent program book of the Boston Symphony Orchestra, warning readers that the conclusions of 'early commentators' who found the Second Symphony of Jean Sibelius expressive of northern nature, revolution, and whatnot of the same sort, should be taken with a grain of salt. How does anybody know that Sibelius was thinking of these things when he wrote the Second Symphony? As a matter of fact, he probably wasn't. How do we know that he probably wasn't? Because, as it transpires, a considerable part of the Second Symphony was written by Sibelius, not when he was roving the wilds of Karelia, but when he was sojourning, in the spring, in sunny Italy.

This shows how careful northern composers should be when they write symphonies. A composer born in Finland who goes to Italy had better be careful. If he doesn't, he'll find that he has composed *Il Trovatore*. The men who discuss his symphonies had better go slow, too, or they will find that just when they thought Sibelius's orchestra was muttering of war and Northern Lights it was really depicting moonlight pouring down upon the Villa d'Este. And anybody with any sense would know that Sibelius wouldn't write like Sibelius if he were in the land of the Villa d'Este. His style would then become that of Monteverdi. It's lucky that he missed Naples, else we might have had hymns with guitar accompaniment to *dolce far niente*.

What music criticism needs, in the above and similar connections, is debunking. Why should music be construed to mean anything? What have a composer's race, past, environment, or individual temperament to do with his creations? Every thoughtful and educated person knows that great art is international, and great music – just music. Sibelius has no more to do with Finland and the north than Tchaikovsky's 'Pathetic' Symphony, with its alleged Slavisms and wails of despair, has to do with the nation that begot Dostoevsky, or Beethoven's Fifth with that composer's ethical or temperamental reactions to his epoch. The Fifth Symphony is simply music, and it is a pity that Schindler's legend of fate knocking at the door was ever promulgated. These people who find 'meanings,' scenes, dramas in music!

What is music, then? Music is a wonderful arrangement of tones in certain positions and patterns which, for reasons we have not successfully analyzed, gives us a certain esthetic pleasure – that is, if we are really cultivated people. We then derive from it, as the Greek philosopher said, a gentlemanlike joy. This orderly and symmetrical arrangement of the tones takes our minds off the real and urgent problems of existence and lifts us above the human equation and the fairy story in art. But Beethoven knew better, and this knowledge is what gives his music universality. Wagner knew it, too, and likewise the youthful Sibelius.

We – the editorial we – that is to say, in this case, good old Downes – should be glad to know these things and to stand corrected, for 'we' were among the erroneous 'early commentators.' What is worse, we are unregenerate. While we are not yet limping, purblind, or of a hoary gray hue, we persist in discovering the elemental northern and magnificently ancestral thing in Sibelius's compositions, at least in the early symphonies and symphonic poems. These appear to us inalienable and unmistakable characteristics of the music. Nor can we easily believe that persons normally responsive to music, with any degree of imagination – a faculty still applicable to that art – and with even a little blood in their veins, can fail to find something of that spirit in the scores.

Whatever its form, music emanates from sources inseparable from the individual and the things deepest and truest in his personality. One or another aspect of the personality may be uppermost at the moment of creation and find expression in a manner that seems incongruous with various factors of the moment. Schubert, nearing his end penniless and in need, shouts his praise to the skies. Beethoven, in the terrible years of the Heiligenstadt Will,[1] creates one of his most joyous works. It is none the less a true emanation of himself, a moment of triumph snatched from the very jaws of tragedy.

Proof and not contradiction of this principle is supplied by Sibelius's frequent denial of the intention of northern nature-painting in his scores. He says that he writes simply the music that comes to him, and perfects it as well as he may in putting it on paper. That is what every composer does. It is not the business, and in many cases it is not in the power, of the composer to explain himself, although it should be said here that when composers such as Schumann, Berlioz, Wagner, Debussy have explained themselves they have not done so in terms of abstract art, but in very vivid word pictures of dramatic or poetic conceptions. When the composer, like a Beethoven, is not given to self-analysis by explication, it may well be the province and usefulness of outsiders to do him and his music this genuine service.

Sibelius, his birth and background being what they are, would have written the music he has written whether it had been composed in Florence or at Niagara Falls. If he had been born in America of Finnish ancestry and lived his life here, he would have produced some other kind of music. As the years have passed, his scores have become far less those of a musical landscapist and romantic revolutionist in his art, and there are good and logical explanations of this. One is that prior to the composition of the Fourth Symphony he drastically changed his conditions of living, getting out of Helsingfors and its many companionships, living a much quieter and more introspective existence than in earlier years, and becoming, as a consequence, always more alone and individual in his music. This was in marked contrast to the period of the Second Symphony, completed at a time of feverish nationalism, when Finland was under Russian rule, and he was one of a young band of artists and writers whose emotions were of a sort – granted the presence of a young composer of genius – to result in a Second Symphony.

There are people, of the paler or academic cast of mind, who persist in attempting to make one rule for everything in music; who would, if they could, put not only limitations but blinders on the art, and fit it to their own limited vision and experience. It is just as ridiculous and unperceptive to close the eyes to patent characteristics of certain compositions and their sources in race and personality as it is to make up silly legends about other works with which officious and impossible tales have obviously no connection. To read events, for example, as many people have, into Beethoven's Seventh Symphony is as impertinent and beside the mark as it would be to deny an implicit meaning to symphonies Six or Nine (in the finale) by the same composer.

To which may be added the following: that the ultimate significance of an art work is determined not only by what its creator intended, or by that of which he was conscious when he produced it, but also by the meanings and the values discovered in it by many individuals and generations.

1 The so-called 'Heiligenstadt Testament' of 1802, in which Beethoven expressed his despair at the realization that he was losing his hearing.

80

Zofia Lissa, 'Karol Szymanowski'

Sygnaly, no. 29 (1937), trans. Mirka Zemanová

One of Poland's leading musicologists, Lissa (1908–80) applied Marxist methodology and the tenets of socialist realism to her study of Polish music and musical aesthetics in general. This obituary of Szymanowski – the most significant Polish composer of the early 1900s – reflects a growing concern on the part of critics and scholars with the composer's relationship to society. Compare the views of Henderson, Schloezer, Sollertinsky and Ivashkin (nos. 59, 66, 77 and 99).

At the moment of a great man's death, society's attitude toward him and his works changes fundamentally. Between the deceased artist and all those with whom he had until recently coexisted and lived, a distance arises such as always exists between that which has ended, been withdrawn, and that which continues and goes on. The deceased artist ceases to be a man and becomes a 'historical fact'.[1] We begin to judge what he created by another scale of value: until recently harnessed to everyday life, which devours us all, until recently one of the weights on the scale of fate, which could turn it to this or that side, it has now already become a myth judged in the light of eternity. What he had created ceases to be an expression of a human being much as we are, ceases to be the sublimation of suffering which we also know, of joy which we also experience. It becomes a 'cultural virtue', a 'historical value' ...

Karol Szymanowski died. And from that moment he became history, a stage of development in Polish music, a national hero for the entire community. But he had long been that stage of development – and its turning point. Like Chopin a hundred years ago, Szymanowski in our own time took Polish music to the world arena, and he took it out there as a specifically Polish music. And yet, how much harder domestic conditions were when Szymanowksi undertook that task than when Chopin was composing and conquering the world!

For the two men have one thing in common which made it easy for one of them, and more difficult for the other, to be understood by the world: a typically Slavic attitude toward music as an art of expression in which the human inner life finds its reflection in the most essential and at the same time the most subtle way. But whereas Chopin composed at a time when such a subjective attitude toward music was the norm, Szymanowski, in bringing this blood-inheritance to the world, faced a difficult struggle: a struggle between his individual and individualistic attitude and the tendencies of our era, whose anti-romantic, anti-subjective, new musical attitude contradicted Szymanowski's tendencies. This is because Szymanowski was a genuine romantic, despite having distanced himself intellectually from romanticism, which he considered 'an open door on which it is no use to bang'. He was a romantic in his need to express himself through his music, and this need distinguished him from other composers of our era.

The early twentieth century, to which the first stage of his creativity belongs, was still marked by the undertones of musical impressionism; it is the beginning of expressionist inspirations against which Szymanowski's individualism could develop by its own lights. Chopinesque lyricism, the ecstasy of Scriabin's egocentric music, only slightly modulated by Brahms's classicist influence – these are the general outlines of the first stage of Szymanowski's creativity. To this period belong Nine Preludes, Variations, Four

Studies, the C minor Sonata, and songs, all lyrical in character. But Szymanowski soon mastered his own creative psychology. He was drawn to the problems of polyphonic construction and monumental form, and these find their expression in the First and Second Symphonies, in three sonatas for the piano, in more songs, in the First Violin Concerto.

The sense of relationship with his era, a historic and social responsibility which Szymanowksi shouldered conscientiously, prompted him to seek further, to disregard his instincts and follow the command of his intellect, to refer to the language spoken by his generation. The consequence was the period of atonal interests and studies, which find their voice in the Third Symphony, in the *Songs of the Infatuated Muezzin*, in *Myths* for violin and *Masques* for piano, in *Słopiewnie*, and partly also in *King Roger*. But even that study is only a stage.

Thereafter follows Szymanowski's contact with folk music from Podhale, as a result of which the composer simplifies his hitherto monumental style and condenses his expressive sound-forms, surrendering them to the discipline arising from inner maturity. In the superb Mazurkas, in *Stabat Mater*, in the Second Violin Concerto, full of feeling through and through, in *Children's Rhymes*, in the Fourth Symphony (*Symphonie Concertante*), and above all in *Harnasie*, a ballet based on motifs from Podhale, which won Szymanowski European recognition – in all these compositions the new, and alas final, stage of Szymanowski's development manifests itself. No one knows whether that stage too might not have been only temporary, had it not been for his untimely death. No one knows what might have followed from the composer's intellectual interest in the stupendously original, genuine melodic material of Podhale. No one knows where this path would have led Szymanowski, who started with the Young Poland movement and got as far as European 'modern' music ...

Did he manage a synthesis? In any case, he stopped not far from the point where two composers who today point most to the future find themselves – Stravinsky and Bartók. To use Norwid's[2] expression, he stopped on the path where 'he raised folk art to humaneness'. This does not mean that there are any stylistic connections between Szymanowski's music and that of these two composers, which is anti-romantic and contemporary through and through. It is only his reaching out for the popular, mass elements – in their crudest form – that links him with them, and his translating of these elements into a contemporary language. But he differs from Stravinsky and Bartók in his attitude toward contemporary reality, an attitude which endeavours to relate the fiction of the 'free man' to the artist's social conscience ...

Karol Szymanowski ... took his talent with him to his grave. But his sense of responsibility for every step, every deed – the only form in which he gave expression to the social problems which reached the summit of his own Olympus – this sense he left as a legacy to the young. It is the only legacy he could have left. Will the younger generation take it up? That is now a matter for their conscience and their spiritual strength to decide. Because only talent, intellect and character together make a creative person into a great artist.

1 That Szymanowski (1882-1937) acutely felt his lack of recognition in Poland is evident from a letter he wrote in 1934, which says in part: 'My funeral will be a different story! I am convinced it will be special! People here love the funeral processions of great men.' *Karol Szymanowski and Jan Smeterlin: Correspondence and Essays*, trans. B. M. Maciejewski and F. Aprahamian (London, 1977), p. 12.
2 Cyprian Norwid, the nineteenth-century Polish writer.

81

Robert Aloys Mooser, 'Works by German Nazi Composers'

(December 1937), from *Regards sur la musique contemporaine* (Lausanne, 1946)

Born in Geneva, Mooser (1876–1969) began his career as a critic in St Petersburg before returning to Switzerland to write for *La Suisse* from 1909 to 1962. Together with Schuh (see no. 87), he was one of the country's most highly respected critics, in part because of his outspoken opposition to fascism before and during the Second World War. The works reviewed here bear out Schloezer's fears for music in a totalitarian society (see no. 66).

The impoverishment visited on musical life in Germany by the repugnant measures the Third Reich has taken with respect to artists who do not enjoy the privilege of being '100 per cent Aryans' cannot be overlooked. Whether composers, orchestra directors, performers or teachers, all Jewish musicians – even those who are simply unlucky enough to count a Jew among their ancestors – have been brutally ousted from their careers and jobs, which have been taken over by men capable of furnishing all the desirable guarantees from the 'racial' point of view.

This 'purification' has had the immediate result of depriving Germany of a host of individuals of real ability who had served their art with distinction and who – whatever the extremists of Hitler's regime may claim – had hitherto done their country the greatest honour.

All the while it was proceeding with these summary executions, the government of the Reich was simultaneously proclaiming its intention of bringing music into line with 'the national-socialist ideal' by restoring it to the 'sacred traditions of great German art', and of mercilessly combating the degenerate tendencies of contemporary music, which, the government asserts in all seriousness, are the work of a 'Jewish junta' and exercise 'a deleterious influence on public taste' (*dixit* Göring) ...

Burdened with the mentality of the primitive who dismisses everything he can't understand as useless, even wicked, the Nazi leaders are following the lead of their counterparts in the USSR, who are also known to have declared war on *avant-garde* composers, under the pretext that their works could hold no interest for the masses and that the only music worthy of the name is music which anyone can grasp without effort.[1]

As a result, a ban was imposed in Germany on all creative artists whose aesthetic didn't conform to Nazi doctrine. So it is that total excommunication has been pronounced against, among others, Paul Hindemith, who has not only been invited to relinquish his chair of composition at the Hochschule für Musik in Berlin but has also seen concert performances of all of his works prohibited under heavy penalties.[2]

Arbitrarily deprived of its most eminent representative, whose name has long shone far beyond the borders of the Reich and who is rightly considered in all countries one of the undisputed masters of our time, what has German music come to today, and where is it going?

A recent concert at the Musik-Collegium of Winterthur, devoted entirely to young composers who toe the Nazi line, has provided the answer. Organized by the Reichsmusikkammer,[3] the session was clearly intended to show the Swiss public what a constellation of German composers free of 'Jewish influence' are up to, and to advertise the tendencies now in vogue at the heart of the German school.

Alas! The concert was a catastrophe.

For it revealed, with blinding clarity, the problem with considering null and void the present evolution of an art whose very essence is to transform itself endlessly, perpetually to seek paths as yet unknown, and to enrich itself every day thanks to experiments which are often rash but almost always profitable, undertaken by spirits enamoured of novelty.

Four orchestral scores by as many composers had been chosen in Berlin to bring us the Nazi gospel; four scores whose identical characters showed that they were not special cases but instead represented an aesthetic conception commmon to present-day German musicians as a group. The pieces were: *Festliches Vorspiel* by Paul Höffer (b. 1895), Three Pieces for string orchestra by Peter Schacht (b. 1901), *Variationen über ein Geusenlied* by Helmut Degen (b. 1911), and Symphony in A minor by Hans Chemin-Petit (b. 1902).

The truly incredible thing is that these four composers, of whom the oldest is barely forty and the youngest just twenty-six, think, feel, and write as if they belonged to the generation at work in the latter half of the nineteenth century. They resolutely disregard everything music has gained – God only knows if it was important and fruitful! – since the time of Brahms and Bruckner.

They seem to be just as ignorant of the art of Debussy and Maurice Ravel – which would still be excusable for composers of the German race – as they are of that of Igor Stravinsky, Arthur Honegger, Paul Hindemith, Arnold Schönberg and Alban Berg. Apparently, none of them has been curious enough to look into the astonishing evolution that music has paraded before our eyes over the last quarter-century, and into the enrichments it has reaped therefrom.

For example, it is (quite understandably) dumbfounding to see Hans Chemin-Petit give us a symphony which remains ingenuously in the Brahmsian line. It might just as well bear the name of some pallid epigone of that master, an epigone content with an incurably out-of-date rhetoric who, like his colleagues, shamelessly exploited every musical cliché and showed himself incapable of development except in accordance with the academic formulas he picked up at the conservatory. In this symphony one often guesses in advance, with virtual certainty, what will become of such and such a theme, how it will be used, and the inferences the composer is going to draw from it.

Peter Schacht's Three Pieces and Helmut Degen's *Variationen* were only slightly less reactionary in their aesthetic conceptions. Sometimes they allowed a glimmer of emancipation and modernism to slip through, though it was quickly repressed. But they too revealed an incoherence which had as much to do with their disdain for logic as with their perpetual fragmentation.

As for Paul Höffer's *Festliches Vorspiel*, it assuredly wins the prize for mediocrity and conventionality, with its inexcusably discredited vocabulary, its noisy, grandiloquent vulgarity, and the overwhelming coarseness of the scoring, which seems to come from the hand of some military-music field sergeant.

This is the overwhelming impression produced by the art which is being worked out today under the eyes and at the behest of the Nazi regime. This is what German music has been reduced to in the second quarter of the twentieth century, by the overweening pretensions of the pedants who set themselves up as its form-masters and who mean to sever it arbitrarily from the natural laws which have governed it from time immemorial.

German music suffers from a deplorable sterility, which can be cured only by an infusion of new blood capable of reviving it and restoring its erstwhile splendour by bringing it back to its authentic traditions. It is very sick ...

1 Shostakovich's condemnation in *Pravda* in 1936 is a case in point; see no. 77.
2 A semi-official boycott of Hindemith's music was imposed in November 1934. The following January he accepted a six-month 'leave of absence' from the Hochschule. He finally gave up his post in 1937 and left Germany a year later.
3 The music division of the Nazi Ministry of Culture.

82

Gianandrea Gavazzeni, 'Cinematic Images and Musical Images'

(1938), from *Trent'anni di musica* (Milan, 1958)

Beginning in the 1920s the possibilities of film music attracted composers such as Prokofiev, Honegger, Britten, Hindemith and Thomson. Gavazzeni (b. 1909) approached the subject from the perspective of a composer and conductor as well as critic. This highly impressionistic piece gives a fresh twist to the old debate about programme music, as well as to discussions of the impact of technology on music. Compare, for example, the articles by Stuckenschmidt and Peterson-Berger (nos. 68 and 78).

When it comes to music and the cinema, the thoughts of a musician who has never scored a film are different, very different, from those of musicians who have composed cinematic music. The difference, I would say, has to do above all with images. However, even in the musician who happens to be composing film music, I believe there is something positively opposed to taking action when the cinema, for him, is the subject of immediate creative work; instead, he watches it and takes it in just as he does other elements of his spiritual life. For the composer, a film to be scored is a chance to make music – passages to be measured out, character expression to be fine-tuned, fleeting images and sonorous figurations. It's a matter of specifics, or rather contingency – with all the resulting problems that we know from the mouth of the man who has experience in such things.

On the other hand, for this musician too the film is one more ingredient on top of the other intellectual and emotional ones: reading the works of novelists and poets for whatever imaginative content they may have to offer, apart from their strictly artistic value.

The cinema runs up against the same limitations: pausing in the musician's life without leaving a vivid imprint; destined to remain above his spiritual, moral and creative problems; yet not passing by him either, like a light entertainment, a sensual and pleasing pastime. A little of both are perhaps present when the composer is not directly engaged in the subject matter of the film. And certainly the musician who has always watched the cinema even as a casual spectator, hardly aware of certain emphases or a murmuring heard in a dreamy haze, feels a little of both: a little arrogance, inner need, precise artistic interest; and a little absentminded pleasure, delight in the black-and-white image which appears and vanishes on the screen, resting, insinuating, barely etched. A value *sui generis*, then; an emotion *sui generis* – this, in a word, is the true nature of the cinema: art and non-art, gimmickry and naturalness, native images and manners and fabrications of the strangest sort …

It is fitting to see those intellectual and emotional elements as a sort of précis of the aesthetic and spiritual harvest that every truly educated musician gathers inside himself. In the film, they are epitomized by the harvest that the film itself is reaping in vanished fields; afterwards, however, they are reduced by the musician as if in a transcription, through the demands and habits which move him. Like music transcribed into unbelievable forms, pure fantasy, chimerical; into other scales, Chinese or Arab; into unknown keys or dead musical languages, arranged for imaginary instruments.

Figures, events, moods that pass on the screen – the musician takes as much as they can give him. They last for a moment and in a trice, no sooner than he has recollected them, they are already different. Just like a memory of life, a memory of images: as so often the screen is made to carry within itself, to recall, to transform the light of a wall, a foreshortened house, the deserted corner of a piazza, and the distant footstep of a lady; the rise and fall and the resonance of that footstep.

The cinematic image being so limited, everyone takes away his own memories and impressions. And once more he hears a certain echo of certain scenes; with the very sound that accompanied them – anonymous, of course, but harmonized at that moment with a triple juncture: its indefinable phonic value, its connection to the scene, and both, afterwards, coming toward us to find the extreme limit of the combination – which may be merely our emotional frame of mind, or our whole aesthetic make-up.

On such occasions, within such devices, after all is said and done, these pieces of truth, poetry or suggestion remain – through allusive meanings, inferences which arise and breathe in the literal or imponderable endings of transfiguration, of evocation. Whereas the music, at that moment, in film, is almost always no more than a phonic reference: sonorous material which lends sounds and timbres to the scene, not music ordered in rhythm and expression. The music the musician extracts from it is different. It is a question of musicality, in some cases, not of music; just as one sometimes speaks of 'poeticity' instead of poetry.

But still these particular pieces have exercised their power. Living in the image, they were inciters of images. From cinema to music.

There will be such moments from time to time: the river in *Mercante d'avorio*, with the sombre drumbeat coming from afar and the caravan led by a ghostly *miss*,[1] passing at night in the forest; and certain northern landscapes in *Eskimo*, barely punctuated by an indefinable musical pedal point; Greta Garbo's 'alone' in *Queen Christina*:[2] the 'alone' of the inn in that famous Nordic morning bathed in snowy whiteness.

There was music accompanying the scene – the sort of anonymous, muted background music which the producers must have requested from the composer, specifying that it be 'music in memory of a love scene, nostalgia for a love scene'. And, let it be said parenthetically, there was the music of the exalters, their signature music, their Sapphic syntax; and that biting, playful music, tedious to those who saw in the inn scene a Garboism that was highly watered down, lax and mannered in the extreme. For the musician, between the reality of the film and the admittedly thriving mannerism, and the pale power of the sounds piercing the light fog – for the musican there was another, a different music: his own; the emotive, sensory life, suspended between the cinematic image and the musical image; a life which is always a life of sounds, of musical spirits, because it springs from an immediate occasion and bows to the musician's moral dominion, enters his world of phonic matchmaking, of rhythmic agglomerations; with the same more or less ephemeral list of the other varied and mixed motives ...

When the position of a musician confronting the cinema is put this way, all the other subjects concerning film music are fatally deficient. On the contrary, one can say that they do not really exist. It would be the same as raising detailed questions about sets, costumes or screenplays to the level of problems; the same as proposing subjects such as: the chair and the cinema; the overcoat and the cinema; overshoes and the cinema. In the same way, the collaboration of authentic musicians in film has never amounted to anything, for either one or the other. It is a marriage that went up in smoke after the relatives' noisy overtures. Music has not brought musical life to the film; the film has not brought cinematic life to the music. Both of them have been integrating elements of a whole which is at the highest level hybrid and capricious. And everything vanished on the perilous thread of contingencies. The only truth rests in the images, lying idle and abandoned. Only here, in the musician's exhaustions, rebirths and impossible loves, are motives and opportunities for fantastic life.

1 English in the original.
2 *Eskimo* and *Queen Christina* were both filmed in the United States and released in 1933. I have not been able to identify *Mercante d'avorio*.

83

Alfred Einstein, 'Universality and Music Today'
Modern Music, vol. 16 (1938–9)

Einstein (1880–1952) was equally eminent as a musicologist and, until he left Germany in 1933, as a critic in Munich and Berlin. After coming to the United States in 1938, he concentrated on scholarly work but continued to write about such broad issues as greatness and universality in music. This stirring plea for 'a new ritual for new men' reflects the resilient optimism of a mind in touch with the past and unbowed by the ascendant nationalism of the 1930s.

In the earlier periods of the history of music, universality was something demanded of the musician. He had no right to follow his inclinations or his impulses. Incorporated into the social order of his age, he was expected as a good craftsman to deliver whatever that order demanded of him – music religious or secular, vocal or instrumental. No one inquired about his special preferences or qualifications. If his craftsmanship was good, it was considered 'art;' the personal qualities he offered over and above the handicraft and art were just those values that might perhaps outlive the age ...

Is universality still possible today? It should be easier to realize, now that the domain of music has become still further restricted. More types of music have died out, or rather, many more retain only the appearance of life. Songs are probably still written but Song exists no longer. For our age, which has properly grown more reticent, song is too uncompromising an expression of emotion. We prefer to escape by stylization, in the masquerade of the cantata. Symphonies are still being written but there no longer is a Symphony. In the symphony, one man attempts to talk to all, perhaps even *for all*, but I am not sure that such a man may be found today, no matter what his name. And so, again quite properly, the attempt is made to write symphonic music within the smaller, less hampering concertante forms, and here too refuge is sought in stylization, preferably in the concerto grosso, and not in the solo concerto with its cultivation of subjectivity. The symphonic form, the 'sonata form,' is a discursive one, and a discourse that reveals too much inner feeling is not popular. All the subjective types of music developed by the nineteenth century are disappearing.

At the beginning of the movement for new music, everything disappeared which had particularly to do with vocal art, most especially opera and choral works. Only gradually did music regain its conception of universality. I believe that the vocal elements today have more vitality than the instrumental. But at the outset, the string quartet was pre-eminent. Any description of the development of this movement must first note the transformation wrought in Schönberg's string quartet. In the period around 1920, a new composer's first opus was usually a string quartet. It was the abstract period of the new music; and the abstract became the dominating style. The paths or bypaths over which Schönberg travels until he arrives at the twelve-tone system are truly remarkable; but once arrived at the goal, Schönberg applies his system to all fields, it becomes universal. It is just as universal in this respect as all the other experiments with tonal materials altered or augmented by arbitrary division. And Hindemith, whose musical nature is so unrelated to Schönberg's – for he is a maker of rhythm and a practising musician – resembles him in this respect: he can and does apply his manner to the whole field of music. A survey of his work will show that Hindemith has been effective in all fields which a composer of new music can cultivate. But he constructs as an instrumentalist, even in his operas or choruses. There are choruses developed from the tonal material of the anti-vocal principle of equal temperament; there are operas in which the drama and the music belong to different spheres. It is really unnecessary to quote Hindemith's remark on the failure of his first opera: never again would he compose an opera without reading the book; one has only to recall *Cardillac*.[1] Even in *Mathis der Maler*, the musical elements, despite all attempts at 'compromise' are only a reflection of the dramatic. It is not a dramatic music.

Quite different, more realistic in nature is Stravinsky's universality. Stravinsky has no style, and even no manner. Each of the 'new musicians' who did not grow up in the era of new music, who are now fifty or sixty, has experienced a 'transformation.' In Schönberg's case it was in the *Gurre-Lieder*, in Stravinsky's, *Le Sacre du printemps*. Since then Stravinsky has become antipodal to all young musicians who compose without preconception, who seek to produce pure expression. He always establishes a hypothesis, a point of support, a circumference to which his line is tangential. Here we must except such purely folk works as *Noces* or an apparently negative work like *L'histoire du soldat* – without in any way commenting on their artistic importance. At a quite early stage he is already in contact with the classicism of the early eighteenth century; in the Pergolesi *Suite*,[2] there is the cheerful style of the opéra bouffe. For a moment he touches the old classical style in *Oedipus Rex*, which is an un-natural, chilling opera. He touches Bach's polyphony in his *Violin Concerto*; the stylized bucolicism of the old French school from Lully to Rameau in his *Duo* for piano and violin; the old music drama and at the same time the oratorio in his *Perséphone*; in *The Card Party* he touches and parodies Rossini's opera and many other stylistic idiosyncrasies of the Empire or Biedermeier period which has almost the same attraction for him, the lure of a mechanistic and puppet-like world, that it exerted on Busoni. It is a universality of relativity and in this respect, Busoni is one of the precursors of Stravinsky.

Can universality again be achieved within our own limits, within the limits of a living music? I believe it can. Change gives us hope. Twenty years ago opera was a field completely abandoned by living, contemporary creators. Young musicians shunned nothing so much as the hypertrophy of materials, the excessive romanticism, the unreality that prevailed in post-Wagnerian opera, Richard Strauss included.

Today it is opera, the unpathetic opera, the opera which addresses itself to a new public, whose first efforts in Germany, as shown in works of Krenek and Weill, were trampled underfoot by the cultural hordes of the Third Reich, that represents perhaps the most fertile activity in the whole sphere of music. Who can tell whether from the chaos of the present there will not be born a new piety, a new desire for religion, which while it may not require sacred music, may still need a new ritual for new men? Whether the period of negation, of tangential music will not be followed by a period in which the demand for a 'direct' music will once again come to life? If such a new music appears will it be without predetermined concepts, divorced from contact with the past? That is the new question, and it is not easily answered.

1 Hindemith wrote his first full-length opera, *Cardillac* (1926), to a ready-made libretto by Ferdinand Lion based on a story by E. T. A. Hoffmann (see no. 19). Later he came to feel that the libretto was weak and revised it himself to bring it closer to the original.
2 The concert suite from the ballet *Pulcinella*.

84

Paul Rosenfeld, 'Ives's *Concord* Sonata'

Modern Music, vol. 16 (1938–9)

American composers between the world wars had no more devoted champion than Rosenfeld (1890–1946). As critic for *The Dial*, *Vanity Fair* and other important journals, he was one of the most eloquent spokesmen for musical progressivism. Although Rosenfeld lacked formal musical training, his writing was respected by experts and lay music-lovers alike. He was among the first to proclaim Ives as a great American original, but the Nazi idolatry of Wagner led him to discountenance cultural chauvinism. Compare Weissmann's remarks on race and nationalism (no. 65).

The scene was The Old House, an ancient lamp-lit mansion near the post-road at Cos Cob. There, before an intrigued, tense, somewhat puzzled little audience on November 28th, John Kirkpatrick gave what to all appearances was the first complete public performance of the work containing possibly the most intense and sensitive musical experience achieved by an American. It is *Concord, Mass., 1840–1860*, the second pianoforte sonata of Charles E. Ives.[1]

Sonorities frequently unique in character and finely veiled, penetrating with a curious sensuous spirituality in which the secretive soul of Puritanism would seem again to have materialized itself, constitute much of its medium. The structure is Beethoven-like in breadth of conception and cyclic, oftentimes in the grand style, elevated in mood and pitch, stirringly rhythmical, melodious with a subtlety not incomparable to that of Debussy or Schönberg; and one of those in which every note during entire pages is rhapsodically alive, tremulously expressive, fraught with special poetic emphasis and meaning.

The exploitation of a pair of melodic germs, one of them actually the tattoo of Beethoven's *Fifth Symphony*, the other a tender, wooing, chromatic little subject, furnishes the principal material of its four extended and complementary movements. They are a broad andante, a fantastically wild scherzo, a simple intermezzo and a slow quiet finale restrained in point of dynamic scale. Various new material, in instances of a folk-song-like character, including *Hail, Columbia!*, the hymn-tunes *Shall We Gather At The River* and a Scotch folk-melody, is texturally introduced into the three latter movements; and the work, which is tonal in spots, polytonal in others and in still others perfectly atonal, is a subtle, sometimes a trifle coarsely but oftentimes exquisitely drawn web of these thematic and melodic wisps. The style in the opening movement is momentarily Lisztianly grand, frequently flighted and oracular, at times prophetically rapturous and wistful, at others almost paroxysmal with the excitements of the instants which untrammel the spirit. That of the scherzo is humorous in the syncopated passages which Kirkpatrick calls 'proto-jazz' but prevalently spookish and dithering to a degree which makes the whole unbridled, extravagantly frolicsome section a supreme bit of spook-romanticism and more than any similar page in Reger the habitation of a *poltergeist*. It is in this scherzo too that Ives, who anticipated European polytonalism and polyrhythmicality in works earlier than this sonata (the date of its publication at least was 1920) surpasses Ornstein and well nigh out-Cowells Cowell in the bold use of tone-clusters, in instances containing as many as sixteen closely-lying notes. However he takes pity on the performer and spares the piano incarnadining effusions of manual blood by prescribing the use in the performance of these chords of a strip of wood fourteen and three-quarter inches long and heavy enough to press the keys down without striking them. The ensuing softly blent sonorities are ghostly.

The contrastingly diatonic intermezzo is a naive movement, almost sentimental but for the nobility of the style and interplay of lofty and majestic and humble, homely sonorities: the *Fifth Symphony* material and the Scotch folk-tune. Then in the stilly mysterious finale with its slow almost monotonously swaying beat, the second cyclic theme, the wooingly chromatic one, attains its fullest development in singularly glamorous music. The subtle melodic invention and veiled elusive quality of tone are at their sublimest here, and the rhythm is profound. Twice the weighted, tremuluous volumes surge gropingly upwards and forwards before culminating in the fluting peroration of the sonata. There might that night at Cos Cob have been some question of the perfect beauty, the fully realized intentions, of the heroically initial movement. There was, indeed there could, be none of that of this finale. It seemed music as beautiful at the very least as any composed by an American.

It thrilled, it touched, again and again, the entire work; releasing something in the depths, restoring enchantment to them and to things. Some of the 'vibrations of the universal lyre,' of the earth itself, seemed in the music; and for more than one conscious member of its audience it brought the body to the state where Nature seemed to flow through it once more, and the whole of it was 'one sense,' and he felt 'a strange liberty in Nature and a portion of herself.' Thus it could be said that the work had transmitted its composer's experience, the comprehension of the forces and values of the Concord transcendentalist band. It was a nationalistic one, this experience: an American instance of the one vocal in all nationalistic music: that of the individual at the stage when, possibly in consequence of some activation of his inmost self, he comprehends his relationship not only to the present life of his group, race or nation, but to its very past. Imaginatively he grasps the forces and the values of the individuals who existed on his soil before him, the forces and values of the group, race or nation incarnate in them; recognizing their survival in the best of himself and comprehending them with love. In the small book *Essays Before a Sonata* with which Ives, Shaw-like, prefaced *Concord, Mass., 1840–1860*, the composer mentions a moment of this mystical fellowship in which 'Thoreau – that reassuring and true friend – stood by him one "low" day when the sun had gone down, long, long before sunset': and *Thoreau* is the title of the sonata's concluding movement, and *Emerson, Hawthorne* and *The Alcotts* those of the other three. For just the frequency of states of sympathy with Nature when 'the whole body is one sense,' of conditions of 'liberty in Nature' when man is a part of her and the self and all which limits it are divinely acceptable, and humblest clay 'instinct with celestial fire' smites upon the infinite: precisely the frequency of these states was the essence of Concord a hundred years since, the genius of the prophetic Emerson, the fantastic Hawthorne, the homely earth-fast Alcotts, the deeply-earth-submissive hermit of Walden Pond, and is the source of the American and democratic idea. But in moving us towards the transcendentalists and their fount, the music moved us towards Ives himself. He seemed the 'Hesper of their throng,' a seer and surely one of the most exquisitely sentient of American artists.

1 Kirkpatrick was a friend and lifelong champion of Ives. On 28 November 1838 he played the *Concord* Sonata before an invited audience at a private house in Cos Cob, Connecticut (on the Boston Post Road). The first public performance – a landmark in American musical history – took place in New York on 20 January 1939.

85

Reynaldo Hahn, 'To Please'

From *Thèmes variés* (Paris, 1946)

A conductor and composer known for his light operas and ballets, Hahn (1874–1947) was music critic of the Paris daily *Le Figaro* from 1934 to 1945, when he became music director of the Opéra. The Gallic virtues of wit and elegance were hallmarks of his writing, establishing a tradition carried on after the war by his successor Bernard Gavoty ('Clarendon'). Many critics protested against the increasingly harsh and cerebral music of the time; see, for example, the articles by Cardus, Pannain and Mila (nos. 89, 90 and 96).

For some time in articles of music criticism I have noticed the recurrence of a phrase once used by certain 'Franckists' (who had very few true affinities with the great and gentle César Franck), at a time when the austere Société Nationale[1] was enacting its first decrees. In this phrase, all music which 'tried to please' was systematically denounced and sternly condemned. This reproach was considered very serious. Nothing, however, could be more absurd. What exceptional and inexplicable law would prohibit music from seeking what the arts of every age have sought and what it has constantly aimed at from its first stammerings? In what sense does music lose favour by striving to attract, to charm, to 'please' when the time is right for it to do so? And how could these exacting judges manage to find fault with affection, loving tenderness, and voluptuous embracing in music, while admitting, nay admiring – as they well deserve to be admired – many enchanting pages of the great musician whom they had taken as master and guide? In the same way they dismissed Gounod and his disciples as entertainers, bogus artists, frivolous and artificial, while on the other hand (heaven knows why) showering exaggerated praise on Monsigny, Grétry and all the minor masters of *opéra comique*, etc.

How many arbitrary and contradictory things were written and spoken in those days! Yet after all the confusion and artistic hurly-burly we've suffered through since that far-off time, people are once again starting to show contempt for music which 'tries to please'. The odd thing is that this ill-humour goes hand in hand with Mozartian snobbishness. If ever a musician felt the need to please, it was the one who, as a child, never tired of asking people who came up to him that touching question: 'Do you love me?' Does that mean that everything he wrote is sweetness and light, as a large number of his recent worshippers seem to believe? I have already had occasion to protest such a false conception of his genius. But when Mozart, having dashed off the tumultuous and violent fresco of the first-act finale of *Don Giovanni*, takes up delicate brushes and refined colours to paint Donna Elvira dreaming in the moonlight, he is 'trying to please'. And he is still trying to please when, after the sombre opening of the Fantasia in C minor for piano, he interrupts his grandiose rambling with two measures of incomparable suavity which anticipate Beethoven – the two measures in B major where a ray of calm hope suddenly appears.

In short, like all musicians who have the gift of pleasing, Mozart tries to please whenever it's called for, whenever the opportunity presents itself or simple logic demands it, in order to stir and captivate the soul, now with gaiety, now with charm, emotion or even sadness. To wish to deprive music of one of its most powerful resources; to prevent it from seducing the heart and mind as it passes through the ear; to force it to remain unapproachable, to put on a grim face when speaking of love or a 'solemn' one when evoking youth; to wish music to be complicated when simple things are to be expressed and austere when it would arouse the idea of pleasure – this is the height of foolishness. The truth is that not everyone can 'please'. So the precepts 'Thou shalt not try to please' and especially 'Thou shalt try to displease' are much easier to observe than the other one. And that's why they muster so many supporters.

1 The Société Nationale de Musique, a concert society established in Paris in 1871 as a forum for contemporary music. Franck was its *de facto* president.

86

Heinrich Strobel, 'Farewell to Schönberg'

Melos, no. 8 (1951)

For nearly half a century, Strobel (1898–1970) was a voice of reasoned progressivism in German criticism. As a newspaper critic in Erfurt and Berlin before the Second World War, and afterwards as editor of *Melos*, a leading journal of contemporary music, he consistently, but not dogmatically, pressed the case for the European *avant-garde*. This posthumous appreciation of Schönberg as a 'romantic of abstraction' contrasts with the revolutionary image conjured by Vuillermoz's review of *Pierrot lunaire* (no. 64).

Musicians the world over are mourning at the bier of Arnold Schönberg.

About the work he created with unwavering logic and the direction he showed to music through his technical compositional inventions, there may be differing opinions. That Schönberg, who has died in Hollywood at age seventy-seven, was one of the greatest and most moving phenomena of the music of this century, there can be no doubt.

Schönberg is the last link in the rich chain of German romanticism. With the utmost singlemindedness, he walked to the end of the road which Richard Wagner had chosen with *Tristan* and then abandoned again – anticipating the revolutionary consequences that the loss of hitherto valid relationships of tonality would call forth ...

Yet as an old man Schönberg still lived to see his scorned art and his derided system find a strong response in all the countries of Europe. Today, every serious musician must come to grips with the twelve-tone system. It is not Schönberg's fault if this coming-to-grips takes an ever more doctrinaire form, which he himself did not wish for and which threatens to become a scribal quarrel antagonistic to art.

How undoctrinaire Schönberg's music is follows from the simple fact that he allowed himself many freedoms in his system, even going so far as to write tonal works again, which show his connection to German late romanticism especially clearly. But even in the atonal works this connection became progressively clearer with the passage of time.

Schönberg, if I may put it this way, was a romantic of abstraction. He created a system to bring order into the chaos of atonal freedom. Yet for him the system was never more than a means of writing a music which corresponded to his expressive need.

Yes, Schönberg's music is music of expression. A music of sublimated, abstracted, intellectualized expression. It is indicative that Schönberg always emphasized the primacy of the heart as against the head – odd enough in a man whose music appears to most as a pure theoretical construction. Yet anyone who is able to hear beyond the novelty of atonal harmony (perplexing even now), to hear more deeply into Schönberg's music, will recognize its romantic expressive essence, especially in the works linked to the word, in the bizarre, unearthly *Ode to Napoleon* and the shocking narration of the 'survivor' of the extermination of the Jews in Warsaw.[1]

Schönberg's close connection to the literary Symbolism of 1900, already so far away from us, is another indication of his deep bond to the late romantic world. And, finally, his incredible sensitivity to sound, which manifests itself in his works time and again, is of romantic origin.

Unquestionably, Schönberg widened the long-standing gap between music and public, almost to the point at which it can no longer be bridged. He seems to have made music a matter for the very few, an art for specialists, once and for all. Even from a sociological point of view, he pursued his goal with his own inexorable singlemindedness.

In the last conversation I must have had with Schönberg, shortly before 1933 at the microphone of the Berlin Radio Hour, he said: 'The past has no interest for me – in 150 years my music will be as understandable as Mozart's is today ... '

That remains for the future to decide.

Today we bow down for the last time before the great man Arnold Schönberg, who, as a genuine master of the musical art, imbued with his mission, took the hard road which his intellect and his conscience prescribed for him.

1 *A Survivor from Warsaw*, written in 1947.

87

Willi Schuh, 'Stravinsky and Tradition'

(1952), from *Von neuer Musik* (Zürich, 1955)

Schuh (1900–86) is generally regarded as Switzerland's foremost critic of the postwar period. Friend and official biographer of Richard Strauss, he was a conscientious and broad-minded commentator, particularly on contemporary music. Most of his articles for the *Neue Züricher Zeitung* and the *Schweizerische Musikzeitung* have been collected in books. Here he reflects on Stravinsky's relationship to tradition – a subject of growing concern to critics as composers' ties to the past became more tenuous and problematic. Compare Thomson's views on the subject (no. 91).

The consideration of Stravinsky's relationship to tradition permits us to describe the precise position he occupies in present-day music. And such precision is essential. 'L'imprécis m'est suspect' (I am suspicious of imprecision): this saying of Stravinsky's, who shares with Paul Valéry the 'horreur du vague', must be borne in mind by anyone who wants to deal with his art. Although Stravinsky is known as one of the great masters of our time, his music is hardly less subject to conflict of opinions today than it was forty years ago, at the time of the Paris scandal over *Le Sacre du printemps*. Only the buzzwords have changed. The early works that have since become celebrated – *Firebird*, *Petruschka*, *Le Sacre du printemps*, *Les Noces*, and (in another way) even *L'Histoire du soldat* – have made the understanding of the later works more difficult. For everything which Stravinsky created subsequently (that is, since *Mavra*) has been seen in relation to the creations of his so-called Russian period – just as Richard Strauss's later works are seen in relation to *Salome* and *Elektra*. In *L'Histoire du soldat* (because the intentions and special circumstances which led to its genesis have scarcely been noted), people saw a revolution, a wholly new idea of musical theatre;[1] and they were disappointed and irritated when Stravinsky gave no thought to developing henceforth exclusively those elements with which the *avant-gardists* had become fascinated because they were seen as new, daring and subversive. People took for music of the future what, more than almost anything else, was created from the present for the present. As with Picasso, with whom he was often compared, the change of 'manners' diverted attention from the essence of Stravinsky's art.

Even when he wrote such aggressive works as *Le Sacre du printemps* and *L'Histoire du soldat*, Stravinsky was no revolutionary, or at least he didn't want to be one – which makes a little difference, after all. It's more likely that in these works, without wishing to – and here too the parallels with *Salome* and *Elektra* hold true – he gave the cue his contemporaries were waiting for in order to topple the old order. 'I was made a revolutionary in spite of myself,' Stravinsky complains in *The Poetics of Music*.[2] The sounds of *Sacre* may be thrilling, its novel idiom may seem harsh, but that doesn't mean this work was revolutionary in the subversive sense of the word. Revolution denotes a fracturing of equilibrium; revolution is synonymous with chaos. Art, however, is the opposite of chaos; if art surrenders to chaos, it sees its living worth, its very existence threatened. Stravinsky laments that we live at a time when revolution enjoys a certain prestige among yesterday's *avant-garde*. Not music but shock value is what they want, i.e., sensation, by which understanding can only be clouded ...

Stravinsky has ranged himself on the side of order, with the utmost resolution and consistency. But the spirit of order is set against the revolutionary. 'Revolution is one thing, innovation another,' says *The Poetics of Music*. For innovation, the development of new methods (whose justification, even necessity, Stravinsky affirms throughout the book) does not destroy the continuity which guarantees the evolution of culture. These new methods do not exclude 'the use of already employed materials and of established forms' – their absence, rather, would have to lead to the musician's 'speaking an idiom without relation to the world that listens to him'.[3] What the continuity of the creative world is capable of ensuring is: tradition. At present, unfortunately, the word has taken on a somewhat enigmatic and ambiguous meaning for the musician, since it almost automatically calls to mind Mahler's epigram 'Tradition is laziness.' That, of course, is nothing but a demand that we take responsibility for ourselves, a battle cry against the complacent who love to appeal to false traditions, that is, to bad habits ... The question is, what is to be understood by tradition? Stravinsky put it precisely in *The Poetics of Music*: tradition (he says there)[4] is something quite different from a habit (even an excellent habit), for habit is acquired unconsciously and has a tendency to become mechanical, while tradition results from a conscious and well-considered predilection. True tradition attests not to a self-contained past but to a living strength which animates and informs the present. Far from signifying the imitation of the has-been, tradition presupposes the reality of the enduring. It resembles a family estate, an inheritance which one receives on condition that its productivity is maintained before it is bequeathed to one's descendants. And Stravinsky adduces an example: Brahms was born sixty years after Beethoven, and in every respect the distance between them was great; but Brahms followed the tradition of Beethoven without borrowing a single piece of his clothing. For – and this seems to me to be the crux of Stravinsky's concept of tradition – borrowing a method has *nothing to do* with preserving a tradition. One adheres to a tradition in order to make something *new*, and this new thing calls for the use of *new methods* ...

Stravinsky breaks with habits that have become mechanical but not with tradition, which signifies the acknowledgment of a certain spiritual order. Radicalism for its own sake seems senseless to him; he considers it more important to sort out in his own mind the still unexploited possibilities in the application of classical forms and formal resources and from them to glean ideas for his own work. This work doesn't stand under the banner of historicism but rather under the strict banner of order and discipline. The use of sharply dissonant chords which are neither prepared nor resolved in no way contradicts this. Dissonance, which has become an 'entity in itself', should, Stravinsky rightly says, be considered just as unimportant as an agent of disorder as consonance is as a guarantee of security. Order in the harmonic and melodic domain is grounded neither in the 'exigencies of tonality' nor in the absolute value of the major–minor system, but in the polar attraction of sounding tones, to which their tonal function is subordinate⁵ ...

Only a few titles from Stravinsky's *oeuvre* need to be called to mind in order to remember how, through the 'high technique of choice', of elimination and wilful self-limitation, a new classical style was founded: *Oedipus Rex*, *Apollon musagète*, *Perséphone*, *Orpheus*, *The Rake's Progress* ... A new *classical* style – which is something quite different from the neo-classicism of the impotent (which, in any case, is neo-Baroquism more often than not). It cannot be stressed enough that Stravinsky's traditionalism is inseparable from the new methods he has developed, which are the constant element in all transformations. One must also reflect, for example, on the new relation between melody and harmony, between rhythm and counterpoint – on methods whose precision and demarcation from the conventional methods still haven't been sufficiently noted. Their significance lies in the creation of new constructive values which compete with the classical ones. By classical, I don't mean to suggest an imitation of historical models; I mean to indicate an attitude, a way of using a style. But the concept of 'classical' should certainly be linked with that of perfection, of the pure crystallization of certain procedures and of the thoroughgoing rationalization of the musical organism. What Jacob Burckhardt said of Voltaire's rationalism holds true of Stravinsky's: it takes on magical features ...

In an American interview Stravinsky sought to explain the relationship between music and drama, as he sees it, with a term from chemistry: his ideal is that of chemical reaction which produces a new element, a third body from the association of two different but equivalent elements – music and drama. For him it is a question of combining music and drama as two individual entities, whereby both are allowed the possibility of living their own lives so that neither is forced to account for the other or to defend itself against the other's claim. For Stravinsky, drama, like ballet, in the first place means an architectonic-musical assignment. This is also true for *The Rake's Progress*, where profession of belief in the Western classical tradition has found its most immediate artistic expression. In conjunction with the choice of subject matter – a moral fable inspired by Hogarth's famous print series, whose figures are clearly related to those of *Faust, Don Giovanni* and *Peer Gynt*, but also to those of early romanticism and Italian comic opera, while the music just as openly acknowledges its affinity with Bach, Mozart, Rossini, Verdi, Tchaikovsky and others – Stravinsky's traditionalism broadens out into a spiritual universalism. Stravinsky seems to want to demonstrate that freedom is not restricted even by the framework of a 'standard opera' – or at any rate that the music, made with extraordinary sensitivity according to the simplest formulas, sacrifices none of its precise new methods. If at first glance many pieces seem like style-copies – in reality, it is more a question of style-'parodies', taking the word *parody* in the serious sense in which it is applied to the art of the early Netherlandish masters – if models show through, one may recall the words Maurice Ravel once wrote about his *Valses nobles et sentimentales*: 'If you have something to say, this something will never make itself clearer than in the unintentional infidelities toward the model.'

The tender lyricism which pervades *The Rake's Progress* and the no-longer-shunned charm of its strong, periodically articulated melodies, along with the distancing, coolness and intellectual intensity which Stravinsky maintains in this wonderfully transparent score, achieve a connection which marks a new and perhaps the last stage in his work. The music's closer relationship not only to the canonical order of the act composed in thrice three scenes, but also to the world of characters and the spirit of the play, now emerges as clearly as can be. *The Rake's Progress* is an aristocratic work; it invites attentive listening, the experiencing of a 'harmony of diversity', which is displayed in a superior organized unity. This is as far from the 'murky inanities of the Art-Religion',[6] which is odious to the rabidly anti-Wagnerian Stravinsky, as it is from making music in a mechanical fashion. Everything is geared to harmony. Comedy and tragedy are in equilibrium. The spirit of order and proportion now seems to be consciously applied to an opera, which brings traditionalism and universalism to life in a *humanistic* sphere. In it Stravinsky's music acquires – in the words of André Gide – 'cette beauté nécessaire et pure de la résolution d'un problème' (that pure and necessary beauty arising from the perfect solution of a problem).

1 See Barilli's review (no. 69).
2 *The Poetics of Music*, trans. Arthur Knodel and Ingolf Dahl (Cambridge, Mass., 1947), p. 10.
3 Ibid., p. 73.
4 Ibid., pp. 56–7.
5 Ibid., pp. 34–7.
6 Ibid., p. 60.

88

Willem Andriessen, 'Two Kinds of Music of the Future'

(1956), from *100 opstellen over muziek* (Amsterdam, n.d.), trans. Jaap Schröder

Andriessen (1887–1964) belonged to one of Holland's most prominent musical families. A composer, like his brother and two nephews, he was also a gifted pianist and wrote criticism in the 1950s for the *Haarlems Dagblad*. The scepticism about electronic music expressed in this article (compare Stuckenschmidt's bold predictions about the 'mechanization' of music in no. 68) were not shared by his nephew Louis, who has written many works for electronic instruments.

I don't know if the expression 'music of the future' was already in use during the lifetime of the classical masters. It has been suggested that it was coined in the nineteenth century, when Richard Wagner transformed his new ideas about musical drama into sounds that were apparently too violent for the ears of his contemporaries. It was then that Wagner's works started to be called, mockingly, music of the future – a phrase that made fun not so much of

Wagner's idealistic motives as of an operatic music which no longer fitted in the beloved traditions and which proposed values that few people could admire. The majority of the nineteenth-century cartoons representing Wagner and his compositions are, it must be said, fairly gentle persiflages of the dissonances which offended the sensitive ears of our greatgrandparents, and also of the (for those same ears) extravagant use of brass instruments.

In 1861 the composer himself appropriated this mocking expression when he published his essay 'Zukunftsmusik'.[1] In this text he explained how his art, under the prevailing circumstances and given the state of musical drama, which was lagging behind in his country, had developed more and more into what he liked to call the artwork of the future: an ideal fusion of the different arts involved in music drama. Discounting the typical Wagnerian grandiloquence, much can still be found in these views even today that is worth considering. One can agree with them or not, one can see the whole essay as an *oratio pro domo*,[2] but in any case the author was sincerely arguing how a certain artwork could in the future be restructured and raised to a higher level. In other words, this was a purely artistic matter.

An article I found in the September 1955 issue of the *Schweizerische Musikzeitung*, written by Fred. K. Prieberg under the title '"Music of the Future" and Its Essence,' was inspired by thoughts of a more material nature. If this is symptomatic for our age, we cannot claim to have made progress. At the outset the writer states, justifiably, that modern man is obsessed by the machine. He then points to the visual arts, most explicitly to cubism, which revealed the anatomical relationship between man and machine, and which transformed veins, muscles and limbs into tubes, rods and ball-bearings. But the visual arts are not the only ones that have long been influenced by the suggestive power of machinery: perhaps this is even more the case with the immaterial art of music. Many of the symptoms which Prieberg still considers to be harbingers of a new spring in the music of the future have in fact already turned out to be dusty artificial flowers of a bygone era. And the reason is that he considers the Futurists of the recent past as heralds of what, in his view, is coming.

However, these pioneers, with their thundering proclamations, are no longer taken seriously. Does anyone remember Marinetti?

And does anyone still believe in Kurt Schwitters?[3] By the way, what is your reaction to the following sentence, uttered in 1913 by the Italian artist-musician Luigi Russolo: 'We Futurists have deeply admired the music of the great masters. For years Beethoven and Wagner made our hearts beat faster. But now it is enough. We enjoy the perfect sound combination of streetcars, motorcycles, automobiles, and noisy crowds much more than yet another performance of, say, the *Eroica* or the *Pastorale* ... '[4]

In Prieberg's parade of innovators of this kind, we also encounter, among many others, John Cage, the 'flower-pottist', if I may call him so.[5] Prieberg quotes an important saying of this composer. In discussing his own work, Cage remarks: 'If you don't want to call it music, that's fine with me. You don't even have to call it art.' Quite another matter is the use of electrical musical instruments, a sure sign of the coming times. They extend the possibilities of sound production which, linked to a machine, fascinates various composers. Arthur Honegger, in the score of *Jean d'Arc au bûcher*, uses the Ondes Martinot, invented by the Frenchman [Maurice] Martenot. Prieberg also mentions Samuel Barber, who includes an electrical tone-generator in his Second Symphony.

In Holland it is Henk Badings who is deeply interested in the most recent experiments. Not long ago, as you may have read, Badings wrote some 'electronic compositions'. It might be more correct to call them 'compositions for electronic instruments (or devices)'. We must wait and see how all this will develop. Rather than music of the future, I would like to talk about instruments of the future, because I am convinced that, essentially, future music will depend less on technological development than on the human spirit. And for the spirit, beauty presents so many aspects that material means, in whatever form, will always be used only as a tool (and not more) in order to reach the ultimate, unchanging goal.

1 Actually published in 1860.
2 i.e., an apology.
3 The Futurist writer Emilio Marinetti and the Dadaist artist and writer Kurt Schwitters.
4 From Russolo's famous manifesto *The Art of Noises*.
5 Apparently an allusion to the found objects that Cage used as percussion instruments.

89

Neville Cardus, 'The Pioneer's Dusty Path'

From *Talking of Music* (London, 1957)

Cardus (1888–1975), long-time critic of the *Manchester Guardian*, has a double claim to fame as a writer on music and on cricket. His style has been likened to Shaw's (see no. 50), though his polemics seldom scaled Shavian heights. As this essay – written at the peak of the postwar infatuation with serially organized music – shows, Cardus was never reluctant to call a spade a spade. For a different opinion of Schönberg, see Strobel's tribute (no. 86).

At an annual conference of the Incorporated Society of Musicians, Mr. Ernest Bradbury, music critic of the *Yorkshire Post*, undertook or threatened to sing quotations from Schönberg throughout the lunch interval, to demonstrate that atonal music can achieve melody. The idea of a vocal music critic is unusual. I have heard all sorts of vocal curiosities – a singing policeman, a singing Irish terrier, a singing barber, a singing tenor; but I have not as a rule expected any burst of song from a music critic except from the bathroom and as a matter of quite unpremeditated art. In passing, assuming that amongst my colleagues there are really a few natural-born singers, how would we suit each of them to parts in opera; which, say, would be the unmistakable Hans Sachs, which the Papageno, which the Loge, which the Klingsor?

Authentic Schönberg, which means music by him coming after *Verklärte Nacht* and *Erwartung* – authentic atonalism, and the tone-row technique derived from it, have not yet produced music appealing to average intelligent and educated listeners who have passed beyond the years of aesthetic adolescence. This kind of composition has been, in different phases of development or arrangement, before the public some thirty years. There is no mystery about it; at any rate deductions from the basic formula do not go beyond the comprehension of an ordinarily perceptive mathematical understanding. But so far, though the system has attracted an increasing number of contemporary professional and amateur

346

musicians, it remains esoteric and apart from the main stream of general musical appreciation. It is still a close corporation, almost a conspiracy. Would sometimes it were a conspiracy of silence. As Mr. Frank Howes[1] pointed out the other day, atonalism or the serial technique which satisfies 'the impulse of construction,' very much and naturally becomes the fashion in a disintegrating period socially, spiritually, and aesthetically. It is easier to construct, to build or add together with factors which can be grasped intellectually and ordered in their sequence by logic, than it is to create, or cause to grow in a traditional soil from seeds of imagination. In other and simpler words, it is easier to be a logician or a mechanic than a poet. The notion of a composer as poet is nowadays old-fashioned. Music criticism seldom nowadays tries – even tries, for the effort is hard and most times doomed to vain failure – to find out if a new composition is 'saying' anything of importance to us as thinking and experiencing beings. Contemporary music criticism ends mainly in technical description and analysis. The sterility of it, taking it by and large, is perhaps excusable. For who can tell whether composers using atonalism and the tone-row technique are indeed saying anything at all? The 'language' of atonalism and the serial method is not yet formulated into symbolical significance; it has not yet acquired 'meanings' or 'associations.' Nobody is in a position to claim of a work composed to this formula or system that it is great, good, indifferent, or bad, as a work of art or as a well-composed work of music. It is almost an impertinence for anybody not a specialist student to discuss experiments in atonalism, to discuss them strictly as laboratory investigators. And to judge or estimate atonal and tone-row compositions as music, with aesthetic verdicts merely implied, is effrontery. By what standard is a critic able to decide that a new work in this latest school is well and truly put together, considered strictly as atonalism or tone-row technique? And by what standard does he rank it in relation to music as we have known music in our different lifetimes? It is perhaps as well that Mr. Bradbury undertook to sing atonally; for if a music critic must on occasion, and under severe provocation, burst into song the composer had better be Schönberg than, say, Mozart. We won't be aware overmuch if he should sing out of pitch or 'off key.'

I am all in favour of the tonal and atonal pioneers; good luck to them. We are not living through the first upheaval of the elements from which so mysteriously emerges the singing sphere of music. Some day a genius will relate the 'new' language to the 'old'; he will find a bridge-passage. The dry or dusty road of the pioneer is for the young and the ingenious, or for those mortals who have been born without the need to mature imaginatively or philosophically. My own personal reluctance to spend much more time with atonalism and the rest than already I have spent is that I have not unlimited years before me now and, more important, experiments of any kind bore me; they do not put into vibration the sense of life that I have developed in a pretty long and arduous experience, human and aesthetic. It is not possible even for a Schönberg to compose a work that means anything to a grown mind while he is working in a musical formula or language not yet spoken by anybody instinctively and not yet known in its parts of speech well enough to be grasped immediately. Technique, said Wagner, is a matter for the composer's private study and discussion; the public should never hear of it. The musical public at the present time hears of little that is not techincal from the multitudinous verbal exponents of the art. It is of course much less difficult to describe and analyse a composition than it is to give an account of it as it has passed through your mind as human being and musician. In the first instance little is needed except some knowledge of the technical set-up. But to try to understand the composition as the composer conceived it calls for the insight which comes, alas, only to few of us, after an accumulation of years and work which in retrospect cause the spirit to quail and the flesh to falter.

There is a danger, much in evidence at the moment, that contemporary critics are inclined to dismiss a new composition as of small account if it does not, directly or indirectly, admit a debt to the 'latest' influences. William Walton's *Troilus and Cressida* has come under the suspicion of the most gifted of our younger critics on the grounds that it reveals a 'reactionary' technical tendency. To call a work 'reactionary' or 'romantic' is, in 1957, apparently a death sentence. We are here face to face with judgments which are really political. The Victorians, we are told, were incapable of looking at any work of art, books, music, or pictures, except as moralists. Today we are, as a people, scarcely more capable than our fathers and grandfathers were to respond to a work of art aesthetically; we have replaced moral with social, psychological, or quasi-political judgments. 'The modern dread of beauty,' wrote Ivor Brown a few months ago, 'is a queer form of cowardice.' The best moments in *Troilus and Cressida* are proof that Walton is able to compose, in a style recognisably traditional, and as recognisably his own, passages as memorable as any in any opera written since [Puccini's] *Turandot*. And that, my young friends, is high praise, praise likely soon to be confirmed by opinion in countries not less musical and not less operatically sophisticated than England, whether the critics there can sing Schönberg or not, before, during, or after lunch.

1 Chief music critic of *The Times*, 1943–60.

90

Guido Pannain, 'To Know Music'

From *L'Opera e le opere* (Milan, 1958)

Musicologist and composer, Pannain (1891–1977) was also one of Italy's liveliest and most opinionated critics. His contributions to the *Rassegna musicale* and other journals range from a review of Menotti's early operas (which he dismissed as 'a catalogue of bad taste') to an erudite discussion of 'criticism and pseudocriticism'. This diatribe against superficial musical 'knowledge' echoes an age-old preoccupation with the dichotomy between emotion and intellect.

A figure of speech on the tongues of musicians nowadays has to do with knowing or not knowing music. When a musician acknowledges that one of those dubbed masters 'knows music', he thinks he's said all there is to say. Likewise, if he says of a contemporary, especially an adversary or rival, 'That man doesn't know music', he is sure of having finished him off for good. And we can even hear it calmly acknowledged that this or that opera is worth little or nothing, but that the author 'knows music'.

'To know music', for the expert steeped in its fetishism, is a profession of absolute wisdom. Someone who listens, then, and who doesn't really know anything about music, gets upset and doesn't know what to think and will continue to repeat 'to know music ... '

to himself, as if in a trance. But who will tell him what that knowing consists of? ...

Now, according to usage and custom, to know music means to know the tricks of the trade – period. First of all, to know the grammar of music and to manipulate the golden formulas with one's eyes shut. Not the knowledge that creates but the knowledge that acts on hard facts, a knowledge squeezed to a pulp and broken into bite-sized pieces, made of expert assurance and trained ability. Schematic knowledge that must exclude many things in order to encompass everything within concise limits: knowledge of classifications, of paradigms, of tailor-made imitations and polished reproductions.

To know music means the wisdom of behaving cleverly, of laying sonorous images out like precision instruments, of moving the chess pieces of counterpoint with shrewd strategy, of arranging harmonic structures with the punctuality of calculus. It means to make a ledger book out of music paper and a calculating machine out of the sonorous apparatus.

Like knowing how to speak, how to write, and how to live, knowing music is a circumscribed wisdom. It is the wisdom of the rhetorician, of the calligrapher, of the puzzle-solver. It means to possess the handbook to all the principles of good workmanship. To know is a fine thing in any case, and always preferable to not knowing: the knowledge which distinguishes the clergyman from the layman and the capable from the inept, as well as the citified man from the peasant and the man who can write his first and last names from the one who marks his name with a cross instead of a signature. And it is a stage of elementary consciousness, a condition of development and growth. But it is not art, and this is where misunderstanding arises. Because it is precisely those who know music in the sense we have been discussing who believe that they are working inside the sphere of art, when in fact they are standing outside it. This knowledge of theirs is a font of illusions, because at bottom they are only postulants; they knock at the door of art and it shall not been opened unto them ...

Dilettantism, in the pejorative sense, is proteiform. There is technical dilettantism, which is content with superficial pleasures; dilettantism which, in the guise of intellectual refinements, imagines that which does not exist; scientific dilettantism, which waters down the formula of knowledge into abstractions. To this last belongs the knowledge of music. A knowledge which is calculated, measured, weighed, acquired and flaunted, but which ignores one's inner feeling along with the means of revealing it.

Music at first appeared to man as a Pythagorean mystery. It had the power of the number, but it was also a magic art because it tended to take possession of sound in place of nature. It went beyond feeling and dreamed of a mystical silence resulting from an immense numerical relationship which symbolized the constitution of the universe. The latest experiments of Schönberg, and of some of his demented exegetes, are connected to these extremely negative aesthetic consequences. The musical interval was an ideal unit of measure. At that time music had a solemn seat in the quadrivium. Its conceptions had a theological and metaphysical character. The horizon of allegory, of an arithmetical symbolism leading to occultism, opened up to them. Musical organization becomes a schematic supermodel of universal harmony. There became ingrained a way of thinking about music which would later be restricted to a trade knowledge. The great theorists of the Quattrocento, such as Tinctoris, were masters of a contrapuntal geometry from which the modern master of music would derive his technicism. But he would stop, lost, before the concept of art ...

Music is a moment of the spirit which is explained in the reality of creating, which the flow of the living being, by day and by night, assembles in audible forms and fixes in the instant which is not fleeting. It is not a murky reflection, a sophism of illusory wisdom which freezes the imagination in numerical symbols or crosses the line into mathematical madness. For music, there are no mysteries to reveal because it is a mystery itself, a mystery revealed in the works where it appeared and was called music. The spirit acquires self-certainty in liberty and overcomes the pain of shapeless existence.

To know music, as the pedants currently define the term, is an artistic pretence, a passive approach to musical experience, emptied and reduced to a simulacrum. It is an ideology of quantity. It is reflection, pondering, calculating which revolves around itself, constructs for the sake of constructing, and poses itself problems that demand a solution merely because they are problems. But they are problems without applications, and solving them is reduced to the simple pleasure of hitting upon a solution. It is a game wrapped in doctrine. Sterile knowledge which signifies nothing beyond the craftsman's expertise, the limitations of pseudo-scientific knowledge, or the artifice of logic without concept. A formula of knowledge which is reduced to the tiniest formula of manoeuvring the sonorous syllable fluently and which is, at heart, a job for grammarians.

91

Virgil Thomson, 'Music's Tradition of Constant Change'

Atlantic Monthly (February 1959)

Thomson (1896–1989) was by common consent the most distinguished musical journalist America has produced. A student of Nadia Boulanger and a life-long francophile, he was a composer better known in Europe than in his homeland when the *New York Herald Tribune* hired him as its chief critic in 1940. The jabs at the Germanic tradition in this article are vintage Thomson; so is the combination of literary flair and an insider's knowledge of music. For contrasting views of musical evolution, see the essays by Fétis, Huneker and Schuh (nos. 24, 62 and 87).

'Tradition' and 'change', as words, are so heavily weighted with hopes and fears that it is impossible to describe with them convincingly any moment of time in music's history. Nevertheless, there have been periods so tranquil that one is tempted to believe no major change was taking place, while during others the evolutionary process was so rapid that, to the casual-minded, change rather than tradition might well seem to have been in the saddle.

Take the European nineteenth century, for instance, after the death of Beethoven. The transformation of musical techniques and expression through Weber, Mendelssohn, Chopin, Schumann, Berlioz, Wagner, Verdi, Moussorgsky, Franck, and Debussy was constant and continuous. At the same time, tradition – the Beethoven tradition – was the basis of musical pedagogy. And none of these composers, not even Debussy, though he complained a little about Beethoven, dreamed of dethroning him as the sun king.

On the contrary, they all aspired to contribute to the tradition that had arrived through Beethoven at so splendid a maturity.

Naturally there were both radical and conservative temperaments around; there always are. Wagner publicized his own music as 'the music of the future', implying by this slogan that everybody else's was of the past. And Brahms, with his own consent, was announced by [Eduard] Hanslick[1] as the defender of the classical tradition against Wagner's irresponsible practices. But both Wagner and Brahms were clearly out for inheriting Beethoven's prestige.

A century later, it looks as if both were wrong about themselves too. Wagner's music had its biggest 'future' between 1890 and 1910. Since the latter date his popularity has declined steadily and by 75 per cent.[2] His orchestration procedures, however, his chromatic harmony, his Germanic declamation, and his symphonico-dramatic textures are still studied in conservatories. Brahms, on the other hand, has enjoyed ever since his death in 1897 a rising incidence of performance, so that today he ranks at the box office second only to Beethoven himself.

There is really no equating the radical with the progressive and the conservative with the reactionary. Saint-Saëns, a conservative type himself, strengthened French music by introducing from Germany the use of sonata form, whereas Richard Strauss, for all his apparent radicalism of style and subject, added very little that is usable today either to the German tradition or to modernism in general.[3] All that one can be sure of, between 1827 and 1914, is that change was rapid and that tradition – the classical tradition of Haydn and Mozart and Beethoven – was firmly respected everywhere. Both tradition and change, indeed, were so strongly entrenched that their representatives could not afford *not* to cooperate. And this is how our century came to assume that the musical tradition creates by its own nature a climate of constant variation in no way destructive to the noble mountains of the past or erosive to the fertile valleys of the present. The truth of this belief is not demonstrable. But its widespread acceptance in our time has assured modern music a hearing and has tended, moreover, to associate the sacred concept 'progressive' with any music that bears any aspect of technical novelty ...

Nevertheless, music's rate of evolution has slowed down noticeably since World War I. Of really powerful works produced in the last forty years I can name you only five: Igor Stravinsky's *L'Histoire du soldat*, Erik Satie's *Socrate*, Honegger's *Pacific 231*, Darius Milhaud's *La Création du monde*, and Alban Berg's *Wozzeck*; and these were all written before 1926. I know nothing of comparable originality composed since then, except possibly some very short pieces by Anton Webern. The music of Sibelius and Bartók, though powerful on the expressive plane, does not seem, technically speaking, to have changed anything.

Today there is little active change going on. There is only tradition, and that tradition includes all the modernisms of yesteryear. The modernist branch of our tradition, now wholly official and more than a little pompous, possesses, as our tradition has always done, a diatonic and a chromatic style. Our century's diatonic style, commonly referred to as neoclassicism, is an eclectic mixture of pre-World-War-I liberties with earlier, tighter syntaxes. Its practitioners dominate pedagogy, publishing, and performance. Twentieth-century chromaticism, as simplified about 1926 by Schönberg into a rule of thumb known as serial dodecaphony (or the twelve-tone row technique), marks the music of a smaller group that essays through a publicity at once pious and pugnacious to seize the positions of power now held by the neoclassic representatives. In neither camp is there much novelty of either expression or method; in both, rather, there is a sectarian adherence to certain parts of the Great Tradition, as if all of it were too much for anybody to live with ...

Now, modernism in music, to begin retracing my argument, is a concept from the late nineteenth century that urges an attitude of receptivity toward anything that may seem progressive either in syntax or in subject matter. It is an open-door policy regarding change, and the official representatives of tradition itself have not always been unfriendly toward it. In any case, modernism long ago won so many of its battles with reaction and won them so decisively that by the end of World War I they were sharing condominium in the conservatories.

Little by little, however, as the supply of musical novelty diminished, the encouragement of novelty was transformed from an open-door policy into a doctrinaire position. This position, as upheld in the magazines of musical modernism and in the programs of the contemporary music concerts, maintained that there could be no authentic or valuable composition that did not embody some technical novelty, the corollary being, of course, that any work which did embody a technical novelty was more valuable than one which did not ...

I do not wish to imply that no musical research today is valid and no expression authentic. But I do consider that both technical advance and expressivity have shown, since World War I, or at least since 1925, a decline in vigor. A parallel situation exists in both painting and poetry. We are living in a time of cultural recession. Politics, economic organization, and the arts of war appear to be on the move. The fine and applied arts, in this epoch of wide cultural distribution, are definitely conservative. This conservatism, at least in music and in painting, is based on a tradition of modernism once radical, now completely academic and official ...

So what do we composers do now? There is only one thing possible: change the assumptions on which we operate. We shall have to forget for a time about novelty and change and tradition and all such great big wordy ideas. I propose to you that every composer has plenty of small ideas, technical and expressive ones, and that these ideas are all valid if sincerely and competently acted upon. It is better to work with the ideas one really has, however minor they may seem, than to try to follow an outworn line like modernism-at-any-price. Especially in a time when there are so few 'modernistic' ideas available at any price. In other words, the tradition of constant change must be thrown overboard and freshness found through other preoccupations.

The standardization of compositional procedures is a fact; we cannot fight that. Anyway, we have produced it ourselves both knowingly and inevitably, through the intense and highly intellectual organization, over centuries, of our whole musical tradition, creative and executional. The standardization of audiences is also a fact; and though composers have contributed toward bringing it about, we are not wholly happy with the result. It is better for business than for creative advance. Our dilemma is that we believe in creative advance but are unable to make very much of it right now through technical innovation. Moreover, we are suspicious, as a source of inspiration, of mere expressivity; in our unconscious it lies uncomfortably close to commercial motivations and the relaxing of standards. So also for the tricky concept of sincerity.

We may well be reduced, all the same, to seeking innovation through expressivity, instead of expressivity through innovation, and to finding expressivity through sincerity, though sincerity at its purest leads straight to anarchy and through anarchy to the destruction of both tradition and progress. It is my belief, regarding musical composition, that today only sincerity and anarchy are valid. There is no good line or bad line, no clearly progressive and no reactionary. We are not fighting from positions any longer, or among ourselves. We are fighting individually against the distributors and the standardizers. We are fighting for our lives and for music's life, because all this vast distribution by phonograph and radio, this amplified inundation of the world with sure-fire classics and banal modernities, can kill the art of music. But till the sad day comes when nobody educated would be caught dead listening to music, it may just be possible to follow for a while the best lesson in the whole classical tradition, which is that individual freedom is honorable, and to succeed by private pushes and private tinkerings in keeping the giant musical machine in some kind of motion. It will require the efforts of many people all over the world to counteract music's present incipient sclerosis. And the time may be short. But I for one should hate to see the day when there will be music, music everywhere – and no surprise or spontaneity in any of it.[4]

1 See no. 43.
2 Typical Virgilian hyperbole, with more than a grain of truth. Cf. Benco's assessment of the 'post-Wagnerians' (no. 54).
3 cf. Krehbiel and Boschot on Strauss (nos. 56 and 71).
4 Thomson is echoing themes sounded by, among others, his musical and literary forebears Berlioz and Debussy (see nos. 33 and 53).

92

Stefan Kisielewski, 'The Seventh Autumn'

(1963), from *Z muzycznej międzyepoki* (From the Middle Epoch of Music) (Cracow, 1966), trans. Mirka Zemanová

Composer and journalist, Kisielewski (1911–91) was well known in Poland and abroad as a writer on music, politics and other subjects. Editor of the musical weekly *Ruch muzyczny*, he was also a columnist for the popular

Polish newspaper *Wprost* and for the Catholic opposition daily *Tygodnik powszechny*. The view of universalism and tradition that he expresses here makes an interesting comparison with those of Einstein, Schuh and Thomson (nos. 83, 87 and 91).

The Seventh Autumn is not only the title of the volume of poetry by Tuwim,[1] it is also the Seventh International Music Festival, the Warsaw Autumn, which recently took place, in Warsaw of course. I have long written extensively about these festivals. This year, for a change, I shall write briefly, in the manner of a *feuilleton* sketch, but at the same time taking a somewhat objective or ideological approach; for here in Warsaw of all places the significance of this festival goes far beyond the problems of pure sound and takes on a universal character to a certain extent. (I use the word *ideological* in a rather specialized sense, and very reluctantly.)

The ideological – that is, extra-musical – significance of the festival therefore lies first of all in the fact, which I have emphasized (a hundred times!) before, that this event brings about a range of meetings and confrontations: between East and West (Communism and capitalism); between traditionalism and *avant-gardism*; between representatives of different psychologies, different aesthetic views, different philosophical systems; and ultimately, quite simply, between different countries and continents. The festival shows that art does not divide but rather unites us, for in the end we have understood each other quite well, despite our many differences. Naturally there have been quarrels, sneers, jealousies, scandalized turning of eyes to heaven (hell?!), and indignant insults. Yet finally we agreed on certain propositions, or better still, self-evident truths – for instance, that Bartók, Stravinsky, Hindemith and Prokofiev already belong to a valid tradition, that dodecaphony and punctualism[2] are history, and that young composers must and do in fact aim at new, mysterious shores, where (as optimists believe) new tonal emotions, new acoustic phenomena, and new principles of organization or disorganization (liberation) of sound surely await us. That's how it is and how it has to be – at least, that was the opinion of the distinguished audience which filled the concert halls twice a day to 120 per cent of capacity, diligently lying in wait for the most extreme and iconoclastic novelties. A nonconformist audience: more than one capital city could envy Poland that! The director of our National Philharmonic would do well to take note, since during the season the hall is so frequently empty and the atmosphere glaringly dull.

Of course, one did boo a little for decency's sake – for instance, during [Franco] Donatoni's *Per Orchestra*. But the boos were merry, not venomous, for the piece itself isn't sad. The composer, if I understood him right, had decided to protest both the excessively inflated dignity of art and its ossification in rounded forms of craftsman-like correctness. Thus he appeared on the platform wearing a casual and rather ill-fitting jacket and conducted in a peculiarly comical manner, while the orchestra played in this way and that, a little from the music, a little by heart. The conductor left the stage and the musicians gradually followed; then they returned, each playing for himself. Then the conductor came back, only to depart again a moment later, his little hand in his pocket, leaving the orchestra to continue playing for itself – even for a day or two. A demonstration of the greatest significance in this era of the *avant-garde*, where extreme organization (punctualism) and extreme freedom and exploitation of chance are neighbours ...

In genuine artistic life, both conservative traditionalism and iconoclastic *avant-gardism* are necessary. My own view of the matter is fairly contradictory, dialectically speaking, and complex; one day perhaps I shall try to give readers an exhaustive (and no doubt exhausting) explanation. True, complex or knotty judgments are not in fashion today; poster-style compendia are more sought after. But never mind – I can wait! ...

Besides, this festival rather predisposed me against tradition. In my opinion, when it comes to writing music that is 'serious' and truly new, the jocular, persiflage-like summing up of the past, such as Stravinsky has achieved, was the last chance of traditionalism. Nothing more is to be found on that path. On the other hand, conventional and universally accessible tonal resources continue to stock the arsenal of light, dance or entertainment music, which is booming today as never before. Personally, I adore this genre. I think it has a real future in our mass-culture age, as well as being a popular recapitulation of the musical achievements of the past. It may be heretical to say so, but in my opinion light music will become the last repository of the great tradition of tonal music and its European evolution. *Signum temporis* – I don't know about you, but I am satisfied with it.[3]

And creative *avant-gardism*? It must go its own way, shedding both the skilful, amusingly intentional traditionalism of Stravinsky and the neo-romanticism and neo-expressionism of all sorts of sanctified serialists, from Schönberg to the punctualists, which are taken so seriously. I discovered, or suspected, the germ of an entirely new kind of sensibility and tonality at this festival, in chamber works by [Francis] Miroglio, [André] Boucourechliew, and the Japanese [Kazuo] Fukushima. It's curious how attentively the audience received some works (each of the ones I've just mentioned was encored) and how bored they were by the counterfeit traditional emotion of [Luigi] Nono's *Sul Ponte di Hiroshima* or by the genuine conventionalism of Bartók's *Cantata profana*, which until recently was generally applauded.

There is no going back from *avant-gardism*, even if the work of individual *avant-garde* composers proves to be an ephemeral phenomenon. 'Our days are like those of the butterfly, the sunrise is our life, noontide our death: better a moment in April than whole Decembers in the autumn of life.'[4]

1 Julian Tuwim's *Seventh Autumn* was published in 1922.
2 i.e., a musical technique akin to pointillism in painting.
3 See Adorno (no. 76) for a different view of light music.
4 From Tuwim, *Seventh Autumn*.

93

Ivan Vojtěch, 'To Change Only Opinions?'

(1963), from *Kommentáře* (Prague, 1988), trans. Mirka Zemanová

Vojtěch (b. 1928), one of Czechoslovakia's leading postwar musicologists and critics, was strongly influenced by Adorno (see no. 76), especially concerning the relationship between music and society. He has translated several of Adorno's works into Czech, along with those of Soviet musicologists. This essay, originally delivered as a lecture at a congress of the Union of Czechoslovak Composers, boldly questions the Marxist orthodoxy represented by Asafyev and Lissa (nos. 67 and 80).

We have been discussing and criticizing things for far too long, and we have a feeling that in practice nothing has changed ... We are still in the situation which has prevailed since the time of the Zhdanov discussions,[1] when we heard and approved criticism of works which most of us had not heard ... But we are also in the same situation as far as the Union of Czechoslovak Composers is concerned. The report,[2] I think, merely skims the surface and does not present a comprehensive picture of the crises which we all feel and which, naturally, have many causes. Some of the causes are of an objective character, in that the Composers' Union has become the focus of more and more responsibility in deciding and influencing the complex problems of our musical culture. As a result, the creative issues which ought to be the alpha and omega of the union have been increasingly marginalized. Moreover, when it comes to expressing opinions about these creative issues, administrative views are taking precedence, proclamations to the contrary notwithstanding – views which are peculiar to the solutions of commercial, management and industrial problems.

These objective problems also have their subjective side ... For, unlike Professor Sychra,[3] who has declared that our congress offers *a unique opportunity to change opinions*, I think it offers a unique opportunity to *change practice* – a change which will naturally be reflected in the management and personnel of the union ...

The Composers' Union originated in the era of revolutionary changes and predicated its work on the following thesis: a revolutionary or a person in a revolutionary situation can do anything, and therefore any means of reaching the goal is justified. This is a false thesis. If at a certain time it can perhaps render valuable services in one sphere of human activity, in other spheres it can be fatal. And we have borne the brunt of this thesis on our own backs for years.

Not every means is justified. In our community of composers it has become apparent that the more a complex, refined sphere of social activity is subjected to management activity, the more important it is to respect the individual's space and right to creative thought, as well as certain rules of democratic relations between people ... In the practice of the union, the problems of ideas and thought naturally are closely linked to the problems of the personal interests of those in positions of responsibility. The latter may conflict with the interests of the musical culture as a whole, to the point where a certain group of people ... performs its duties in such a way as wittingly or unwittingly to suppress the democratic rights of other members in its own favour ...

I would like to draw attention to one of the key issues which comes up continually: the relationship of music and society. If this relationship is to be elucidated in theory and solved in the present situation, it must be done on the basis of concrete sociological research ... At every step we encounter conflicts separating the mass of our listeners from new music. But as far as I know, no one in our country has given deep consideration to the basis of these conflicts. They are not of an artistic nature; *they are social conflicts, created by a certain stage in the development of social order.* Jan Kapr[4] has touched on the problem of alienation. It must be said that the term *alienation*, which Adorno uses, was invented by Hegel and further elaborated by Marx.[5] It describes the situation of man undergoing a certain kind of distribution of labour which exhausts him, alienating him from the products of his work and vice versa, and thus alienates man from himself.

Of course, the problem of alienation is more complicated than this, but the process is reflected, on the social plane, in a diminishing of the listener's activity, preventing him from fully reacting to the work at hand. That is, even today most listeners turn to art primarily for relaxation, recreation, entertainment and repose, and are much less willing to consider works whose perception demands intellectual effort.

This fact which confronts us, and which still exists even in our society, must be taken into consideration. Otherwise it makes no sense to talk about the problems of audiences or of the so-called little genres, about the contacts between the composer and the people, and so on ...

It is also a matter of elucidating for ourselves the issues of deepening and realizing the necessary *democratic* relations between the union's members and its elected officials, in order to forestall the situation to which Jan Kapr has drawn attention, in which the officials are often under the impression that the members are here for them and not they for the members, so as to make them realize that we vote for them and that they are obliged to work for the good of all of us.

On the other hand, it is also a matter of us, as members, having at all times a guaranteed right not only to express ourselves at any gathering but also to demand that the conclusions discussed and accepted there be put into practice – having *the right to control* how the resolutions and conclusions which we have reached are reflected in practice. This, to my mind, is the greatest weakness [of the present system] ... and one of the least pleasant consequences of the era in which false theory distorted the practice of the Union of Czechoslovak Composers.

1 The campaign of vilification of artists and intellectuals launched after the Second World War by Andrei Zhdanov, the Communist Party boss in Leningrad.
2 The union's annual report.
3 Antonín Sychra, the Czech Marxist musicologist.
4 The Czech composer.
5 Adorno uses both *Entfremdung*, in the Marxist sense of alienation from the means of production, and *Verfremdung*, signifying spiritual alienation.

94

Martin Cooper, 'Composers and the Influence of Politics'

Daily Telegraph (10 May 1969)

Among Britain's postwar critics, few wrote better or had more to say than Cooper (1910–86). As critic for the *Daily Telegraph* and editor of the *Musical Times*, he addressed a wide range of issues with grace and integrity. In this article he takes a characteristically wide-angled view of the composer's position *vis-à-vis* politics and society at large. For the rather different view from the Communist world, see the comments of Schloezer and Vojtěch (nos. 66 and 93).

The meeting of extremes, which is a marked feature of art as well as society today, has puzzled to distraction the ordinary music-lover who hankers for the lost 'middle of the road' which he associates (not always quite rightly) with the great art of the past. Was it not Schoenberg who said that all roads lead to Rome except the *via media*? And that has been the principle of his disciples, though they now find themselves rudely jostled by newcomers on the Left into just that middle way their master declared to be a blind alley. Certainly to an outsider it was an amusing, if puzzling spectacle to see, for example, René Leibowitz, Schoenberg's strongest propagandist in France, concerning himself enthusiastically with the performance of Offenbach's operettas, when these returned to favour in the 1950s; and to witness the gradual building up of Kurt Weill and Charles Ives, two of the avant-garde OK composers, into 'major' figures of music between the two wars.

It is very difficult to distinguish, in what seems to be developments of taste of this kind, aesthetic from political elements. These have often been quite as strong among avant-garde musicians as among Russian party-liners, though similar social and political sympathies have led to diametrically opposed aesthetic conclusions. Anti-serialism, for instance, which counted as a Nazi hallmark in Germany after the war, has until recently been the keystone of Soviet, anti-Western aestheticians. Recent controversy over Pfitzner[1] suggests that his right-wing political philosophy still looms so large that it effectively obscures any final, objective rating of his music; and on the other hand, the social-political attitudes expressed in the works of Offenbach, Weill, or Ives – anti-establishment, anti-war, anti-capitalism, anti-religion, anti-bourgeois, or whatever it may be – certainly account for the atmosphere of benevolence in which their music is judged today.

If Offenbach remains as much performed in Russia as he was until very recently, it is an anomaly which must become increasingly obvious as the Soviet regime grows visibly more like the French Second Empire, Offenbach's original target, and the Second Reich, the achievement of Offenbach's great admirer, Bismarck. It is perhaps worth remembering that in the late eighteenth century Catherine the Great showed her strong, if very partial, sympathy with the French *encyclopédistes* (the European 'progressives' of the day) by introducing into Russia the French *opéra comique*, the musical form most closely associated with social criticism. It has always been 'little' music – parody, *opéra comique*, cabaret song, operetta, revue – that has lent itself to the expression of party political sentiment and social rancour. When political motives have consciously inspired a composer in the big forms – symphony, opera, cantata – the result has always been to diminish or trivialize the music.

How many of the 'revolutionary' works of the 1790s in France have survived? Or the Komsomol symphonies, Five-Year-Plan opera, and odes to Stalin from the Russian 1930s? Even a composer of Shostakovich's stature slackens the rein, lowers the tone, coarsens the thought-texture in his politically based symphonies; and it is hardly possible to believe that Prokofiev's opera *The Story of a Real Man*[2] – where the glorification of war and the patriotic sentiment would today count as out-and-out 'fascist' – is by the same composer who wrote *Romeo and Juliet* or *The Love for Three Oranges*.

Is Beethoven an exception to this rule? I believe not. Neither the planned dedication of the Third Symphony to Napoleon, nor the finale of the Ninth Symphony committed Beethoven to any closer political or social programmes than the idea of 'liberty,' which meant for him the destruction of feudalism rather than the establishment of an egalitarian democracy. Neither of these works argues, or even implies, his approval of Napoleonic policies in Central Europe or a sympathy with early Socialism, any more than we can argue from Palestrina's Masses a sympathy with the aims and methods of the Counter-Reformation; or from Bach's Passions an approval of Lutheran church policy in Saxony. *Fidelio*, with its French libretto, French *opéra comique* first act, and naive oratorio finale, is the closest that Beethoven ever came to subordinating his 'big' music to social or political preaching (*The Battle of Vittoria* and *Der glorreiche Augenblick* were frankly occasional, frankly pot-boilers); and is it not just the disparity of these features that prevents *Fidelio* from ranking among Beethoven's very greatest works?

The sign that this is so is that we find ourselves making allowances and adjusting our sights historically with *Fidelio* in a way that never occurs to us during the *Missa Solemnis* or the greatest piano sonatas and string quartets. Beethoven's fundamentally unpolitical attitude can be seen from his accepting a commission to write *Der glorreiche Augenblick* to celebrate the gathering of the Congress of Vienna, the greatest triumph of legitimist reaction, which imposed on Europe for another half century exactly those regimes against which *Fidelio* had been a protest. Beethoven did not foresee this; he was an idealist, not a politically minded man, and he needed the money.

To look for such hard distinctions today, when the transvaluation of values and the confusion of genres prophesied by Nietzsche have become actualities, is unrealistic. That Nietzsche himself considered both as indubitable marks of decadence is beside the point. What we still need is a 'big' music that is unequivocally human and a 'little' music in which wit and style are not sacrificed to easy popularity.

1 The centenary of Hans Pfitzner's birth in 1969 occasioned a reassessment of his career. Once regarded as Strauss's peer, Pfitzner saw his reputation decline and, having supported the Nazis during the war, died in disgrace in 1949.
2 Composed in 1947–8, around the time of Prokofiev's denunciation by Andrei Zhdanov (see no. 93) as a 'formalist' in February 1948. *The Story of a Real Man* succeeded in restoring Prokofiev to official grace, although it was not performed publicly until 1960. For the views of two major Soviet critics on Prokofiev and Shostakovich, see nos. 67 and 77.

95

Joachim Kaiser, 'Music and Recordings'

Suddeutsche Zeitung (1 June 1973), from *Erlebte Musik* (Hamburg, 1977)

Kaiser (b. 1928) has been one of Germany's most prominent critics in recent years. Writing for the *Suddeutsche Zeitung* in Munich, he first attracted attention with his outspoken reviews of Wieland Wagner's radical opera productions at Bayreuth. A radio and television personality as well, Kaiser here views records as forging an important bond between performers, listeners and scholars – unlike Stuckenschmidt (no. 68), who predicted that recording technology would put an end to live performance.

Have we really stopped to evaluate, quite consciously, how tremendously our whole relationship to music, to the interpretation of music, has changed since the institution of the record came to be taken for granted? ...
We live with records. There are specialists whose only contact with music has been made via records. The record enshrines the one-time performance; it also enshrines a specific mood and interpretation. It has emerged as a call to standards – a threat to standards even – in the most remote village, the most private dwelling.

There it is. Anyone concerned with music today must give records a large share of his attention, his interpretive commitment, his capacity for work, and his willingness to record (in both senses of the word) his impressions. Anyone who doesn't do this is letting the reality of our musical life pass him by. But anyone who does must ask himself some questions. Otherwise he turns into the plaything of the record business, the slave of the Bielefelder catalogue. Otherwise he confuses Frau Musica with an industry which is, all in all, honourable. And he doesn't even notice it ...

Even a Karajan, a Friedrich Gulda or an Elisabeth Schwarzkopf can't make a new recording of the masterpieces of the literature whenever he or she wants. When Karajan records Beethoven's symphonies, Gulda Beethoven's piano sonatas, Schwarzkopf her Marschallin, even these world-renowned artists know that they may perhaps have another crack at Beethoven's symphonies and sonatas, or even at *Der Rosenkavalier*, in five or ten years. But they also know that, all in all, the chances are slim. In the meantime – and this is still truer of the interpretations of less renowned artists – the record holds the essence of an artistic existence: this is how fast Gulda plays the *Waldstein* Sonata, this is how slowly Schwarzkopf sings the Marschallin's monologue, this is how lucidly Karjan interprets the Maestoso of the Ninth.

What consequences does this have? Well, the fact that records can't be remade every two years (as, for instance, Horowitz recorded Chopin's *Funeral March* Sonata twice within a few years, because the first version was too undisciplined for him) inevitably leads to a classicism of interpretation. When they commit themselves, artists quite unconsciously choose the middle course. On records they don't risk the extreme or ecstatic interpretations, the captivating blend of manic and depressive which a live but none the less transitory concert sometimes still provokes – under the right, exhilarating circumstances. Records encourage the 'middle way'. Horace, who was no musician, spoke of the golden mean, of course, but Schönberg, a real musician, said that the middle way was the only one which didn't lead to Rome. Thus, one must deal with the fact that records, so to speak, appease us. They encourage care, caution.

Then too, contrary to current belief, only in rare cases does virtuosity make such a spontaneous and compelling impression on records as it does in concert. On records, successes which are merely virtuosic have as weak an effect as a conjuring trick in a film. After all, one must be able to keep a close eye on the conjuror! To put it more positively, only the expression of the compellingly vehement virtuoso makes an impression on the recording, not the flawless facility one naturally expects from the (correctable) electroacoustical product. Perhaps, too, we assume much too thoughtlessly that the recording can 'manipulate' us. I know of no truly first-class, great and important recording which has been produced by a merely second-class, mediocre and unimportant artist. Stature can't be gained surreptitiously, even with ever so many refinements.

In concert there is coughing; your neighbour wears a necklace that tinkles at the slightest movement; the soloist has to warm up; by his second aria, Radames's B natural [in *Aida*] may be no joy to listen to; the stage floor creaks; a cellist drops his bow; and in the middle of a pianissimo an explosion hisses out when a spotlight gives up the ghost. The man who only, 'only' listens to records knows nothing about these live accompaniments. He is alienated from corporeal music making. Half-way through a concert he suddenly longs for the abstraction of his stereo set. In a certain way he's like a living thing in which the sense of public life and presence is dangerously stunted. Late Proust was like that. In hindsight, this has serious consequences for public musical life. It hasn't been made sufficiently clear what it means that every record collector (or borrower) can hold his own ghost-Olympics. He can set the volume on his machine to a specific level, pick up the score and then have ten *Siegfried*s sung one after another, under conditions which are (so he thinks) completely identical ... If these ten performances are pulled out of the context of their respective *Ring*s, if they are isolated, if no consideration is given to what the conductor wanted, what the relation between orchestra and tenor was like, how the protagonist was portrayed, and in what light the silly sot should be seen at just this point, then *playing* records turns into *playing them off* against each other. And in the end one will long for an ideal figure who is a combination of ten tenors. I once read an essay by someone who had heard Schumann's A minor Piano Concerto twenty-two times in a row and then, Arrau, Cortot, Lipatti, Rubinstein and Serkin notwithstanding, decided that if the young Edwin Fischer had made a recording with Furtwängler (which never happened, unfortunately), it certainly would have been the best of the lot.

Certainly? To be sure, one can also run a marriage ad: 'Wife wanted. Specifications: the legs of the young Marlene, Brigitte Bardot's derrière, Marilyn Monroe's bosom, Marcia Haydée's neck, Elizabeth Taylor's eyes and Hannah Arendt's brains.' As far as we know, a woman built like that is nowhere to be found. And if one does turn up, who knows whether she might not be a repulsive monster? In other words, the playing off against each other leads to an ideal type which is far from ideal – it leads to irrefutable smart-aleckiness: tenor X's attack isn't quite as light as Caruso's, his change of register isn't as free as Nicolai Gedda's, and Dietrich Fischer-Dieskau is better at penetrating the meaning of the text.

Are we becoming so impossibly hard to please? Answer: no one can simply ignore his hearing experiences, his experience of standards. Often enough famous singers and instrumentalists are afraid not only of being measured against the recordings of their rivals (for they can always fall back on their own individuality) but still more of meeting the spectre of their own recordings on the stage: 'You must be as good and as perfect as you were six years ago in the studio!'

Precisely because I am convinced that only a constant alternation between live concerts and recordings (which are just as serious) makes it possible for us to listen to and partake of music in a reasonably responsible fashion, I must close by calling attention to the various possibilities opened up by recordings. We won't discuss the obvious availability of beautiful things which is now part and parcel of our existence: after the day's trials and tribulations, one can share a glass of red wine with a small group of friends as midnight approaches, listening to a Mozart string quartet, Verdi's Requiem, the Bible Scene from *Wozzeck*, or an aria from *Norma* in peace and quiet (and one probably gets more of such music that way than under any other conditions whatsoever). So far, so good.

But one can also – and this is the record's pedagogical function – learn to experience the complex masterworks. No one who doesn't know how to read scores like a professional, even if he's a diligent concertgoer, can do a reasonable job of internalizing Bruckner's Sixth Symphony or Schönberg's Violin Concerto or the complete works of Webern or Messiaen, unless he studies music and records equally seriously. The Lasalle Quartet's Schönberg–Berg–Webern cassette must have been epoch-making. And our descendants will be able to hear how Strauss or Stravinsky or Boulez saw themselves as interpreters of their own music.

The third possibility which recordings open up is much too seldom perceived, astonishingly. At the moment we have a culture of musicological analysis (one professor refers to others, and they all refer to the music) as well as an active culture of interpretation. (The great pianists of our time plunge into the Op. 111 Sonata [of Beethoven] and bring to light, often after a labour of decades, connections, gestures, interpretations and insights.) Doesn't it stand to reason, for example, that a bond will eventually be forged between the professor's and the pianist's image of Beethoven? Doesn't it stand to reason that everyone who thinks about our culture's supreme musical works will also give thought to the ineffable insights of these interpreters, who are certainly no stupider or more unmusical or poorer in experience than the professors of musicology? Nothing, however, can be more beneficial to such a broadened outlook on works and tendencies than the careful and urgently comparative consideration of recorded interpretations.

96

Massimo Mila, 'Benjamin Britten Is Dead'

Stampa (5 December 1976), from *Terza pagina* (Turin, 1985)

Mila (1910–88), long-time critic of *L'Espresso* and *La Stampa*, was a prolific, entertaining and insightful writer. Like many of his compatriots, he was particularly drawn to Italian opera, but both his writing and his teaching reflected a remarkably international outlook. In this obituary appreciation, published the day after Britten's death, he depicts the English composer as representing a 'third force' between the neo-romantics and the exponents of twelve-tone music.

Britten burst on to the scene right after the war with the memorable performance of *Peter Grimes* in London on 7 June 1945. It not only marked the appearance of a new opera composer – and just where you would least expect to find one – but actually seemed to betoken the rebirth of the values of art and civilization. The ruins were still smoking, yet here was opera – the most complex and laborious genre of musical production – already setting off bright fireworks, as if to assert that the creative hiatus of the five war years had been caused merely by the force of external cirumstances, but that nothing had been compromised, nothing lost, nothing really destroyed. *Peter Grimes* was just this: the sudden revenge of man's creative forces. Art which had been shunted aside, stigmatized and burrowed in anti-aircraft shelters suddenly leaped forth to proclaim: 'Never fear, I am here.'

That the good news came from a country which in the past had been an importer rather than a producer and exporter of operas, and from a virtually unknown thirty-two-year-old musician, seemed to make the intrinsically happy event even more thrilling. In reality, only the closing of the borders had prevented notice being taken of concert works like *Les Illuminations* for soprano and strings (1939) and the Serenade for tenor, horn and strings (1943) – works which in other circumstances would have brought the young musician to the attention of Europe. We would already have encountered, in large part, that blend of old and new experiences fused in the fire of a personality which was not overly powerful but highly informed and cultured – a personality which in *Peter Grimes* seemed to express itself in its own language, eclectic as you please, yet never before heard in its entirety. Mallarmé and English poetry, Purcell and Monteverdi, Verdi and Wagner, Mahler and Alban Berg, Stravinsky and Schönberg – these and others were the springs from which the musician drank with eager impartiality. Britten was no casual plunderer; on the contrary, he reduced everything to the common denominator of an up-to-date culture, musical and otherwise, and above all of a distinctively personal taste.

In England, then, Britten's appearance was greeted with special enthusiasm. The laborious birth, or rebirth, of English music had been protracted for more than half a century: from Elgar to Vaughan Williams, from Frederick Delius to Edmund Rubbra, from Arnold Bax to Gustav Holst, from Arthur Bliss to Walton, from Frank Bridge to John Ireland (both Britten's teachers), the gestation was prolonged and fitful. What was still lacking for the new English music really to begin to exist? You might say it was the joy of making music, the ease and naturalness of spontaneity. Britten may have been highly sophisticated and steeped in historical culture, but with him English music recognized, perhaps for the first time since the Elizabethan age (and always excepting the special case of Gilbert and Sullivan), that sinful dimension which the Victorian mentality had held at arm's length: pleasure.

As a result, the path to maturity was no bed of roses for the young musician. The marvel of *Peter Grimes* blossomed at a very special historical moment, when no one yet knew which way the winds of contemporary music were blowing. It may have been the last moment when the single front of 'modern music' still held out against the classic/romantic dictatorship, a single front in which Schönberg and Stravinsky (despite some grumbling on the former's part), Bartók and Hindemith, Casella and Milhaud felt united. That unity shattered just when the restoration of peace and of freedom of expression and communication made it possible for them all to lay their cards on the table. And they were clearly playing different games: some continued to play with the old tarot cards, while others had new tricks up their sleeves. Britten, hailed at first as a modern musician, soon saw himself detailed to another unit: neither that of a discredited reactionary conservatism nor that of the *avant-garde*, which would shortly replace old-fashioned 'modern music' on the front line of progress. He became the most influential exponent of the third force. He wasn't a follower of Strauss or Puccini, though he didn't overlook either the Bavarian or the Italian and occasionally put them to good use. Nor did he join the twelve-tone camp at any time, even if now and then his thirst for new experiences and sensations prompted him to lean out over the dangerous abyss of atonality, approached via the intricate and tricky paths of modality and of so-called extended tonality.

The good luck which had favoured his first essay seemed to desert him, and only in the dark and disquieting *Turn of the Screw* of 1954 did he match the success of *Peter Grimes* (with superior artistic results). The intervening operas – *The Rape of Lucretia* (revived this year in two Italian productions, to an acclaim which would have been unimaginable thirty years ago), *Albert Herring*, *Billy Budd* (also staged in Italy), and *Gloriana* (celebrating the coronation of Queen Elizabeth), were not substantially successful. What did succeed, beyond their deserts, were the little one-act operas designed to be performed by reduced forces in churches and other makeshift spaces – works such as *Noye's Fludde* of 1958 (which may have suggested *The Flood* to Stravinsky but was overwhelmed by it), *Curlew River* (1964), *The Burning Fiery Furnace* (1966), and *The Prodigal Son* (1968). Written with one eye on the medieval mystery play and the other on Japanese Noh theatre, these amiable little works exposed what was probably the greatest danger to Britten's art: a slightly affected elegance, a worldly cultural trendiness. And yet *Death in Venice* (1973) was another great and serious undertaking, though an unfortunate production may have cost it the esteem it deserved. It represented what was always the main thrust of Britten's music: the deepening of the voice's expressive resources in union with the phonic and semantic resources of texts in English or other languages (French, Latin, Italian) – resources which he explored with the tenor Peter Pears, his chosen interpreter and artistic soulmate, and by studying all the greats who have sown in that field, from Monteverdi to Purcell, from Verdi to Puccini, from Wagner to Debussy, from Schönberg to Berg.

One thing at least has to be said in Britten's favour: although he sided with Stravinskyan neo-classicism rather than Viennese expressionism, he hardly ever practised the neo-classicists' favourite exercise: music raised to the second degree, that is, the reworking of styles of the past – parody. Even when he modelled Peter Grimes's great monologues ('Now the Great Bear and Pleiades') on the 'elevated' style of Purcell, his object was always to draw sustenance for a language that was new and of today, never to ape the old style by mischievously appealing to the 'history gap'.

As a man, Britten was undeniably one of the most civilized musical figures of this century. He was never known to take part in polemical debates. Superior historical understanding gave him insight into the motivations of musicians who were different from himself, and he always felt a genuine and unquenchable curiosity about their work. It was the disinterested curiosity of a historian, of a man of culture, not the curiosity of the composer who is willing to investigate other people's work only if it happens to offer something he can use. Britten did not flaunt his faith, and in the little works masquerading as theatre pieces which I mentioned before, his approach to religious themes may be open to a suspicion of aestheticism. Nor did he tax his art with political commitment. Yet the

War Requiem (1962), probably his masterpiece outside of the theatre, is not the work of a man who was lukewarm or indifferent.

97

Jorge Velazco, 'Television Music'

Excélsior (February 1977), from *De Música y músicos*
(Mexico, 1983)

Velazco (b. 1942) has conducted widely throughout Europe and the Americas, especially in his native Mexico. As critic for the daily *Excélsior* in Mexico City, he is notable for his wide-ranging interests and lively, accessible style. These reflections on the incompatibility between television and the 'static' medium of music offer a different slant on the issue of music and technology. Compare Gavazzeni's essay on film music (no. 82).

Music is an art which, by its nature, lacks a spatial dimension. No one could define the visual parameters of music in space. It's clear that air in vibration, the basic and immediate manifestation of music, occupies a determined space, but to the human eye such a property is overly subtle and totally invisible. Besides, the most important point is that music is an art which links thoughts via a system of predetermined relations, a linkage which is essentially invisible to the human eye.

This confronts the twentieth century, which in terms of mass communication might be described as the century of television, with a problem (a genuine dilemma at times) of a most curious form: music, one of the most effective media of mass communication, is unsuited to transmission by television, which is basically a visual medium, one whose effectiveness is rooted in the possibility of transmitting images and whose possibilities are defined by spatial parameters.

What a bizarre situation! Music, which according to the romantics says everything because it says nothing concrete,[1] is a limited and incomplete 'spectacle' on television, which is accustomed to use it as an element of decoration and emphasis, as accompaniment and stimulant, but never as a starting point or foundation.

This 'never' has an exception. The necessity of disseminating culture among great masses of people (another characteristic reflection of the twentieth century) has meant that music is televised fairly often, though never often enough. Confronted with television's inadequacy *vis-à-vis* the musical phenomenon, programme directors, producers and consultants are used to tearing their hair and fuming: 'What use are its cameras and their possibilities for movement, in the face of a static spectacle? What use are its immense lighting resources in the face of a source [of music] which doesn't require a great deal of movement?' Music is usually produced with the executant sitting down, and the movement required to produce it is extremely delicate and subtle in terms of physical spectacle. The muscular feats of the cellist or pianist are of narrow spatial dimensions; the trumpet or horn's most delicate and complicated problems are practically invisible. The most extraordinary horn player in the world is an absolute bore, tedious and wearisome, from the perspective of movement which is perceptible for television. And that's because what that or any other musician produces is a thought manifested in sound, which occurs in time and not in space.

The thought is the hero of concerts. Music lives and transpires in time, while television lives and transpires in the dynamic of movement, in the image of which sound is merely an auxiliary. One still has recourse to constantly varying the camera angles and takes, but this doesn't solve the basic problem, and it causes endless bother for the public and the artists: the possibility of a physical attack on the cameraman (threatening words and gestures are common) is always in the air at televised concerts. To the musical *aficionado*, it's clear, the visual aspect of a musical programme is not of great concern. But this specialist public is the least important and least interesting segment of the television audience, now that the mass media's primary mission has to be acculturating and educating people who are remote from cultural events. In the present state of society, satisfying *aficionados* is less useful and interesting than capturing a new public.

The simultaneous transmission of images which 'relate' to the music being played is an invitation to the affected gentility which has been accepted all too often. The appearance on screen of interesting views of the public, sitting quietly listening to a concert, produces the apotheosis of tedium. The storms that music excites are inside the listeners' heads; except in extreme cases, they don't usually provoke easily visible external reactions.

Concert 'commentators' constitute a distinguished and exclusive fauna. Luckily, they come in all kinds, but there is an abundance of pedantry, lack of intellectual capacity, a want of adequate culture if not of a laughable one, a virtually absolute ignorance of music, an inability to express themselves coherently, clearly and fluently when it comes to general or specific thoughts, emotional problems which relieve frustrations at the slightest provocation. More than one commentator could justify the nickname 'boob tube' that many television people find so irritating. In reality, it's not the tube that is the boob ...

Perhaps radio is the natural medium for transmitting music. Since it doesn't raise problems of image, but only of sound and time, it's more naturally related to music than is television, which is captivating but anti-musical (in being bound to the image). For many years, radio was the primary vehicle of social bonding and the most important musical mass medium. Today it continues to be a medium of overriding importance in the dissemination of music, but it's addressed to the specialist public, whether for art music or for rubbish. Television is the medium of general communication, the one which is addressed to the whole world, which reaches every member of society – the one which is most important and therefore must necessarily contribute to the dissemination of the artistic discipline that is most crucial to man's formation and education: music.

Perhaps an abundance of cameras, virtually unrestricted movement, mobile platforms for obtaining particularly interesting angles, high-resolution cameras for avoiding the unfortunate light of reflectors, zoom lenses which permit close-ups without sticking the cameras under the musicians' noses, ultra-sensitive microphones placed cleverly and appropriately, expert musical advice, possibilities for editing and polishing – perhaps these can produce programmes that *aficionados* will find immensely interesting. But the basic problem with this kind of programme still stands: the transmission of physically static situations, which only a specialist musician can appreciate – without the possibility of the newscaster who communicates sought-after ideas and fills a general need – and which therefore lacks general interest.

These difficulties must stimulate creative minds. There is no reason to stop or retard the rhythm of the search for the solution to reconciling music and image, time and space.

1 See, for example, Schumann's essay (no. 25).

98

Gérard Condé, 'Consonances for Tomorrow'

Monde (22 November 1986)

Condé (b. 1947) is one of the most respected French critics of the younger generation. Since 1975 he has written for *Le Monde*, a newspaper known for its intellectual depth and independence and its literary stylishness. Condé's longer essays carry on the tradition of the great *feuilletonists* like Castil-Blaze, Berlioz and Boschot (see nos. 27, 33 and 71). This review attests to his skill at working within the stringent space limitations of modern daily journalism.

The evolution of music is like the evolution of clouds in a calm sky: so long as you stare at them they scarcely seem to move, but when you take your eyes away you can never be sure of being able to look up again and find the head of a dog or whale you thought you saw. Nothing is in its place any more ...

Ten years from now we may see a wholesale return to tonality, long since pronounced dead, and hence a convergence of language between 'serious' music and the other kind. Like it or not, everything is pointing in that direction, and less commercial composers should seriously set about recapturing a broader public, to avoid seeing their conquests reclaimed by 'easy-listening' confectioners. To be surprising is no longer enough – audiences aren't turned on by making an effort. For composers, seducing their listeners is a matter of artistic life or death.[1]

Nothing is more significant in this regard than the confrontation, in the same concert of the Groupe Vocal de France at the Auditorium des Halles, between Xenakis's *Nuits*, the signature piece of this ensemble, which gave its première at the Royan Festival in 1968, and the latest work of Hugues Dufourt (b. 1943),

La Mort de Procris, unveiled at Musica 86 in Strasbourg, of which this was the first Parisian performance. Apart from the abrupt violence of the homage Xenakis was rendering to all political prisoners, what was striking in *Nuits* were the moments when the skein of the voices unravelled to produce more defined effects, when the onomatopoeias were contrived with a stark clarity which composers at that time were avoiding.

Almost the opposite effect was produced earlier when we heard *La Mort de Procris*, which is all order, transparency and beauty. It contains dissonances, to be sure, but they are mitigated by the disposition of the voices; melodies which are atonal but composed of intervals conducive to intonation; no vocal eccentricity; a certain languor which allows the listener to let himself be charmed by the harmony; in short, a climate of sober serenity that is quite explicit. For a while, it seemed more obviously related to Debussy's *Chansons de Charles d'Orléans*.[2]

Another notable première, by the same performers, at the Eglise Saint-Vincent-de-Paul, the *Missa brevis* of Philippe Hersant (b. 1948), took place within the framework of the Festival of Sacred Art, and its power of immediate seduction conquered an audience which was hardly expecting it. Without a doubt, the concern for establishing powerful centres of harmonic attraction is even clearer in this piece. Still, a composer can hardly be blamed for looking to the past: he searches inside himself and finds chords which others have repudiated for fifty years, melodic formulas which, like Bartók's, renew contact with popular traditions, and a taste for full sonorities in which consonance inevitably wins out over dissonance.

These shared concerns, the convergence one notices at certain points, don't prevent Philippe Hersant and Hugues Dufourt from presenting sharply different personalities through their music. But what strikes you is the evolution they illustrate and to which they contribute by the success of their works.

1 Compare Hahn's plea for 'pleasing' music (no. 85).
2 The *Trois Chansons de France*, two of which are set to poems by Charles d'Orléans. Vuillermoz (no. 64) similarly saw a link between the vocal music of Debussy and Schönberg.

99

Alexander Ivashkin, 'The Paradox of Russian Non-Liberty'

Musical Quarterly (Winter 1992)

Since the demise of state Communism, critics in the former Soviet Union and elsewhere in Eastern Europe have been searching for a new role. Ivashkin (b. 1948), one of Russia's outstanding younger critics, has written insightfully about the opportunities and dangers of the new freedom of expression. Former president of the Bolshoi Theatre Orchestra in Moscow, he now teaches cello and music history in New Zealand. See no. 66 for the views of an earlier émigré critic, Schloezer.

The last years of Perestroika and Glasnost brought many changes to the cultural life of the Soviet Union. The changes began in an atmosphere of cautious optimism and included new freedoms to travel, to demonstrate publicly, and to write without the threat of censorship. So far, the changes of the past seven years have yet to produce any significant cultural results, only a re-evaluation and a new understanding of old ideas in life, politics, and art. Foremost among these is the idea of traditional Russian non-liberty, which remains as prominent today as it was before the August coup of 1991 and the Second Russian Revolution.

Perhaps the most successful and productive year of Perestroika was 1989. Many new publications and newly published archival materials appeared, and there was also a great increase in the sale of Russian paintings. Soviet composers made many trips abroad, and musicians from all over the world were invited to perform in the Soviet Union. But then disappointment came, and at the moment many things simply do not work any more. Many musicians and painters have since left the Soviet Union for different Western countries, and their former workshops and basements are now empty ... You will not meet Alfred Schnittke and Sofia Gubaidulina in Moscow, Valentin Silvestrov in Kiev or Gia Kancheli in Tbilisi any more. To reach them, you have to go to Germany or even to the Canary Islands. In fact, one can say that Russian culture exists more now in the West than in Russia itself.

Of course, the cultural context changed completely after the Second Russian Revolution of August 1991: there is no longer any pressure, control or censorship. Russia has become a new country, but in spite of its new freedom, something is definitely missing. The strong inner tension inherent in most Russian music is disappearing. Art and literature, like today's music, are tending to be less and less social, becoming more and more cold or academic ...

Russian art seldom goes in the same direction as real life. Primarily, that has been because of the very individual, personal and sometimes even selfish character of Russian music, poetry, prose and painting: each work of art always carries both a new message, a new concept, and a very personal one. That is why we do not properly understand modern French or British music; it seems to Russians too dietetic, too vegetarian. Their conception of art is different – to them art is a game, an entertainment, a competition of rational forces. Russian music is much more irrational, controversial, further removed from this 'game conception'. A work of Russian art is a confession. There is nothing commonplace in it, nothing decorative, well balanced or moderate. Everything is extreme, somtimes shocking, strange. We treat music as something more than just music; it is a means to express something spiritual.[1] This does not mean that our musical language is not significant. The Russian school has always been very advanced in the technical sense, but in Russia we have never had an art for the sake of art. Even the Russian *avant-garde* at the beginning of the twentieth century only used their extreme means to express a new metaphysical image, for the Russian style is, first of all, a metaphysical one. It tries to ensure that all the events, all the written notes, all the words or colours do not conceal the content of the work. The real content, the real tensions are *between* the words, the colours or the sounds ...

Russian music is always in touch with its roots – roots of significance, and meaning. And in that sense Russian art is destructive, for it is concerned more with accidence and morphology than with syntax. This is also true in social life; Russians are more prone to self-examination and introspection than to formal social contacts.

That is why all the changes of the last year have not affected Russian music too much. It is, paradoxically, that music was more profound and interesting in an atmosphere of harsh political pressure and social discomfort than today, when Russians have the freedom to travel, to bargain and to sell. In other words, less freedom, more creativity; more freedom, less creativity. Russian art does not flourish under conditions of total freedom; it is (and was) usually more productive in an atmosphere of social and political contradictions. The long periods of social suppression in Russian history produced music of symbolic character, symbolic with 'hidden' levels of meanings, which require investigation and interpretation. Many things in Russian life and art are like an iceberg, and one needs to be experienced to catch the important hints, situated below the surface. The language of Russian art and music is, in many respects, Aesopian language ...

The fateful role of Russia is to join West and East, in both a social and a cultural sense. In the past, there was no real contact between the culture of the West and Russia. While the West experienced democracy, Russia remained under the Tartar yoke. We had no real bourgeoisie; the best of our intelligentsia was lost during the Stalin repressions. Finally, the Communists destroyed many cultural institutions and traditions. Russia never had freedom. And life in Russia was never so scheduled, so well organized, as in the West, so the perception of Western traditions and cultural patterns could not be direct; there was always some Russian amendment, some modification ...

Usually there is a close connection between the social climate and musical forms at any period of history. For instance, sonata form emerged during the age of rationalism and enlightenment. The Russian philosopher Georgy Gachev considers sonata form to be a child of the era of the great geographical discoveries, when the ideas of space, contrasts and development became dominant. You travel – this is the exposition; you are away from native Europe – the development section; you return – the recapitulation.

The fugue was more suitable for small cities, expressing the idea of fixed rules and a guaranteed course of events. Of course, there were the possibilities of irrational, mystical occurrences, but in general, the fixed rules in the arts – as the stable events in life – were a warranty and condition for access to the opposite.

But in the sonata and in the fugue, the idea of development – the idea of time – was connected with the idea of a circle, or a spiral. If you do not come back from your journey, your journey is a disaster. If you write a work without a recapitulation, that is a disaster too.

The gap between the rational and irrational spheres, depending on the requirements of a particular period of history, sometimes became quite wide. Sonatas by Liszt or Scriabin demonstrate a very free treatment of the idea of development and return. But still, the basic idea of logical perfection in a work of art was closed, not open; pattern was very powerful. Then, one can find the most tragic contradiction between an irrational landscape in music and an extremely rational serial technique in Schoenberg's last works, such as his String Trio, op. 45. This contradiction demonstrates an already changed perception of the world's order and disorder. The twentieth-century conception of the world is far from being just rationalistic; to many theorists the world consists of quite well-known, investigated components, but connections between these components are indiscernible – irrational – especially on micro levels.

Let me briefly comment on Russian 'amendments' to this concept of musical forms as a reflection of global order and disorder. Of course, irrational and personal elements of disorder were always part of classical music forms. What do Mozart's codas mean? They are an attempt to cross all the previous development, to use a pedal point, to let us enjoy, by irrational repetition, something that has already been accomplished. From the structural point of view, such a coda means nothing, but often, these codas are the most important and expressive sections of Mozart's music. Later in the nineteenth century even the finales of symphonies are merely contemplative codas; their traditional functions of 'explanation of everything' and successful conclusion are transformed into something different ...

In the symphonies and quartets of Dmitry Shostakovich, the entire finale appears to be a big, non-structural coda. Sometimes the whole work is only coda (like the Fifteenth String Quartet). The Russian attitude tends toward this development. The large form becomes more and more irrational, less and less structural. And that is because nowhere, except in Russia, have art and music been so firmly bound to the political and social situation. Nowhere, except in Russia, has art been such a substitute for real life. Nowhere, except in Russia, has the real life of a great country with enormous intellectual potential also been so empty and hopeless ...

In the 1970s, at the time of [Leonid] Brezhnev, under terrible political pressure, Soviet composers began to write large musical compositions; they started to organize a large musical space. It was an attempt to create an ideal sound model for the emptiness and darkness of real life. Very often, searching for the ideal image, composers descended to the utmost depth of linguistic simplicity, then invested it with greater strength, and turned it back into a sign, or symbol, imbued with the light of current history. Russian music, since Shostakovich, has rejected the importance of logical development and replaced it with an irrational shimmering (exactly what Mozart did in his classical codas) of the most important symbolic elements. To a Russian music is not a text, not a construction; it is a special kind of reality. Music emerges in organic juxtapositions of important elements, rather than in a mechanical, strictly logical development of the main theme or idea. Simple elements play a very important role in the symphonies of Schnittke, Gubaidulina, [Avet] Terterian, Kancheli, Silvestrov, [Boris] Tishenko, [Nikolay] Korndorf. Those elements – in different contexts – practically organize musical form, becoming points of orientation in the flow of different and contrasting events. The spaces (and the time) in Soviet music of the 1970s and 1980s are living, real spaces, not just abstractions ...

The present period of Russian history is very unclear. We do not know what will happen to Russian music. But the big 'coda', I hope, is certainly over now, and we are standing at the door of new beginnings. Now we can export our music and art; Russian music and Russian composers are known everywhere. Sometimes it seems to be not far away from our own century's very common stream of *fin de siècle*, the end of both the century and of the millennium. 'Everything must be sold' is the typical attitude for such transitional periods. And, as has happened before in history during similar 'ends' and 'transitions', we just think about the modifications of what we have already accomplished. We just do not notice something new; perhaps it has already been born.

But I do not think this 'new' is just an attempt to establish a pure, abstract, Western-like art, which seems at the moment to be acceptable for post-August Russia. I believe Russia will never be a typical Western country. Moreover, musicians, composers, artists who leave Russia now will produce a huge Russian irrational invasion in the West. Borders of Russian culture, as never before, will be extremely wide.

Russian culture is very strong. But for Western civilized cultures it might be dangerous. It combines art and life and presents a completely different attitude to creative work. For Western art, unfamiliar with Russian 'amendments', Russian influence might be very painful. Russian art always contains elements of 'illness' which can be very productive, but could also destroy a very well organized tradition of Western art.

Of course, there are positive examples of the influence of Russian mentality on Western artists. I see this influence in the works of George Crumb, Olivier Messiaen, György Kurtág. But a new wave of Russian immigration might produce a huge invasion of Russian irrationalism in all the arts. Be sure, it is not so easy to deal with. Be careful.

1 Compare Stasov's discussion of the Russian school (no. 44).

100

Andrew Porter, 'A Feast for the Willing Ear'

Observer (4 July 1993)

No English-language critic of the past quarter-century has had a wider influence than Porter (b. 1928). A native of South Africa, he served as critic of England's *Financial Times* and editor of the *Musical Times* before moving to the United States to write long essay-reviews for the *New Yorker*. In 1991 he returned to London as critic for the *Observer*. Porter's writing is distinguished by its clarity, measured eloquence and attentiveness to detail.

Andrew Lloyd Webber may be the British composer most often played. By champions of new music in Europe and America, Brian Ferneyhough – Coventry-born, 50 last January – is the British composer most highly regarded. In the annals of Royan, Donaueschingen, La Rochelle, the Venice Biennale, he is prominent. His *Carceri d'invenzione*, a 90-minute cycle, had its first London performance last week, in the BBC Concert Hall. The place was thronged, the listeners rapt. A wider audience can enjoy the concert when Radio 3 broadcasts it on 18 July, at 10.45 p.m.

I heard my first Ferneyhough in 1968, at the Palermo festival, but didn't hear much: the Two-Piano Sonata was abandoned after a page or two amid a storm of barracking – not at the music but because that day censorship had banned a showing of Markopoulos's film *Illiac Passion*.[1] It was an heroic time. By then the post-war waves of pointillism, total serialisation, timbre structures, and chance procedure had broken. Drenched composers were building as best they could amid the debris on music's beach.

Who could have foreseen that ricky-tick minimalism, soupy neo-romanticism, and holy monotony would be the next waves? In Palermo, individual voices – [Luigi] Nono, [Franco] Donatoni – sang strongly. Morton Feldman's *False Relationships and the Extended Ending* was an orderly, seductive piece. At the last minute Feldman asked the conductor, who had prepared it carefully, not to conduct; he wanted a performance approximate, not precise.

Ferneyhough's music, unlike Feldman's, thrives on accurate execution. Making uncommonly high performance demands, it yields little but confusion when it is clumsily played ...

Carceri d'invenzione was composed between 1981 and 1986. The imaginary prisons, like Piranesi's, are filled with intricate, overlapping, contradictory incidents and perspectives. Eye or ear, running along one path, encounters another, wonders which to follow. Within confining forms, invention is fierce and free. Three orchestral *Carceri* are preceded by a brilliant, fine-line *Superscriptio*, for solo piccolo; divided by two *Intermedi*; and closed by *Mnemosyne* (Memory, mother of the Muses), for bass flute and tape.

Sometimes the *Carceri* suggest transcendental birdsong – a bewildering, glorious chorus of high, clear voices, exuberant and joyful, irregular in rhythms, microtonal in pitches, each individual and distinct. Listeners cannot hope to apprehend them all or discern the pattern, but somehow everything seems to make sense as, with ear and mind alert and delighted – using Roger Sessions's 'willing ear', which is all a composer expects – they respond to now one detail, now another.

Ferneyhough composes, he has said, for active, collaborative auditors prepared to jump between levels of texture and tolerate multiple meanings. Imagery and objects are presented so swiftly and profusely that they outrun the ability to assimilate; a listener is left behind while already new things are happening. The composer packs in all he can.

So at each hearing there will be new perceptions, until from details newly discovered a sense of the whole gradually forms. *Superscriptio*, the two *Intermedi*, and *Mnemosyne*, which are recorded on an Etcetera CD, make a good starting point, for they have fewer voices. The first *Intermedio, alla ciaccona*, is for solo violin. The second, entitled *Etudes transcendentales*, is a 27-minute cycle of nine songs for soprano and flute, oboe, and harpsichord in various combinations.

The first song, with long chains of short oboe motifs, is like an intoxicated nightingale outpouring, the singer as long, marvelling listener. The fourth, like 'Der kranke Mond' in [Schönberg's] *Pierrot lunaire*, is for flute and voice – but rapid and rhapsodical, not slow. The eighth is a dark, dense solo, harpsichord-accompanied. By the ninth, instruments have become so eloquent that the singer resorts to rapping claves or percussive phonemes, and speech.

The first of the *Carceri* is a dazzling labyrinth for 16 players, the second a flute concerto, string-accompanied except when members of a wind septet add bold colours, contrasts, new directions. The third, for excited winds and percussion, passes without break into *Mnemosyne* – a long coda calm and quiet. High bright busyness is stilled at last. The bass flute sings. The tape, in gentle flute tones that move toward those of an organ, plays chords. A single flute note dies away into silence. The final sound world, Ferneyhough suggests, is that of Debussy's *Cathédrale engloutie*.

Carceri d'invenzione had its first complete performance at Donaueschingen in 1985. A Dutch ensemble brought it to the 1987 Huddersfield Festival. Components of the cycle have been heard here before. (*Carceri I* was a London Sinfonietta commission.) The complete London performance was given by Lontano and the London Chamber Symphony, conducted by Odaline de la Martinez, along with three soloists versed in Ferneyhough's music: the flautist Pierre-Yves Artaud; the violinist Irvine Arditti, who had given the first performance of the *Intermedio all ciaccona*; and the Canadian soprano Brenda Mitchell, delicate and exact, who had given the first performance of the *Etudes transcendentales*.

The performances were thrilling – bold, enthusiastic, passionate, each player making much of his or her virtuoso line. Special praise to Ingrid Culliford (flute, and glittering piccolo in *Superscriptio*), Chris Redgate (oboe, initiator of *Carceri III*), and Sophie Langdon (first violin). And to Martinez. By putting on such a concert – it must have been costly to prepare – Radio 3 maintains its high purpose. Ferneyhough's *Terrain* (1992), for violin solo (Arditti) and instrumental octet, has its first London performance at the late-night Prom on 2 September.

1 *Prometheus Bound – The Illiac Passion* (1966) by the American underground film-maker Gregory Markopoulos, most of whose films centre on the theme of homosexual love.

Further Reading

A full-scale bibliography of collections of music criticism is outside my brief. The following is a selective guide to general anthologies of journalistic criticism in English, and to other writings by critics represented in this anthology. I have bent the rules a little by citing dissertations and secondary works dealing with critics whose work is not otherwise accessible in English.

Anthologies

Amis, John, and Michael Rose, eds, *Words about Music: An Anthology* (London, 1989).

Aprahamian, Felix, ed., *Essays on Music: An Anthology from 'The Listener'* (London, 1967).

Barzun, Jacques, ed., *Pleasures of Music: A Reader's Choice of Great Writing about Music and Musicians from Cellini to Bernard Shaw* (New York, 1951).

Demuth, Norman, ed., *An Anthology of Musical Criticism from the Fifteenth to the Twentieth Century* (London, 1947).

Kolodin, Irving, ed., *The Critical Composer: The Musical Writings of Berlioz, Wagner, Schumann, Tchaikovsky, and Others* (New York, 1940).

– *The Opera Omnibus: Four Centuries of Critical Give and Take* (New York, 1976).

Ledermann, Minna, *The Life and Death of a Small Magazine ('Modern Music,' 1924–46)* (Brooklyn, N.Y., 1983).

Sablovksy, Irving, ed., *What They Heard: Music in America, 1852-1881: From the Pages of 'Dwight's Journal of Music'* (Baton Rouge, La., and London, 1986).

Scholes, Percy A., *The Mirror of Music, 1844–1944: A Century of Musical Life in Britain as Reflected in the Pages of the 'Musical Times'* (London, 1947).

Slonimsky, Nicolas, ed., *Lexicon of Musical Invective: Critical Assaults on Composers since Beethoven's Time* (New York, 1953).

Strunk, Oliver, ed., *Source Readings in Music History from Classical Antiquity through the Romantic Era* (New York, 1950; revised and expanded edition forthcoming).

Sullivan, Jack, ed., *Words on Music: From Addison to Barzun* (Athens, Ohio, 1990).

Wallace, Robin, *Beethoven's Critics* (Cambridge, 1986).

Weiss, Piero, and Richard Taruskin, eds, *Music in the Western World: A History in Documents* (New York, 1984).

Individual Critics

Addison, Joseph, Richard Steele, et al., *The Spectator: 1711–14*, ed. Donald F. Bond, 5 vols (Oxford, 1965).

Adorno, Theodor, *Prisms*, trans. Samuel and Shierry Weber (Cambridge, Mass., 1981).

– *Quasi una fantasia: Essays on Modern Music*, trans. Rodney Livingstone (London, 1992).

Apthorp, William Foster, *By the Way*, 2 vols (Boston, 1898).

– *Musicians and Music-Lovers and Other Essays* (New York, 1895).

Asafyev, Boris, *A Book about Stravinsky*, trans. Richard French (Ann Arbor, Mich., 1982).

– *Russian Music from the Beginning of the Nineteenth Century*, trans. Alfred J. Swan (Ann Arbor, Mich., 1953).

Bellaigue, Camille, *Musical Studies and Silhouettes*, trans. Ellen Orr (New York, 1900).

– *Portraits and Silhouettes of Musicians*, trans. Ellen Orr (New York, 1897).

Berlioz, Hector, *The Art of Music and Other Essays*, trans. Elizabeth Csicery-Ronay (Bloomington, Ind., 1994).

– *Beethoven: A Critical Appreciation of Beethoven's Nine Symphonies and His Only Opera, 'Fidelio,' with its Four Overtures*, trans. Ralph De Sola (Boston, 1975).

– *Evenings with the Orchestra*, trans. Jacques Barzun (New York, 1956).

(Berlioz, Hector) H. Robert Cohen, 'Berlioz on the Opera (1829–49): A Study in Music Criticism', Ph.D. diss., New York University, 1973.

– Kerry Murphy, *Hector Berlioz and the Development of French Music Criticism* (Ann Arbor, Mich., 1988).

Burney, Charles, 'Essay on Musical Criticism', in *A General History of Music* (London, 1776–89).

(Burney, Charles) Kerry S. Grant, *Dr. Burney as Critic and Historian of Music* (Ann Arbor, Mich., 1983).

Cardus, Neville, *Cardus on Music: A Centenary Collection*, ed. Donald Wright (London, 1988).

– *Composers Eleven* (London, 1958).

– *The Delights of Music* (London, 1966).

– *Full Score* (London, 1970).

— *Talking of Music* (London, 1957).

– *Ten Composers* (London, 1957).

(Chabanon, Michel Paul Guy de) Harry Robert Lyall, 'A Music Aesthetic of the Eighteenth Century: A Translation and Commentary on Michel Paul Guy de Chabanon's "Musique considérée en elle-même et dans ses rapports avec la parole, les langues, la poésie, et le théâtre" (1785)', Ph.D. diss., North Texas State University, 1975.

Chorley, Henry, *Modern German Music: Recollections and Criticisms* (London, 1862).

– *Thirty Years' Musical Recollections* (London, 1862).

Cooper, Martin, *Judgements of Value* (New York, 1988).

(Davison, J. W.) *From Mendelssohn to Wagner: Being the Memoirs of J. W. Davison, Forty Years Music Critic of 'The Times'*, ed. Henry Davison (London, 1912).

Debussy, Claude, *Debussy on Music*, trans. Richard Langham Smith, ed. François Lesure (New York, 1977).

Downes, Olin, *Olin Downes on Music*, ed. Irene Downes (New York, 1957).

Einstein, Alfred, *Alfred Einstein on Music: Selected Music Criticisms*, trans. Catherine Dover (New York and London, 1991).

Fétis, François-Joseph, *Music Explained to the World* (Boston, 1842).

(Fétis, François-Joseph) Peter A. Bloom, 'François-Joseph Fétis and the "Revue musicale" (1827–1835)', Ph.D. diss., University of Pennsylvania, 1972.

(Fry, William Henry) W. T. Upton, *William Henry Fry: American Journalist and Composer-Critic* (New York, 1954).

Hahn, Reynaldo, *On Singers and Singing*, trans. Leopold Simoneau (Portland, Ore., 1990).

(Hale, Philip) Jean Ann Boyd, 'Philip Hale, American Music Critic, Boston, 1889–1933', Ph.D. diss., University of Texas, 1985.

Hanslick, Eduard, *Music Criticisms, 1846–99*, trans. Henry Pleasants (Baltimore, 1963).

– *Vienna's Golden Years of Music*, trans. Henry Pleasants (New York, 1950).

(Heine, Heinrich) Oscar Sonneck, 'Heinrich Heine's Musical Feuilletons,' trans. Frederick H. Martens, *Musical Quarterly* 8 (1922): 119–59, 273–95 and 435–68.

Henderson, W. J., *The Art of Singing* (New York, 1938).

– *Preludes and Studies* (New York, 1891).

Hoffmann, E. T. A., *E. T. A. Hoffmann's Musical Writings*, trans. Martyn Clarke, ed. David Charlton (Cambridge, 1989).

Huneker, James Gibbons, *Americans in the Arts, 1890–1920: Critiques by James Gibbons Huneker*, ed. A. T. Schwab (New York, 1985).

– *Essays*, ed. H. L. Mencken (New York, 1929).

– *Melomaniacs* (New York, 1902).

– *Mezzotints in Modern Music* (New York, 1899).

– *Old Fogy: His Musical Opinions and Grotesques* (Philadelphia, 1913).

– *On Music and Musicians*, ed. Mortimer H. Frank (St. Paul, Minn., 1978).

– *Overtones: A Book of Temperaments* (New York, 1902).

– *Variations* (New York, 1921).

(Hunt, Leigh) Thedore Fenner, *Leigh Hunt and Opera Criticism: The 'Examiner' Years* (Lawrence, Kan., 1972).

Janáček, Leoš, *Janáček's Uncollected Essays on Music*, trans. Mirka Zemanová (London, 1989).

Kodály, Zoltán, *The Selected Writings of Zoltán Kodály*, trans. Lili Halápy and Fred Macnicol (London, 1974).

Krehbiel, H. E., *Chapters of Opera* (New York, 1908).

– *More Chapters of Opera* (New York, 1919).

– *Review of the New York Musical Season, 1885–1890*, 4 vols (New York and London, 1886–1890).

(Marpurg, Friedrich Wilhelm) Howard Serwar, 'Friedrich Wilhelm Marpurg (1718–1795): Music Critic in a Galant Age,' Ph.D. diss., Yale University, 1969.

(Mattheson, Johann) Beekman C. Cannon, *Johann Mattheson: Spectator in Music* (New Haven, Conn., 1947).

Newman, Ernest, *Essays from the World of Music* (London, 1956).

– *More Essays from the World of Music* (London, 1958).

– *A Musical Critic's Holiday* (London, 1925).

– *A Musical Motley* (New York, 1925).

– *Musical Studies* (London, 1905).

– *Testament of Music* (London, 1962).

(Odoyevsky, Vladimir) James S. Campbell, *V. F. Odoyevsky and the Formation of Russian Musical Taste in the Nineteenth Century* (London, 1989).

– David Lowe, 'Vladimir Odoevskii as Opera Critic', *Slavic Review* 1982: 306–15.

Pannain, Guido, *Modern Composers* (New York, 1933).

Porter, Andrew, *Music of Three Seasons* (New York, 1978).

– *Music of Three More Seasons* (New York, 1981).

- *Musical Events* (New York, 1987).
- *A Musical Season* (New York, 1974).

(Reichardt, Johann Friedrich) N. B. Reich, 'A Translation and Commentary of Selected Writings of Johann Friedrich Reichardt', Ph.D. diss., New York University, 1973.

(Rochlitz, Friedrich) Charles Paul Nolte, '"Allgemeine musikalische Zeitung": A Study in Music Criticism', Ph.D. diss., Syracuse University, n.d.

Rosenfeld, Paul, *By Way of Art: Criticisms of Music, Literature, Painting, Sculpture, and the Dance* (New York, 1928).
- *Discoveries of a Music Critic* (New York, 1936).
- *Musical Chronicle, 1917–1923* (New York, 1923).
- *Musical Impressions: Selections from Paul Rosenfeld's Criticism*, ed. Herbert A. Liebowitz (New York, 1969).
- *Musical Portraits* (New York, 1920).

Runciman, John F., *Old Scores and New Readings* (London, 1901).

Salazar, Adolfo, *Music in Our Time: Trends in Music Since the Romantic Era*, trans. Isabel Pope (New York, 1946).

(Scheibe, Johann Adolph) Imanuel Wilheim, 'Johann Adolph Scheibe: German Musical Thought in Transition', Ph.D. diss., University of Illinois, 1964.

Schloezer, Boris de, *Scriabin: Artist and Mystic*, trans. Nicolas Slonimsky (Berkeley, Calif., 1987).

Schumann, Robert, *On Music and Musicians*, trans. Paul Rosenfeld, ed. Konrad Wolff (New York, 1946).

(Schumann, Robert) Leon Plantinga, *Schumann as Critic* (New Haven, Conn., 1967).

Shaw, George Bernard, *The Great Composers: Reviews and Bombardments by Bernard Shaw*, ed. Louis Crompton (Berkeley, Calif., 1987).
- *How to Become a Musical Critic*, ed. Dan H. Laurence (New York, 1961).
- *Shaw's Music: The Complete Musical Criticism in Three Volumes*, ed. Dan H. Laurence (New York, 1981).

Stasov, Vladimir, *Selected Essays on Music*, trans. Florence Jonas (London, 1968).

(Stasov, Vladimir) Richard A. Hoops, trans. and ed., 'V. V. Stasov: Selected Articles on Mussorgsky', Ph.D. diss., Florida State University, 1977.
- Yuri Olkhovsky, *Vladimir Stasov and Russian National Culture* (Ann Arbor, Mich., 1983).

Strobel, Heinrich, *Stravinsky: Classic Humorist*, trans. Hans Rosenwald (New York, 1955).

Stuckenschmidt, Hans Heinz, *Ferruccio Busoni: Chronicle of a European*, trans. Sandra Morris (London, 1970).

- *Maurice Ravel*, trans. Samuel Rosenbaum (Philadelphia, 1968).
- *Schoenberg: His Life, Music, and Work*, trans. Humphrey Searle (London, 1977).

Tchaikovsky, Peter Ilich, *Tchaikovsky: A Self-Portrait*, trans. R. M. Davison, ed. Alexandra Orlova (New York, 1990).

Thomson, Virgil, *The Art of Judging Music* (New York, 1948).
- *Music Reviewed* (New York, 1967).
- *Music Right and Left* (New York, 1951).
- *The Musical Scene* (New York, 1945).
- *The Virgil Thomson Reader*, ed. John Rockwell (Boston, 1988)

Vuillermoz, Emile, *Gabriel Fauré*, trans. Kenneth Schapia (Philadelphia, 1969).

Weissmann, Adolf, *Music Come to Earth*, trans. Eric Blom (London, 1930).
- *Problems of Modern Music*, trans. M. M. Bozman (London, 1925).

Wolf, Hugo, *The Music Criticism of Hugo Wolf*, trans. Henry Pleasants (London, 1968).

Index